PICTORIAL
PRICE GUIDE
TO AMERICAN ANTIQUES

and Objects Made for the American Market

2000-2001 EDITION

PICTORIAL PRICE GUIDE TO AMERICAN ANTIQUES
and Objects Made for the American Market

ILLUSTRATED AND PRICED OBJECTS

By

Dorothy Hammond

VIKING STUDIO
Published by the Penguin Group
Penguin Putnam Inc., 375 Hudson Street,
New York, New York, 10014, U.S.A.

Penguin Books Ltd, 27 Wrights Lane,
London W8 5TZ, England

Penguin Books Australia Ltd, Ringwood,
Victoria, Australia

Penguin Books Canada Ltd, 10 Alcorn Avenue,
Toronto, Ontario, Canada M4V 3B2

Penguin Books (N.Z.) Ltd, 182-190 Wairau Road,
Auckland 10, New Zealand

Penguin Books Ltd, Registered Offices:
Harmondsworth, Middlesex, England

First published in the United States by Viking Studio, a member of Penguin Putnam Inc.

First printing, October 1999

10 9 8 7 6 5 4 3 2 1

ISBN: 0-14-028529-6

CONTENTS

INTRODUCTION

This is the twenty first edition of Pictorial Price Guide to American Antiques and Objects Made for the American Market. The book is recognized by collectors as one of the most authoritative and up-to-date references on the market. The format is designed to provide the collector and antiques dealer with an accurate market value of items sold at auction galleries from June 1998 through June 1999. A selection of approximately 5,000 illustrated items were chosen for this edition. Entries are keyed to the auction gallery where an item actually sold with state abbreviation because prices vary in different regions of the country. The year and month the item sold is also included.

Again, auction houses have enjoyed another great year with a very healthy and diversified buyer response. To recognize a bargain and to avoid buying unwisely, it is vital that the collector understand today's marketplace. During the past three decades, interest in antiques and collectibles has increased tremendously, making it increasingly difficult to keep abreast of current values. Therefore, serious collectors look to auctions as the ultimate price determinant because they reflect market trends. When comparing similar pieces within this edition, the reader must always take into consideration that fluctuations in the market as well as quality of an object, the region in which it is sold, as well as popularity will determine the auction price.

Among the major trends were an increase in values of upper end collectibles and fine period furniture, with continued dominance of the formal look. Enthusiasm for Centennial and early twentieth century furniture continues to increase. Although some are not technically antiques, items from later periods are finding their way into the marketplace. As our population increases and collectors become more knowledgeable these well made pieces are in demand. Surprisingly, even restoration and repairs have become more acceptable. However, when the original finish or decoration has been removed from a period or elderly piece of furniture, it reduces the value substantially. And because of the quality of later mass produced furniture, there has become an increased demand for custom made furniture from all periods by well recognized cabinetmakers. When these pieces find their way into the market place, they are not only well received because of their quality, but fetch strong prices. Afterall, everything collected these days was new once.

Record prices have been set during the year for all periods of furniture, shore birds, lighting, art glass, toleware, movie and sports memorabilia, pottery, porcelain, toys, textiles and dolls.

Collectibles produced during the late nineteenth century and well into the present century continue to dominate a large segment of the market. Collecting continues to be a very highly sociable pastime all across the country. It is fascinating, enjoyable and educational because of the seemingly endless categories.

Although every effort has been made to record prices accurately and describe each entry within the space allotted to our format, the writer cannot be responsible for any clerical or typographical error that may occur.

– Dorothy Hammond

ACKNOWLEDGMENTS

Most auction galleries charge a buyer's premium which is a surcharge on the hammer or final bid price at auction. For the reader's convenience we have included the buyer's premium following the name and location of each auction gallery.

I would like to express my appreciation to the following, without whose help this publication would not have been possible:

Bill Bertoia Auctions, Vineland, NJ 10%; Cincinnati Art Galleries, Cincinnati, OH 10%; Conestoga Auction Co., Lancaster, PA 10%; Craftsman Auctions, Putnam, CT and Pittsfield, MA 10%; CYR Auction Co., Gray, ME 10%; David Rajo Auctions, Inc. Lambertville, NJ 10%; Davies Auctions, Lafayette, IN 13%; DeCaro Auction Sales, Inc., Easton, MD 15%; Early Auction Company, Milford, OH 10%; Garth's Auctions, Inc., Edie Preece, Delaware, OH 10%; Gene Harris Auction Center, Marshalltown, IA 10%; Guyette & Schmidt, Inc., W. Farmington, ME 10%; Horst Auction Center, Clarence E. Spohn, Ephrata, PA n/c; Hunt Auctions Inc., Wayne, PA 10%; International Toy Collectors Association, (ITCA), Athens, IL 10%; Jackson's Auctioneers and Appraisers, Cedar Falls, IA 10%; James D. Julia, Fairfield, ME 15%; Ken Farmer Auctions, Inc., Radford, VA 10%; Maritime Auctions, York, ME 10%; New England Auctions of Brookfield, David R. Ayers 15%; Northeast Auctions, Hampton, NH 15%; Pook & Pook, Inc., Downingtown, PA 10%; Rafael Osona Auctions, Nantucket, MA 10%; Richard Opfer Auctioneering, Inc., Timonium, MD 10%; Richard W. Withington, Inc., Hillsboro, NH 10%; Skinner, Inc., Bolton & Boston, MA 10%;

I am especially grateful to Steve Philip, President of Hi-Rz Graphics and his staff, and Jean Israel, for their dedication to this book throughout it's preparation. And I am very grateful to Mell Cohen for her editorial assistance.

ABBREVIATIONS USED IN THIS BOOK AND THEIR MEANINGS

Am. . . . . American	hex. . . . . hexagon	pc. . . . . piece
attrib. . . . . attributed	illus. . . . . illustrated/illustration	pcs. . . . . pieces
batt. . . . . battery	imper. . . . . imperfections	prob. . . . . probably
blk. . . . . black	impr. . . . . impressed	prof. . . . . professional
br. . . . . brown	int. . . . . interior	Q.A. . . . . Queen Anne
C. . . . . century	irid. . . . . iridescent	reconst. . . . . .reconstructed
ca. . . . . circa	lrg. . . . . large	ref. . . . . . . refinished/refinishing
compo. . . . . composition	L. . . . . length/long	repr. . . . . repair/repaired
const. . . . . . constructed/construction	lt. . . . . light	repl. . . . . replaced
dk. . . . . dark	litho. . . . . lithograph	replm . . . . replacement
dec. . . . . decorated/decoration	mah. . . . . mahogany	repro . . . . reproduction
diam. . . . . diameter	mfg. . . . . manufactured	rev. . . . . reverse
emb. . . . . embossed	mkd. . . . . marked	sgn. . . . . signed
Eng. . . . . England	mech. . . . . mechanical/mechanism	sm. . . . . small
engr. . . . . engraved	mono. . . monogram/monogrammed	sq. . . . . square
escut. . . . . escutcheon	N.E. . . . . New England	T. . . . . tall
Euro. . . . . Europe/European	N/S . . . . No Sale	unmkd. . . . . unmarked
ext. . . . . exterior	opal. . . . . opalescent	unsgn. . . . . unsigned
Fed. . . . . Federal	oper. . . . . operate	W. . . . . wide
Fr. . . . . France/French	ora. . . . . orange	w/ . . . . with
gal. . . . . gallon	orig. . . . . original	wrt. . . . . wrought
Ger. . . . . German/Germany	pr. . . . . pair	yel. . . . . yellow
gr. . . . . green	pat. . . . . patent	The common and accepted abbreviations are used for states.
H. . . . . high	patt. . . . . pattern	

A-ME Sept. 1998   Cyr Auction Co. Inc.
Sign, "We Ride The Flying Yankee", Eastern Cycle Mfg. Co. Ad, 14" x 11" $1,200.00

A-ME Sept. 1998   Cyr Auction Co. Inc.
Labels, lot of eight, "J.C. Norris & Co's" $425.00

A-ME Sept. 1998   Cyr Auction Co. Inc.
Poster, "Pe-ru-na For Catarrh", 18" x 30" $300.00

A-ME Sept. 1998   Cyr Auction Co. Inc.
"Slade's Pure Spices", tin spice wall display, 1906, 12" x 7" x 2" .$1,100.00

A-ME Sept. 1998   Cyr Auction Co. Inc.
Sign, "Select Society Cigarettes", litho on paper, framed 25" x 19" . .$750.00

A-ME Sept. 1998   Cyr Auction Co. Inc.
Sign, "National Accident Society", gold frame, 25" x 30" $275.00

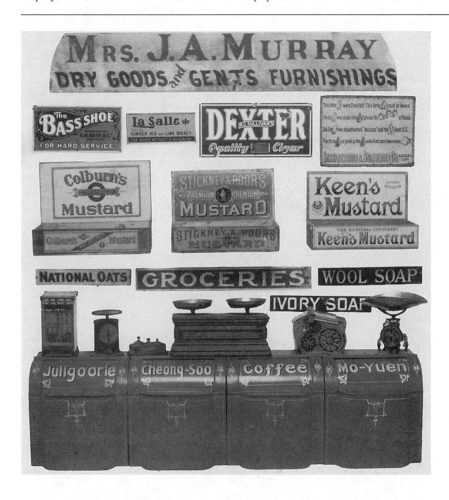

A-ME Sept. 1998   Cyr Auction Co. Inc.
Sign, "Mrs. J.A. Murray...", painted wood, 69" x 11½" $300.00
Sign, "The Bass Shoe", porcelain, 18" x 9" $160.00
Sign, "La Salle Ginger Ale", rev. on glass, 6" x 14" $65.00
Sign, "Dexter Quality Cigar", porcelain, 10½" x 23" $80.00
Sign, "Little Pig Went To Market", emb. tin, 9½" x 13½" $400.00
Box, wooden, "Colburn's Mustard", paper labeled $125.00
Box, wooden, "Stickney & Poor's", paper labeled $150.00
Box, wooden, "Keen's Mustard", paper labeled $300.00
Sign, "National Oats", metal, 3" x 19" $85.00
Sign, "Groceries", sand painted wood, 4" x 34" $425.00
Signs, two porcelain soap signs, "Wool Soap" & "Ivory Soap" . .$115.00
Scale, "Turnbull's Fancy Scale", fancy brass feet & dial, 11½" x 14" .$500.00
Register Machine, metal, 11" x 9" x 7" $75.00
Balance Scale, w/ weights, walnut, 19½" x 9" x 10" $200.00
Scale, iron & brass, "US Scale Patented 1877", 9" x 6" x 6" . . .$55.00
Dispenser, "Mansfield's Choice Pepsin Gum", 7" diam., 12" T .$850.00
Tea Bins, set of four roll top, res. orig. design, ea. 19" x 16" x 20" . . .$460.00

A-ME Sept. 1998   Cyr Auction Co. Inc.
Die Cut, "Don't Monkey W/ Imitations...1896", 12" x 15" .$225.00

A-ME Sept. 1998   Cyr Auction Co. Inc.
Sign, "In The Swim" The Hoffman House Little Cigars, 15" x 25" $2,000.00

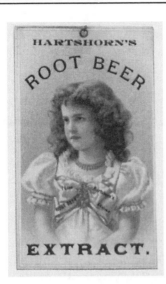

A-ME Sept. 1998   Cyr Auction Co. Inc.
Sign, "Hartshorn's Root Beer Extract", 6½" x 10" $325.00

A-ME Sept. 1998   Cyr Auction Co. Inc.
Die Cut, lady golfer "Compliments of James Clark, Fall River, MA", 11½" x 22" $450.00
Die Cut, a high stepper", "Compliments of Charles Lawrence Co.", 8½" x 14" $70.00

A-ME Sept. 1998   Cyr Auction Co. Inc.
Sign, "King Arthur Flour", 16¼" x 27" $225.00

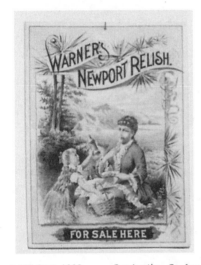

A-ME Sept. 1998   Cyr Auction Co. Inc.
Sign, "Warner's Newport Relish", 10½" x 14" $115.00

A-ME Sept. 1998   Cyr Auction Co. Inc.
Sign, "King Arthur Flour", 27¾" x 17¾" $100.00

A-ME Sept. 1998   Cyr Auction Co. Inc.
Sign, "Heinz Pure Food Products", 14" x 24" $425.00

A-ME Sept. 1998   Cyr Auction Co. Inc.
Sign, "Totem 5 Cent Cigar", round, 6" diam. $125.00

A-ME Sept. 1998   Cyr Auction Co. Inc.
Sign, "Mayo's Plug", 31" x 18" $450.00

A-ME Sept. 1998   Cyr Auction Co. Inc.
Sign, "Old Honesty Plug", litho on paper w/ walnut frame, 33½" x 23" $325.00

A-IA Mar. 1999   Jackson's Auctioneers & Appraisers
Poster, promoting "Buffalo Bill's Wild West Show", dated 1905, 30" x 40" $9,240.00

A-ME Sept. 1998   Cyr Auction Co. Inc.
Sign, "Learn to Drink Moxie", die cut, some roughness, 37" x 20" . .$250.00

A-PA Oct. 1998   York Town Auction Inc.
Cigar Store Indian Princess, attrib. to Robb of NYC, ca. 1890, standing on base w/ iron wheels, old repaint, base 27" x 22" $38,000.00

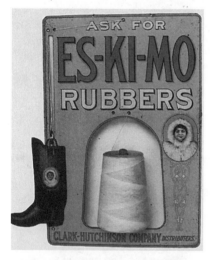

A-ME Sept. 1998   Cyr Auction Co. Inc.
Sign, ES-KI-MO Rubbers mech. string holder, 13½" x 19½" $3,700.00

A-ME Sept. 1998   Cyr Auction Co. Inc.
Pumpkin Trade Stimulator, key wind, clockwork mech., 12" T w/o hat, 13" diam. $8,750.00

A-ME Sept. 1998   Cyr Auction Co. Inc.
Sign, "Old Virginia Cheroots", Uncle Sam litho on paper, 29" x 21" $950.00

A-NJ Oct. 1998   Bill Bertoia Auctions

Left to Right

Change Tray, 1903 Coca-Cola, "Hilda Clark", minor wear, 6" diam. $1,870.00
Change Tray, 1906 Coca-Cola, "Delicious & Refreshing", minor crazing, 4" diam. $550.00
Change Tray, 1909 Coca-Cola, St. Louis Fair in background, minor crazing, 6⅛" diam. $550.00

A-NJ Oct. 1998   Bill Bertoia Auctions

Row 1, Left to Right

Change Tray, 1910 Coca-Cola, "Coca-Cola Girl", sgn. by Hamilton King, minor edge rubs, 6⅛" H,$440.00
Change Tray, 1913 Coca-Cola, Hamilton King image, crazing 6⅛" H, ...$385.00
Change Tray, 1914 Coca-Cola, "Betty", crazing, 6⅛" H $165.00

Row 2, Left to Right

Change Tray, 1916, Coca-Cola, "World War I Girl", 6¼" H $132.00
Change Tray, 1920 Coca-Cola, paint flakes, 6⅜" H $132.00

A-NJ Oct. 1998   Bill Bertoia Auctions

Serving Tray, 1905 Coca-Cola, Lillian Russell in center, minor edge wear & flakes, 13" H $3,630.00
Serving Tray, 1925 Coca-Cola, flapper girl, overall surface pitting, 13¼" H $198.00

A-NJ Oct. 1998   Bill Bertoia Auctions

Serving Tray, 1913 Coca-Cola Hamilton King, 15¼" H $935.00
Serving Tray, 1914 Coca-Cola, "Betty", pastel colors, surface faded & worn, 13¼" H $193.00

A-NJ Oct. 1998   Bill Bertoia Auctions

Row 1, Left to Right

Serving Tray, 1920 Coca-Cola, paint flakes, 13¼" H $462.00
Serving Tray, 1922 Coca-Cola, "Summer Girl" image, edge wear, 13¼" H $715.00

Row 2, Left to Right

Serving Tray, 1921 Coca-Cola, "Autumn Girl", edge paint flakes, 13¼" H $468.00
Serving Tray, 1923 Coca-Cola, Flapper girl, br. rim, minor rust to edge, 13¼" H $242.00

A-NJ Oct. 1998   Bill Bertoia Auctions

Serving Tray, 1933 Coca-Cola, "Francis Dee", in bathing suit, minor paint loss, 13¼" H $352.00
Serving Tray, 1934 Coca-Cola, Johnny Weismuller "Tarzan & Jane" fame, minor surface scratches, rim wear, 13¼" W $770.00

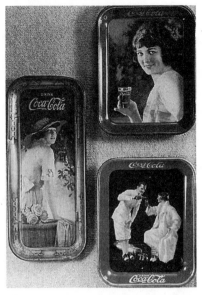

A-NJ Oct. 1998   Bill Bertoia Auctions

Top to Bottom

Serving Tray, 1924 Coca-Cola, red rim w/ blue ground, edge wear, 13¼" H $990.00
Serving Tray, 1916 Coca-Cola, World War I girl image, denting to left rim, surface pitting, 8½" x 19" $220.00
Serving Tray, 1926 Coca-Cola, The Golfers, surface pitting, paint rubs, 13¼" H $440.00

A-NJ Oct. 1998   Bill Bertoia Auctions

Row 1, Left to Right

Serving Tray, 1927 Coca-Cola, Curb Service, minor paint flakes, edge wear, 13¼" W $605.00
Serving Tray, 1928 Coca-Cola, minor edge wear, 13¼" H $605.00

Row 2, Left to Right

Serving Tray, 1927 Coca-Cola, Soda Jerk, edge wear, 13¼" H $484.00
Serving Tray, 1929 Coca-Cola, girl in yel. swimsuit, minor edge skin, 13¼" H $605.00

A-NJ Oct. 1998   Bill Bertoia Auctions

Row 1, Left to Right

Serving Tray, 1930 Coca-Cola, Girl in white Bathing Suit, minor edge wear, 13¼" H $495.00

Serving Tray, 1930 Coca-Cola, "Meet Met at the Soda Fountain", minor scratch, 13¼" H $330.00

Row 2, Left to Right

Serving Tray, 1931 Coca-Cola, Norman Rockwell boy w/ dog, minor edge wear, rim rubs, 13¼" H .$715.00

Serving Tray, 1932 Coca-Cola, sgn. Haydon, young lady in yel. swimsuit, 13¼" H $770.00

A-NJ Oct. 1998   Bill Bertoia Auctions

Row 1, Left to Right

Serving Tray, 1937 Coca-Cola, running girl wearing beach cape & suit, 13¼" H $220.00

Serving Tray, 1938 Coca-Cola, young girl w/ bottle, minor denting, 13¼" H $176.00

Row 2

Serving Tray, 1940 Coca-Cola, "Sailor Girl", 13¼" H $440.00

A-NJ Oct. 1998   Bill Bertoia Auctions

Serving Tray, 1935 Coca-Cola, "Madge Evans", scratches, overpainted rim, 13¼" H $220.00

Serving Tray, 1936 Coca-Cola, hostess w/ tray, w/ gold rim, surface pitting & edge wear, 13¼" H . . .$220.00

A-NJ Oct. 1998   Bill Bertoia Auctions

Row 1

Serving Tray, 1941 Coca-Cola, The Ice Skater, 13¼" H $308.00

Serving Tray, 1942 Coca-Cola, two girls by roadster, 13¼" H $308.00

Row 2

Serving Tray, 1939 Coca-Cola, Springboard girl minor edge scratches, 13¼" H $242.00

A-NJ Oct. 1998   Bill Bertoia Auctions

String Holder, Red Goose Shoes, cast iron, painted red overall w/ yel., orig. puzzle card, emb. on sides, 10¾" H x 15" L $6,050.00

A-NJ Oct. 1998   Bill Bertoia Auctions

Left to Right

Syrup Dispenser, Green River, milk glass w/ acid etched logo, pump top reads "Ginger", 13¾" H $4,620.00

Syrup Dispenser, Viccola, w/ ornate gold trim, incl. orig. pump, 16" H $8,800.00

Syrup Dispenser, Howel's Cherry Julep, ca. 1920, red overall w/ logo & wording in white, orig. pump, 15" H $3,960.00

A-NJ Oct. 1998   Bill Bertoia Auctions

Left to Right

Syrup Dispenser, Christo Ginger Ale, barrel shaped in br. hues w/ chrome bands & lettering, orig. pump, 15" H $1,320.00

Syrup Dispenser, wording on two sides, incl. orig. pump, emb. top reads "Fowler's Root Beer", 15¾" H $1,980.00

A-NJ Oct. 1998   Bill Bertoia Auctions

Syrup Dispenser, Cherry Smash, ceramic w/ colorful decal, metal plunger contains ceramic insert, 14" H $1,980.00

Salesman Sample, Eureka Hoosier, stained wood, hinged top, decals, 16" H $1,320.00

Salesman Sample, Ice Box, wood, exact scale model, nickel hardware, inter galvanized, 18" H, 15" W $660.00

Salesman Sample, Ice Box, made for Kleen Kold Co., wood w/ intricate hardware & insulated doors, 11½" H $880.00

Salesman Sample, Chickering baby grand, wood in exacting scale, 17½" x 18" $2,200.00

Left to Right

Sample Stove, "Charter Oak", St. Louis, Pat. 1867, lrg. scale cast iron, nickeled panel w/ oak leaf embossing, 24" W, 33" H to pipe $605.00

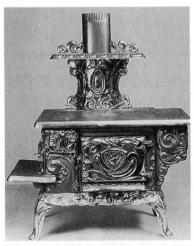

Salesman Sample, "Bucks Junior 2", elaborate cast iron, painted blk. w/ nickeled iron stove doors, removable lids, ref., 22" W x 27" H $935.00

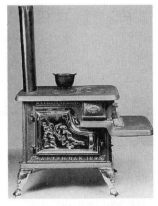

Salesman Sample, "Charter Oak", stove, cast iron, painted blk. w/ nickeled cast iron doors, removable top lids, cast iron pot incl., 19" W x 26" $880.00

Salesman Sample, Karr Range Co. stove, cast iron, blue enameled w/ nickeled doors, trim & feet, emb. front panel, 21½" H $5,500.00

Salesman Sample, Quick Meal Stove Co., cast iron painted blk. overall, stove doors nickeled overall, removable range lids, 17" W, x 26" H $4,950.00

A-NJ Oct. 1998   Bill Bertoia Auctions

Left to Right

Still Bank, Punch & Judy, Ger., litho. tin, 2⅞" H $220.00
Still Banks, two dog banks, incl. dog w/ clock, made of lead & steel & dog w/ doghouse, made of lead w/ tin $495.00

Still Banks, two, both silvered lead, incl. woman's shoe & a hinged back swan, approx. 4½" L $176.00
Still Banks, lot of two, incl. Euro. teapot, made of metal & wood & camel w/ hinged back made in Ger. of silvered lead, 3⅝" to 5" H . . .$176.00
Still Bank, bell, white metal, emb. florals, 5½" H $143.00

A-NJ Oct. 1998   Bill Bertoia Auctions

Left to Right

Still Banks, two pigs, both of cast iron, one painted blk. & one painted gold, 4" to 4⅜" L overall $330.00
Still Banks, tiny elephant w/ Howdah, painted gold overall & Hubley camel painted in multi colors, 2½" to 4¾" H $132.00
Still Banks, two, both cast iron, one sm. pig painted blk. & sm. buffalo painted gold, 4" to 4⅜" $220.00

A-NJ Oct. 1998   Bill Bertoia Auctions

Row 1, Left to Right

Still Banks, two, cast iron & painted blk., embossing, 4⅜" to 5½" .$165.00
Still Banks, two, both cast iron & painted blk., gold trim & combination lock on doors, 5¼" to 5½" H .$385.00
Still Banks, two, both nickeled cast iron, incl. Independence Bank w/ comb. lock & urn casting design safe bank, 3⅜" to 6⅜" $132.00

Row 2, Left to Right

Still Bank, security safe, cast iron, painted blk. overall comb. lock on door, emb., gold trimmed, 4³⁄₁₆" $165.00
Still Bank, security safe, possibly Ives, cast iron, painted blk. overall w/ gold highlights, brass dial comb. lock, emb. lions, 8¼" H x 5⅝" W . .$143.00
Still Bank, keyless safety deposit, cast iron, electroplated, features two comb. dials on front door, 5⅞" H $110.00
Still Bank, coin deposit, nickeled cast iron, ornate emb., comb. lock on front door, 6¾" H $110.00

A-NJ Oct. 1998   Bill Bertoia Auctions

Left to Right

Horse, cast iron, blk. overall w/ gold highlights, emb. "Beauty", 4¾" to 4⅞" $352.00
Still Bank, Arcade cast iron horse, painted blk., 4⅛" x 4¾" $424.00
Still Banks, two horses, both cast iron, ea. done in blk., 4⅞" L .$154.00
Still Banks, two horses, both cast iron, ea. painted gold, 2¾" to 5" $308.00
Still Banks
two reindeer, both cast iron & painted gold overall, 6¼" H $88.00

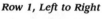

A-NJ Oct. 1998   Bill Bertoia Auctions

Left to Right

Still Bank, red ball, cast iron, red overall, emb. comb. door, 3" H $121.00
Still Bank, globe w/ hinged door, Kenton, electroplated, comb. lock on front door, 5" H $242.00

Still Bank, moon & star bank, cast iron, blk. overall w/ gold highlights, emb. moon & star, 5⅛" x 3⅞" $110.00
Still Bank, nickeled cast iron, comb. lock, emb. "State Safe", 4⅛" H .$88.00
Still Banks, two safes, both cast iron, incl. nickeled "CZAR" safe & "the Rival", painted silver w/ sheet metal sides, 3⅜" H $88.00

A-NJ Oct. 1998   Bill Bertoia Auctions

Left to Right

Still Banks, two lion, both cast iron & painted gold, 2½" to 4½" . .$462.00
Still Banks, two lion, both cast iron & painted gold, 3⅝" to 4" $44.00
Still Banks, two Lion, both cast iron & painted gold, 3" to 3¹³⁄₁₆" . . .$66.00
Still Banks, both cast iron, blk. Scottie & gold cow, 3⁵⁄₁₆" to 3⅜" $330.00
Still Banks, both cast iron, incl. Wire-haired Terrier painted white & red Newfoundland, 3⅝" to 4⅝" . .$220.00

A-NJ Oct. 1998   Bill Bertoia Auctions

A-NJ Oct. 1998   Bill Bertoia Auctions

Row 1, Left to Right

Still Bank, A.C. Williams, cast iron, red w/ nickeled wheels, 6" L .$440.00
Still Bank, trolley car, Kenton, cast iron, silver overall, 2¹¹⁄₁₆" x 5¼" $825.00
Still Bank, A.C. Williams, cast iron, exact scale of Graf Zeppelin, silver, 6½" L $198.00
Trolley, ca. 1889, cast iron, japanned overall, 3¹⁵⁄₁₆" x4⅝" $198.00

Row 1, Left to Right

Still Bank, plane made of nickeled sheet metal, brass tag, inscribed "Spirit of Thrift", 7½" L $550.00
Still Bank, Beverly Hills savings bank plane, Geo. Hunter, casted aluminum, prop of brass, 7¼" L $264.00
Still Bank, trolley, w/ people, A.C. Williams, cast iron, painted gold overall, 3" x 6¾" $352.00

Row 1, Left to Right

Still Bank, John Harper, Eng., cast iron, emb. "City Bank", japanned, 4⅛" H $242.00
Still Bank, John Harper, Eng., cast iron, japanned overall, 4¼" H $264.00
Still Bank, Washington Monument, A.C. Williams, cast iron, painted gold overall, 6⅛" H $242.00
Still Banks, two bldgs., Kenton, both cast iron, silver overall w/ gold trim, 3¼" to 4⅝" $462.00
Still Banks, two bldgs., both cast iron, one Cupola by J & E Stevens, & 1876 Bank ca. 1895, by Judd Co., 2⅞" to 4⅛" $198.00

Row 2, Left to Right

Still Banks, two bldgs., both cast iron, incl. Double Door bank, silver & gold overall & Home Savings w/ dog finial bank, japanned overall, 5⁷⁄₁₆" to 5¾" $528.00
Still Banks, two spaceheaters, Chamberlain & Hill, Eng., both cast iron, one japanned overall, one in blk., 6½" H $198.00
Still Banks, two bldgs., J & E Stevens, both cast iron, incl. four tower bank & a roof bank, japanned overall, 5¼" to 5¾" $528.00

A-NJ Oct. 1998   Bill Bertoia Auctions

A-NJ Oct. 1998   Bill Bertoia Auctions

Bank, Prudential "nickel" savings, pat. 1890, nickeled cast iron, intricate mech., 7¼" H $154.00
Bank, Prudential "dime" savings, pat 1890, nickeled cast iron, drawer pulls out, 7¼" H $154.00
Bank, Prudential "quarter" savings, pat. 1890, nickeled cast iron, 7¼" H $220.00

Row 1, Left to Right

Still Bank, globe savings, Kyser & Rex, ca. 1889, cast iron, japanned overall, 7⅛" x 5¹¹⁄₁₆" $1,650.00
Still Bank, Independence Hall, Enterprise, ca. 1875, cast iron, 8⅞" x 6¹¹⁄₁₆" x 6¼" $330.00
Still Bank, Eiffel Tower, Sydenham & McOustra, Eng., ca 1908, cast iron, japanned overall, gold highlights, 8¾" H $1,045.00

Still Bank, tower, Kyser & Rex, cast iron, japanned overall w/ red roof & gold highlights, 6⅞" x 6⅞" x 2½" $264.00
Still Bank, triangular bldg., Hubley, cast iron, silver overall, letters in gold 6" x 3⅜" $1,650.00

Row 2, Left to Right

Still Bank, Home Savings, cast iron, multi gabled bldg., painted gr. overall w/ br. roof, 10½" x 6¼" x 8⅛" $3,520.00

Still Bank, church, Ger., litho. & hand painted tin, clock tower, 11½" H $418.00
Still Bank, Eagle Bank, US, cast iron, gold overall, 9¾" x 5½" x 4¼" $1,760.00
Still Bank, Independence Hall, Enterprise, ca. 1875, cast iron, japanned overall w/ gold highlights, 10" x 9⅜" $3,080.00

A-NJ Oct. 1998   Bill Bertoia Auctions

Row 1, Left to Right

Still Bank, aluminum monoplane, slot on wing, trap on fuselage, rubber tires $385.00

Still Bank, yel. cab, arcade, cast iron, 7¾" L $770.00
Still Bank, tank savings, Ferrosteel, ca. 1919, cast iron, emb. on sides, 9½" L x 4" W $385.00

A-NJ Oct. 1998   Bill Bertoia Auctions

Row 1, Left to Right

Steamboat, Arcade, cast iron, painted gold overall, 7½" L $286.00
Sailboat, Brighton, cast iron, painted yel. overall, emb. "When My Fortune Ship Comes In,", 5⅜" L $518.00
Steamboat Bank, Arcade, cast iron, painted silver overall, paddle wheel which allows bank to be pulled, 7½" L $275.00

Row 2, Left to Right

The Maine, Grey Iron Casting Co., cast iron, japanned overall, 4⅝" x 4½" $528.00
Battleship, J & E Stevens, early 19th C., painted gray overall w/ gold highlights, emb. "Oregon", 6" L . .$330.00
Still Bank, battleship, J & E Stevens, cast iron, white overall, elaborate castings w/ great detail, repl. trap & masts, 10¼" L $1,430.00

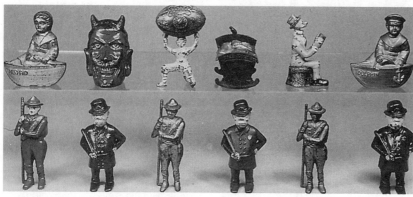

A-NJ Oct. 1998   Bill Bertoia Auctions

Row 1, Left to Right

Still Bank, mermaid, U.S., cast iron, painted gold overall, 4 -9/16" .$660.00
Still Bank, two faced devil, A.C. Williams, cast iron, red & blk., 4¼" H $605.00
Still Bank, boy w/ football, Hubley, cast iron, gray overall, 5⅛" x 3¼" $1,320.00
Still Bank, baby in cradle, ca. 1890, nickeled cast iron & steel bed, 3¼" x 4" $1,320.00
Still Bank, Andy Gump, Arcade, cast iron, colorful, 4⅜" x 2⅞" . . .$1,760.00
Still Bank, "Dolphin" boat, U.S., cast iron, gold overall, 4½" $825.00

Row 2, Left to Right

Still Bank, Boy Scout, Hubley, cast iron, br. overall w/ gold highlighted scarf, 7" H $1,100.00
Still Bank, Mulligan Policeman, cast iron, blue & flesh color, emb. "None So Good", 5¾" $880.00
Still Bank, Boy Scout, A.C. Williams, cast iron, gold overall w/ red hat band, 5⅞" $154.00
Still Bank, Mulligan Policeman, cast iron, blue w/ flesh color, emb. "Bennet & Fish", 5¾" H $352.00
Still Bank, Boy Scout, A.C. Williams, cast iron, painted gold overall, emb. "Made in Canada", 5⅞" H . .$154.00
Still Bank, Mulligan Policeman, A.C. Williams, cast iron, painted blue w/ flesh color, 5¾" H $242.00

Still Bank, Policeman safe, JM Harper, cast iron, crack at base, 5¼" H $2,640.00
Still Bank, baseball player standing on baseball, Hubley, gold overall w/ red stocking & cap, 5¹³/₁₆" . .$3,740.00
Still Bank, two faced indian, A.C. Williams, cast iron, headdress in gold, 4⁵/₁₆" H $2,640.00
Still Bank, Mary & Little Lamb, cast iron, white overall w/ red stockings & red trim on dress, 4⅜" H $352.00

Row 2, Left to Right

Still Bank, Dutch girl, Grey Iron Casting Co., cast iron, painted gold overall, 6½" H $385.00
Still Bank, football player, A.C. Williams, cast iron, gold overall, 5⅞" H $385.00
Still Bank, Statue of Liberty, Kenton, cast iron, gr. overall w/ gold highlights, mkd. "Liberty", 6⅜" H .$385.00
Still Bank, Minute Man, Hubley, cast iron, 6" H $555.00
Still Bank, sailor, Hubley, cast iron, silver overall w/ blue scarf, 5¼" H $55.00
Still Bank, Cadet, Hubley, cast iron, bright blue w/ gold accents, 5¾" H $990.00

A-NJ Oct. 1998   Bill Bertoia Auctions

Row 1, Left to Right

Still Bank, eggman, Arcade, caricature of Wm. Howard Taft, cast iron, gold overall, 4⅛" H $2,640.00
Still Bank, King Midas, Hubley, cast iron, colorful, emb. "King Midas", 4½" x 3⅜" $1,650.00

A-NJ Oct. 1998   Bill Bertoia Auctions

Left to Right

Banks, Scottie grouping, all white metal, incl. six in basket & one blk. & one white, approx. 4¾" H . . .$286.00

Goat, cast iron, painted blk. overall w/ br. horns & silver beard, 7¾" to 9¼" $110.00

Still Bank, Scottie, Hubley cast iron, painted blk. w/ red collar, 4⅞" x 6" $308.00

A-NJ Oct. 1998   Bill Bertoia Auctions

Row 1, Left to Right

Still Bank, owl, Vindex, cast iron, gray & white, 4¼" H $308.00

Still Bank, elephant on wheels, A.C. Williams, cast iron, gold overall w/ Howdah on back, 4⅛" x 4⅜" .$165.00

Still Bank, elephant, A.C. Williams, cast iron, silver, red & gold paint, 5⅜" H $275.00

Still Bank, possum, Arcade, cast iron, gold overall, 2⅜" x 4⅜" $495.00

A-NJ Oct. 1998   Bill Bertoia Auctions

Row 1, Left to Right

Still Banks, two geese, Arcade, cast iron, one emb. "Red Goose Shoes", other painted white w/ red bill & webb feet, 3⅜" to 4" H $275.00

Still Bank, cat w/ ball, A.C. Williams, cast iron, gray w/ gold ball, 2½" x 5¹¹⁄₁₆" $286.00

Still Banks, two, elephant on bench painted gold & sm. lion on tub also gold, 3⅞" to 4⅛" H $198.00

A-NJ Oct. 1998   Bill Bertoia Auctions

Left to Right

Still Bank, three wise monkeys, A.C. Williams, cast iron, painted gold, 3¼" x 3½" $352.00

Still Bank, Teddy Bear, Arcade, cast iron, painted gold, emb. "Teddy", 2½" x 3⅞" $286.00

Still Bank, rabbit, Hubley, wing nut version, ca 1906, cast iron, gray & white, 4⅝" x 4⅜" $176.00

Horse, w/ belly band, cast iron, painted gold, 4½" x 5" $220.00

Still Bank, duck, A.C. Williams, cast iron, painted gold, 4⅞" H $330.00

Still Bank, rooster, Hubley cast iron, gold w/ red comb, 4⅞" H . . .$352.00

Still Bank, lion, A.C. Williams, cast iron, hand painted in blue, red & gold, 5½" $330.00

Still Bank, horse, A.C. Williams, cast iron, hand painted, blk. over all w/ red & gold saddle, 5⁵⁄₁₆" H $265.00

Row 2, Left to Right

Still Banks, turkeys, two, A.C. Williams, cast iron, one japanned & one painted gold, 3⅜" $330.00

Still Banks, two elephants w/ howdahs, A.C. Williams, both cast iron & painted gray overall w/ gold highlights, 3½" to 4¾" $275.00

Still Banks, two lions, both cast iron & painted gold, 3½" to 5¼" H $132.00

Still Banks, two St. Bernards w/ packs, A.C. Williams, both cast iron & japanned w/ gold highlights on pack straps, 3¾" to 5½" H $242.00

Still Bank, "Be Wise Owl", A.C. Williams, cast iron, painted gold overall, 4⅞" H $198.00

Still Banks, two, A.C. Williams, both cast iron, incl. cat on tub & dog on tub, both gold, 4⅕" to 4⅛" H .$176.00

Row 2, Left to Right

Still Bank, Boston Bull Terrior, Vindex, cast iron, br. & white, 5¼" x 5¾" $198.00

Still Bank, lamb, Grey Iron Casting, japanned overall, 3¼" x 5½" .$220.00

Still Bank, bear, painted br. overall w/ red mouth, 5⅞" H $220.00

Still Bank, Holstein, Arcade, cast iron, white & blk. overall, 2½" x 4⅝" $110.00

Still Bank, lamb, cast iron, painted gold overall, 3³⁄₁₆" x 4⅛" $330.00

Still Bank, cat w/ finely cast hair, blk., Arcade, 4¼" H $204.00

A-NJ Oct. 1998   Bill Bertoia Auctions

Row 1, Left to Right

Still Bank, elephant, Hubley, cast iron, colorful, 3⅞" $242.00

Still Bank, squirrel w/ nut, cast iron, gold overall, 4⅛" $770.00

Still Bank, rhino, Arcade, cast iron, blk. overall w/ gold horn & painted features, 2⅝" x 5" $198.00

Still Bank, pelican, Hubley, cast iron, white overall w/ yel. bill & gr. base, 4¾" H $880.00

Still Bank, rabbit, cast iron, br. overall, 2⅛" x 5⅛" $220.00

Still Bank, songbird, A.C. Williams, cast iron, gold overall, 4¾" x 4¹¹⁄₁₆" $242.00

Row 2, Left to Right

Still Bank, rabbit, A.C. Williams, cast iron, gold overall, 6¼" x 5⅝" .#308.00

Still Bank, donkey, A.C. Williams, cast iron, colorful, 6¹³⁄₁₆" X 6¼" $352.00

Still Bank, duck, lrg. Kenton trap, cast iron, colorful in yel. & red, 4" x 4⅞" $330.00

Still Bank, pig in blk. "A Christmas Roast", cast iron, emb., 3¼" x 7⅛" $198.00

Still Bank, reindeer, A.C. Williams, cast iron, gold overall, overpainted, 9½" H x 5¼" $66.00

A-NJ Oct. 1998   Bill Bertoia Auctions

Left to Right

Sewing Machine, Singer, Ger., made of tin & iron, w/ decal & done in true scale, 5⅛" x 4¼" $495.00

Still Bank, beehive "Industry Shall Be Rewarded", John Harper, Ltd., Eng., ca. 1897, cast iron, electroplated base, 4⅛" x 5½" $528.00

Gas Pump, U.S., cast iron, red overall, gold globe, 5¹¹⁄₁₆" x 2⅛" . .$275.00

Still Bank, parlor stove, Schneider & Trenkamp, cast iron, red inserts simulate fire, 6¼" H $264.00

Street Clock, A.C. Williams, cast iron, red pedestal w/ gold painted face, 6" x 2½" $550.00

Still Bank, world time, Arcade, cast iron w/ paper time-tables, 4⅛" x 2⅝" $352.00

A-NJ Oct. 1998   Bill Bertoia Auctions

Row 1, Left to Right

Still Bank, Tabernacle, Keyless Lock Co., cast iron, copper finish, 2¼" x 5" x 2½" $2,860.00

Still Bank, West Side Church, cast iron, silver overall, depicts church from PA, cast iron, silver overall, 3¾" W x 4" H $330.00

Still Bank, The Alamo, Alamo Iron Works, cast iron, 1⅞" x 2¾" x 3⅜" $330.00

Still Bank, log cabin, Kyser & Rex, ca. 1882, cast iron, painted red, 2½" x 3¼" $176.00

Still Bank, Zepplin Dock, emb. "Duralumin used in Airship 'Akron'", 7¼" L $330.00

A-NJ Oct. 1998   Bill Bertoia Auctions

Row 1, Left to Right

Still Banks, two houses, A.C. Williams, blue & gr. roofs, both one story, ea. painted gold overall, 3¹⁄₁₆" H $143.00

Still Banks, two houses, cast iron, incl. Quatrefoil house painted white & one painted gold, 3¹⁄₁₆" $132.00

Still Bank, Cupola bank, J & E Stevens, cast iron, gr. w/ red trim on embossing, 3¼" H $330.00

Still Bank, Cupola bank, J & E Stevens, cast iron, br. w/ red trim, blue roof, 4⅛" H $286.00

Still Bank, Presto bank, A.C. Williams, cast iron, silver overall w/ gold top, 3⅝" H $66.00

Still Bank, Presto bank, cast iron, silver w/ gold dome, 3¼" H $66.00

Still Bank, The Fort, Kenton, cast iron, blk. overall, emb. "Fort", 4⅛" H x 2⅜" $495.00

Row 2, Left to Right

Still Banks, four domed, A.C. Williams, cast iron features various sizes & color schemes, 3" to 4¼" H $285.00

Still Banks, houses, cast iron incl. Colonial House w/ porch, two car garage & sm. Colonial house w/ porch, 2½" to 4" H $385.00

A-NJ Oct. 1998   Bill Bertoia Auctions

Row 1, Left to Right

Still Bank, Boston State House, Smith & Egge, U.S., late 1800's, cast iron, painted gold & red overall, 5⅛" x 3½" x 3⅜" $2,860.00

Still Bank, triangular "Bank", Hubley, cast iron, silver overall, emb. clock, 6" H $528.00

Still Bank, US Treasury, Grey Iron Casting Co., cast iron w/ sheet metal base, white & red overall, 3⅓" x 3¾" $440.00

A-NJ Oct. 1998   Bill Bertoia Auctions

Left to Right

Still Bank, hen on next, U.S., ca. 1900's, cast iron, gold overall, red highlights, 3" x 3⅜" $1,540.00

Still Bank, elephant, U.S., cast iron, gold overall, 4¼" H $880.00

Still Bank, possum, JM Harper, emb. base, gray overall, 3" x 4¾" $3,960.00

Still Bank, basset hound, cast iron, blk. overall, 3⅛" H $1,045.00

Still Bank, camel, Kyser & Rex, cast iron, japanned overall, missing retainer, 2½" x 4¹³⁄₁₆" $495.00

Still Bank, bear, cast iron, gold overall, 2½" x 2⅝" $715.00

A-NJ Oct. 1998   Bill Bertoia Auctions

Left to Right

Still Bank, Puppo, Hubley, cast iron, white & blk., emb. fly, 5⅝" x 6" $462.00

Still Bank, "Wise Pig", Hubley, cast iron & hand painted, 6⅝" H ..$110.00

Still Banks, Hubley, both cast iron, Kitty Bank & Fido, approx. 5" H $154.00

Still Bank, Puppo, Hubley, emb. fly, cast iron, white & blk., 5" H .$176.00

Still Bank, bear w/ honey pot, Hubley, cast iron, br. w/ blue & yel. coin pot, 6½" H $220.00

Still Bank, Marietta Silo, cast iron, white & silver, 5½" H $440.00

Still Bank, Eng. Church, facade in cast iron & japanned, colored tin stained simulating stained glass windows, reads "Bank", 5⅝" H .$1,430.00

Row 2, Left to Right

Still Bank, Fidelity Trust Vault, J. Barton Smith Co., cast iron, gr. overall, w/ dog cashiers on sides, 4⅞" x 3⅞" $418.00

Still Bank, Church Towers, USA, cast iron, blk. overall, center contains cross, 6¾" x 6⅛" W $1,045.00

Still Banks, two domed mosque banks, Grey Iron Casting Co., both cast iron, gold overall, 3⅛" to 5⅛" $528.00

Still Bank, Home Bank, HL Judd, ca. 1895, cast iron, japanned, 4" x 3½" $605.00

A-NJ Oct. 1998   Bill Bertoia Auctions

Row 1, Left to Right

Still Bank, State Bank, Kenton, ca. 1890, cast iron, japanned overall w/ gold highlights, 3" H $220.00

Still Banks, both cast iron, japanned overall w/ gold highlights, incl. State Bank & Deposit Bank, ea. 4⅛" H $242.00

Still Bank, Kenton, cast iron, japanned overall w/ gold & bronze trim, emb. "State Bank", 5⅞" .$198.00

Still Bank, State Bank, U.S., ca. 1897, cast iron, japanned & gold gilded, 6¾" H x 4⅝" $990.00

Still Bank, State Bank, Kenton, cast iron, japanned overall w/ gold highlights, 9" H $770.00

Row 2, Left to Right

Still Bank, Litchfield Cathedral, Chamberlain & Hill, Eng., ca. 1908, cast iron japanned overall, 6½" H $308.00

Still Bank, bear stealing honey from beehive, Sydenham & McOustra, Eng., 7" H $176.00

Still Bank, High Rise, Kenton, cast iron, painted silver overall w/ gold tiered top, 5¾" H $660.00

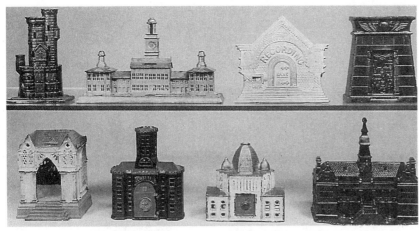

A-NJ Oct. 1998   Bill Bertoia Auctions

Row 1, Left to Right

Still Bank, castle, John Harper Ltd., Eng., cast iron, japanned overall, 7" H $1,650.00

Still Bank, Independence Hall, U.S., late 1800's, cast iron, gold overall, 6⅜" x 11" H $990.00

Still Bank, pat. 1891, cast iron, emb. "Recording", 6⅝" x 4¼" $275.00

Still Bank, Egyptian tomb, cast iron, japanned overall, 6¼" H $352.00

Row 2, Left to Right

Still Bank, J & E Stevens, cast iron, white, red & blue, int. w/ mirrors making money double in appearance, 6½" H x 4½" W $1,760.00

Still Bank, tower, John Harper Ltd., cast iron, japanned overall, 9¼" x 3⅞" $990.00

Still Bank, World's Fair, U.S., cast iron, painted white & red overall, 6" x 6" x 2½" $1,210.00

Still Bank, palace, Ives, ca. 1885, cast iron, japanned & hand painted, gold highlights overall, 7½" x 8" x 5" $2,090.00

Still Bank, two Woolworth Bldgs, Kenton, both cast iron, gold overall, 5¾" to 8⅛" $330.00

Still Bank, triangular bldg., Kenton, cast iron, emb. "Flat Iron Bank", 5¾" H $352.00

Still Bank, triangular bldg., Kenton, cast iron, 3³⁄₁₆" $385.00

A-NJ Oct. 1998   Bill Bertoia Auctions

Row 1, Left to Right

Still Bank, camel, U.S., cast iron, painted blk. w/ gr. rocking base, 3¾" x 5⅜" $935.00

Still Bank, rooster, cast iron, handsomely painted overall, 5½" H $1,045.00

Still Bank, rabbit, U.S., "1884", cast iron, white on gr. base, 2¼" x 2¹³⁄₁₆" $825.00

Still Bank, bear stealing pig, cast iron painted gold, 5½" H $1,430.00

Still Bank, Spitz, Grey Iron Casting, cast iron, br. overall, 4¼" x 4½" $275.00

Still Bank, lost dog, U.S., cast iron, 5⅜" H $385.00

Row 2, Left to Right

Still Bank, camel, A.C. Williams, cast iron, painted gold, 7¼" H $220.00

Still Bank, horse,, A.C. Williams, cast iron, blk. overall, 7³⁄₁₆" x 6⁹⁄₁₆" $264.00

Still Bank, buffalo, ca. 1930's, emb. "Amherst Stoves, 5¼" x 8" . . .$275.00

Still Bank, cow, bronze version, J.E. Stevens, ornate base, 4³⁄₁₆" .$418.00

A-NJ Oct. 1998   Bill Bertoia Auctions

Still Bank, Bell Telephone, Kantor Co., tin w/ stenciling, complete w/ receiver, 10" x 4⅜" $330.00

Mail Box, electroplated bronze, stamped "US Mail", glass view front panels, 4¾" x 5¼" $66.00

Still Bank, Mail Box Savings, Nicols, cast iron, electroplated bronze, attached wooden frame w/ orig. ad for bank, 3½" x 6¼" $1,100.00

A-MA Jan. 1999   Skinner, Inc.

A-MA Jan. 1999   Skinner, Inc.

Row 1, Left to Right

Cupola Bank, by J. & E. Stevens Co., w/ red roof, gray/blue walls, & yel. & red details, 4¼" H $1,150.00

Hall's Excelsior Bank, by J. & E. Stevens w/ maroon walls, string-pull mech., wood figure & paper label, 5¼" H $431.25

Hall's Liliput Bank, by J. & E. Stevens Co., lacking trap, 4½" H $4,600.00

Old South (Boston) Church Bank, w/ gr. roof, white walls, & spire, damage, spire top rusted, 9½" H . . .4,600.00

Flat Iron Building Bank, by Kenton, triangular w/ silver finish, lacking trap, paint wear, 5¾" H $345.00

Home Savings Bank, by J. & E. Stevens, w/ dog's head finial, 6" H $546.25

Ironmaster's House Bank, still, by Kyser & Rex Co., w/ combination trap, 4½" H $2,530.00

Row 2, Left to Right

Bank of Industry, by Kenton, w/ combination door cast w/ a blacksmith, nickel mostly worn off, 5½" H $86.25

Mosque Bank, by the Judd Mfg. Co., blk. w/ blue wipe, w/ rotating gorilla, lacking finial, 6¾" H $1,380.00

Multiplying Bank, by J. & E. Stevens Co., in form of a Gothic-style bldg., cream, br. & red, lacking trap, 6½" H $4,887.50

Tower Bank 1890, by Kyser & Rex Co., w/ inner & outer alphabetic combination door lock, 7" H $1,035.00

Watchdog Safe, mech., by J. & E. Stevens, sides cast w/ a classical head, 5¾" H $546.25

Row 3, Left to Right

Jewel Chest Bank, still, w/ hinged lid, combination lock & bronzed foliate dec., 6½" W $316.25

Fidelity Trust Vaults Bank, still by J. Barton Smith, ornate bank kiosk, front w/ coin-slot & Little Lord Fontleroy-style "cashier", br. painted w/ gilt highlights, 7" H $431.25

State Bank, by Kenton w/ cupola dormer windows & locking door, 8¾" H $1,380.00

Independence Hall Bank, by Enterprise Mfg. Co., PA, w/ removable tower, tied reed plinth w/ gilt finish, 10¼" H $977.50

Time Safe, by E.M. Roche Novelty Co., NJ, nickel plated, clock hand operated opening mech., w/ orig. instruction sheet, 7¼" H $575.00

Row 1, Left to Right

World's Fair Bank, by J. & E. Stevens Co., "Columbus" cast into base, worn, 8¼" W $1,150.00

Indian & Bear Bank, lacks trap, paint loss, 10½" L $5,290.00

William Tell Bank, mech., by J. & E. Stevens Co., lacking balcony & trap, some chipping, 10½" L $373.25

Row 2, Left to Right

Bank, Lion hunter mech., by J. & E. Stevens Co., w/ firing rifle, moving head, & rearing lion, rifle inoperative, 11" W $3,220.00

Creedmoor Bank, by J. & E. Stevens Co., w/ red trousers, firing rifle & bell, mkd. "Bowden Series", 10" W . . .$920.00

Creedmoor Bank, by J. & E. Stevens Co., w/ firing rifle, paint chips, 10" L $575.00

Row 3, Left to Right

Lion & Monkeys Bank, by Kyser & Rex Co., lacks baby monkey & trap, much paint loss $488.75

Trick Pony Bank, by Shepard Hardware Co., chipping, 7" W $1,610.00

Speaking Dog Bank, by J. & E. Stevens Co., lacks trap, poor paint, 7" W $747.50

Lion & Monkeys Bank, by Kyser & Rex Co., lion lacking one eye, paint loss, 9¹⁄₁₆" L $1,160.00

A-MA Jan. 1999   Skinner, Inc.

Ferris Wheel Bank, the wheel finished in ora. & blk. w/ six yel. gondolas ea. carrying two male riders, finished in blk. w/ red highlights, underside mkd. "Bowen's Pat. Apd For", chipping to wheel & gondolas, 22" H $12,650.00

A-ME July 1998   Cyr Auction Co. Inc.
Box, dometop, molded & painted
pine w/ marbleized paint, gr. banding,
yel. pinstriping w/ simulated drawer,
18" x 8" x 10" $1,750.00

A-ME July 1998   Cyr Auction Co. Inc.
Box, red & blk. grained dovetailed
pine w/ brass handle, 18" x 8" x
10" $350.00

A-ME July 1998   Cyr Auction Co. Inc.
Box, vinegar grained pine w/ dometop, split on top, 22" x 9½" x
12" $800.00

A-ME July 1998   Cyr Auction Co. Inc.

Top to Bottom

Hat Box, floral, white roses on blk.
ground, wood, 5" H x 7½" W .$300.00
Bandbox, "Cows & Ruins", 10" H x
12" W $350.00
Bandbox, w/ drapery swag w/ roses
& vase, ca. 1830, blue w/ cream 11" H
x 16" W $600.00
Bandbox, "Joys of Rural Life", 11½" H
x 16½" W $100.00
Bandbox, "Laisser Courre", ca. 1830-
1840, 11½" H x 16½" W . . .$1,900.00
Bandbox, "Sandy Hook, ca. 1830-35,
12" H x 24" W $250.00

A-ME July 1998   Cyr Auction Co. Inc.

Shaker

Top to Bottom

Box, round covered, one finger dk.
blue, 2½" diam., 1½" H $450.00
Pantry Box, one finger dk. blue, 3" L,
1½" H $700.00
Pantry Box, one finger, 5½" L,
2¼" H $400.00
Pantry Box, one finger, gray, 5½" L,
2" H $350.00
Pantry Box, one finger, red, 6½" L,
2¾" H $350.00
Pantry Box, one finger late gr., 6" L,
2¾" H $250.00
Pantry Box, two finger, dk. gr., 8" L,
2¾" H $500.00
Pantry Box, two finger dk. mustard,
8" L, 2¾" H $850.00
Pantry Box, three finger, dk. gr.,
10¼" x 4" H $400.00

A-ME July 1998   Cyr Auction Co. Inc.
Box, salmon painted pine w/ finger
joints, gilt stenciled w/ fruit, oval
base, 11" x 7" x 7" $400.00

A-ME Jan. 1999   Cyr Auction Co. Inc.
Shaker Boxes, oval w/ orig. surface
paint, top 6½" x 9", mid. 7½" x 10½",
bottom 8¼" x 11½" $3,250.00

A-ME July 1998   Cyr Auction Co. Inc.
Box, paint dec. pine w/ molded
base & dovetailed corners, 12" x 10"
x 10" $350.00

A-PA Sept. 1998   Pook & Pook Inc.

Row 1, Left to Right

Tea Caddy, Regency, ca. 1790, lid w/ inlaid conch shell on gr. reserve & dk. border, int. w/ orig. lids & ivory handles, 4¾" H, 7½" W, 4½" D $2,100.00

Dresser Box, lacquerware, M.O.P. & gilt dec., ca. 1803, fitted int. w/ ivory needlecase, 3½" H, 9¾" W $200.00

Tea Caddy, Georgian tortoise shell, late 18th C., w/ domed lid & a fan carved front, retains silver mounts, 4½" H, 5½" W, 3¾" D $1,700.00

Tea Caddy, Birdseye maple, ca. 1800 w/ int. fitted lid & inlaid escut., 5" H, 5" W, 4" D $650.00

Tea Caddy, George III, fruitwood apple form, 4" H $1,600.00

Tea Caddy, Georgian satinwood octagonal w/ pearwood inlays & int. fitted lid, 5" H, 6¾" W, 4" D $450.00

Row 2, Left to Right

Tea Caddy, lacquerware, ca. 1830, ebonized surface w/ vine & marbleized bands & fitted int., 2½" H, 11" W, 7" D $175.00

Tin Box, 19th C. w/ floral tole dec. lift lid sgn. "C.F. Feurer", 1½" H, 4" W, 2½" D $100.00

Tea Caddy, Georgian apple form w/ iron escut., 5" H .$2,300.00

Dresser Box, lacquerware, early 19th C., w/ overall gilt dec. lift lid, hand-painted scene of 'Goolsbure Castle', 3½" H, 8" W, 6½" D $550.00

Tea Caddy, Georgian apple form, w/ an iron escut., 4¼" H $950.00

Dresser Box, lacquerware, early 19th C., lift lid w/ gilt & M.O.P. inlays, incl. 6 gilt & gr. glass bottles, 5¼" H, 5½" W, 6½" D $750.00

A-NH Nov. 1998   Northeast Auctions

Box, wood, N. Eng., w/ gray painted surface, 40" H, 21" W $1,300.00

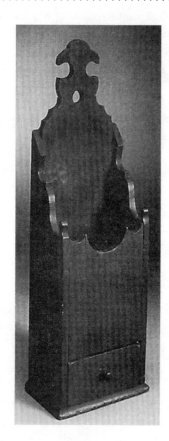

A-MA Feb. 1999   Skinner, Inc.

Pipe Box, pine w/ red wash, early 19th C., nailed const. reprs., 21¼" H, 5½" W $2,990.00

A-ME July 1998   Cyr Auction Co. Inc.

Wall Box, red painted , 14" H, 13" W, 6" D $1,200.00

ABC PLATES — Alphabet plates were made especially for children as teaching aids. They date from the late 1700s and were made of various material including porcelain, pottery, glass, pewter, tin and ironstone.

AMPHORA ART POTTERY was made at the Amphora Porcelain Works in the Teplitz Tum area of Bohemia during the late 19th and early 20th centuries. Numerous potteries were located there.

ANNA POTTERY — The Anna Pottery was established in Anna, IL, in 1859 by Cornwall and Wallace Kirkpatrick, and closed in 1894. The company produced utilitarian wares, gift wares and pig-shaped bottles and jugs with special inscriptions, which are the most collectible pieces.

BATTERSEA ENAMELS — The name "Battersea" is a general term for those metal objects decorated with enamels, such as pill, patch, and snuff boxes, doorknobs, and such. The process of fusing enamel onto metal—usually copper—began about 1750 in the Battersea District of London. Today the name has become a generic term for similar objects—mistakenly called "Battersea."

BELLEEK porcelain was first made at Fermanagh, Ireland, in 1857. Today this ware is still being made in buildings within walking distance of the original clay pits according to the skills and traditions of the original artisans. Irish Belleek is famous for its thinness and delicacy. Similar type wares were also produced in other European countries as well as the United States.

BENNINGTON POTTERY — The first pottery works in Bennington, Vermont, was established by Captain John Norton in 1793; and, for 101 years, it was owned and operated by succeeding generations of Nortons. Today the term "Bennington" is synonymous with the finest in American ceramics because the town was the home of several pottery operations during the last century—each producing under different labels. Today items produced at Bennington are now conveniently, if inaccurately, dubbed "Bennington." One of the popular types of pottery produced there is known as "Rockingham." The term denotes the rich, solid brown glazed pottery from which many household items were made. The ware was first produced by the Marquis of Rockingham in Swinton, England—hence the name.

BESWICK — An earthenware produced in Staffordshire, England, by John Beswick in 1936. The company is now a part of Royal Doulton Tableware, Ltd.

BISQUE — The term applies to pieces of porcelain or pottery which have been fired but left in an unglazed state.

BLOOR DERBY — "Derby" porcelain dates from about 1755 when William Duesbury began the production of porcelain at Derby. In 1769 he purchased the famous Chelsea Works and operated both factories. During the Chelsea-Derby period, some of the finest examples of English porcelains were made. Because of their fine quality, in 1773 King George III gave Duesbury the patent to mark his porcelain wares "Crown Derby." Duesbury died in 1796. In 1810 the factory was purchased by Robert Bloor, a senior clerk. Bloor revived the Imari styles which had been so popular. After his death in 1845, former workmen continued to produce fine porcelains using the traditional Derby patterns. The firm was reorganized in 1876 and in 1878 a new factory was built. In 1890 Queen Victoria appointed the company "Manufacturers to Her Majesty" with the right to be known as Royal Crown Derby.

BUFFALO POTTERY — The Buffalo Pottery of Buffalo, New York, was organized in 1901. The firm was an adjunct of the Larkin Soap Company, which was established to produce china and pottery premiums for that company. Of the many different types produced, the Buffalo Pottery is most famous for its "Deldare" line which was developed in 1905.

CANARY LUSTER earthenware dates to the early 1800s, and was produced by potters in the Staffordshire District of England. The body of this ware is a golden yellow and decorated with transfer printing, usually in black.

CANTON porcelain is a blue-and-white decorated ware produced near Canton, China, from the late 1700s through the last century. Its hand-decorated Chinese scenes have historical as well as mythological significance.

CAPO-di-MONTE, originally a softpaste porcelain, is Italian in origin. The first ware was made during the 1700s near Naples. Although numerous marks were used, the most familiar to us is the crown over the letter N. Mythological subjects, executed in either high or low relief and tinted in bright colors on a light ground, were a favorite decoration. The earlier wares had a peculiar grayish color as compared to the whiter bodies of later examples.

CARLSBAD porcelain was made by several factories in the area from the 1800s and exported to the United States. When Carlsbad became a part of Czechoslovakia after World War I, wares were frequently marked "Karlsbad." Items marked "Victoria" were made for Lazarus & Rosenfeldt, Importers.

CASTLEFORD earthenware was produced in England from the late 1700s until around 1820. Its molded decoration is similar to Prattware.

CELEDON — Chinese porcelain having a velvet-textured greenish-gray glaze. Japanese and other oriental factories also made celedon glazed wares.

CHELSEA — An early soft paste porcelain manufactured at Chelsea in London from around 1745 to 1769. Chelsea is considered to be one of the most famous of English porcelain factories.

CHELSEA KERAMIC ART WORKS — The firm was established in 1872, in Chelsea, MA, by members of the Robertson family. The firm used the mark CKAW. The company closed in 1889, but was reorganized in 1891, as the Chelsea Pottery U.S. In 1895, the factory became the Dedham Pottery of Dedham, MA, and closed in 1943.

CHINESE EXPORT PORCELAIN was made in quantity in China during the 1700s and early 1800s. The term identifies a variety of porcelain wares made for export to Europe and the United States. Since many thought the product to be of joint Chinese and English manufacture, it has also been known as "Oriental" or "Chinese Lowestoft."

As much as this ware was made to order for the American and European market, it was frequently adorned with seals of states or the coat of arms of individuals, in addition to eagles, sailing scenes, flowers, religious and mythological scenes.

CLARICE CLIFF POTTERY — Clarice Cliff (1899-1972) was a designer who worked at A.J. Wilkinson, Ltd.'s Royal Staffordshire Pottery at Burslem, England. Cliff's earthenwares were bright and colorful Art Deco designs which included squares, circles, bands, conical shapes and simple landscapes incorporated with the designs. Cliff used several different printed marks, each of which incorporated a facsimile of her signature—and generally the name of the pattern.

CLEWS POTTERY — (see also, Historical Staffordshire) was made by George Clews & Co., of Brownhill Pottery, Tunstall, England, from 1806-1861.

CLIFTON POTTERY — William Long founded the Clifton Pottery in Clifton, NJ, in 1905. Pottery was simply marked CLIFTON. Long worked until 1908, producing a line called Crystal Patina. The Cheasapeake Pottery Company made majolica marked Clifton Ware, which oftentimes confuses collectors.

COALPORT porcelain has been made by the Coalport Porcelain Works in England since 1795. The ware is still being produced at Stroke-on-Trent.

COORS POTTERY — Coors ware was made in Golden, CO, by the Coors Beverage Company from the turn of the century until the pottery was destroyed by fire in the 1930s.

COPELAND-SPODE — The firm was founded by Josiah Spode in 1770 in Staffordshire, England. From 1847, W.T. Copeland & Sons, Ltd., succeeded Spode, using the designation "Late Spode" to its wares. The firm is still in operation.

COPPER LUSTER — See Lusterwares.

CORDEY — Boleslaw Cybis was one of the founders of the Cordey China Company, Trenton, NJ. Production began in 1942. In 1969, the company was purchased by the Lightron Corporation, and operated as the Schiller Cordey Company. Around 1950, Cybis began producing fine porcelain figurines.

COWAN POTTERY — Guy Cowan produced art pottery in Rocky River, OH, from 1913 to 1931. He used a stylized mark with the word COWAN on most pieces. Also, Cowan mass-produced a line marked LAKEWARE.

CROWN DUCAL — English porcelain made by the A.G. Richardson & Co., Ltd. since 1916.

CUP PLATES were used where cups were handleless and saucers were deep. During the early 1800s, it was very fashionable to drink from a saucer. Thus, a variety of fancy small plates was produced for the cup to rest in. The lacy Sandwich examples are very collectible.

DAVENPORT pottery and porcelain were made at the Davenport Factory in Longport, Staffordshire, England, by Joan Davenport from 1793 until 1887 when the pottery closed. Most of the wares produced there—porcelains, creamwares, ironstone, earthenwares and other products—were marked.

DEDHAM (Chelsea Art Works) —The firm was founded in 1872 at Chelsea, Massachusetts, by James Robertson & Sons, and closed in 1889. In 1891 the pottery was reopened under the name of The Chelsea Pottery, U.S. The first and most popular blue underglaze decoration for the desirable "Cracqule Ware" was the rabbit motif—designed by Joseph L. Smith. In 1893 construction was started on the new pottery in Dedham, Massachusetts, and production began in 1895. The name of the pottery was then changed to "Dedham Pottery," to eliminate the confusion with the English Chelsea Ware. The famed crackleware finish became synonymous with the name. Because of its popularity, more than 50 patterns of tableware were made.

DELFT — Holland is famous for its fine examples of tin-glazed pottery dating from the 16th century. Although blue and white is the most popular color, other colors were also made. The majority of the ware found today is from the late Victorian period and when the name Holland appears with the Delft factory mark, this indicates that the item was made after 1891.

DORCHESTER POTTERY was established by George Henderson in Dorchester, a part of Boston, Massachusetts, in 1895. Production included stonewares, industrial wares, and, later, some decorated tablewares. The pottery is still in production.

DOULTON — The pottery was established in Lambeth in 1815 by John Doulton and John Watts. When Watts retired in 1845, the firm became known as Doulton & Company. In 1901 King Edward VII conferred a double honor on the company by presentation of the Royal Warrant, authorizing their chairman to use the word "Royal" in describing products. A variety of wares has been made over the years for the American market. The firm is still in production.

DRESDEN — The term identifies any china produced in the town of Dresden, Germany. The most famous factory in Dresden is the Meissen factory. During the 18th century,

English and Americans used the name "Dresden china" for wares produced at Meissen which has led to much confusion. The city of Dresden which was the capital of Saxony, was better known in 18th century Europe than Meissen, which was fifteen miles away. Therefore, Dresden became a generic term for all porcelains produced and decorated in the city of Dresden and surrounding districts including Meissen. By the mid-19th century, about thirty factories in the city of Dresden were producing and decorating porcelains in the style of Meissen. Therefore, do not make the mistake of thinking all pieces marked Dresden were made at the Meissen factory. Meissen pieces generally have crossed swords marks and are listed under Meissen.

FLOWING BLUE ironstone is a highly glazed dinnerware made at Staffordshire by a variety of potters. It became popular about 1825. Items were printed with patterns (Oriental) and the color flowed from the design over the white body so that the finished product appeared smeared. Although purple and brown colors were also made, the deep cobalt blue shades were the most popular. Later wares were less blurred, having more white ground.

FRANKOMA — The Frank Pottery was founded in 1933, by John Frank, Sapulpa, Ok. The company produced decorative wares from 1936-38. Early wares were made from a light cream-colored clay, but in 1956 changed to a red brick clay. This along with the glazes helps to determine the period of production.

FULPER — The Fulper mark was used by the American Pottery Company of Flemington, NJ. Fulper art pottery was produced from approximately 1910 to 1930.

GALLÉ — Emile Gallé was a designer who made glass, pottery, furniture and other Art Nouveau items. He founded his factory in France in 1874. Ceramic peices were marked with the initials E.G. impressed, Em. Gallé Faiencerie de Nancy, or a version of his signature.

GAUDY DUTCH is the most spectacular of the gaudy wares. It was made for the Pennsylvania Dutch market from about 1785 until the 1820s. This softpaste tableware is lightweight and frail in appearance. Its rich cobalt blue decoration was applied to the biscuit, glazed and fired—then other colors were applied over the first glaze—and the object was fired again. No luster is included in its decoration.

GAUDY IRONSTONE was made in Staffordshire from the early 1850s until around 1865. This ware is heavier than gaudy Welsh or gaudy Dutch, as its texture is a mixture of pottery and porcelain clay.

GAUDY WELSH, produced in England from about 1830, resembles Gaudy Dutch in decoration, but the workmanship is not as fine and its texture is more comparable to that of spatterware. Luster is usually included with the decoration.

GOUDA POTTERY — Gouda and the

surrounding areas of Holland have been one of the principal Dutch pottery centers since the 17th century. The Zenith pottery and the Zuid-Hollandsche pottery, produced the brightly colored wares marked GOUDA from 1880 to about 1940. Many pieces of Gouda featured Art Nouveau or Art Deco designs.

GRUEBY — Grueby Faience Company, Boston, MA, was founded in 1897 by William H. Grueby. The company produced hand thrown art pottery in natural shapes, hand molded and hand tooled. A variety of colored glazes, singly or in combinations were used, with green being the most prominent color. The company closed in 1908.

HAEGER — The Haeger Potteries, Inc., Dundee, IL, began making art wares in 1914. Their early pieces were marked with the name HAEGER written over the letter "H." Around 1938, the mark changed to ROYAL HAEGER.

HAMPSHIRE — In 1871 James S. Taft founded the Hampshire Pottery Company in Keene, NH. The company produced redware, stoneware, and majolica decorated wares in 1879. In 1883, the company introduced a line of colored glazed wares, including a Royal Worcester-type pink, blue, green, olive and reddish-brown. Pottery was marked with the printed mark or the impressed name HAMPSHIRE POTTERY or J.S.T. & CO., KEENE, N.H.

HARKER — The Harker Pottery Company of East Liverpool, OH, was founded in 1840. The company made a variety of different types of pottery including yellowware from native clays. Whiteware and Rockingham-type brown-glazed pottery were also produced in quantities.

HISTORICAL STAFFORDSHIRE — The term refers to a particular blue-on-white, transfer-printed earthenware produced in quantity during the early 1800s by many potters in the Staffordshire District. The central decoration was usually an American city scene or landscape, frequently showing some mode of transportation in the foreground. Other designs included portraits and patriotic emblems. Each potter had a characteristic border which is helpful to identify a particular ware, as many pieces are unmarked. Later transfer-printed wares were made in sepia, pink, green and black but the early cobalt blue examples are the most desirable.

HULL — In 1905, Addis E. Hull purchased the Acme Pottery Company in Crooksville, OH. In 1917, Hull began producing art pottery, stoneware and novelties including the Little Red Riding Hood line. Most pieces had a matte finish with shades of pink and blue or brown predominating. After a flood and fire in 1950, the factory was reopened in 1952 as the Hull Pottery Company. Pre-1950 vases are marked HULL USA or HULL ART USA. Post-1950 pieces are simply marked HULL in large script or block letters. Paper labels were also used.

HUMMEL — Hummel items are the original creations of Berta Hummel, born in 1909 in Germany. Hummel collectibles are made by W. Goebel Porzellanfabrik of Oeslau, Germany, now Rodenthal, West Germany. They were first made in 1934. All authentic Hummels bear both the signature, M.I. Hummel, and a Goebel trademark. However, various trademarks were used to identify the year of production.

IRONSTONE is a heavy, durable, utilitarian ware made from the slag of iron furnaces, ground and mixed with clay. Charles Mason of Lane Delft, Staffordshire, patented the formula in 1823. Much of the early ware was decorated in imitation of Imari, in addition to transfer-printed blue ware, flowing blues and browns. During the mid-19th century, the plain white enlivened only by embossed designs became fashionable. Literally hundreds of patterns were made for export.

JACKFIELD POTTERY is English in origin. It was first produced during the 17th century; however, most items available today date from the last century. It is a red-bodied pottery, often decorated with scrolls and flowers, in relief, then covered with a black glaze.

JASPERWARE — A very hard, unglazed porcelain with a colored ground, varying from blues and greens to lavender, red, yellow or black. White designs were generally applied in relief to these wares, and often times reflect a classical motif. Jasperware was first produced by Wedgwood's Etruria Works in 1775. Many other English potters produced jasperware, including Copeland, Spode and Adams.

JUGTOWN POTTERY — This North Carolina pottery has been made since the 18th century. In 1915 Jacques Busbee organized what was to become the Jugtown Pottery in 1921. Production was discontinued in 1958.

KING'S ROSE is a decorated creamware produced in the Staffordshire district of England during the 1820-1840 period. The rose decorations are usually in red, green, yellow and pink. This ware is often referred to as "Queen's Rose."

LEED'S POTTERY was established by Charles Green in 1758 at Leed, Yorkshire, England. Early wares are unmarked. From 1775 the impressed mark "Leeds Pottery" was used. After 1880 the name "Hartly, Green & Co." was added, and the impressed or incised letters "LP" were also used to identify the ware.

LIMOGES — The name identifies fine porcelain wares produced by many factories at Limoges, France, since the mid-1800s. A variety of different marks identify wares made there including Haviland china.

LIVERPOOL POTTERY — The term applies to wares produced by many potters located in Liverpool, England, from the early 1700s, for American trade. Their print-decorated pitchers—referred to as "jugs" in England—have been especially popular. These featured patriotic emblems, prominent men, ships, etc., and can be easily identified as nearly all are melon-shaped with a very pointed lip, strap handle and graceful curved body.

LONHUDA — In 1892, William Long, Alfred Day, and W.W. Hunter organized the Lonhuda Pottery Company of Steubenville, OH. The firm produced underglaze slip-decorated pottery until 1896, when production ceased. Although the company used a variety of marks, the earliest included the letters LPCO.

LOTUS WARE — This thin Belleek-like porcelain was made by the Knowles, Taylor & Knowles Company of Easter Liverpool, OH, from 1890 to 1900.

LUSTERWARE — John Hancock of Hanley, England, invented this type of decoration on earthenwares during the early 1800s. The copper, bronze, ruby, gold, purple, yellow, pink and mottled pink luster finishes were made from gold painted on the glazed objects, then fired. The latter type is often referred to as "Sunderland Luster." Its pinkish tones vary in color and pattern. The silver lusters were made from platinum.

MAASTRICHT WARE — Petrus Regout founded the De Sphinx pottery in 1835 at Maastricht, Holland. The company specialized in transfer painted earthenwares.

MAJOLICA — The word MAJOLICA is a general term for any pottery glazed with an opaque tin enamel that conceals the color of the clay body. It has been produced by many countries for centuries. Majolica took its name from the Spanish island of Majorca, where figuline (a potter's clay) is found. This ware frequently depicted elements in nature: birds, flowers, leaves and fish. English manufacturers marked their wares and most can be identified through the English Registry mark, and/or the potter-designer's mark, while most continental pieces had an incised number. Although many American potteries produced majolica between 1850 and 1900, only a few chose to identify their wares. Among these were the firm of Griffen, Smith, and Hill; George Morely; Edwin Bennett; Cheaspeake Pottery Company; and the new Milford-Wannoppe Pottery Company.

MARBLEHEAD — This hand thrown pottery had its beginning in 1905 as a therapeutic program by Dr. J. Hall for the patients of a Marblehead, MA, sanitarium. Later, production was moved to another site and the factory continued under the management of A.E. Baggs until it closed in 1936. The most desirable pieces found today are decorated with conventionalized designs.

MATT-MORGAN — By 1883 Matt Morgan, an English artist, was producing art pottery in Cincinnati, OH, that resembled Moorish wares. Incised designs and colors were applied to raised panels, then shiny or matte glazes were applied. The firm lasted only a few years.

McCOY POTTERY — The J.W. McCoy Pottery was established in 1899. Production of art pottery began after 1926 when the name was changed to Brush McCoy.

MEISSEN — The history of Meissen porcelain began in Germany in 1710 in the Albrechtsburg fortress of Meissen, about twelve miles from Dresden. The company was first directed by Johann Boettger, who developed the first truly white porcelain in Europe. The crossed swords mark of the Meissen factory was adopted in 1723.

METTLACH, Germany, located in the Zoar Basin, was the location of the famous Villeroy & Boch factories from 1836 until 1921 when the factory was destroyed by fire. Steins (dating from about 1842) and other stonewares with bas relief decorations were their specialty.

MINTON — Thomas Minton established his pottery in 1793 at Stroke-on-Trent, Hanley, England. During the early years, Minton concentrated on blue transfer painted earthenwares, plain bone china, and cream colored earthenware. During the first quarter of the 19th century, a large selection of figures and ornamental wares were produced in addition to their tableware lines. In 1968, Minton became a member of the Royal Doulton Tableware group, and retains its reputation for fine quality hand painted and gilted tablewares.

MOCHAWARE — This banded creamware was first produced in England during the late 1700s. The early ware was lightweight and thin, having colorful bands of bright colors decorating a body that is cream colored to very light brown. After 1840 the ware became heavier in body and the color was often quite light—almost white. Mochaware can easily be identified by its colorful banded decorations—on and between the bands—including feathery ferns, lacy trees, seaweeds, squiggly designs and lowly earthworms.

MOORCROFT — William Moorcroft established the Moorcroft Pottery, in Burslem, England in 1913. The majority of the art pottery wares were hand thrown. The company initially used an impressed mark, MOORCROFT, BURSLEM, with a signature mark, W.MOORCROFT, following. Walker, William's son, continued the business after his father's death in 1945, producing the same style wares. Contemporary pieces are marked simply MOORCROFT with export pieces also marked MADE IN ENGLAND.

NEWCOMB — William and Ellsworth Woodward founded Newcomb Pottery at Sophie Newcomb College, New Orleans, LA, in 1896. Students decorated the high quality art pottery pieces with a variety of designs that have a decidedly southern flavor. Production continued through the 1940s. Marks include the letters NC and often have the incised initials of the artist as well. Most pieces have a matte glaze.

NILOAK POTTERY with its prominent swirled, marbelized designs, is a 20th century pottery first produced at Benton, Arkansas, in 1911 by the Niloak Pottery Company. Production ceased in 1946.

NIPPON porcelain has been produced in quantity for the American market since the late 19th century. After 1891, when it became obligatory to include the country of origin on all imports, the Japanese trademark "Nippon" was used. Numerous other marks appear on this ware identifying the manufacturer, artist or importer. The hand-painted Nippon examples are extremely popular today and prices are on the rise.

NORSE POTTERY was founded in 1903 in Edgerton, WI. The company moved to Rockford, IL, in 1604, where they produced a black pottery which resembled early bronze items. The firm closed in 1913.

OHR POTTERY was produced by George E. Ohr in Biloxi, Mississippi, around 1883. Today Ohr is recognized as one of the leading potters in the American Art Pottery movement. Early work was often signed with an impressed stamp in block letters—G.E. OHR, BILOXI. Later pieces were often marked G.E. Ohr in flowing script. Ohr closed the pottery in 1906, storing more than 6,000 pieces as a legacy to his family. These pieces remained in storage until 1972.

OLD IVORY dinnerware was made in Silesia, Germany during the late 1800s. It derives its name from the background color of the china. Marked pieces usually have a pattern number on the base, and the word "Silesia" with a crown.

OTT & BREWER — The company operated the Etruria Pottery in Trenton, NJ, from 1863 to 1893. A variety of marks were used which incorporated the initials O & B.

OWENS — The Owens Pottery began production in Zanesville, OH, in 1891. The first art pottery was made after 1896, and pieces were usually marked OWENS. Production of art pottery was discontinued about 1907.

PAUL REVERE POTTERY — This pottery was made at several locations in and around Boston, MA, between 1906 and 1942. The company was operated as a settlement house program for girls. Many pieces were signed S.E.G. for Saturday Evening Girls. The young artists concentrated on children's dishes and tiles.

PETERS & REED Pottery Company of Zanesville, Ohio, was founded by John D. Peters and Adam Reed about the turn of the century. Their wares, although seldom marked, can be identified by the characteristic red or yellow clay body touched with green. This pottery was best known for its matte glaze pieces—especially one type, called Moss Aztec, combined a red earthenware body with a green glaze. The company changed hands in 1920 and was renamed the Zane Pottery Company. Examples marked "Zaneware" are oftentimes identical to earlier pieces.

PEWABIC — Mary Chase Perry Straton founded the Pewabic Pottery in 1903 in Detroit, MI. Many types of art pottery was produced here including pieces with matte green glaze and an iridescent crystaline glaze. Operations ceased after the death of Mary Stratton in 1961, but the company was reactivated by Michigan State University in 1968.

PISGAH FOREST POTTERY — The pottery was founded near Mt. Pisgah in North Carolina in 1914 by Walter B. Stephen. The pottery remains in operation.

QUIMPER — Tin-glazed, hand-painted pottery has been produced in Quimper, France, dating back to the 17th century. It is named for a French town where numerous potteries were located. The popular peasant design first appeared during the 1860s, and many variations exist. Florals and geometrics were equally as popular. The HR and HR QUIMPER marks are found on Henriot pieces prior to 1922.

REDWARE is one of the most popular forms of country pottery. It has a soft, porous body and its color varies from reddish-brown tones to deep wine to light orange. It was produced in mostly utilitarian forms by potters in small factories, or by potters working on their farms, to fill their everyday needs. The most desirable examples are the slip-decorated pieces, or the rare and expensive "sgraffito" examples which have scratched or incised line decoration. Slip decoration was made by tracing the design on the redware shape with a clay having a creamy consistency in contrasting colors. When dried, the design was slightly raised above the surface.

RED WING ART POTTERY AND STONEWARE — The name includes several potteries located in Red Wing, MN. David Hallem established his pottery in 1868, producing stoneware items with a red wing stamped under the glaze as its mark. The Minnesota Stoneware Co. began production in 1883. The North Star Stoneware company began production in 1892, and used a raised star and the words Red Wing as its mark. The two latter firms merged in 1892, producing stoneware until 1920, when the company introduced a pottery line. In 1936, the name was changed to Red Wing Potteries. The plant closed in 1967.

RIDGWAY — Throughout the 19th century the Ridgway family, through partnerships held positions of importance in Shelton and Hanley, Staffordshire, England. Their wares have been made since 1808, and their transfer-design dinner sets are the most widely known product. Many pieces are unmarked, but later marks include the initials of the many partnerships.

RIVIERA — This dinnerware was made by the Homer Laughlin Company of Newell, WV, from 1938 to 1950.

ROCKINGHAM — See Bennington Pottery.

ROOKWOOD POTTERY — The Rookwood Pottery began production at Cincinnati, Ohio, in 1880 under the direction of Maria Longworth Nichols Storer, and operated until 1960. The name was derived from the family estate, "Rookwood," because of the "rook" or "crows" which inhabited the wooded areas. All pieces of this art pottery are marked, usually bearing the famous flame.

RORSTRAND FAIENCE — The firm was founded in 1726 near Stockholm, Sweden.

Items dating from the early 1900s and having an "art noveau" influence are very expensive and much in demand these days.

ROSE MEDALLION ware dates from the 18th century. It was decorated and exported from Canton, China, in quantity. The name generally applied to those pieces having medallions with figures of people alternating with panels of flowers, birds and butterflies. When all the medallions were filled with flowers, the ware is identified as Rose Canton.

ROSE TAPESTRY — See Royal Bayreuth.

ROSEVILLE POTTERY — The Roseville Pottery was organized in 1890 in Roseville, Ohio. The firm produced utilitarian stoneware in the plant formerly owned by the Owens Pottery of Roseville, also producers of stoneware, and the Linden Avenue Plant at Zanesville, Ohio, originally built by the Clark Stoneware Company. In 1900 an art line of pottery was created to compete with Owens and Weller lines. The new ware was named "Rozane," and it was produced at the Zanesville location. Following its success, other prestige lines were created. The Azurine line was introduced about 1902.

ROYAL BAYREUTH manufactory began in Tettau in 1794 at the first porcelain factory in Bavaria. Wares made there were on the same par with Meissen. Fire destroyed the original factory during the 1800s. Much of the wares available today were made at the new factory which began production in 1897. These include Rose Tapestry, Sunbonnet Baby novelties and the Devil and Card items. The Royal Bayreuth blue mark has the 1794 founding date incorporated with the mark.

ROYAL BONN — The tradename identifies a variety of porcelain items made during the 19th century by the Bonn China Manufactory, established in 1755 by Elmer August. Most of the ware found today is from the Victorian period.

ROYAL CROWN DERBY — The company was established in 1875 in Derby, England, and has no connection with the earlier Derby factories which operated in the late 18th and early 19th centuries. Derby porcelain produced from 1878 to 1890 carry the standard crown printed mark. From 1891 forward, the mark carries the "Royal Crown Derby" wording, and during the present century, "Made in England" and "English Bone China" were added to the mark. Today the company is a part of Royal Doulton Tableware, Ltd.

ROYAL DOULTON wares have been made from 1901, when King Edward VII conferred a double honor on the Doulton Pottery by the presentation of the Royal Warrant, authorizing their chairman to use the word "Royal" in describing products. A variety of wares has been produced for the American market. The firm is still in production.

ROYAL DUX was produced in Bohemia during the late 1800s. Large quantities of this decorative porcelain ware were exported to the United States. Royal Dux figurines are especially popular.

ROYAL RUDOLSTADT — This hard paste ware was first made in Rudolstadt, Thuringen, East Germany, by Ernt Bohne in 1854. A second factory was opened in 1882 by L. Straus & Sons, Ltd. The ware was never labeled "Royal Rudolstadt" originally, but the word "Royal" was added later as part of an import mark. This porcelain was imported by Lewis Straus and Sons of New York.

ROYAL WORCESTER — The Worcester factory was established in 1751 in England. This is a tastefully decorated porcelain noted for its creamy white lusterless surface. Serious collectors prefer items from the Dr. Wall (the activator of the concern) period of production which extended from the time the factory was established to 1785.

ROYCROFT POTTERY was made by the Roycrofter community of East Aurora, New York, during the late 19th and early 20th centuries. The firm was founded by Elbert Hubbard. Products produced included pottery, furniture, metalware, jewelry and leatherwork.

R.S. GERMANY porcelain with a variety of marks was produced at the Tillowitz, Germany, factory of Reinhold Schlegelmilch from about 1869 to 1956.

R.S. PRUSSIA porcelain was produced during the mid-1800s by Erdman Schlegelmilch in Suhl. His brother, Reinhold, founded a factory in 1869 in Tillowitz in lower Silesia. Both made fine qualtiy porcelain, using both satin and high gloss finishes with comparable decoration. Additionally, both brothers used the same R.S. mark in the same colors, the initials being in memory of their father, Rudolph Schlegelmilch. It has not been determined when production at the two factories ceased.

RUSKIN is a Brittish art pottery. The pottery, located at West Smethwick, Birmingham, England, was started by William H. Taylor. His name was used as the mark until around 1899. The firm discontinued producing new pieces of pottery in 1933, but continued to glaze and market their remaining wares until 1935. Ruskin pottery is noted for its exceptionally fine glazes.

SAMPSON WARE dates from the early 19th century. The firm was founded in Paris and reproduced a variety of collectible wares including Chelsea, Meissen and Oriental Lowestoft, with marks which distinguish their wares as reproductions. The firm is still in production.

SATSUMA is a Japanese pottery having a distinctive creamy crackled glaze decorated with bright enamels and often with Japanese figures. The majority of the ware available today includes the mass-produced wares dating from the 1850s. Their quality does not compare to the fine early examples.

SEWER TILE — Sewer tile figures were made by workers at sewer tile and pipe factories during the late nineteenth and early twentieth centuries. Vases and figurines with added decorations are now considered folk art by collectors.

SHAWNEE POTTERY — The Shawnee Pottery Company was founded in 1937 in Zanesville, OH, The plant closed in 1961.

SHEARWATER POTTERY — was founded by G.W. Anderson, along with his wife and their three sons. Local Ocean Springs, MS, clays were used to produce their wares during the 1930s, and the company is still in business.

SLEEPY EYE — The Sleepy Eye Milling Company, Sleepy Eye, MN, used the image of the 19th century Indian chief for advertising purposes from 1883 to 1921. The company offered a variety of premiums.

SPATTERWARE is a softpaste tableware, laboriously decorated with hand-drawn flowers, birds, buildings, trees, etc., with "spatter" decoration chiefly as a background. It was produced in considerable quantity from the early 1800s to around 1850.

To achieve this type of decoration, small bits of sponge were cut into different shapes—leaves, hearts, rosettes, vines, geometrical patterns, etc.—and mounted on the end of a short stick for convenience in dipping into the pigment.

SPONGEWARE, as it is known, is a decorative white earthenware. Color—usually blue, blue/green, brown/tan/blue, or blue/brown—was applied to the white clay base. Because the color was often applied with a colorsoaked sponge, the term "spongeware" became common for this ware. A variety of utilitarian items were produced—pitchers, cookie jars, bean pots, water coolers, etc. Marked examples are rare.

STAFFORDSHIRE is a district in England where a variety of pottery and porcelain wares has been produced by many factories in the area.

STICKSPATTER — The term identifies a type of decoration that combines hand-painting and transfer-painted decoration. "Spattering" was done with either a sponge or brush containing a moderate supply of pigment. Stickspatter was developed from the traditional Staffordshire spatterware, as the earlier ware was time consuming and expensive to produce. Although most of this ware was made in England from the 1850s to the late 1800s, it was also produced in Holland, France and elsewhere.

TEA LEAF is a lightweight stone china decorated with copper or gold "tea leaf" sprigs. It was first made by Anthony Shaw of Longport, England, during the 1850s. By the late 1800s, other potters in Staffordshire were producing the popular ware for export to the United States. As a result, there is a noticeable diversity in decoration.

TECO POTTERY is an art pottery line made by the Terra Cotta Tile works of Terra Cotta, Illinois. The firm was organized in 1881 by William D. Gates. The Teco line was first made in 1885 but not sold commercially until 1902 and was discontinued during the 1920s.

UHL POTTERY — This pottery was made in Evansville, IN, in 1854. In 1908 the pottery was moved to Huntingburg, IN, where their stoneware and glazed pottery was made until the mid-1940s.

UNION PORCELAIN WORKS — The company first marked their wares with an eagle's head holding the letter "S" in its beak around 1876; the letters "U.P.W." were sometimes added.

VAN BRIGGLE POTTERY was established at Colorado Springs, Colorado, in 1900 by Artus Van Briggle and his wife, Anna. Most of the ware was marked. The first mark included two joined "As," representing their first two initials. The firm is still in operation.

VILLEROY & BOCH — The pottery was founded in 1841 at Mettlach, Germany. The firm produced many types of pottery including the famous Mettlach steins. Although most of their wares were made in the city of Mettlach, they also had factories in other locations. Fortunately for collectors, there is a dating code impressed on the bottom of most pieces that makes it possible to determine the age of the piece.

VOLKMAR pottery was made by Charles Volkmar, New York, from 1879 to around 1911. Volkmar had been a painter, therefore many of his artistic designs often look like oil paintings drawn on pottery.

WALRATH — Frederick Walrath worked in Rochester, NY, New York City, and at the Newcomb Pottery in New Orleans, LA. He signed his pottery items "Walrath Pottery." He died in 1920.

WARWICK china was made in Wheeling, WV, in a pottery from 1887 to 1951. The most familiar Warwick pieces have a shaded brown background. Many pieces were made with hand painted or decal decorations. The word ILGA is sometimes included with the Warwick mark.

WEDGWOOD POTTERY was established by Josiah Wedgwood in 1759 in England. A tremendous variety of fine wares has been produced through the years including basalt, lusterwares, creamware, jasperware, bisque, agate, Queen's Ware and others. The system of marks used by the firm clearly indicates when each piece was made.

Since 1940 the new Wedgwood factory has been located at Barleston.

WELLER POTTERY — Samuel A. Weller established the Weller pottery in 1872 in Fultonham, Ohio. In 1888 the pottery was moved to Piece Street in Putnam, Ohio—now a part of Zanesville, Ohio. The production of art pottery began in 1893 and by late 1897 several prestige lines were being produced including Samantha, Touranda and Dicken's Ware. Other later types included Weller's Louwelsa, Eosian, Aurora, Turada and the rare Sicardo which is the most sought after and most expensive today. The firm closed in 1948.

WHEATLEY — Thomas J. Wheatley worked with the founders of the art pottery movement in Cincinnati, Ohio. He established the Wheatley Pottery in 1880, which was purchased by the Cambridge Tile Manufacturing Company in 1927.

A-OH Oct. 1998   Early Auction Company

Row 1, Left to Right

B70-Vase, purple w/ white iris dec., Belleek, 12½" H $500.00

B37-Vase, hand painted pink orchid, sgn. Willets Belleek, 8½" H . .$350.00

B62-Tankard, gr. & purple grapes, gold handle, Lenox mark, 14" H $275.00

B52-Cookie Jar, w/ cover, blue w/ gold dec., Ott & Brewer, 6" H $100.00

B68-Pitcher, gray w/ birds, Belleek, 10½" H $200.00

B10-Three Pieces, Willets Belleek creamer 2½" H, covered sugar 3" H & vase w/ enameled pink roses in blk. vase, 8" H, artist sgn. & dated 1917 . . . .$40.00

B31-Cracker Barrel
Lenox covered, colorful pastel enameled "mums", gold trim pallette mark, 7" H $175.00

B25-Bowl, Belleek w/ gold dragon handles, ruby & pink roses w/ foliage, 4"H $200.00

B72-Vase, lifesize yel. roses on br. & gr. ground, gold dec., Belleek, 15½" H $400.00

B51-Coffee Pot, w/ cover, br. w/ clouds, fish scale porcelain design, Ott & Brewer china, 8½" H $50.00

B64-Tankard, gr. & purple grapes, gold handle, CAC mark, 14" H $400.00

Row 2, Left to Right

B39-Loving Cup, three handled, rose dec., hand dec., CAC mark, 7¼" H $250.00

B55-Vase, dec. w/ poppies, artist sgn., Willets Belleek, 8" H . . .$100.00

B31A-Creamer, 3¾" H & berry bowl, raised gold floral branches, gold trim, CAC mark, 2" H $55.00

B35-Mug, white Toby undec., Lenox Wreath, 6½" H $50.00

B18-Tumblers, six Lenox, colorful della-robia asst. fruit on gold ground, palette mark, 4¾" H $250.00

B40-Jug, yel. & purple pansies, hand dec., artist sgn., gold spout & handle, CAC mark, 6" diam. $250.00

B24-Two Pieces, RCA Victor dog salt shaker, Lenox, 3" H, Lenox hexagonal gold textured bud vase, 2½" H $60.00

B7-Bowl & Nappie, circular bowl mkd. Belleek w/ enamel dec. bird on berried branch, 1¾" H, 5" diam., & Pickard handled nappie w/ lake & pagoda, sgn. Marker, 6½" diam. $250.00

B28-Creamer, Belleek, 4¾" H & covered sugar, pink wild roses, gold dragon handles, 4½" H $75.00

B34-Vase, all over gold w/ white bamboo dec., Belleek, 8¼" H . .$70.00

B32-Cider Jug, hand dec. w/ red currants & gr. foliage, CAC mark, 5¾" H $225.00

B60-Vase, yel. roses & lilacs, Belleek, 14" H $525.00

B27-Creamer, Belleek, 3" H & covered sugar, rims w/ gold lacy design & gold handles, 3¾" H $75.00

Row 3, Left to Right

B13-Plates, six Willets Belleek, dec. w/ amethyst & blue pansies w/ raised gold leaves, gilt emb. border, 7" diam. $150.00

B41-Mug, dk. gr., monk drinking beer, Willets Belleek, 5¾" H . . .$60.00

B42-Mug, pink & blue, manls portrait, Belleek, 5½" H $70.00

B43-Mugs, two, gr. & purple grapes, gr. & gold handles, hand painted, one w/ rim chip, Belleek, 5" H $50.00

B57-Salt Cellars, 3 silver overlay, 2 matching w/ 3 ball feet, Willets Bellek & Lenox, 2" diam. $75.00

B44-Mug, br. & red berries, gold handle, CAC mark, 5" H $45.00

B45-Mug, br. w/ musketeer, CAC mark, 5½" H $80.00

B46-Mug, red currants w/ gr. leaves, Belleek, 5½" H $90.00

B20-Four Pieces, 3 Lenox swans, 2 cream, 1½" H & 3½" H & pink 3" H & oval sauce bowl w/ blue enamel beaded rim w/ gold trim, 2¼" H, 5" diam. $70.00

B47-Mug, gr. hops dec., hand painted, artist sgn., CAC mark, 4¾" H $40.00

B48-Mug, irid. Bird of Paradise, Lenox mark, 7½" H $225.00

B50-Mug, rose design, gold handle, CAC mark, 5½" H $55.00

B49-Mug, blk. ground w/ Dutch figures, Belleek, 7¼" H $70.00

B19-Two Pieces, Willets Bellek bowl, yel. fruit w/ foliage, gold trim, 8¾" diam., & oval bowl w/ pink scalloped rim dec. w/ blue & amethyst floral swags w/ gold flowers, 3 gold feet, 3" H, 8½" diam. $125.00

Row 4, Left to Right

B38-Vase, red poinsettia w/ gold & blk., Willets Belleek, 8½" H . .$125.00

B16-Creamer, 3¾" H & sugar w/ raised gold floral branches, cream grounds, 3½" H $125.00

B17-Pitcher, Lenox palette mark, hand dec. w/ blk. raspberries, pink blossoms & gr. foliage, gold beaded handle, artist initials, 5½" H . .$175.00

B22-Creamer, & covered sugar, Willets Belleek, ea. w/ colorful floral sprays, gold dragon handles, both 4" H $175.00

B26-Plates, 3 oyster, molded w/ shells, crab legs & foliage, mkd. Union Porcelain Works, 2-8½" L, 1-10¼" L $600.00

B1-Tea Service, Lenox, cream w/ gold Art Deco handles, covered coffee 11" H, covered teapot 7" H, creamer 5¾" H, covered sugar 6" H . . .$175.00

Row 5, Left to Right

B11-Two Pieces, Belleek, shell form oval nappie w/ scroll handle, scattered pink roses, gold rim, 2½" H, 6" L & ribbed shell form pitcher w/ gold bamboo handle, 6" H $250.00

B20-Four Pieces, 3 Lenox swans, 2 cream, 1½" H & 3½" H & pink 3" H & oval sauce bowl w/ blue enamel beaded rim w/ gold trim, 2¼" H, 5" diam. $70.00

B4-Lenox Ware, 4 pcs., all cream w/ gold trim, pr. salt & pepper shakers, 2½" H, oval footed compote, 3¼" H, circular bowl w/ 3 gold ball feet, 1¾" H, 4¾" diam. $25.00

B12-Cups & Saucers, four Lenox chocolate cups 3¼" H & saucer 5¼" diam., gold trims, one cup chipped $50.00

B33-Dresser Set, seven pcs., tray, 8" x 11½", powder shaker 5" H, ring tree 3" H, 2 circular & 1 oval covered boxes, trinket tray 2½" x 6: L, all w/ raised gold stylized roses on cream palette mark $300.00

A-OH July 1998   Garth's Auctions

Pearlware w/ Blue & White Peony Dec.

Row 1, Left to Right

Sugar Bowl, Caughley, mismatched lid has applied flower & leaves finial, repr., 5½" H $275.00

Waste Bowl, Caughley, 4¾" diam. $165.00

Teapot, Worcester, mismatched lid, applied finial, chips, unmkd., 5¼" H $275.00

Row 2, Left to Right

Milk Jug, Worcester sparrow-beak, sm. chips & hairline in spout, 4½" H $192.50

Waste Bowl, Caughley, chips on foot, 6⅛" diam. $247.50

Cup & Saucer, Worcester handleless $181.50

A-OH Oct. 1998　　Early Auction Company

Row 1, Left to Right

B54-Vase, Japanese girl, artist sgn., Lenox mark, 10¼" H $250.00

B130-Three Pieces, demi-tasse cup, 2" H, saucer 4½" diam., yel. & white w/ shell-like surface, Ott & Brewer & coffee cup, yel. int., gold twig handle w/ pink flower $105.00

B66-Tankard, Troubadour & girl, hand painted D'Arcy Decorators, JH Schindle artist, Belleek, 15" H, age line $300.00

B123-Pitcher, bamboo & lotus blossom dec., w/ bamboo handle, Belleek $100.00

B128-Pitcher, gargoyle w/ ornate handle & dec., Belleek, pierced masked spout $750.00

B71-Vase, w/ Grecian handles, gr. & gold, CAC mark, 19" H $400.00

B91-Finger Vase, white w/ silver overlay, Lenox, 8½" H $170.00

B77-Vase
gold w/ red poppies, Pickard dec., Willets Belleek, 13" H $350.00

B79-Demi-tasse, six, white w/ gold & blue enamel dec., sterling holders, CAC wreath $275.00

B63-Tankard, gr. & purple grapes, gold handle, Belleek, 14" H . .$250.00

B75-Vase, white w/ enamel nymphs & deer w/ silver overlay, Lenox, Rockwell silver mark, 10¼" H . . .$175.00

B125-Creamer, lavender flowers w/ raised gold flowers, ornate shape, CAC palette mark, 4¾" H $50.00

B61-Tankard, apple blossoms, gold handle, CAC mark, 14" H $350.00

B85-Mug, br. w/ silver overlay, CAC wreath, 5½" H $250.00

Row 2, Left to Right

B121-Bowl, twig gold handles, multi-colored flowers, Belleek, 4¾" H $275.00

B136-Vase, floral design, double scroll handles, K.T. & K. Lotus, 7½" H $375.00

B129-Vase, gr. base & top w/ heavy gold bands, center white w/ gold clouds, Ott & Brewer, 9¾" H . .$200.00

B88-Sugar, w/ cover & creamer, br. w/ silver overlay, web & scroll design, Lenox, 4" H $125.00

B113-Bowl, dragon handles, gold bands & blackberry & foliage dec., Belleek, 11" diam. $500.00

B109-Three Pieces, coffee pot, 8½" H, sugar & creamer, 3" H, white w/ silver overlay, Oriental motif, Lenox, Rockwell silver mark $450.00

B99-Vase, red poppies w/ gr. ground, Belleek, 13½" H . . . . .N/S

B103-Dish, covered, gr. w/ silver overlay, Lenox, 6¼" diam. . . .$275.00

B76-Urns, pr., Grecian design, white w/ silver overlay, Lenox $175.00

B80-Jug, br. & gr. w/ silver overlay, "RYE", CAC mark $200.00

B81-Jug

"Scotch", br. w/ silver overlay, CAC wreath $100.00

Row 3, Left to Right

B110-Four Pieces, teapot, 6" H, sugar & creamer & ceramic infuser & covered condiment jar, br. w/ silver overlay, Lenox wreaths $330.00

B127-Ewer, Belleek, gold cactus handle, pink Christmas flower dec., angled bamboo spout, 8" H . . . . .N/S

B102-Decanter, cobalt blue w/ silver overlay, "Scotch", handle & stopper, CAC wreath, 4" H $300.00

B144-Vase, Truscan, gr. fish net design w/ nasturtiums, gr. & gold ground, K.T. & K. Lotus $360.00

B135-Cup, 2" H & saucer 5½" diam., shell surface w/ raised gold flower branches, Ott & Brewer $75.00

B124-Bowl, w/ twig gold handles, thistle dec., creamy textured surface, Belleek, 5" H, 6½" diam. . . .$300.00

B141-Rose Bowl, covered, multi-covered art deco dec., K.T. & Lotus $800.00

B148-Cider Pitcher, Belleek, mkd. Darcy, hand dec., lrg. pink water lily & buds w/ gr. pods, gold handle, artist sgn., 7" H $350.00

B147-Salt & Pepper, & mustard jar, lt. gr. w/ silver overlay, 3" H, CAC wreath $200.00

Row 4, Left to Right

B122-Pitcher, white w/ molded bamboo gold motif, Belleek, 5½" H $125.00

B134-Bowl, Columbia, fish net design w/ raised gold flower blossoms, K.T. & K. Lotus $350.00

B132-Three Pieces, Demi-tasse cup, 2" H, saucer 4½" diam., pink int. glaze, white w/ raised gold flowers & butterfly, Ott & Brewer & creamer 3" H, pink lustre shell surface $150.00

B100-Vase, cobalt blue w/ silver overlay CAC wreath, 8" H . . .$450.00

B67-Cups & Saucers, 9 sets, floral dec., ea. pc. different factory dec., all styles of period, Willets Belleek $810.00

B133-Sugar & Creamer, covered, white w/ gold fish net design, gold twig handles, K.T. & K. Lotus, 2½" H $225.00

B105-Three Pieces, coffee pot, 7½" H, sugar bowl & creamer, 2¾" H, gold wash w/ silver overlay, CAC Pegasus silver mark $175.00

B84-Candlesticks, 2 white w/ silver overlay, Lenox Wreath, 8½" H .$125.00

B139-Bowl, Columbia, undec., molded flowers & knobs, K.T. & K. Lotus $300.00

B111-Three Pieces, teapot, 7½" H, sugar & creamer, 2½" H, cobalt blue w/ silver overlay, hexagonal shape, Lenox wreath $575.00

Row 5, Left to Right

B92-Creamer, & covered sugar, cobalt blue w/ silver overlay, CAC wreath, 2" H $175.00

B82-Two Pieces, salt shaker, cobalt blue w/ silver overlay, 1¾" H, CAC Wreath & demi-tasse silver overlay mug, 3" H $75.00

B67-Cups & Saucers, 9 sets, floral dec., ea. pc. different factory dec., all styles of period, Willets Belleek $810.00

B90-Teapot, br. w/ silver overlay, CAC Pegasus silver mark, inside rim chip, 4½" H $100.00

B138-Bowl, Columbia, raised lavender flowers w/ gold fish scale design, K.T. & K. Lotus $300.00

B131-Demi-tasse Cup, 2" H & saucer, 4" diam., dec. w/ Palmer Cox Brownies, CAC mark $275.00

B89-Sugar, & creamer, br. w/ silver overlay, 2½" H $160.00

A-OH Sept. 1998　　Garth's Auctions

Staffordshire Miniatures

Left to Right

Cat, seated, sponged blk. & br. on white, glazed over crack, 4½" H $275.00

Cats, two similar facing, blk. & yel. on white, one damaged, 3⅞" H . .$357.50

Cat, seated, sponged blk. & yel., wear & chips, 4¼" H $275.00

A-OH Nov. 1998　　Garth's Auctions

Old Sleepy Eye Pottery in Cobalt Blue & White

Creamer, 2¼" H $27.50

Creamer, stains, 4" H $137.50

Cigarette Jar, mkd. "WS. Co....Ill", chips, 3" H $27.50

Creamer, wear & crazing, 4" H $137.50

Mug, mkd. "W.S. Co....Ill.", 4⅜" H $275.00

Row 2, Left to Right

Pitcher, repr. to handle, 8⅞" H $165.00

Pitcher, int. stains, 7⅞" H . . .$220.00

Pitcher, stains & hairlines, 6½" H $275.00

Pitcher, minor stains & crazing, 5⅜" H $165.00

A-PA Oct. 1998   Conestoga Auction
Co., Inc.

Gaudy Dutch

Row 1, Left to Right

Waste Bowl, Butterfly patt., 3¾" H, x
6½" diam. $3,080.00
Cup Plate, War Bonnet pattern, 3⅞"
diam. $1,540.00
Teapot, Dahlia pattern, minor use,
6" H $12,100.00
Cup Plate, Grape patt., 3⅜" diam-
eter $1,540.00
Plate, Urn patt., 7½" diam. . .$1,870.00

Row 2, Left to Right

Plate, Dove patt., 10" diam. .$4,510.00
Coffee Pot, Dove patt., dome top,
11" H $20,350.00
Plate, Butterfly patt., 9¾" . .$4,290.00

Row 3, Left to Right

Cup & Saucer, handleless, War Bon-
net patt. $660.00
Plate, Grape patt., 7¼" diam. . .$385.00
Plate, War Bonnet patt., hairline, 7¼"
diam. $880.00
Cup & Saucer, handleless Gaudy
Dutch, Dove pattern, minor pin
nips $385.00

A-PA Oct. 1998   Conestoga Auction
Co., Inc.

Historical Blue Staffordshire

Row 1, Left to Right

Plate, "Arms of New York" by T.
Mayer, 10" diam. $880.00
Plate, "Woodlands near Philadelphia",
6¾" diam. $247.50
Plate, "Park Theater New York", 10"
diam. 357.50

Row 2, Left to Right

Plate, "Arms of R.I.", designed by T.
Mayer, 8¾" diam. $550.00
Soup Plate, "Oltagon Church, Boston"
by J. & W. Ridgway, 9¾" diam. .$660.00
Plate, "Gulpin Mills on the Brandywine Creek", impr. Wood & Son, 9¼"
diam. $357.50

Row 3, Left to Right

Soup Plate, "United State Hotel
Philadelphia", 10¼" diam. . . .$825.00
Plate, "Fairmont near Philadelphia",
impr. Stubbs, 10¼" diam. $247.50
Plate, "Table Rock Niagara", impr.
Wood & Sons, 10¼" diam. . . .$632.50

A-PA Oct. 1998   Conestoga Auction Co., Inc.

Spatterware

Row 1, Left to Right

Plate, blue triple yel. Acorn patt., 9¼" diam. $3,080.00

Sugar, covered, child's gr. peafowl dec. repr., incl. pitcher $330.00
Plate, red w/ blue, gr. & red peafowl on branch w/ gr. leaves, 8⅝" $880.00

Pitcher, child's gr. peafowl dec. repr., incl. sugar $330.00
Plate, purple w/ triple br. acorn design, 9¼" diam. $1,320.00

Row 2, Left to Right

Plate, blue w/ red schoolhouse w/ yel. roof, gr. & blk. foreground, 8½" diam. $4,070.00
Plate, purple paneled w/ double yel. acorn design, 5" diam. $3,190.00
Pitcher, blue, Castle pattern, 7¾" H $1,210.00
Plate, blue w/ primrose design, 5" diam. $440.00
Plate, blue & gr. rainbow plate w/ ora./br. flowers, blue buds & gr. leaves, 8" diam. $687.50

Row 3, Left to Right

Plate, purple, Holly Berry patt., chip on backside of rim $220.00
Cup Plate, blue, w/ blue, gr. & red peafowl & gr. foreground, 4" diam. $990.00
Plate, yel. border Morning Glory patt., blue flower w/ blk. highlights & gr. leaves, 9¾" diam. $4,070.00
Plate, blue & purple Bull's Eye patt. w/ rainbow, hairline & sm. chip, 4⅛" diam. $93.50
Plate, blk. & purple Bull's Eye w/ rainbow, repr., 9½" diam. $302.50

A-PA Oct. 1998   Conestoga Auction Co., Inc.

Gaudy Dutch

Row 1, Left to Right

Cream Pitcher, Single Rose patt., 4½" H $660.00
Waste Bowl, Dove patt., sm. hairline, 3¼" H x 6½" diam. $440.00
Waste Bowl, Single Rose pattern, tiny chip on base rim, 3" H, 6¼" diam. $770.00
Plate, "Double Rose" patt., 4,⅜" diam. $1,210.00

Row 2, Left to Right

Plate, Double Rose patt., 7¼" $440.00
Cream Pitcher, Dove pattern, 4¼" H $1,650.00
Plate, Zinnia patt., 8½" . . .$2,860.00
Cream Pitcher, Carnation patt., 4½" H $1,375.00
Plate, Single Rose patt., 7" .$522.50

Row 3, Left to Right

Plate, Grape patt., 9¾" . . .$2,310.00
Plate, Double Rose patt., 10" $935.00
Plate, War Bonnet patt., 9¾" diam. $1,127.50

A-PA Oct. 1998   Conestoga Auction Co., Inc.

Canary Yellow Earthenware

Row 1, Left to Right

Tea Bowl, ora. br. floral & cherry & gr. foliage design, 2½" H, 4½" diam. $605.00

Pitcher, mask form w/ blk. & orange/brown dot design, repr. spout, 6" H $467.50

Planter, w/ underplate, canary yel. having ora./br. flowers w/ lt. blue centers $1,045.00

Pitcher, double sided ora. flowers w/ ora. & blk. leaves & foliage, tiny hairline, 6½" H $1,320.00

Mug, polychrome foliate dec. band, 2½" H $385.00

Row 2, Left to Right

Mug, lrg. w/ double sided ora. / br. flowers & buds w/ silver lustre leaves & band dec., 5" H $990.00

Vase, ora. br. & blue gr. vine w/ flared top, minor pin nips, 4¼" H $935.00

Pitcher, polychrome transfer & hand dec., sgn. "R. Johnson, Hanley Staffordshire", bruise & glaze loss, 5¼" H $2,750.00

Pepper Pot, w/ incised zig-zag design, minor pin nips, 4¼" H $1,485.00

Bowl, reddish br. floral & foliate dec. w/ gr. highlights, 3⅝" H, 6⅞" diam. $400.00

Row 3, Left to Right

Cup & Saucer, handless w/ ora. br. transfer depicting mother w/ children, impr. Sewell, sm. chip $467.50

Mug, child's w/ blk. transfer of woman, rabbits & dog, 2½" H $357.50

Bowl, w/ ora. & br. flowers, buds & gr. leaf running patt., pin nip & sm. flaw on inside rim $1,017.50

Mug, w/ LaFayette/Washington blk. transfer, 2½" H $2,310.00

Cup & Saucer, handleless cup w/ ora. & br. transfer of fishing scene, impr. Sewell $412.50

Row 4, Left to Right

Plate, polychrome dec. w/ emb. floral border, foliate & floral dec. in center, 8¼" diam. $1,595.00

Mug, child's w/ blue & ora./br. flowers & lt. blue leaves, hairline, 2½" $176.00

Plate, stylized King's Rose w/ blue flowers & orange/brown & gr. leaves, minor paint loss, 9½" H . . .$1,540.00

Mug, child's w/ orange/brown floral & blue/green leaf dec., 2½" H .$357.50

Plate, ora. br. floral & gr. foliage dec., approx. 8⅝" diam. $990.00

A-PA Oct. 1998   Conestoga Auction Co., Inc.

Spatterware

Row 1, Left to Right

Waste Bowl, gr. Tulip patt., sm. hairline, 4" H, 5⅞" diam. $3,850.00

Cup & Saucer, handleless, red w/ blue, yel. & gr. peafowl dec. .$357.50

Cup & Saucer, handleless, blue Rooster patter $2,640.00

Cream Pitcher, blue, Castle patt. w/ double sided dec., 4½" H . .$1,100.00

Row 2, Left to Right

Cup & Saucer, handleless w/ gr., blue & red criss-cross stripe design . . .$3,808.00

Cup & Saucer, handleless, blue, purple & gr. rainbow dec. $1,705.00

Cup & Saucer, handleless yel. .$1,650.00

Cup & Saucer, handleless blue & gr. $2,640.00

A-PA Oct. 1998   Conestoga Auction
                                      Co., Inc.

Mochaware

Row 1, Left to Right

Pepper Pot, dome top, w/ ora., br., gr. & blue/gray band dec., repr., 4" H $522.50

Master Salt, footed w/ cat's eye design on green/gray ground, br. bands, 2¼" H, 2¾" diam. $605.00

Pepper Pot, dome top w/ br. squiggle line & dot bands on cream ground, 4¼" H $770.00

Bowl, dk. br., blue/gray & opaque white zig zag earthworm dec. on ora./br. ground, 3½" H, 7⅜" diam. $797.50

Pepper Pot, dome top w/ ora./br. opaque white & dk. br. zig zag earth-worm & cat's eye design, 4" H $1,100.00

Master Salt, footed w/ br. seaweed dec. on gray ground, & dk. br. bands, 2" H, 3" diam. $357.50

Mustard Pot, br. bands & design on white ground, chips on lid, 3½" H $110.00

Row 2, Left to Right

Bowl, opaque white, blk. lt. blue looping earthworm dec. on gray ground, tin chips, 2¾" H x 4¾" W $467.50

Mug, straight sided w/ dk. br. & tan bands, sm. chips, 3¼" H $275.00

Chamber Pot, Yellowware, child's w/ br. seaweed mocha dec. & br. bands, 4" H, 8" diam. $220.00

Pepper Pot, earthworm design w/ blue feather edge dome top, opaque white & br. zig zag on blue/gray ground, 5" H $1,320.00

Pepper Pot, dome top w/ br./ blk. seaweed dec. on orange/tan ground, w/ orange/brown bands, repr., 3½" $385.00

Bowl, Earthworm patt., blue, tan & br. zig zag on white ground & br. bands, 2" hairline, 3" H, 5½" diam. $330.00

Row 3, Left to Right

Pitcher, Cat's Eye dec. w/ multiple & random blk., br., opaque white & lt. blue design on gray gr. ground, repr., 7" H $1,100.00

Bowl, Earthworm patt., int. opaque white, tan, br. & blk. on med. blue/gray ground, ext. in opaque white br. & blk. on a gray gr. ground w/ blk. bands, chip, 4¼" H, 10¾" diam. . . .$2,200.00

Pitcher, earthworm & cat's eye patterns, opaque white, br. & blue criss-crossing patt. on brown/ orange ground, chip on spout, 7¼" H $3,410.00

Row 4, Left to Right

Mug, blue & blk. cat's eye design on br. bands w/ blk. bands, repr., 4¾" H $550.00

Pitcher, opaque white & blk. cat's eye design on gray/green ground flanked by tan & blue bands, repr. $1,072.50

Pitcher, blk. dot dec. on white ground w/ blk. & blue/gray bands, hairline & repr., 6" H $302.50

Mug, blue, gr. & blk. sprigs on opaque white ground, w/ blk. & green/gray band dec., 5½" H $440.00

Mug, straight sided, dk. br., blue/ gray & opaque white looping earth-worm dec. on ora./br. ground, 3¼" H $522.50

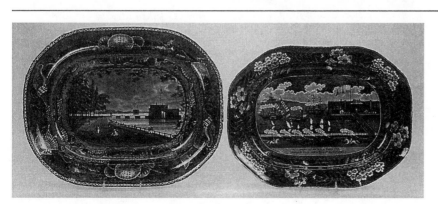

A-PA Oct. 1998   Conestoga Auction
                                      Co., Inc.

Historical Blue Staffordshire

Row 1, Left to Right

Platter, "Castle Garden Batt., NY", impr. "Wood & Sons", 16¼" x 20½" $3,410.00

Platter, "Landing of Gen. Lafayette", impr. Clews, 14½" x 19" . . .$1,265.00

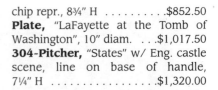

chip repr., 8¾" H $852.50
Plate, "LaFayette at the Tomb of Washington", 10" diam. . . . $1,017.50
304-Pitcher, "States" w/ Eng. castle scene, line on base of handle, 7¼" H $1,320.00

Row 2, Left to Right

Sauce Tureen, covered, ladle depicting "Savannah Bank" & "Charleston Exchange" on base & "Insane Hospital, Boston" on lid, 7" H, 8¼" W . . . . ,. $1,265.00
Bowl, "Beauties of Am. City Hall NY", scrolled open handle, footed, sgn. J&W Ridgway, 5" H, 11" diam. . . $4,180.00
Sauce Dish, w/ underplate, "Landing of Lafayette", impr. Clews, minor chip on lid, dish 5½" H, 4½" W, plate, 5¾" x 9¼" $1,375.00

Row 3, Left to Right

Cup & Saucer, handleless, "Landing of Gen. Lafayette" $357.50
Vegetable Dish, "States", covered w/ English castle scene impr. Clews, 6½" H, 12½" W, 9½" L $5,770.50
Cup & Saucer, Am. eagle & shield handless, sm. chip on base rim of cup $522.50

A-PA Oct. 1998   Conestoga Auction Co., Inc.

Historical Blue Staffordshire

Row 1, Left to Right

Pitcher, "Landing of Gen. LaFayette",

Row 1, Left to Right

Cup & Saucer, handleless, red, Dahlia patt. $715.00
Cream Pitcher, blk. & yel. rainbow, 4" H $2,310.00
Cream Pitcher, blue w/ red, yel. & gr. peafowl design, 3⅝" H . $1,320.00
Cup & Saucer, handleless, red & yel. rainbow, cluster of buds, red flowers w/ gr. leaves $3,410.00

Row 2, Left to Right

Plate, blue Castle patt., 9¾" diam. $1,100.00
Pitcher, blue w/ pinwheel patt. & sunburst border, 10¼" H $990.00
Plate, red, Dahlia patt., 9¼" diam. $1,320.00

Row 3, Left to Right

Plate, yel., thistle patt., repr., 7⅜" diam. $467.50
Sugar Bowl, three color rainbow, red, yel. & blue, covered, handles in rose dec., minor int. use & wear, 7¼" H $5,610.00
Sugar Bowl, covered red & yel. rainbow, w/ double sided thistle design, repr. & hairlines, 5¼" H $935.00
Plate, blue w/ red, yel. & gr. peafowl dec. $440.00

A-PA Oct. 1998   Conestoga Auction Co., Inc.

Spatterware

A-OH Nov. 1998   Cincinnati Art Galleries

Roseville Pottery

Row 1, Left to Right

Vase, Clematis w/ br., emb. "Roseville USA..." $75.00
Basket, Zephyr Lily in gr., emb., 10¼" H $300.00
Floor Vase, Clematis in gr., emb., nick, 15¼" H $300.00
Vase, Wincraft in blue, emb., 12¼" H $175.00
Vase, Wincraft vase w/ pine cone dec., emb., 8⅜" H $75.00

Row 2, Left to Right

Vase, Clematis, two handled in gr., emb., 6⅛" H $100.00
Bowl, Zephyr Lily in br., emb., 2¾" H, 9⅞" Diam. $50.00
Vase, Wincraft w/ pine cone dec., emb., sm. flake, 6⅛" H . . . . .N/S

A-OH Nov. 1998   Cincinnati Art Galleries

Roseville Pottery

Row 1, Left to Right

Vase, Clemana in br., impr. "Roseville", glaze skips, 6¼" H $250.00
Vase, Carnelian II in rich gr., mauve br. & tan glaze combo., unmkd., bruise on foot, 8" H $200.00
Wall Pocket, Vista, 9⅜" H . .$600.00
Vase, Bushberry in br., emb., 8⅛" H $150.00

Row 2, Left to Right

Ash Tray, creamware w/ decal "K. of P. Grand Lodge Zanesville, OH, 1915", mkd., sm. rim bruise, 2⅛" H . .$50.00
Flower Frog, Bushberry in gr., emb. "Roseville U.S.A. 45", 4⅞" H . .$150.00
Vase, Laurel in persimmon color, mkd. w/ "x", painted in blue slip, repr. rim chip, 6⅛" H $150.00

A-OH Nov. 1998   Cincinnati Art Galleries
Vase, Iris glaze w/ sailboat scene on peach colored ground, ca. 1911 by Kataro Shirayamadani, sm. glaze flaws repr., 14" H $13,500.00

A-OH Nov. 1998   Cincinnati Art Galleries
Vase, Vellum glaze w/ white irises, ca. 1927 by Ed Diers, Rookwood logo, 14¼" H $7,250.00

A-OH Nov. 1998   Cincinnati Art Galleries
Vase, Iris glaze w/ lilac dec., pale blue flowers & pale gr. leaves on purple ground, ca. 1901 by John Dee Wareham, mkd. Rookwood, minor glaze imper., 11⅞" H $4,000.00

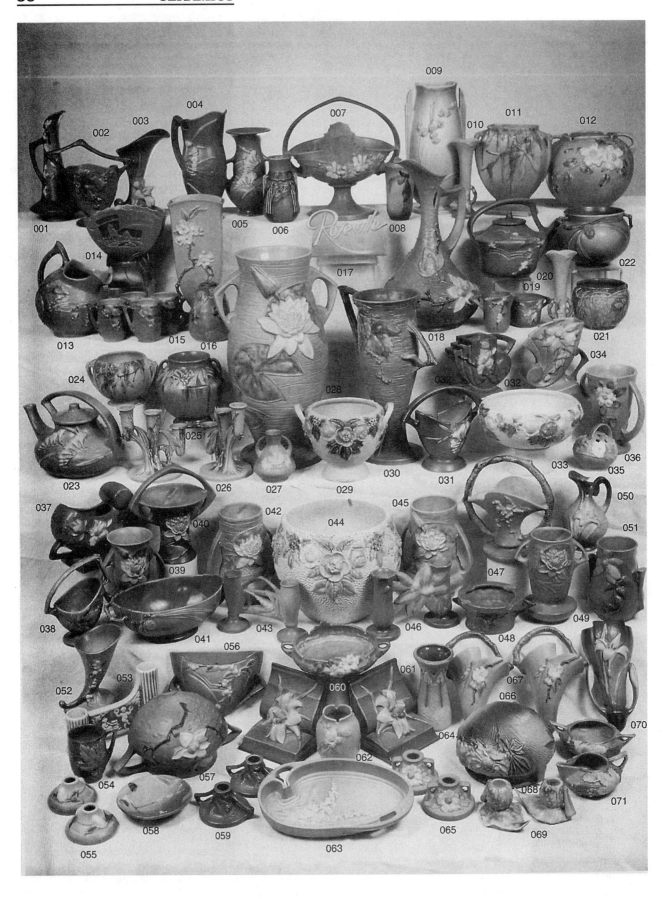

A-IA July 1998   Jackson's

Roseville Pottery

Row 1, Left to Right

1-Ewer, "Snowberry", blue w/ emb. mark, minor rim flake $110.00
2-Basket, "Bushberry", russet, emb. mark, 8½" H $181.50
3-Lilly Vase, "Zephyr", evergreen, emb. mark, 8½" H $137.50
4-Pitcher, "Freesia", delft blue, emb. mark, chip on base, 10½" H . .$176.00
5-Vase, "Freesia", 2-handled in delft blue, emb. mark, chip on base, 8" H $71.50
6-Vase, "Laurel", persimmon, paper label, 6" H $247.50
7-Basket, "Cosmos", gr., handled, impr. mark, minor foot rim flakes, 11" H $231.00
8-Tumbler, "Pinecone", gr., emb. mark, 5" H $148.50
9-Vase, "Ixia", gr., impr. mark, minor foot rim flake, 12½" H $220.00
10-Bud Vase, "Apple Blossom", gr., emb. mark & shape, 7½" H . .$126.50
11-Vase, "Moss", tan & blue, impr. mark & shape, 8½" H, minor flake under foot, ...$275.00
12-Bowl/Vase, "White Rose", blue, emb. mark & shape, 7½" H . .$192.50

Row 2, Left to Right

13-Cider Set, "Bushberry", 5-pc., blue, w/ pitcher & four mugs, emb. mark, 9" H & 3½" H $495.00
14-Vase, "Silhouette", rose w/ dec. emb. mark & shape, 7½" H . .$412.50
15-Vase, "Apple Blossom", pink, emb. mark & shape, 12" H $192.50
16-Vase, "Blackberry", gr., paper label, 5"H $440.00
17-Dealer Sign, pink w/ molded trademark script, 7½" L . . .$1,925.00
18-Ewer, "Magnolia", tan, emb. mark & shape, chip on base & rim flake, 16" H $137.50
19-Tea Set, "Snowberry", 3 pc., blue, tea pot, cream & sugar, emb. mark & shape, damage to sugar handle, 7" H, 3½" H 220.00
20-Vase, "Apple Blossom", blue, emb. mark & shape, 7½" H $104.50
21-Bowl, "Wisteria", br. w/ gr. vines & lavender wisteria, paper label, 4" H $375.50
22-Jardiniére, "Pinecone", br., impr. mark & shape, 5" H $220.00

Row 3, Left to Right

23-Teapot, "Freesia", covered in tangerine, emb. mark & shape, minor foot flake, 7" H $115.50
24-Rose Bowl, "Moss", tan & blue, impr. mark & shape, 4½" H . .$165.00
25-Vase, "Baneda", handled in gr. & blue, 6½" H $440.00

26-Candle Holders, "Moss", pr. 3 socket in pink & gr., impr. mark & shape, 7" H $495.00
27-Vase, "Cosmos", 2 handled in gr., emb. mark & shape, 4" H $82.50
28-Floor Vase, "Waterlily", handled in blue, emb. mark & shape, prof. repr. to foot & handle, 18½" H $220.00
28A-Vase, "Rozane Patt." turquoise, emb. mark & shape, 15" H . . .$330.00
29-Urn, "Rozane 1917", footed in yel., printed circle mark, minor glaze flakes, 6" H $49.50
30-Vase, "Bushberry", handled in gr., emb. mark & shape, 14½" H .$522.50
31-Basket, "Freesia", handled in blue, emb. mark & shape, 7" H $137.50
32-Cornucopia, "Magnolia", gr., emb. mark & shape, minor glaze loss, 5" H $66.00
33-Bowl, "Rozane 1917", footed in ivory, minor hairline & flake, 9" diam. $38.50
34-Cornucopia, "Clematis", blue, emb. mark & shape, 6" H . . .$104.50
35-Flower Frog, "Cosmos", blue, impr. mark & shape, 3½" H . .$220.00
36-Vase, "White Rose", handled in blue, emb. mark & shape, 7" H $110.00

Row 4, Left to Right

37-Vase, "Magnolia" in gr., emb. mark & shape, 6" H $110.00
38-Basket, "Bushberry", gr., emb. mark & shape, 7" H $159.50
39-Vase, "Waterlily", tan & br., emb. mark & shape, 7" H $104.50
40-Basket, "Waterlily", tan & br., emb. mark & shape, 8" H . . .$115.50
41-Bowl, "Pinecone", br., impr. mark & shape, 11" L $220.00
42-Vase, "Waterlily", 2 handled in blue, emb. mark & shape, 8" H$110.00
43-Double Bud Vase, "Foxglove", blue, emb. mark & shape, 5" H $137.50
44-Jardiniére, "Rozane 1917", in ivory, printed mark, minor glaze flakes, 11" diam. $82.50
45-Vase, "Waterlily", 2 handled in blue, emb. mark & shape, 8" H$110.00
46-Double Bud Vase, "Clematis", gr., embossed $66.00
47-Basket, "Apple Blossom", gr., emb. mark & shape, 8½" H . .$192.50
48-Ash Tray, "Bushberry", russet, emb. mark & shape, 5½" diam. $99.00
49-Vase, "Waterlily", handled in pink & gr., emb. mark & shape, 7½" H $137.50
50-Ewer, "Zephyr Lily", gr., emb. mark & shape, 6½" H $115.50
51-Vase, "Clematis", tan, emb. mark & shape, 6" H $66.00

Row 5, Left to Right

52-Cornucopia Vase, "Snowberry", blue, emb. mark & shape, 6" H $44.00
53-Double Bud Vase, "Donatello", 5" H $82.50
54-Mug, "Bushberry", gr., emb. mark, 3½" H $82.50
55-Candle Holders, "Peony", pr. in blue & br., emb. mark & shape, 2" H $82.50
56-Wall Pocket, "Snowberry", emb. mark & shape, sm. chip on rim, 7½" L $165.00
57-Hanging Basket, "Magnolia", gr., 11" L $137.50
58-Ash Tray, "Snowberry", blue, impr. mark, 5½" diam. $110.00
59-Candle Holders, "Bushberry", pr., russet, emb. mark & shape, 2" H $99.00
60-Bowl, "White Rose", tan & gr., emb. mark & shape, 7" diam. .$66.00
61-Bookends, "Freesia", tangerine, emb. mark & shape, chip on one flower, 5" H $104.50
62-Vase, "White Rose", blue, emb. mark & shape, 4½" H $77.00
63-Tray, "Foxglove", blue, impr. mark, 11' L $104.50
64-Vase, "Mostique", tan, 6"H .$82.50
65-Candle Holders, "Peony", pr. in pink, emb. mark & shape, 2" H $71.50
66-Wall Pocket, "Apple Blossom", gr., emb. mark & shape, 9" H . . .$192.50
67-Wall Pocket, "Apple Blossom", emb. mark & shape, 9" H . . .$192.50
68-Hanging Basket, "Peony", yel., emb. U.S.A., 7" diam. $104.50
69-Candle Holders, "Thornapple", pr. in gr., impr. mark & shape, 2½" H $110.00
70-Wall Pocket, "Zephyr Lily", Bermuda blue, emb. mark & shape, 8½" H $275.00
71-Cream & Sugar, "Bushberry", blue, emb. mark & shape, 2"H $137.50

A-PA Oct. 1998   Conestoga Auction Co., Inc.

Row 1, Left to Right

Plate, gr. border stick spatter ironstone w/ columbine, rosebud & thistle design, 8¾" diam. $275.00
Plate, blue sponge border ironstone plate w/ yel., red & gr. peafowl dec., impr. Cotton & Barlow, 8¾" diam. $660.00

A-IA July 1998   Jackson's

Roseville Pottery

Row 1, Left to Right

72-Vase, "Zephyr Lily", Bermuda blue, emb. mark & shape, 6½" H . . .$110.00

73-Ewer, "Zephyr Lily", Bermuda blue, emb. mark & shape, 10½" H $192.50

74-Vase, "Snow Berry", blue, emb. mark & shape, 6½" H $137.50

75-Vase, "Freesia", Delft blue, emb. mark & shape, 2 glaze flakes, 10½" H $104.50

76-Basket, "Freesia", handled in Delft blue, emb. mark & shape, 7" H $137.50

77-Basket, "Snowberry", emb. mark & shape, 12½" H $247.50

78-Vase, "Snowberry", blue, emb. mark & shape, 7" H $115.50

79-Pitcher, "Freesia", Delft blue, emb. mark & shape, 10½" H $192.50

80-Basket, "Snowberry", handled in blue, emb. mark & shape, 8"H $148.50

81-Ewer, "Snowberry", blue, emb. mark & shape, minor flake on foot rim, 10½" H $110.00

82-Vase, "Zephyr Lily", Bermuda blue, emb. mark & shape, 6" H $121.00

Row 2, Left to Right

83-Vase, "Florentine", br., printed "R" mark, 6" H $60.50

84-Urn, "Freesia", handled in Delft blue, emb. mark & shape, chip under foot rim, 8" H $82.50

85-Bowl, "Magnolia", tan, emb. mark & shape, 3" H $38.50

86-Bowl, "Bleeding Heart", handled in pink, emb. mark & shape . . .$198.00

87-Basket, "Zephyr Lily", handled in Bermuda blue, emb. mark & shape, 10" H $220.00

88-Ewer, "Snowberry", blue, emb. mark & shape, 6½" H $110.00

89-Cookie Jar, "Zephyr Lily", Bermuda blue, emb. mark & shape, 10" H $687.50

90-Basket, "Pinecone", gr., impr. mark & shape, 6½" H $253.00

91-Basket, "Snowberry", handled in blue, emb. mark & shape, 10½" H $165.00

92-Vase, "Zephyr Lily", handled in Bermuda blue, emb. mark & shape, 12½" H $187.00

93-Window Planter, "Freesia", tangerine, emb. mark & shape, 10½" H $82.50

94-Vase, "Snowberry", handled in blue, emb. mark & shape, minor roughness, 8½" H $82.50

95-Cornucopia, "Snowberry", blue, emb. mark & shape, 6½" H . . .$93.50

96-Ewer, "Zephyr Lily", Bermuda blue, emb. mark & shape, 6½" H $132.50

Row 3, Left to Right

97-Double Cornucopia, "White Rose", blue, emb. mark & shape, 8" H $195.50

98-Bowl, "Peony", handled in yel., emb. mark & shape, 4" H $66.00

99-Vase, "Snowberry" blue, emb. mark & shape, 8" H $165.00

100-Jardiniére, "Blackberry", gr., 4" H $357.50

101-Floor Vase, "Zephyr Lily", Bermuda blue, emb. mark & shape, 15½" H $440.00

102-Cornucopia, "Snowberry", blue, emb. mark & shape, 8½" H . .$110.00

103-Bowl, "Snowberry", blue, emb. mark & shape, 11½" diam. . .$165.00

104-Teapot, "Snowberry", gr., emb. mark & shape, no lid 7" H 82.50

105-Vase, "Dawn", pink, emb. mark & shape, minor flake, 6" H . . .$137.50

106-Basket, "Freesia", handled in Delft blue, emb. mark & shape, minor chip, 8½" H $110.00

107-Basket, "Gardenia", handled in sea foam, emb. mark & shape, 8" H $247.50

108-Vase, "Snowberry", emb. mark & shape, 7½" H $132.00

109-Vase, "Zephyr Lily", Bermuda blue, emb. mark & shape, minor flake on foot rim, 7½" H $77.00

110-Flower Pot, & underplate, "Apple Blossom", gr., emb. mark & shape, 6" H $148.50

111-Bud Vase, "Snowberry", blue, emb. mark & shape, 7½" H . .$110.00

Row 4, Left to Right

112-Vases, "Snowberry" pr. in blue, emb. mark & shape, 7½" H . .$203.50

113-Vase, "columbine", blue, emb. mark & shape, 6" H $165.00

114-Basket, "Zephyr Lily", handled in Bermuda blue, emb. mark & shape, 8½" H $220.00

115-Jardiniére, "Freesia", gr., emb. mark & shape, minor glaze flake, 5" H $110.00

116-Vase, "Snowberry", handled in blue, emb. mark & shape, 12½" H $247.50

117-Flower Pot, & underplate, "Apple Blossom", blue, emb. mark & shape, 5" H $165.00

118-Center Bowl, "Cosmos", blue, impr. mark & shape, 11½" diam. $385.00

119-Cornucopia Vase, "Snowberry", blue, emb. mark & shape, 7½" H $110.00

120-Floor Vase, "Waterlily", blue, emb. mark & shape, 24" H . . .$440.00

121-Jardiniére, "Peony", gr. emb. mark & shape, 3" H $60.50

122-Basket, "Zephyr Lily", handled in Bermuda blue, emb. mark & shape, 7" H $165.00

123-Pillow Vase, "Snowberry", blue, emb. mark & shape, 7" H . . .$110.00

124-Ewer, "Freesia", Delft blue, emb. mark & shape, 6½" H $137.50

125-Ewer, "Zephyr Lily", Bermuda blue, emb. mark & shape, 6½" H $110.00

Row 5, Left to Right

126-Ewer, "Snowberry", blue, emb. mark & shape, 6" H $110.00

127-Wall Pocket, "Zephyr Lily", Bermuda blue, emb. mark & shape, minor glaze flake, 8" H $192.50

128-Vase, "Freesia", Delft blue, emb. mark & shape, chip on base . .$66.00

129-Wall Pocket, "Columbine", blue, emb. mark & shape, 9" H . . .$286.00

130-Bookends, "Zephyr Lily", Bermuda blue, emb. mark & shape, repr. chip $99.00

131-Jardiniére, "Peony", pink & gr., emb. mark & shape, 7" diam. $121.00

132-Shell Planter, "Foxglove", gr., emb. mark & shape, 4½" H . .$192.50

133-Planters, pr. "Snowberry" in blue, emb. mark & shape, one handle repr., 5½" H $330.00

134-Vase, "Zephyr Lily", Bermuda blue, emb. mark & shape, 8½" H $154.00

Row 6, Left to Right

135-Candle Sticks, "Snowberry", pr. in blue, emb. mark & shape, 4" H $132.50

136-Planter, "Apple Blossom", pink, emb. mark & shape, 12" L $77.00

137-Vase, "Columbine", blue, emb. mark & shape, 3" H $104.50

138-Ash Tray, "Magnolia", emb. mark & shape $110.00

139-Console Set, "Bushberry", 3 pc., blue, emb. mark & shape, minor flake, 11" diam. $203.50

A-PA Oct. 1998   Conestoga Auction Co., Inc.

Historical Blue Staffordshire

Plate, "Landing of Gen. LaFayette", impr. Clews, 10" diam. $330.00

Plate, "Commodore MacDonough's Victory", 10" diam. $770.00

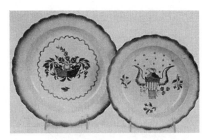

A-PA Oct. 1998   Conestoga Auction Co., Inc.

Leeds Soft Paste

Plate, gr. feather edge w/ polychrome flowers & foliate design, 9⅝" diam. $1,100.00

Plate, gr. feather edge w/ br., tan & blue Am. spread wing eagle & shield dec., 8" diam. $1,650.00

A-OH Nov. 1998   Cincinnati Art Galleries

Roseville Pottery, Row 1, Left to Right

Vase, Apple Blossom in blue, emb. "Roseville...", chip, 10⅜" H . . $175.00
Vase, Poppy two-handled in gray, impr. "Roseville...", sm. chip off base, rim repr., 12¼" H $100.00
Floor Vase, Apple Blossom in pink, emb. "Roseville...", 15⅜" H . .$650.00
Ewer, Poppy w/ white poppies on a gray ground, impr. "Roseville...", 10¼" H $250.00
Basket, Thornapple in blue, impr. "Roseville...", tight line at rim, 10½" H $75.00

Row 2, Left to Right

Vase, apple Blossom in gr., emb. "Roseville...", glaze nick, 7¼" H $100.00
Ewer, Apple Blossom in blue, emb. "Roseville...", 8⅛" H $250.00
Vase, Apple Blossom, two-handled in gr., emb. "Roseville...", minor roughness, 6" H $175.00

A-OH Nov. 1998   Cincinnati Art Galleries

Roseville Pottery

Row 1, Left to Right

Wall Pocket, Sunflower, unmkd., several cracks, 7¼" H $600.00
Vase, Cherry Blossom in br., two-handled, unmkd., 7⅛" H $400.00
Vase, Sunflower, two-handled, unmkd., 9⅛" H $1,700.00
Vase, Sunflower, unmkd., sm. rim chip repr., 8⅛" H $1,000.00
Vase, Sunflower w/ two wing-like handles, unmkd., 6" H $600.00

Row 2, Left to Right

Bowl, Wisteria in tan, unmkd., 2¼" H, 7¾" Diam. $300.00
Candlesticks, pr. Wisteria in tan, mkd. w/ gold foil label, one w/ repr. neck, 4½" H $250.00

A-OH Nov. 1998   Cincinnati Art Galleries
Vase, Iris glaze, winter scene on blue/gray ground, ca. 1912 by Carl Schmidt, two large. cracks profesionally repr. $3,600.00

A-OH Nov. 1998   Cincinnati Art Galleries
Vase, Iris glaze w/ white storks on blk. ground shading to cream, ca. 1907 by Carl Schmidt, mkd. w/ Rookwood logo, glaze bubble, 9½" H $3,400.00

A-OH Nov. 1998   Cincinnati Art Galleries
Vase, Vellum glaze w/ detailed pink & white carnations, ca. 1925 by Ed Ediers, w/ Rookwood logo, drilled bottom, 13⅜" H $3,100.00

A-OH Nov. 1998   Cincinnati Art Galleries

Hull Pattern Pottery

Row 1, Left to Right

Vase, in pink, impr. "U.S.A. Hull Art…", 8½" H $175.00
Basket, in blue, emb. "U.S.A. Hull Art…", 10½" H $475.00
Vase, in blue, pink & gr., emb. "U.S.A. Hull Art…", minor glaze skips & imper., 8½" H $150.00
Vase, in pink, impr. "Hull Art U.S.A.…", 5⅞" H $75.00

Row 2, Left to Right

Candlesticks, pr. in blue, impr. "Hull Art…U.S.A.", minor grinding chips, 3⅞" H $125.00
Flower Frog, Muncie "Duck" in pink & teal mat glaze, unmkd., 5½" H $100.00

A-OH Nov. 1998   Cincinnati Art Galleries

Rookwood

Vase, sharp high glaze w/ fruit blossoms, ca 1919 by Lorinda Epply, int. is slightly grainy, lemon yel. mat glaze, Rookwood logo, 5⅜" H $900.00
Vase, Vellum glaze w/ sailboats scene, ca. 1914 by Sallie Coyne, Rookwood logo, minor peppering, tiny glaze flake, 7" H $650.00
Jug, w/ sprigged tree dec. ca. 1883, impr. "Rookwood" on red clay bottom, 2⅜" H $425.00
Vase, emb. Art Deco ferns, blue on cream, ca. 1947, sgn. Jens Jensen, Rookwood logo, 11¾" H . . .$1,300.00
Vase, standard glaze, wild rose., ca 1894, Carrie Steinle, Rookwood logo, pin head glaze nick, 3" H $400.00
Vase, emb. leaves w/ colors from 1932 period, mkd. w/ Rookwood logo, 9⅜" H $475.00
Vase, emb. pine dec. w/ crystalline gr. mat glaze, ca. 1923, w/ Rookwood logo $500.00

A-OH Nov. 1998   Cincinnati Art Galleries
Vase, standard glaze w/ portrait of Native Am. girl, ca. 1898 by Artus Van Briggle, w/ Rookwood logo & artist's initials, minor glaze scratches, 8" H $7,250.00

A-OH Nov. 1998   Cincinnati Art Galleries
Vase, high glaze in blues, grays & cream of Venetian harbor scene, ca. 1923 by Carl Schmidt, int. in med. blue high glaze, Rookwood logo & artist mono., 7⅞" H $4,700.00

A-OH Nov. 1998   Cincinnati Art Galleries
Vase, landscape scene covered with Vellum glaze, ca. 1912 by Kataro Shirayamadani, Rookwood logo, date, incised cypher of artist, small bruise on rim, 15" H $4,000.00

A-ME Jan. 1999   Cyr Auction Co. Inc.
Chalkware, reclining deer, pr., 3½" x 8½" x 11 . . . .$750.00

A-MA Sept. 1998   Craftsman Auctions
Vase, Grueby, gr. glaze, sgn., 12" H $3,000.00

A-NH Nov. 1998   Northeast Auctions

English Pearlware

Row 1

Figure, Horse & rider on domed base, 9¼" H $9,000.00

Row 2, Left to Right

Figural Groups, pr., one w/ milk-maid & calf, other w/ farmer & dog, 6" H $1,600.00

Row 3, Left to Right

Figures, milkmaids & cows .$1,600.00

A-MD Sept. 1998   Richard Opfer
Auctioneering, Inc.

Row 1, Left to Right

Leeds Coffee Pot, blue & white flo-ral, chips & crazing, 9¼" H . .$650.00
Leeds Coffee Pot, blue & yel. floral design, several chips, 12¼" H $675.00

Row 2, Left to Right

Gaudy Welsh Coffee Pot, flakes & crazing, 9¾" H $450.00
Leeds Tea Pot, dome top, blue & yel. floral design, crazing, early repr., 10" H $700.00

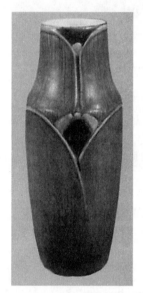

A-MA Sept. 1998   Craftsman Auctions
Vase, Newcomb College, carved & dec., sign. w/ NC logo, 8½" H $3,300.00

A-MD Sept. 1998   Richard Opfer
Auctioneering, Inc.

Row 1

Lions, pr. of Staffordshire, reclining, one w/ base repr., one w/ hairlines & base chip, 4¾" L $725.00

Row 2, Left to Right

Cats, pr. Staffordshire, mottled dec., minor base chips, 7" H $925.00
Cats, pr., Staffordshire, slight surface wear, minor base flakes, 7" H $975.00

A-MA Sept. 1998   Craftsman Auctions
Candlestick, Moorcroft, sgn., 8" H $250.00

A-MA Sept. 1998   Craftsman Auctions
Wall Pockets, Teco Pottery, by Fritz Albert w/ mkd. sign., 17" x 6¾" $5,000.00

A-MA Oct. 1998   Skinner, Inc.

Left to Right

Vase, Grueby Faience Co., Boston, thin matte gr. glaze trailing & gathering at dec. edges & base, pale matte yel. glaze on buds, impr. marks & incised artist's initials, spider hairline in base, 11¾" H, 8" diam. $5,750.00
Vase, Grueby Faience Co., Boston, leathery matte gr. glaze w/ applied tendril ribs, impr. marks & artist's cipher, minor rim nick, 5⅞" H $3,737.50
Vase, Grueby pottery, Boston, dec. w/ matte yel. glazed buds on elongated stems w/ leaf blades under matte gr. glaze, impr. marks & incised artist's cipher, 9⅞" H, 4¼" diam. . .$4,887.50

A-MA Oct. 1998   Skinner, Inc.

Left to Right

Vase, Marblehead pottery, matte blue glaze, impr. mark, minor glaze scratches, 6¼" H, 5¼" diam. $460.00
Vase, dk. gr. matte glaze, impr. Marblehead cipher, 7" H $575.50
Vase, Hampshire pottery designed by Cadmon Robertson, matte two-tone blue glaze highlighted w/ strands of pale blue, impr. & incised marks, 3" H, 6" diam. $546.25
Vase, Hampshire pottery, designed by Cadmon Robertson, matte marbleized blue glaze on body w/ impr. marks, 9½" H $977.50
Wall Pocket, Paul Revere pottery, dk. sage gr. glaze, mkd. "S.E.G." & paper label, 6" L, 4" W $287.50

A-MA Sept. 1998   Craftsman Auctions
Low Bowl, Newcomb College, carved & dec. w/ minor glaze chip, 2" x 4¼" $900.00

A-PA Mar. 1999   Horst Auctioneers
Platter, historic blue "Landing of Lafayette At Castle Garden, NY", 16 Aug., 1824, mkd. "Clews Warranted Staffordshire", minor knife marks & minor glaze wear on rim, 17" x 13½" $1,250.00

A-MA Mar. 1999   Skinner, Inc.
Belleek, four strand oval basket, ca 1925 w/twig handles & applied flowers, 8½" L $1,380.00

A-MA Oct. 1998   Skinner, Inc.
Cider Jug, covered, rose mandarin, China, 19th C., w/ woven double strap applied handle, lid w/ foo dog finial, glaze wear, 9½" H $2,990.00

A-MA Oct. 1998   Skinner, Inc.
Garden Seats, two rose medallion hex-form, China, 19th C., glaze wear, 18¼" H $5,175.00

A-MD Sept. 1998   Richard Opfer
                                  Auctioneering, Inc.

Left to Right

Pitcher, Shenandoah, minor roughness, 6" H $1,250.00
Water Jug, Shenandoah, some glazing imperf., badly cracked, 8¼" H $325.00
Wall Pocket, Shenandoah, dec. w/ applied bird, rosette-type flowers & leaves, part of beak missing, 7¼" H $3,200.00

A-MA Oct. 1998   Skinner, Inc.

Row 1, Left to Right

Box & Cover, enamel, Eng., late 18th C. w/ polychrome dec., 4¾" L $920.00
Box, enamel, Staffordshire, Eng., late 18th C., w/ polychrome dec., 5¾" L $1,725.00

Row 2, Left to Right

Bodkin Holder, Staffordshire, late 18th C., 5" L $977.50
Bodkin Holder, late 18th C., 5" L $1,150.00

A-MD Sept. 1998   Richard Opfer
                                  Auctioneering, Inc.

Row 1, Left to Right

Creamer, Lotus ware, pink & white floral w/ gold accents, 3½" H .$90.00
Creamer, Lotus ware, fish net design, 5¼" L $1,030.00

Row 2, Left to Right

Vase, Lotus ware, yel. floral w/ gold beading & reticulated button handles, 6½" L $425.00
Rose Bowl, Lotus ware, footed, leaf & berry design, 4" H $375.00

Row 1, Left to Right

Tureens, pr., Nanking sm. lidded, early 19th C., w/ under-trays, 6" H, together w/ blue Fitzhugh fruit basket, 9" L & undertray $3,100.00
Platter, oval blue Fitzhugh, early 19th C. $550.00
Porcelain, group of 4 pcs. of Chinese export blue & white, early 19th C., incl. Nanking tea caddy, pot de creme & 2 Canton serving dishes, chips & reprs. $1,000.00
Basket, & undertray, Canton blue & white, early 19th C., 8½" L $800.00
Porcelain, group of 4 pcs. of Chinese export blue & white, early 19th C., incl. Nanking tea caddy, pot de creme & 2 Canton serving dishes, chips & reprs. $1,000.00
Tureen, sm. Canton blue & white covered w/ rabbits head handles & undertray, 7¾" L, w/ sm. covered vegetable dish, 7¾" L $650.00

Row 2, Left to Right

Tureen, lrg. Canton blue & white, early 19th C., w/ boars head handles, 7½" H, 12" L $1,700.00
Tureens, pr., Nanking sm. lidded, early 19th C., w/ under-trays, 6" H, together w/ blue Fitzhugh fruit basket, 9" L & undertray $3,100.00
Platter, Chinese export blue & white, w/ pierced drain board, 16" L $275.00
Platter, Chinese export blue & white porcelain, Fitzhugh patt., 14½" L, together w/ 2 sm. Chinese export trays & approx. 20 sm. Canton plates, 6½" diam. $900.00
Tureen, sm. Canton blue & white covered w/ rabbits head handles & undertray, 7¾" L, w/ sm. covered vegetable dish, 7¾" L $650.00
Tureen, lrg. Canton blue & white covered, early 19th C., w/ boars head handles, 12" L $450.00
Tureens, pr., Nanking sm. lidded, early 19th C., w/ under-trays, 6" H, together w/ blue Fitzhugh fruit basket, 9" L & undertray $3,100.00
Platter, Canton blue & white porcelain, early 19th C., 13¾" L $325.00

Spatterware

Left to Right

Teapot, inside lid rim minor chips, 10" H $1,250.00
Teapot, finial & handle repr., 9" H $225.00

Spatterware

Left to Right

Teapot & Sugar Bowl, rim chip on teapot, lid repr. & rim flake on sugar, 7" H $450.00

Row 1, Left to Right

Ink Well, Faience, colorful glaze w/ hungers, sm. chips, 5¼" x 5¼" $137.50
Dishes, three Delft, polychrome, pr., one w/ repr., 6⅝" diam., & single w/ hairline, 6½" diam., all have chips $132.00
Tiles, three blue & white delft, one is religious, edges chipped, 5¼" x 5¼", one has monk w/ stick, 4⅞" x 4⅞", & blue & white Adam & Eve, 5¼" x 5¼" $165.00

Row 2, Left to Right

Plate, Eng. polychrome delft, flowers & bird, sm. chips, 8¾" diam. $385.00
Tiles, two delft w/ floral designs, purple & white, & blue & white w/ yel. & gr., both 5⅛" x 5⅛" $110.00
Charger, delft, polychrome floral, chips & hairline, 12¾" diam. $275.00
Chicken, shaped jar, delft, polychrome w/ pink & gr., sgn., chips, 8¼" H $396.00

Left to Right

Poodle, pottery by Bennington, ca. 1890, overall mottled br. glaze & coleslaw mane, 8½" H, 9½" L $2,900.00
Creamer, Bennington, cow form, ca. 1875, overall mottled br. glaze, retains orig. lid, repr., 5½" H, 7" L $200.00
Spittoon, Bennington, mkd. "Lyman Fenton, pat. 1849", w/ overall mottled br. glaze, 4¼" H, 9½" diam. $75.00
Bottle, Bennington figural in form of monk, mkd. "Lyman Fenton, pat. 1849", overall mottled br. glaze, 10½" H $750.00

A-MD Sept. 1998   Richard Opfer
Auctioneering, Inc.

Row 1, Left to Right

Plate, Deldare ware, "The Fallowfield Hunt", 12" diam. $400.00

Plate, Deldare ware, "Ye Olden Times", artist S. Rowley, 9¼" diam. $140.00

Row 2

Plates, Deldare ware, lot of 2, "Ye Village Gossips", artist A. Jentsen, slight crazing, 10" diam., & "Ye Village Gossips", artist W. Fizter, 10" diam. $200.00

A-MD Sept. 1998   Richard Opfer
Auctioneering, Inc.

Row 1, Left to Right

Pitcher, Deldare ware, "Ye Lion Inn,", Olde English Village, chip on lip, 10" H $250.00

Vase, Deldare ware, "Ye Village Schoolmaster", artist: J. Nekola, 8¼" H $500.00

A-ME July 1998   Cyr Auction Co. Inc.
Jug, 4-gal. J & E Norton, Bennington VT, dec. w/ two peacocks $7,750

A-MA Aug. 1998   Robert C. Eldred Co., Inc.

Stoneware

Jug, by J & E Norton w/ cobalt blue dec. of nightingale on branch, 3 gal. $605.00

Crock, mkd. Norton & Fenton East Bennington, w/ cobalt blue dec., 11" H $121.00

Jug, mkd. F.T. Wright & Son, w/ cobalt blue dec., chip on spout, 2 gal. .$165.00

Crock, mkd. Taunton, MA, w/ bird dec., 7½" H $176.00

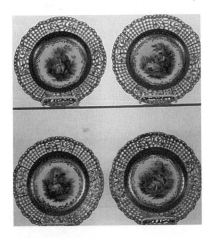

A-MD Sept. 1998   Richard Opfer
Auctioneering, Inc.

Dresden Plates, set of 12, four shown, 12 different courting scenes, reticulated borders, gilt dec., 3 have minor chips, 9" diam. $1,600.00

A-MD Sept. 1998   Richard Opfer
Auctioneering, Inc.

Candlesticks, pr. of Deldare ware, artist: O. S., crazing, 9" H . . .$475.00

A-MD Sept. 1998   Richard Opfer
Auctioneering, Inc.

Row 1, Left to Right

Tankard Pitcher, Deldare ware, "The Great Controversy", sgn. "Stiner", 12¼" H $725.00

Pitcher, Deldare ware, "The Fallonfield Hunt", sgn. "A. Delaney", 8½" H $625.00

Row 2, Left to Right

Candlesticks, Deldare ware, Village scene, crazing, 9" H $450.00

Humidor, Deldare ware, "Ye Lion Inn", sgn. "W. Fozter", 6½" H .$750.00

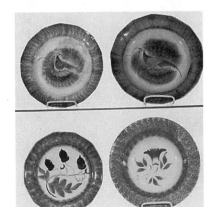

A-MD Sept. 1998   Richard Opfer
Auctioneering, Inc.

Row 1

Spatterware Plates, two peafowl dec., lrg. w/ repr. back, smaller is stained, approx. 9½" diam. . .$625.00

Row 2, Left to Right

Leeds Plates, pr., Acorns, 1 shown, has repair, 9" diam. $1,600.00

Bowl, Sunderland-type, ca. 1930, transfer & pink lustre ship scene & verse, 12" diam. $1,600.00

A-NH Nov. 1998   Northeast Auctions

Battersea Enamel Boxes

Row 1, Left to Right

Pug, on lid & base, 2¼" diam. $2,100.00
Oval Box, depicting draftsman's implements, 2" L .$2,200.00
Rabbit form box, oval base w/ flowers, 2½" L . . .$4,100.00
Book-form Etui, dec. w/ birds & gilt, 3½" L . . .$2,100.00
Crouching Rabbit, on lid, oval, 1½" L $1,100.00
Rabbit, form box depicting a rabbit chase on underside, 1¾"
L $1,000.00

Row 2, Left to Right

Box, modeled as a bird, 3" L $900.00
Box, depicting a village scene & floral cards on pink ground,
2" diam. $1,000.00
Box, recumbent dog form w/ pink ground & floral dec. base,
2" diam. $900.00
Box, circular w/ floral spray dec., 1¾" diam. $100.00
Box, bird form w/ bird in flight on base, 2¼" L . . .$700.00
Box, circular w/ enameled bird & fruit on lid, 2"
diam. $1,000.00

A-PA Sept. 1998   Pook & Pook Inc.

Row 1, Left to Right

Stein, Ger. stoneware, inscription & blue floral dec.,
15" H $150.00
Stein, Ger. stoneware 3-liter, w/ relief tavern scene,
16½" H $150.00
Stein, Ger. Mettlach, w/ drinking men scene, 17" H . .$475.00
Stein, Ger. 2-½ liter, w/ central dec. of elves drinking, 15½"
H $200.00

Row 2, Left to Right

Stein, Ger. w/ overall floral dec. & rust banding, 20½"
H $225.00
Charger, round Mettlach w/ fish & seaweed dec., 17½"
diam. $650.00
Stein, Ger. Mettlach, w/ tavern scene on rust field, 16½"
H $800.00

A-PA Feb. 1999   Pook & Pook Inc.

Row 1, Left to Right

Sugar Bowl, spatterware, covered, mid 19th C., w/ red, yel.
& gr. peafowl dec. on blue ground, 5½" H, w/ another covered sugar bowl w/ red carnation on gray & br. rainbow
ground, 3¾" H $200.00
Teapot, Staffordshire Gaudy Dutch, War Bonnet patt., ca.
1820, repr., 5½" H, 10¼" L $2,200.00
Sugar Bowl, covered spatterware, ca. 1830, red, blue & gr.
peafowl dec., chips, 4½" H, 4¾" diam., w/ blue, gr. & mini.
red peafowl spatter cup & saucer, 4⅜" diam. $375.00
Sugar Bowl, spatterware, covered, mid 19th C., w/ red, yel.
& gr. peafowl dec. on blue ground, 5½" H, w/ another covered sugar bowl w/ red carnation on gray & br. rainbow
ground, 3¾" H $200.00

Row 2, Left to Right

Coffee Pot, spatterware, ca. 1830, w/ red, yel. & gr. peafowl
dec. on blue ground, 9" H $500.00
Sugar Bowl, covered spatterware, ca. 1830, red, blue & gr.
peafowl dec., chips, 4½" H, 4¾" diam., w/ blue, gr. & mini.
red peafowl spatter cup & saucer, 4⅜" diam. $375.00
Coffee Pot, w/ lid, blue & red rainbow spatterware, ca.
1830, 10" H, chip & repr., w/ matching sugar bowl,
7½" H $550.00

A-MA Oct. 1998   Skinner, Inc.

Left to Right

Coffee Cups & Saucers, six Clarice Cliff items, honeydew
patt., incl. coffee pot, creamer, open sugar bowl & three cups
& saucers, pot mkd. "Clarice Cliff", all others mkd. "Made in
Eng., Wilkinson Eng." $460.00
Vase, Clarice Cliff, dec. w/ vine, leaves & clouds in relief in
gr., br., & gold on a beige oval-shaped vase, mkd. "Clarice
Cliff Newport Pottery Eng.", 7" H $230.00
Jar & Sugar, covered condiment jar & sugar shaker,
bands of yel., gr. & ochre dec. w/ crocuses in ora., blue, &
purple, mkd. "Bizarre by Clarice Cliff", some staining, 3½" H,
5½" H $373.75
Vases, pr., w/ colored bands of gr., br., & yel., dec. w/ crocuses in ora., blue, purple, mkd. "Bizarre by Clarice Cliff", sm.
glaze chip, 8" H $690.00

A-OH July 1998   Garth's Auctions

Row 1, Left to Right

Washbowl, & pitcher, Gaudy Welsh tulip patt., minor wear, 4⅜" diam., 3⅞" H $330.00

Pottery, two pcs. w/ polychrome enamel, "Leed's Pottery" cottage, repr., 3½" H, & Staffordshire monkey, 4⅛" H $357.50

Pottery, two pcs., Staffordshire cup plate w/ red transfer, molded floral rim w/ polychrome enamel, impr. "Wood, chip & hairline, 4½" H, & porcelain figure of woman, polychrome, mkd. "God", chips, 3¼" H $159.50

Pepper Pots, two Staffordshire, red transfer, blue transfer, chips, 4⅝" H $165.00

Row 2, Left to Right

Pepper Pot, Mocha, blue & white stripes w/ dk. br. band w/ white leaves & dots, blue top, chips, 4¾" H .$715.00

Pepper Pots, two, Gaudy Staffordshire w/ floral design in red, blue, gr. & blk., chips, 4⅝" H, & white w/ two shades of blue stripes, 4⅝" H . .$385.00

Pepper Pots, two yellowware, white, br. & blk., repr., 4⅛" H & blue & white stripes, chips, 4⅜" H $1,072.50

Pepper Pots, four, three are blue & white, one is blue, white & blk., all have damage, 4" to 4⅝" H . . .$412.50

Pepper Pots, four blue & white feather stripe, stains & damage, 3⅝" to 4¾" H $330.00

A-OH July 1998   Garth's Auctions

Row 1, Left to Right

Shelves, pine w/ old gray paint, cut out feet & sq. nailed const., 35" W, 35½" H $522.50

Pitcher, blue & white stoneware, molded leaves & old w/ beard, 8" H $137.50

Pitcher, blue & white stoneware, molded roses & bust of man w/ beard, 8" H $137.50

Pitchers, two blue & white stoneware, molded roses & crane, hairlines, 8" H, & roses only, crazing & minor hairlines, 6¾" H $165.00

Row 2, Left to Right

Pitcher, blue & white stoneware, molded dog's heads, old woman & man w/ beard, Ger. "Trink mas Klar 1st", 10¾" H $220.00

Crocks, two blue & white stoneware covered, deer hunt scenes, "3" & "2", larger has repr. to lid, 6½" & 8" diam. $412.50

Row 3, Left to Right

Pitchers, two blue & white, deer hunt scenes, one is labeled "Flemish Jugs, The Cincinnati Glass & China Co.", minor chips, 7¾" H $880.00

A-OH Sept. 1998   Garth's Auctions

All Historical Blue Staffordshire

Row 1, Left to Right

Plate, dk. blue transfer, "St. Paul's School, London", impr. "Adams", 7¾" diam. $165.00

Plate, med. blue transfer, Boston State House, wear & scratches, 8½" diam. $110.00

Pitcher, dk. blue transfer, City Hall NY & Insane Asylum, NY w/ flower & foliage border, wear & hairline, 6¼" H . . .$550.00

Plate, med. blue transfer, "The Landing of the Father at Plymouth, 1620", mkd. "Enoch Wood", wear & sm. edge chips, 10⅛" diam. $38.50

Plate, dk. blue transfer "Fall of Montmorenci, Near Quebec", impr. "Wood", wear & scratches, 8⅜" diam. $165.00

Row 2, Left to Right

Plate, med. blue transfer "The Landing of the Fathers at Plymouth, Dec. 22, 1620", impr. "Wood", wear, scratches w/ sm. flake, 7½" diam. $49.50

Plate, med. blue transfer, "Fair Mount Near Phila.", wear & minor scratches, 10¼" diam. $148.50

Sauce Tureen, & tray, med. blue transfer Boston State House, tray impr. "Wood", stains & chip, 8⅜" L $715.00

Plate, med. blue transfer, Boston State House, wear & scratches, 9¾" diam. $121.00

Plate, dk. blue transfer "St. Paul's School, London" impr. "Adams", scratches, crazing & minor stains, 7¾" diam. $115.50

A-OH July 1998   Garth's Auctions
Hanging Shelves, pine w/ old blk. paint, sq. nail const., edge damage, 29" W, 8" D, 34½" H $1,100.00

Row 1, Left to Right

Food Mold, redware scalloped w/ sponged rim, hairline, 8½" diam. $165.00

Jugs, two redware w/ straps, reddish glaze, 6⅜" H, & blk. w/ sm. chips, 5½" H $275.00

Row 2, Left to Right

Redware, two pcs., flower pot w/ lt. gr. slip spots, chip & hairline, 5¼" H, & mug w/ mottled glaze, hairlines, 4½" H $192.50

Clay Pot, VA buff w/ strap handle & spout, lt. gr. w/ br. sponging, chips, 4¾" H $165.00

Row 3, Left to Right

Flask, redware, 7½" H $137.50

Jar, Redware ovoid, hairlines, mismatched lid, 8⅛" H $165.00

Jug, grotesque redware w/ gr. glaze, illegible incised signature, 7¾" H $110.00

Jug, redware w/ strap handle, blk. glaze, chips on base, 7¾" $55.00

A-OH Nov. 1998   Cincinnati Art Galleries
Garden Ornament, two dancing frogs, incised "Weller Pottery", 13⅞" H $9,500.00

A-PA Oct. 1998   York Town Auction Inc.
Bracket Clock, Eng. musical eight-day bracket clock, 3 train movement w/ 12 bells, 5 gongs, & a 6" musical cylinder w/ silvered 11" diam mkd. J E. Caldwell & Co., PA, ca. 1880, wood probably linden, minor wood blemish, overall 45" H, 23" W $13,000.00

A-PA Oct. 1998   York Town Auction Inc.
Table Clock, carved walnut Blk. Forest, great detail, carved wooden dial w/ applied brass numerals, 8 day Fr. movement, few minor breaks, ca. 1850's, overall 35½" H, 33" W . .$6,000.00

A-PA Oct. 1998   York Town Auction Inc.
Wall Clock, walnut Blk. Forest, 8 day movement w/ blk. glass dial & old numerals, movement & dial prob. replm., 47" T, 27" W, 12½" dial $5,100.00

A-PA Oct. 1998   York Town Auction Inc.
Bracket Clock, Fr. Empire boulle bracket, emb. gilt brass dial w/ sunburst, inset porcelain shield numerals, gilt sunburst pendulum, 8 day movement, ca. 1820, damage to bottom of case, Athena's spear missing, overall 45" H $2,900.00

A-MA Oct. 1998   Skinner, Inc.
Banjo Clock, Fed., Simon Willard, Roxbury, MA, ca. 1810, mah. case w/ inlay & gilt gesso, 29¼" H .$12,650.00

A-NH Nov. 1998   Northeast Auctions
Clock, pillar & scroll, CT, mah. case w/ eglomise panel by Ephraim Downes of Bristol, 31" H . . .$2,750.00

A-NH Nov. 1998   Northeast Auctions
Shelf Clock, NH, Fed., mah., works by Joseph Chadwick of Boscawen, 42" H $14,000.00

A-MD Sept. 1998　　　Richard Opfer
Auctioneering, Inc.

Row 1, Left to Right

Clock, mini., pink enamel & gold trimmed clock, made in Fr., Schamanns & Sons, N.Y. in orig. case w/ orig. key, faded, 2" H $750.00
Carriage Clock, mini., blue enamel & sterling,　　　Swiss movement, in leather case, sm. chip, not working, 1¾" H $225.00
Carriage Clock, mini., Waterbury, brass case, beveled glass, runs, 3" H $140.00

Row 2, Left to Right

Carriage Clock, mini., pale blue & pink enamel & brass clock, some discoloration on enamel, not working, 3" H $425.00
Clock, mini., Fr. works, silver case, not working, no crystal, 2½" H $130.00
Carriage Clock, mini., footed gr. enamel on bronze w/ exposed pendulum, Swiss movement, mkd. Lanceldore, sprung, 1¾" H $425.00

A-NH Nov. 1998　　　Northeast Auctions
Tall Case Clock, early Am., cherry case, 98" H $2,800.00

A-NH Nov. 1998　　　Northeast Auctions
Tall Case Clock, N. Eng., birch, 80" H $2,100.00

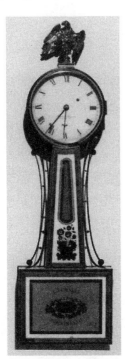

A-MA Aug. 1998　Robert C. Eldred Co., Inc.
Banjo Clock, sgn. Elmer Stennes, in mah. w/ brass side arms, 34½" H $1,870.00

A-NH Nov. 1998　　　Northeast Auctions
Tall Case Clock, PA, cherry & mah. case, 93" H $2,500.00

A-NH Nov. 1998　　　Northeast Auctions
Tall Case Clock, Am. Fed., cherry case, 86" H $2,600.00

A-MA Aug. 1998   Robert C. Eldred Co., Inc.
Tall Case Clock, maple case, painted floral spandrels, date hand missing, brass works, dial mkd. "Timo, Chandler, Concord", 87" H .$3,500.20

A-MA May 1999   New England Auctions
of Brookfield
Tall Case Clock, Fed., cherry w/ inlay, George Holbrook, Brookfield, MA, mid-18th C., rep. finials, old refinish, 89½" H $31,000.00

A-PA Dec. 1998   Pook & Pook Inc.
Tall Case Clock, PA, mah. veneer, ca. 1830 w/ 8-day moon phase works by "Nicholas Le Huray Jr., Philad", feet reduced, 94¾" H $4,000.00

A-PA June 1998   Pook & Pook, Inc.
Tall Case Clock, by John Martin, Kincardine, Scottish, mah., ca. 1800, 8-day brass movement, 88" H $3,500.00

A-NH Nov. 1998   Northeast Auctions
Tall Case Clock, MA, Roxbury case, mah., w/ inlay, by Ephraim Willard, 86" H $16,000.00

A-PA Sept. 1998   Pook & Pook Inc.
Tall Case Clock, PA, walnut, ca. 1800, 30-hour brass works w/ white dial inscribed "John Saml Krause, Bethlehem", 89" H $4,000.00

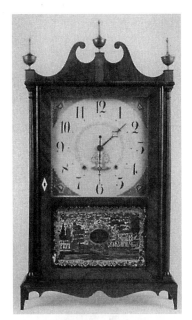

A-MA Oct. 1998 Skinner, Inc.
Mantle Clock, Fed. pillar & scroll, Seth Thomas, CT., ca. 1825, mah. case, old finish, tablet loss, wooden 30 hr. weight-driven movement, 31½" H $2,415.00

A-OH July 1998 Garth's Auctions
Clock, Sheraton, exotic wood veneer, pine secondary wood, reddish mah. colored stain, brass works & painted metal face w/ phases of moon dial, face worn & flaked, cracks, repr., 97" H $3,300.00

A-ME July 1998 Cyr Auction Co. Inc.
Tall Case Clock, mah. inlaid w/ capitals & brass finials, sgn. on moon phase dial "Hodson Dudley", 8' 8" T $8,000.00

A-OH Aug. 1998 Garth's Auctions
Clock, PA grandfather, walnut case w/ old worn finish, dovetailed bonnet, brass works w/ calendar movement, painted steel face, crazed w/ old retouch, label "Wm. Maus Quakertown", back of bonnet & weights & pendulum missing, height loss, replms., 90" H $4,950.00

A-OH Nov. 1998 Garth's Auctions
Clock, Hepplewhite grandfather, mah. case w/ inlay, brass finials, inlays of two shells, ten fans, urn, banding & eight stars, brass works w/ phases of moon dial, calendar movement & second hand, metal face w/ worn orig. paint, minor reprs. to feet, no weights or keys, replms., 8' 2¾" H $7,425.00

A-ME Jan. 1999 Cyr Auction Co. Inc.
Tall Case Clock, ME, mah. case, brass works, 85" H $3,500.00

A-MA Oct. 1998 Skinner, Inc.
Tall Case Clock, Fed., ca. 1790, eight-day brass weight driven movement, old ref., dial repainted, 90″ H $14,950.00

A-MA Oct. 1998 Skinner, Inc.
Tall Case Clock, Simon Willard, Roxbury MA, ca. 1790-1810, old refinish, imper., case 89″ H . . .$42,550.00

A-MA Oct. 1998 Skinner, Inc.
Tall Case Clock, Fed., mah. w/ inlay, ca. 1810, old ref., imper., 89″ H $14,950.00

A-MA Oct. 1998 Skinner, Inc.
Tall Case Clock, John Potter, Brookfield, MA, 1781, tiger maple, w/ brass weight driven movement, old finish, 83″ H $80,600.00

A-MA Oct. 1998 Skinner, Inc.
Tall Case Clock, Fed., cherry & mah. veneer case, possibly MA, ca. 1820, 8 day brass weight-driven movement, minor imper., 88″ H $9,200.00

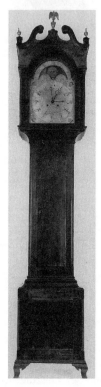

A-PA June 1998 Pook & Pook, Inc.
Tall Case Clock, Chippendale, PA, ca. 1800, mkd. John Heilig, Germantown, old repr. to bonnet door, 102″ H $5,500.00

A-ME Nov. 1998   Guyette & Schmidt, Inc.

Row 1, Left to Right

Mallard Drake, hollow by Ken Greenlee, IA, ...$175.00
Mallards, pr. oversized by Carl Sattler, IA, both have old repaint, dents & rough areas $250.00

Row 2, Left to Right

Mallard Drake, preening by Robert Elliston, IL, res. paint, cracks in base of neck, repr. $100.00
Mallard Drake, ca 1930 by Heck Whittington, IL, old repaint $200.00
Bluebill Drake, by Christie Brothers, MI, ca 1920, old in-use repaint, sm. crack $75.00

Row 3, Left to Right

Mallard Drake, from Chilicothe area, appealing old in-use paint w/ minor shrinkage & wear $400.00
Crow, hollow by Charles Perdew, IL, three pc. boy w/ glass eyes, repaint & wear, wire leg missing $400.00
Canvasback Drake, balsa body by Jim Kelson, . .$300.00

A-ME Nov. 1998   Guyette & Schmidt, Inc.

Left to Right

Pigeon, English wood by unknown maker, flaking & blistered paint, cracks but overall good . . . . .N/S
Yellowlegs, three decoys, one contemporary oversized by Reggie Birch, VA, & pr. of yellowlegs, Birch decoy has two stick holes for upright & feeding positions, stressed to look old, excellent $150.00

A-ME Nov. 1998   Guyette & Schmidt, Inc.

Left to Right

Yellowlegs & Skimmer, by David Personius, both sgn. & dated, 1988 & 1990, glass eyes $200.00
Shorebirds, two by Hurley Conklin, Yellowlegs & peep, near mint $475.00
Yellowlegs, w/ turned head by David Ward, CT, relief wing carving near mint, orig. paint $175.00

A-ME Nov. 1998   Guyette & Schmidt, Inc.

Row 1, Left to Right

Canvasbacks, pr. by Madison Mitchell, reprs. $275.00
Flat Bottom Pintails, pr. by R. Madison Mitchell, MD, lead weights removed, minor wear $550.00

Row 2, Left to Right

Bluebill Drake, early, ca. 1950 by Madison Mitchell, average wear, head lifted slightly from body $300.00
Ruddy Duck Drake, by Robert Litzenberg, MD, .$300.00
Coot, by Madison Mitchell, MD, excellent & orig. .$375.00
Coot, by Robert Litzenberg, MD, sgn. & dated 1975, mint & unused $350.00

Row 3, Left to Right

Bluewing Teal Hen, by Madison Mitchell, MD, sgn. & dated 1981, sep. at knot, otherwise mint $350.00
Coot, by Robert Litzenberg, MD, sgn. & dated 1984, mint & unused $300.00
Drake & Hen, Greenwing Teal Drake & Cinnamon Teal Hen both by Robert Litzenberg, Greenwing sgn. & dated 1980, Cinnamon dated 1989 . . . .$300.00

A-ME Nov. 1998   Guyette & Schmidt, Inc.

Left to Right

Curlew, contemporary in Cobb Island style by Reggie Birch, VA, sgn., natural flaw in wood $400.00
Curlew, oversized contemporary in Cobb Island style by Reggie Birch, VA, sgn., ...$165.00
Curlew, contemporary in running pose by Reggie Birch, VA, in Cobb Island style & sgn., excellent $200.00
Curlew, lrg. contemporary made in Luther Lee Notthingham style by Reggie Birch, VA, sgn. & dated 1993, painted & stressed $225.00

A-ME Nov. 1998   Guyette & Schmidt, Inc.

Shorebirds, five contemporary, four half-sized by William Johnson, sgn. & dated 1996 & one full size hollow blk. bellied plover, excellent $150.00

A-ME Nov. 1998   Guyette & Schmidt, Inc.

Row 1, Left to Right

Bluewing Teal Drake, by Mason Decoy Factory, premier grade, w/ wear $1,100.00
Bluewing Teal Drake, by Mason Decoy Factory, w/ minor to moderate wear $750.00

Row 2, Left to Right

Bluebill Drake, by Mason Decoy Factory, premier grade, minor wear $900.00
Canvasback Hen, by Mason Decoy Factory, Seneca Lake Model, premier grade, minor wear $900.00

Row 3, Left to Right

Bluebill Drake, by Mason Decoy Factory, challenge grade, minor wear $400.00
Mallard Hen, by Mason Decoy Factory, challenge grade, minor discoloration & wear $400.00

A-ME Nov. 1998   Guyette & Schmidt, Inc.
Canvasback Hen, by Mason Decoy Factory, premier grade, wear $850.00

A-ME Nov. 1998   Guyette & Schmidt, Inc.

Row 1, Left to Right

Redhead Hen, by Mason Decoy Factory, standard grade w/ glass eyes, very slight wear $400.00
Canvasback Drake, by Mason Decoy Factory, standard grade, glass eye model, minor wear $500.00
Mallard Drake, by Mason Decoy Factory, standard grade, glass eye model, average wear $265.00

Row 2, Left to Right

Mallard Drake, by Mason Decoy Factory, challenge grade, minor discoloration & wear $450.00
Bluebill Drake, by Mason Decoy Factory, premier grade, minor wear $400.00
Redhead Drake, by Mason Decoy Factory, premier grade, old in-use repaint on most of decoy, two cracks in back $350.00

A-ME Nov. 1998   Guyette & Schmidt, Inc.

Row 1, Left to Right

Mallards, two by Wildfowler Decoy Factory, CT, boy have balsa bodies, near mint $325.00
Blk. Duck & Goldeneye Drake, duck is standard grade, drake is challenge grade, both w/ moderate wear w/ sm. cracks & dents $375.00

Row 2, Left to Right

Drakes, standard grade redbreasted merganser & challenge grade canvasback, both res., struct. good . . .$375.00
Mallards, pr. from Animal Trap Decoy Factory, MS, near mint, hen has one eye missing $125.00

Row 3, Left to Right

Redheads & Blk. Duck, by Wildfowler Decoy Factory, all w/ minor wear, redheads heavily hit by shot $275.00
Bluebill Drake, by Mason Decoy Factory, standard grade w/ glass eyes, minor wear $200.00

A-ME Nov. 1998   Guyette & Schmidt, Inc.

Row 1, Left to Right

Bluebill Drake, by Peterson Decoy Factory, MI, ca. 1880's, very minor wear $950.00
Redhead Drake, "Back Bay" model oversized, by Mason Decoy Factory, premier grade, paint res. w/ moderate wear $300.00
Canvasbacks, pr., oversized "Back Bay" model, by Mason Decoy Factory, premier grade, res., cracks $500.00

Row 2, Left to Right

Drakes & Blk. Duck, lot of 3, by Downeast Sportscraft Co., ME, all orig. condition $850.00
Greenwing Teal Drake, by Wildfowler Decoy Factory, near mint, crack in back, eye missing $250.00

Row 3

Canvasbacks & Drake, three decoys by Wildfowler Decoy Factory, minor to moderate wear $275.00

A-ME Nov. 1998   Guyette & Schmidt, Inc.

Hollow Carved Swan, by Bob White, PA, sgn. & dated 1985, ...$2,850.00

A-ME Nov. 1998   Guyette & Schmidt, Inc.

Row 1, Left to Right

Squaw Drake, by Mark McNair, slight wear $1,300.00

Am. Merganser Drake, by Mark McNair, hollow, near mint, well aged $700.00

Row 2

Drake & Hen, pr., by Bob White, PA, sgn., near mint $750.00

A-ME Nov. 1998   Guyette & Schmidt, Inc.

Row 1, Left to Right

Goldeneye, pr. by John Holloway, NJ, paint shrinkage .$150.00

Redbreasted Mergansers, pr., by John Holloway, NJ, near mint $145.00

Row 2, Left to Right

Pintails, by John Holloway, NJ, DE River style, near mint .$175.00

Drakes, Hollow Bluebill by Ed Cassedy & Hooded Merganser by B D Rodier, both sgn., near mint ...$170.00

Row 3, Left to Right

Blk. Duck, by Leo MacIntosh, NY, mint $400.00

Drakes, pr. Greenwing Teal & Bufflehead by William Geonne, CA, all near mint $325.00

A-ME Nov. 1998   Guyette & Schmidt, Inc.

Canada Goose, w/ turned head & raised crossed wing tips, by John McLoughlin, NJ, near mint $2,500.00

A-ME Nov. 1998   Guyette & Schmidt, Inc.

Left to Right

Canada Goose, by John McLoughlin, NJ, preening w/ lifted wings & crossed tips, minor flaws $6,500.00

Blk. Brant, by John McLoughlin, NJ, near mint ..$3,500.00

A-ME Nov. 1998   Guyette & Schmidt, Inc.

Left to Right

Cackling Goose, by John McLoughlin, NJ, Gunning model, near mint $5,000.00

Canada Goose, by John McLoughlin, NJ, working decoy style, near mint, hairline & "dog chew" $5,500.00

A-ME Nov. 1998   Guyette & Schmidt, Inc.

Row 1

Mergansers, four, pr. of swimming by Bob Biddle PA & pr. Mergansers by F Dobbins, ME, near mint, Dobbins has slight damage to tip of hen's crest $375.00

Row 2

Wigeon & Drakes, pr. of Wigeon by Bob Biddle, PA, Pintail by Shannon Smith, ME, & Canvasback by Carlton McGee, VA, slight wear $275.00

Row 3, Left to Right

Drakes, three by John Holloway, NJ, Bufflehead, Bluebill & pinball, near mint $200.00

Snow Goose, carved in DE River tradition by Herb Miller, mint $475.00

A-MA Jan. 1999   Skinner, Inc.

Bed, Renaissance style, carved oak, double, late 19th C. $1,840.00

A-NH Nov. 1998   Northeast Auctions

Bed, N. Eng., country Sheraton w/ red paint, posts 93" H, 76" L, 53" W $2,500.00

A-PA Mar. 1999   Horst Auctioneers

Rope Bed, Low-post, early 19th C., softwood, reprs. & ref., 52¼" W, 82" L, 61" H $900.00

A-MA Jan. 1999   Skinner, Inc.

Bedroom Suite, faux bamboo, 3 pcs., 4th qtr. 19th C., bureau w/ mirror, double bed frame & bedside table, losses $3,200.00

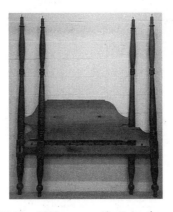

A-PA Mar. 1999   Horst Auctioneers

Rope Bed, w/ plain tester, Sheraton, rails retain orig. turned rope pegs, ref., 76½" H, 52" W, 78" L $800.00

A-MA Feb. 1999   Skinner, Inc.

Bed, Shaker maple & pine, N. Eng., first half of 19th C., old refinish, 30¼" H, 29" W, 64" L $690.00

A-PA Mar. 1999   Horst Auctioneers

Rope Bed, early to mid-19th C., w/ red stain, cannonball finials, wear to finish on bed rails, 52½" W x 78½" L 46" H $375.00

A-MA Aug. 1998   Rafael Osona Auctioneer & Appraiser

Rope Bed, tiger maple, ca. 1830, 85½" L, 55" W, 61" H $3,000.00

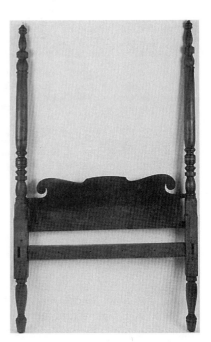

A-MA Feb. 1999   Skinner, Inc.

Tall Post Bed, cherry, N. Eng., ca. 1825, old refinish, 90" H, 45" W, 70" D .$1,955.00

A-ME Jan. 1999 Cyr Auction Co. Inc.
Side Chair, Q.A. mah. w/ trifid feet,
19" x 18" x 40" $3,750.00

A-MA Aug. 1998 Rafael Osona Auctioneer
& Appraiser
Chairs, Chippendale Centennial, set
of 10, 2 arm & 8 side, Irish, mah., 19th
C., 38" H $9,000.00

A-IA June 1998 Jackson's
Parlor Set, 3 pc., mah. finish .$230.00

A-IA June 1998 Jackson's
Chair, gothic revival, walnut w/
pierced & foliate carved back, burled
panels, 70" H $517.50

A-MA May 1999 New England Auctions
of Brookfield
Wing Chair, Q.A., AM., last qtr. 18th
C., pin const $4,000.00

A-MA Aug. 1998 Rafael Osona Auctioneer
& Appraiser
Chaise Lounge, Sheraton, mah., ca.
1810, w/ silk damask upholstery,
76½" L, 28" W, 37¼" H : ...$1,000.00

A-MA Aug. 1998 Rafael Osona Auctioneer
& Appraiser
Daybed, N. Eng., Q.A., ca. 1740, birch
& maple w/ adj. headboard, 71½" L, 3
stretchers are early replms. $2,750.00

A-MA May 1999 New England Auctions
of Brookfield
Lolling Chair, Fed., Am., mah. w/
stretcher base & line inlay to front of
arms & front legs $3,500.00

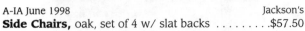

A-IA June 1998 Jackson's
Side Chairs, oak, set of 4 w/ slat backs $57.50

A-IA June 1998 Jackson's
Side Chairs, four oak w/ "T" shaped backs $80.50

A-NH Nov. 1998 Northeast Auctions
Chair Set, Q.A. assembled set of 10, N. Eng., painted
blk. $5,500.00

A-MA Aug. 1998 Skinner, Inc.
Side Chairs, Rod-back, set of 6, ca. 1800, w/ old dk. br.
surface, branded "W. Dalton,", Boston, working
1799-1800 ....$4,212.50

A-ME Jan. 1999 Cyr Auction Co. Inc.
Chairs, Chippendale w/ ribbon back, set of 12 ..$5,700.00
Table, Hepplewhite, centennial, 3 part w/ string & bell
flower inlay, 2 shaped ends & dropleaf center, 24" x 48" x
29½" $3,750.00

A-MA Jan. 1999 Skinner, Inc.
Side Chairs, George III w/ shield back, 19th C.,
restored $2,070.00

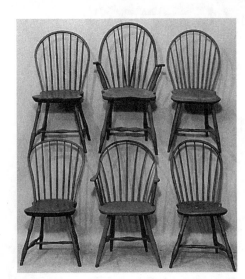

A-OH July 1998 Garth's Auctions

Row 1, Left to Right

Side Chair, bamboo Windsor bowback, sage gr. repaint,
36¾" H $467.50
Armchair, bamboo Windsor, sage gr. repaint, 39" H $742.50
Side Chair, bamboo Windsor bowback, sage gr. repaint,
mismatched cross "H" stretcher, 35½" H $440.00

Row 2, Left to Right

Side Chair, bamboo Windsor bowback, sage gr. repaint,
reprs., 36¼" H $440.00
Chairs, two of three bamboo Windsor, one arm & two sides,
sage gr. repaint, reprs. & replms., 34½" to 36" H .$1,205.00

A-PA Jan. 1999   York Town Auction Co.
Arm Chair, Windsor, Lancaster Co., w/ blue primer under coat w/ orig. gr. paint oxidized to dk. gr. & blk., sa. 1760-80, seat ht. 17" H $6,000.00

A-IA June 1998   Jackson's
Horn Stool, w/ cow hide uphol., 49" H $316.25

A-OH Aug. 1998   Garth's Auctions
Armchair, NH Q.A., hardwood w/ old blk. repaint, old rush seat, feet have lost height, 41" H $4,125.00

A-IA June 1998   Jackson's
Chair, sack-back Windsor, N. Eng., ca. 1780, painted salmon, red & blk. over earlier gr., loss of height, 37½" H $1,840.00

A-MA May 1999   New England Auctions
                        of Brookfield
Corner Chair, Chippendale, walnut, MA,   mid-18th   C.,   loose joints $2,600.00

A-ME July 1998   Cyr Auction Co. Inc.
Rocker, DE, five slat w/ early br. finish, orig. rockers, 44" T $2,250.00

A-MA Feb. 1999   Skinner, Inc.
Side Chairs, Windsor, set of 6, ca. 1810, old refinish, late dec., reprs. $1,150.00

A-MA May 1999   New England Auctions
                        of Brookfield
Rocking Chair, Windsor, Am., 19th C., w/ orig. gr. paint & stencil on crest rail, 44" H $675.00

A-MA May 1999   New England Auctions
                        of Brookfield
Chairs, Windsor bow back, matching set of 6, sgn. "Shove Berkley", ca. 1800-1805, Bristol Co., MA, partial old ref. $17,000.00

A-MA May 1999   New England Auctions
of Brookfield

Arm Chair, Windsor, sack back, painted gr., N. Eng., late 18th C., orig. paint, 38¼" H $32,000.00

A-ME Jan. 1999   Cyr Auction Co. Inc.

Chair, RI, brace back Windsor w/ bulbous turnings, 15" x 18" x 39" $2,000.00

A-MA May 1999   New England Auctions
of Brookfield

Arm Chair, Windsor w/ comb back, orig. grain paint & stencil dec., 47" H $4,700.00
High Back Chair, Windsor, old finish, reprs., RI, early 19th C. .$1,900.00

A-MA May 1999   New England Auctions
of Brookfield

Side Chairs, Windsor, set of 8, painted blk., chicken coop style back, 1 w/ crack in seat $6,000.00

A-NH Nov. 1998   Northeast Auctions

Corner Chair, MA, walnut w/ turned x-stretcher $11,000.00

A-MA May 1999   New England Auctions
of Brookfield

Side Chair, Windsor fanback, 38½" H $1,000.00
Side Chair, Windsor fanback, 37" H $1,800.00

A-MA May 1999   New England Auctions
of Brookfield

High Chair, child's arrow back Windsor, N.Eng., early 19th C., w/ old blk. paint over yel. $500.00
Rocker, arrow back, N. Eng., 1st qtr. 19th C., old paint but not orig., imper. $110.00

A-MA May 1999   New England Auctions
of Brookfield

Left to Right
Side Chair, Windsor, bowback, brace back w/ saddle seat, orig. gr. paint, sgn. "E. Tracy", late 19th C. .$8,250.00
Side Chair, Windsor, fan back, brace back, VT, late 18th C., w/ old blk. finish, 35" H $1,600.00

A-ME Jan. 1999   Cyr Auction Co. Inc.
Chair Set, four half spindle w/ grained & stenciled dec., 34" H $2,200.00

A-ME July 1998   Cyr Auction Co. Inc.
Bench, Windsor w/ bamboo turnings in gr. paint, 81" L, 36" H, 18½" D $4,500.00

A-ME Jan. 1999   Cyr Auction Co. Inc.
Side Chairs, Windsor, bird cage style w/ finials .$3,750.00

A-ME July 1998   Cyr Auction Co. Inc.
Mammy Bench, w/ orig. baby gate & paint., 51" L $4,000.00

A-ME Jan. 1999   Cyr Auction Co. Inc.
Chairs, Windsor, arrow back, 4 side, 1 arm, mkd. "Benjamin Bennet", NY, w/ gr. paint $5,500.00

A-MA Oct. 1998   Skinner, Inc.
Settle Bench, Arrow-back, PA, 1820-31, w/ some old repaint, minor imper., 36" H, 78" L $1,092.50

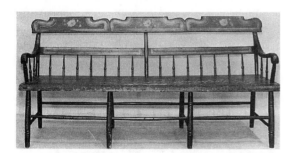

A-OH July 1998   Garth's Auctions
Settle Bench, dec., worn orig. olive br. paint w/ lt. gr. & cream colored striping & rose dec. on three section crest, stenciled label "E.D. Jeffries...PA", plank seat worn, repr., 73½" L $1,430.00

A-PA Sept. 1998   Pook & Pook Inc.
Settee, Windsor, PA, ca. 1800, w/ bamboo turnings & old surface, 33" H, 70" L $6,000.00

A-MA Aug. 1998 Rafael Osona Auctioneer & Appraiser
Settee, Windsor, ca. 1804, PA, w/ bamboo turned spindles, plant seat, 37½" H, 77¼" L $5,500.00

A-NH Nov. 1998 Northeast Auctions
Settee, N. Eng. birdcage Windsor w/ bamboo turnings, 78" L $3,000.00

A-MA Feb. 1999 Skinner, Inc.
Chairs, Windsor, birdcage style, set of four, ca. 1810 w/ bamboo turnings & old blk. paint $1,552.50

A-MA Feb. 1999 Skinner, Inc.
Side Chairs, Windsor bow-back, assembled set, N. Eng., ca. 1810, all w/ bamboo turnings $1,955.00

A-ME Jan. 1999 Cyr Auction Co. Inc.
Chair Set, four half spindle w/ grained & stenciled dec., 34" H $2,200.00

A-ME Jan. 1999 Cyr Auction Co. Inc.
Side Chairs, Windsor, bird cage style w/ finials .$3,750.00

A-ME Jan. 1999 Cyr Auction Co. Inc.
Chairs, Windsor, arrow back, 4 side, 1 arm, mkd. "Benjamin Bennet", NY, w/ gr. paint $5,500.00

A-MA Aug. 1998 Skinner, Inc.
Side Chairs, bowback Windsor, assembled set of 8, N. Eng., 1780-1810 w/ various finishes $747.50

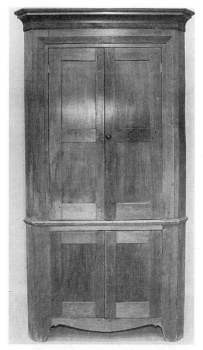

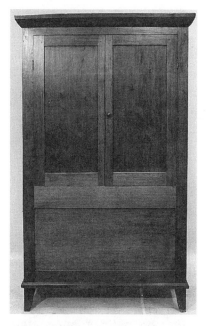

A-OH Sept. 1998   Garth's Auctions
Corner Cupboard, one pc., ref. walnut, poplar secondary wood, reprs. & hinges repl., 49½" W, 88¾" H $1,980.00

A-OH Sept. 1998   Garth's Auctions
Shaker Cloak Cupboard, walnut w/ old soft finish, open int. has two rows of wooden peg knobs, one board poplar ends & secondary wood, 20" x 46¾", 77¾" H $935.00

A-OH Sept. 1998   Garth's Auctions
Shaker Corner Cupboard, one piece, walnut w/ old finish, replm., poplar secondary wood, int. has partially removed yel. & white paint, 49½" W, 86½" H $1,210.00

A-OH Sept. 1998   Garth's Auctions
Shaker Cabinet, ref. walnut, int. has shelves w/ worn gray repaint, pine secondary wood, reprs., feet have lost height, bottom door repl., 37" W, 13½" D, 77" H $2,750.00

A-OH Nov. 1998   Garth's Auctions
Corner Cupboard, dec. two pc., by Rupp of Yorktown, PA, pine & poplar w/ orig. red flame graining, two dovetailed drawers in base, top shelves serpentine & have cut outs for spoons, repl. hardware, wear & flaking, 49½" W, 86¾" H $8,800.00

A-PA Oct. 1998   Pook & Pook, Inc.
Secretary, George III, Mah., late 18th C., orig. brasses, 40" W, 23" D, 81" H $9,500.00

A-PA Sept. 1998   Pook & Pook Inc.

Corner Cupboard, architectural, pine, ca. 1800, 90" H, 37" W $2,750.00

A-MA Feb. 1999   Skinner, Inc.

Desk & Bookcase, Fed., NH, bird's-eye maple, early 19th C., rep. brasses, old ref., imper., 83½" H, 40" W, 20" D ..$10,350.00

A-PA Sept. 1998   Pook & Pook Inc.

Dutch Cupboard, Chippendale, PA, ca. 1775, backboards of base, bottom board & one sm. drawer face res., 64" H, 63½" W $13,000.00

A-IA June 1998   Jackson's

Cabinet, oak w/ curved glass on front, 3 drawers below, 40" W, 50" H $373.75

A-MA Feb. 1999   Skinner, Inc.

Cupboard, N. Eng., early 19th C., painted white w/ salmon red int., loss of height, 70" H, 54½" W $920.00

A-NH Nov. 1998   Northeast Auctions

Dresser, MA, North Shore, 77" H, 64" W $16,000.00

A-IA June 1998   Jackson's

China Cupboard, oak w/ 2 curved glass panes, adj. shelves, 59" H $402.50

A-IA June 1998   Jackson's

China Cupboard, oak w/ curved glass side panels, 48" W, 65" H $1,092.00

A-PA Apr. 1999   York Town Auction Inc.

Corner Cupboard, PA, softwood, 2-pc., old finish, 88″ H $3,250.00

A-PA Mar. 1999   Horst Auctioneers

Corner Cupboard, Architectural, early 19th C., 2 pcs., ref. & repl., 88″ H, 34″ D, 48½″ W $3,900.00

A-MA Feb. 1999   Skinner, Inc.

Desk & Bookcase, Fed., cherry & cherry veneer, N. Eng., ca. 1820, repl. brasses, old refinish, minor imper., 81½″ H, 39″ W $5,175.00

A-PA Sept. 1998   York Town Auction Inc.

Dutch Cupboard, PA, walnut & cherry, two-part, untouched condition, ca. 1830-40, 53″ W, 83″ H, 18½″ D $8,000.00

A-PA Sept. 1998   Pook & Pook Inc.

Corner Cupboard, PA or DE, pine, ca. 1750 w/ rattail hinges, res. to cornice, 82½″ H, 41¼″ W $5,000.00

A-MA Aug. 1998   Rafael Osona Auctioneer & Appraiser

Dutch Cupboard, PA, cherry, ca. 1840, 2 pcs. w/ orig. mustard paint on int., 86½″ H, 50″ W, 19½″ D $2,250.00

A-ME Jan. 1999   Cyr Auction Co. Inc.

Secretary, ME, red painted case w/ tiger grained drawer fronts & cornice panels, 74″ H, 38″ W, 18″ D .$8,500.00

A-ME July 1998   Cyr Auction Co. Inc.
Bookcase, Hepplewhite mah. two part, w/ two eight lt. doors above a four drawer base, 92" H, 52" W, 14" D $9,000.00

A-MA Feb. 1999   Skinner, Inc.
Corner Cupboard, pine w/ barrel-back, N. Eng., late 18th C., butterfly hinges & shaped shelves, minor imper., 93½" H, 46" W $3,450.00

A-PA Sept. 1998   Pook & Pook, Inc.
Secretary, Q.A., DE Valley, ca. 1750, feet res., 89" H, 39¼" W . . .$8,000.00

A-PA June 1998   Pook & Pook, Inc.
Secretary, Chippendale desk, DE Valley, ca. 1790, 83" H, 40" W, minor repr. & losses $4,500.00

A-MA Aug. 1998   Rafael Osona Auctioneer & Appraiser
Cabinet, faux bamboo & pine glazed, Eng., late 19th C., 93½" H, 56¼" W $5,000.00

A-MA Aug. 1998   Robert C. Eldred Co., Inc.
Secretary, cherry, 2-part w/ tambour doors, 80" H, 42" W, 19½" D $2,860.00

A-ME Jan. 1999   Cyr Auction Co. Inc.
Butlers Desk, tiger maple & croch mah. w/ mah. post & feet, 21" D x 5' H $3,850.00

A-MA Oct. 1998   Skinner, Inc.
Chest of Drawers, tiger maple, ca. 1830, old finish, 49½" H, 46" W $2,185.00

A-MA May 1999   New England Auctions
of Brookfield
Spice Chest, Chippendale, tiger maple, all drawers w/ locks, old ref., 18" x 11" x 24" $6,000.00

A-ME Jan. 1999   Cyr Auction Co. Inc.
Tall Chest, six drawer, pine, grain painted, 36" W x 55" T x 16½" D $2,500.00

A-ME Jan. 1999   Cyr Auction Co. Inc.
Tall Chest, PA walnut w/ bracket base, 3 over 2 over 5 drawer, pine secondary, good old finish, repl. brasses, 38" W x 63" H x 21½" D . . .$4,750.00

A-PA Sept. 1998   Pook & Pook Inc.
Blanket Chest, Fed., walnut, PA ca. 1810 w/ inlaid fan corners, 29" H, 49½" L $3,000.00

A-ME Jan. 1999   Cyr Auction Co. Inc.
Cupboard, Quebec "Diamond Point", missing part of back, 66" H, 52" W, 19" D $2,000.00

A-MA Oct. 1998   Skinner, Inc.
Cupboard, paneled pine, Canada, late 18th C., painted blue, res., 71½" H, 53½" W $1,725.00

A-ME July 1998   Cyr Auction Co. Inc.
Chest, mini. three drawer w/ turned feet, 14" H, 11" W, 7" D $1,300.00

A-NH Nov. 1998   Northeast Auctions
Chest-on-Chest, CT, Chippendale, cherry, two parts, 77" H, 38" W $16,500.00

A-NH Nov. 1998   Northeast Auctions
Linen Press, PA, Fed., 2 parts, mah., 84" H, 48" W $7,000.00

A-PA Sept. 1998   York Town Auction Inc.
Blanket Chest, PA, w/ dec., untouched cond., ca. 1850, 49½" W x 27" H x 22" D $15,000.00

A-PA Mar. 1999   Horst Auctioneers
Chest of Drawers, Soap Hollow, PA, w/ Ger. paint dec., softwood, paint shows some wear & soiling, wooden Quaker lock broken on top drawer, 38½" W, 20⅞" x 53½" H . .$14,000.00

A-PA Mar. 1999   Horst Auctioneers
Chest of Drawers, Mini. Chippendale, PA, late 18th C., imper. & repl., 20¼" x 13¼" x 16" H $3,500.00

A-MA Oct. 1998   Skinner, Inc.
Butler's Desk, mah. veneer, ca. 1825, rep. brasses, old finish, imper., 48" H, 45" W, 22" D $920.00

A-PA Mar. 1999   Horst Auctioneers
High Chest of Drawers, PA, late 18th C., PA Chippendale, walnut, imper., 42½" x 26¼" x 67¼" H $18,500.00

A-PA Mar. 1999   Horst Auctioneers
High Chest of Drawers, poplar & walnut, Quaker locks, repr., shows wear, 63½" H, 45½" W $6,000.00

A-MA Oct. 1998   Skinner, Inc.
Desk, Chippendale slant lid, w/ rev. serpentine front, ca. 1780, mah., old ref., minor imper., 44" H, 40" W, 41" D $2,875.00

A-MA Oct. 1998　　　　　Skinner, Inc.
Chest of Drawers, bowfront, Fed., mah., ca. 1800, repl. brasses, ref., restorations, 38" H, 41" W, 23" D $1,725.00

A-MA Oct. 1998　　　　　Skinner, Inc.
Bureau, mah. carved veneer, ca. 1825, old finish, minor imper., 47" H, 45½" W, 23½" D $920.00

A-PA June 1998　　　Pook & Pook, Inc.
Chest of Drawers, Chippendale, PA, cherry, ca. 1800, Fr. feet, 38½" H, 41½" W, minor losses $2,400.00

A-MA May 1999　　New England Auctions
of Brookfield
Blanket Chest, Chippendale, grain painted, 6 board, minor res., 37½" W x 16" D , 21½" H $1,500.00

A-MA May 1999　　New England Auctions
of Brookfield
Bow Front Chest, Fed., N. Eng., tiger maple, 3rd qtr. 18th C., old ref., scratches to top, 35½" H . . .$5,750.00

A-MA May 1999　　New England Auctions
of Brookfield
Chest of Drawers, ox bow, Fed., cherry, early 19th C., orig. brass, old ref., 32" H $6,500.00

A-MA Feb. 1999　　　　　Skinner, Inc.
Chest of Drawers, Fed., mah. & mah. veneer, bow-front, MA, ca. 1815-20, minor imper., old ref., 39" H, 37½" W $2,300.00

A-MA Feb. 1999　　　　　Skinner, Inc.
Chest over Drawers, MA, pine, early 18th C., imper., 32½" H, 42" W .$4,600.00

A-IA June 1998　　　　　　Jackson's
Roll Top Desk, walnut w/ paneled cylinder top & false privacy panel w/ locking door, 48" W, 56" H .$2,587.50

A-MA May 1999　　New England Auctions
of Brookfield
Desk, Chippendale, maple & curly maple w/ slant lid, 6 visible drawers & 3 hidden, old rep. brasses, ref., 41" H $4,250.00

A-MA Oct. 1998　　　　　Skinner, Inc.
Desk, Chippendale slant lid, N. Eng., late 18th/early 19th C., maple, repl. brasses, ref., imper., 40½" H, 35" W, 17½" D $1,840.00

A-ME July 1998   Cyr Auction Co. Inc.
Highboy, Q.A., CT cherry, w/ full bonnet top, 85" H, 38" W, 21" D $15,000.00

A-MA May 1999   New England Auctions of Brookfield
Q.A. Highboy, tiger maple, late 18th C., old ref., minor imper., 75½" H $18,000.00

A-MA May 1999   New England Auctions of Brookfield
Q.A. Highboy, maple, old but not orig. brass, old ref., repr. to back leg, 74¼" H $11,500.00

A-MA May 1999   New England Auctions of Brookfield
Chest of Drawers, Chippendale, tiger maple, N.Eng., late 18th C., old ref., dovetailed pine top, 56¾" H $7,500.00

A-MA Feb. 1999   Skinner, Inc.
Desk, Q.A., child's w/ slant lid, ca. 1750, maple, old ref., res., 20" H, 19¼" W $2,530.00

A-MA May 1999   New England Auctions of Brookfield
Chest on Chest, w/ bonnet top, Chippendale, tiger maple, late 18th C., old brass, ref., 83¾" H $25,000.00

A-MA Feb. 1999   Skinner, Inc.
Chest-On-Chest, Chippendale, NH, maple, ca. 1760-80, minor reprs., 76" H, 36" W $14,950.00

A-MA May 1999   New England Auctions of Brookfield
Chest of Drawers, Chippendale, tiger maple, rep. brass, N. Eng., late 18th C., old ref., 55" H $51,000.00

A-MA Feb. 1999   Skinner, Inc.
Chest of Drawers, tiger maple & cherry, PA or OH, ca. 1825, imper., 56" H, 42½" W $2,760.00

A-IN Mar. 1999   Davies Auctions
Sugar Chest, Sheraton, KY, tiger-maple w/ dovetailed case & drawer, 32" H, 23" W, 17½" diam. . .$5,775.00

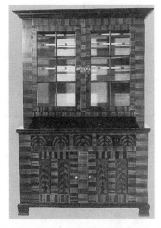

A-PA Sept. 1998   York Town Auction Inc.
Dutch Cupboard, York Co., PA w/ flamed dec., 55" W x 82" H x 19" D $30,000.00

A-NH Nov. 1998   Northeast Auctions
Armoire, Fr. Provincial, Louis XV, fruitwood, 85" H, 53" W . . .$4,250.00

A-MA Oct. 1998   Skinner, Inc.
Panel Cupboard, PA or OH, ca. 1834-45, orig. blue surfaces, unpainted int., orig. cond. 59½" H, 36¼" W, 14¼" D $4,600.00

A-MA Oct. 1998   . Skinner, Inc.
Corner Cupboard, Fed., walnut, early 19th C., Fr. feet, old finish, imper., 94¼" H, 44" W, 22" D $8,625.00

A-MA Oct. 1998   Skinner, Inc.
Corner Cupboard, ca. 1830, tulipwood, old refinish, some imper., 84½" H, 41" W $3,910.00

A-OH Aug. 1998   Garth's Auctions
Chest on Chest, Chippendale, cherry w/ old mellow ref., dovetailed cases, nine dovetailed overlapping drawers, pine secondary wood, int. drawers varnished, old brasses, reprs., replms., 77¾" H $13,200.00

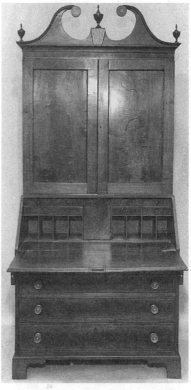

A-OH Aug. 1998   Garth's Auctions
Secretary, Hepplewhite two pc., walnut & figured walnut veneer w/ inlay, old finish, four dovetailed drawers, top has adjustable shelves & removable cornice, pine & poplar secondary wood, brasses are period replms., reprs., & finials repl., cornice base 21" x 40½", 90" H . . .$20,900.00

A-OH Sept. 1998   Garth's Auctions
Corner Cupboard, Hepplewhite, two pc., curly maple w/ old ref., dovetailed case, pine secondary wood, old glass, int. has pale yel. repaint, repl. brass hardware, edge damage to feet, reprs., 49" W, 83" H $7,920.00

A-OH Aug. 1998   Garth's Auctions
Corner Cupboard, Hepplewhite one pc., ref. cherry w/ inlay, feet repl., reprs., 42½" W, cornice 45¼", 82¼" H $3,300.00

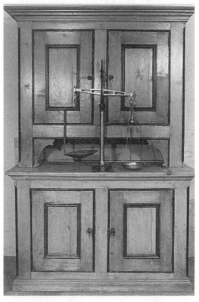

A-OH Aug. 1998   Garth's Auctions
Wall Cupboard, two pc., ref. pine w/ moldings in blk., base molding added & cornice repl., 55" W, cornice 22" x 62½", 88" H $1,760.00
Scales, Eng. balance, cast iron & brass, "Birmingham" label, 33¾" H $275.00

A-OH Sept. 1998   Garth's Auctions
Highboy, Q.A., ref. maple w/ curly facade, dovetailed drawers in base, top dovetailed, pine secondary wood, brasses orig., base reworked & several brasses on base are incomplete, one escut. missing, 35" W, cornice 20⅞" x 39", 70¼" H $7,370.00

A-OH July 1998   Garth's Auctions
Corner Cupboard, Hepplewhite two pc., cherry w/ old finish, old glass, reeded frieze & cove molded cornice, feet repl. & minor reprs., 49½" W, 89¾" H $5,225.00

A-OH July 1998   Garth's Auctions
High Chest, PA Hepplewhite, ref. walnut, dovetailed case, four overlapping dovetailed drawers, pine secondary wood, repl. oval brasses, damage & reprs., 22¼" x 41½", 53¼" H $3,300.00
Jug, stoneware w/ strap handle, impr. "Fort Edward Pottery Co. 2", floral dec. in cobalt blue, 15" H $478.50

A-OH Aug. 1998   Garth's Auctions
High Chest, PA Hepplewhite, walnut w/ old worn refinish, orig. wood facade & line inlay, nine dovetailed drawers, pine & poplar secondary wood, repl. brasses, 41" W, cornice 21½" x 44⅝", 60¾" H $3,850.00

A-OH Sept. 1998   Garth's Auctions
Corner Cupboard, one pc., ref. walnut w/ inlay, reprs., replm. & door edges restored, backboards renailed, 47" W, 85" H $2,090.00

A-OH July 1998   Garth's Auctions
Bookcase, on chest, Hepplewhite, walnut w/ inlay on base, old soft finish, four dovetailed drawers, mismatched top, removable cornice, poplar secondary wood, repl. brasses, minor edge damage, 39" W, 19½" D, 89½" H $2,970.00

A-OH Sept. 1998   Garth's Auctions
Corner Cupboard, one pc., curly maple w/ old ref., poplar secondary wood, replm. & restorations, 44½" W, 99½" H $10,450.00

A-PA Mar. 1999   Horst Auctioneers
Bench, or settle table, early 19th C., softwood w/ red wash, repl., scrubbed top, 30" H, top 38" x 71¼" . . .$2,800.00

A-MA Oct. 1998   Skinner, Inc.
Sideboard, Limbert, oak w/ copper pulls, branded, ref., 41¼" H, 51" L, 19½" D $4,025.00

A-IA June 1998   Jackson's
Library Table, oak w/ single drawer, 42" L, 30" D., 26" H $316.25

A-MA Feb. 1999   Skinner, Inc.
Table, Fed., N. Eng., ca. 1800-10, tiger maple, old ref., minor imper., 28" H, top 19¼" x 19½" $4,312.50

A-IA June 1998   Jackson's
Table, oak, ext., 46" diam. . .$143.75

A-IA June 1998   Jackson's
Parlor Table, oak w/ curio shelf, 26" sq., 30" H $149.50

A-MA May 1999   New England Auctions
                     of Brookfield
Stand Table, Fed. w/ inlay, top damaged $3,500.00

A-ME July 1998   Cyr Auction Co. Inc.
Stand, Sheraton, w/ cookie corners in tiger maple & pine-embellished w/ primitive scenes, flowers & fruit baskets, top 15½" x 19", 30" T $15,000.00

A-IA June 1998   Jackson's
Library Table, oak w/ bookend panels & drawer, 30" H, 36" L . . .$143.75

A-MA May 1999   New England Auctions
                     of Brookfield
Stand Table, Fed., cherry w/ inlay, N. Eng., late 18th C., old refinish, slight warp to top $2,100.00

A-MA Feb. 1999 Skinner, Inc.
Tea Table, Q.A., N. Eng., late 18th C., old refinish, minor imper., 27½" H, 32½" W, w/ 26½" drop $5,462.50

A-MA Feb. 1999 Skinner, Inc.
Table, Pembroke, Fed., mah. w/ inlay, Southeaster US., ca. 1790-1800, rep. brass pulls, old refinish, minor imper., 28½" H, 37" W $3,335.00

A-MA Feb. 1999 Skinner, Inc.
Dining Table, Chippendale, walnut, MA, ca. 1780, ref., imper. . . $2,070.00

A-IA June 1998 Jackson's
Dining Table, oak & oak veneer w/ 4 leaves, 45" sq. $345.00

A-IA June 1998 Jackson's
Library Table, oak w/ pressed designs on drawer $172.50

A-ME Jan. 1999 Cyr Auction Co. Inc.
Sideboard, Hepplewhite w/ serpentine front & bellflower inlay, centennial, 6' L, 38½" H, 25" D $3,000.00

A-MA Jan. 1999 Skinner, Inc.
Sideboard, bowfront, George III, mah. w/ inlay, late 18th C., w/ repr., 37½" H, 54½" L $1,725.00

A-MA May 1999 New England Auctions of Brookfield
Wash Stand, Sheraton, tiger maple, same as above but has some sun bleaching $8,250.00

A-ME Jan. 1999 Cyr Auction Co. Inc.
Work Table, Sheraton w/ drawer, mah., 28" H $1,750.00

A-ME July 1998 Cyr Auction Co. Inc.
Stand, Sheraton, w/ cookie corners in tiger maple & pine-embellished w/ primitive scenes, flowers & fruit baskets, top 15½" x 19", 30" T $15,000.00

A-MA Feb. 1999 Skinner, Inc.
Tavern Table, Wm. & Mary, N. Eng., 18th C., old refinish, imper., 26½" H, 37½" W $2,070.00

A-IA June 1998   Jackson's
Parlor Table, walnut, 29" H, 31"
sq. $201.25

A-IA June 1998   Jackson's
Parlor Table, walnut w/ inlaid floral
medallion, carved skirt & legs,
30" H $345.00

A-MA Oct. 1998   Skinner, Inc.
Table, tilt-top tripod, Irish, George III,
late 18th C. w/ piecrust top, res., 27"
H, top 26½" diam. $4,025.00

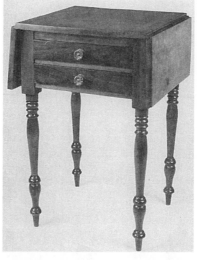

A-MA Aug. 1998   Skinner, Inc.
Work Table, tiger maple & mah.
veneer, N. Eng., ca. 1825, old refinish,
imp. 29" H $862.50

A-MA Aug. 1998   Skinner, Inc.
Sewing Table, Fed., MA, ca. 1805,
mah. veneer w/ sliding bag frame,
old brass, old refinish, reprs.,
28¼" H $1,610.00

A-MA Oct. 1998   Skinner, Inc.
Table, carved & veneer mah., ca.
1825, w/ cock-beaded skirt, acanthus
& scroll carved feet, refinish, minor
imp., 28½" H, 44" diam., exc.
leaf $3,325.00

A-MA Oct. 1998   Skinner, Inc.
Dressing Table, Fed., mah. & mah.
veneer w/ inlay, ca. 1825, ref., reprs.,
55" H, 36½" W, 21½" D $1,725.00

A-MA Oct. 1998   Skinner, Inc.
Card Table, Fed., prob. MA, ca.
1790, mah. w/ inlay, old finish,
minor imper., 30½" H, 35½" W,
17" D $5,175.00

A-MA Oct. 1998   Skinner, Inc.
Sewing Table, Fed., N. Eng., mah.,
top fitted for writing, bottom w/ sliding sewing bag frame, old finish, repl.
brass, reprs., 29¼" H $1,150.00

A-PA Sept. 1998   Pook & Pook, Inc.

Card Table, PA, mah., ca. 1800 w/ serpentine line inlaid edge folding top, inlaid cartouches, tapering legs w/ inlaid capitals, string inlays & banded cuffs, 29½" H, 35½" W $5,500.00

A-PA Sept. 1998   Pook & Pook, Inc.

Card Table, MD, mah., ca. 1800 w/ line inlaid folding top, sq. legs w/ eglomise inset panels of gilt vases & flowers on blue rev., minor losses, 28½" H, 36" W $3,750.00

A-MA Oct. 1998   Skinner, Inc.

Card Table, Fed., NH, tiger maple birch & bird's eye maple veneer, ca. 1820, old ref., imper., 28" H, 36" W, 18" D $1,495.00

A-MA May 1999   New England Auctions of Brookfield

Table, Q.A. oval drop leaf w/ old red wash, N. Eng., mid-18th C., half of 1 foot missing, 31¾" x 30½" x 26" H $30,000.00

A-MA May 1999   New England Auctions of Brookfield

Table, drop leaf oval Q.A., w/ old red wash, half of one foot missing $30,000.00

A-MA Feb. 1999   Skinner, Inc.

Dining Table, Chippendale, MA, mah. old refinish, reprs., 28" H, 47" W, 46¼" $4,600.00

A-PA June 1998   Pook & Pook, Inc.

Dining Table, Chippendale. walnut, ca. 1780, 28½" H, 44½" L . .$4,900.00

A-PA Sept. 1998   Pook & Pook, Inc.

Dining Table, MA, ca. 1780, mah., retains a prob. orig. surface, res. to one knee, 28¼" H, 47" W, open, 48" D $6,500.00

A-PA Sept. 1998   York Town Auction Inc.

Work Table, Q.A., walnut w/ pin-top, DE Valley, ca. 1770, 28½" H x 56" W x 32½" D, w 6" overhang, hardware repl., lip reprs. $14,000.00

A-MA May 1999   New England Auctions of Brookfield

Dining Table, drop leaf, Fed., tiger maple & maple inlay, late 18th C., old refinish $1,900.00

A-MA May 1999   New England Auctions
of Brookfield
Dining Table, drop leaf, tiger maple,
1st qtr. 19th C., old finish . .$6,900.00

A-MA May 1999   New England Auctions
of Brookfield
Dining Table, Q.A. drop leaf, tiger
maple, N. Eng., mid 18th C., w/
remnants of old finish scrubbed
down $11,000.00

A-MA May 1999   New England Auctions
of Brookfield
Pembroke Table, Hepplewhite,
cherry w/ one inlaid drawer, MA, late
18th C., new drawer front, old ref.,
28" H $1,200.00

A-MA Feb. 1999   Skinner, Inc.
Tea Table, Q.A., N. Eng., maple & pine
w/ breadboard ends, top not orig., imper.,
27" H, top 38¼" x 26" $2,875.00

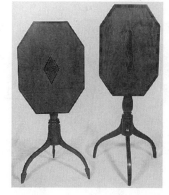

A-MA May 1999   New England Auctions
of Brookfield
Tilt Top Table, Fed., mah. w/ inlay,
ca. 1810 . . . .$3,100.00
Candlestand, Fed., cherry w/ inlay,
Am., late 18th C., old refinish, repr. to
block $3,400.00

A-MA May 1999   New England Auctions
of Brookfield
Game Table, Fed., MA, satinwood,
inlaid old ref. cherry, late 18th
C., ...$3,500.00

A-NH Nov. 1998   Northeast Auctions
Candlestand, PA, walnut w/ birdcage, 29" H, 22" diam. $7,500.00

A-NH Nov. 1998   Northeast Auctions
Tea Table, PA, Chippendale w/ birdcage, walnut, 28½" H, 31"
diam. $6,250.00

A-NH Nov. 1998   Northeast Auctions
Sideboard, N. Eng., Hepplewhite w/
inlay, mah., 43" H, 70" L . .$19,000.00

A-NH Nov. 1998   Northeast Auctions
Gateleg Table, N. Eng., Wm. &
Mary, maple w/ red wash & one
drawer $1,750.00

A-NH Nov. 1998   Northeast Auctions
Dining Table, Q.A., 2-part, English,
84" L $1,000.00

A-MA Aug. 1998   Skinner, Inc.
Chair Table, painted pine & maple, early 19th C., old red painted finish, feet pieced, 29" H, 46" diam. $2,415.00

A-MA Oct. 1998   Skinner, Inc.
Sawbuck Table, N. Eng., pine w/ old redbrown paint, nail const., 30" H, 50" W, 28" D $2,070.00

A-PA June 1998   Pook & Pook, Inc.
Tavern Table, PA, pine & walnut, mid 18th C., w/ old red stained surface & blk. checkerboard dec., minor reprs., 28½" H, 53½" W, 35¼" D $1,800.00

A-ME Jan. 1999   Cyr Auction Co. Inc.
Tavern Table, w/ one drawer, walnut 26" W, 48" L, 26½" H . .$1,250.00

A-MA Oct. 1998   Skinner, Inc.
Chair Table, shoefoot, pine w/ red paint over earlier paint, prob. N. Eng., 18th C., 26¼" H, 31" diam. .$6,900.00

A-ME Jan. 1999   Cyr Auction Co. Inc.
Tap Table, N.H., button foot, w/ shaped top & apron, 24" x 32" x 27" H $4,000.00

A-PA Mar. 1999   Horst Auctioneers
Miller's Desk, softwood, early 19th C., w/ lift top, 1 drawer has repr., ref. $300.00

A-PA Sept. 1998   York Town Auction Inc.
Cutlery Box, walnut, dovetailed w/ cut-outs $350.00
Coffeepot, tin, gooseneck w/ flared base & strap handle, 10½" H .$675.00
Work Table, PA, walnut w/ pin-top, untouched condition, chestnut & poplar secondary wood, ca. 1820-40, 29" H, 34½" D, 50" W, 9" over-hang $4,000.00

A-ME July 1998   Cyr Auction Co. Inc.
Chair Table, ME, w/ one drawer in red, 47" diam., 28½" T $8,000.00

A-ME Jan. 1999   Cyr Auction Co. Inc.
Tavern Table, w/ splayed legs & button feet, 28" x 34", 27" H .$9,000.00

A-MA Aug. 1998   Robert C. Eldred Co., Inc.
Mirror, convex, ca. 1820, 12½" diam., w/ 2 candle arms, eagle pediment & carved giltwood frame, mkd. Thomas Fentham, No. 136, 34" H, 21½" W $6,600.00

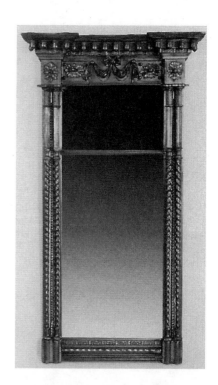

A-OH Jan. 1999   Garth's Auctions
Mirror, worn orig. gilt, top panel w/ figures in molded compo., orig. beveled mirror has worn silvering, damage, 44" H, 26¾" W . . .$1,705.00

A-MA Aug. 1998   Rafael Osona Auctioneer & Appraiser
Mirror, Girandole Cheval, mah., ca. 1820, 36½" W, 69¼" H $4,100.00

A-MA Oct. 1998   Skinner, Inc.
Tabernacle Mirror, Fed. w/ gilt gesso, ca. 1815-20, possibly Salem, MA, imper., 52" H, 29" W . .$2,070.00

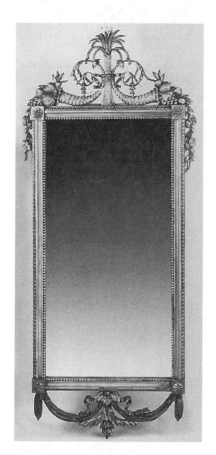

A-OH Jan. 1999   Garth's Auctions
Mirror, ref. mah. & veneer, orig. glass has worn silvering, bottom panel cracked, reprs., & replms., 36¼" H, 20½" W $440.00
Mirror, old gold repaint, applied compo. medallions, repl. rev. glass painting & mirror, some edge damage, 39¾" H, 24" W $220.00

A-MA Jan. 1999   Skinner, Inc.
Mirror, Pier, giltwood, losses, 67½" H, 29½" W $4,312.00

A-MA Oct. 1998   Skinner, Inc.
Mirror, Chippendale, mah. w/ parcel gilt mirror, prob. Eng., ca. 1790 w/ gilt incised concave shell in crest above gilt liner, old finish, 27", 14½" W $632.50

A-IA June 1998   Jackson's
Settee, walnut w/ medallion back, new upholstery, 48" L $575.00

A-MA Jan. 1999   Skinner, Inc.
Settees, pr., regency ebonized & parcel-gilt, early 19th C., paint loss, 51" L $9,200.00

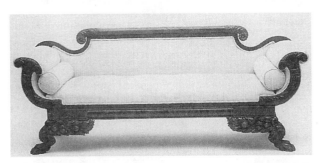

A-NH Nov. 1998   Northeast Auctions
Sofa, NY, carved mah., 89" L $1,500.00

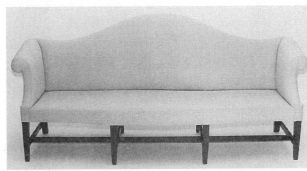

A-NH Nov. 1998   Northeast Auctions
Sofa, Fed., mah. w/ camel back, 86" L $3,250.00

A-MA Jan. 1999   Skinner, Inc.
Settees, Renaissance revival, rosewood w/ bronzed & parcel gilt, 3rd qtr. 19th C., w/ restoration, 36½" H, 72" L $6,900.00

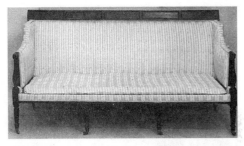

A-OH Jan. 1999   Garth's Auctions
Sofa, Sheraton, mah. frame w/ dk. finish, brass castors, worn reupholstery & repl. cushion 78" L $2,200.00

A-IA June 1998   Jackson's
Bench, Eastlake style, walnut w/ gr. mohair sculpted freize upholstery, 38" L $661.25

A-MA Feb. 1999   Skinner, Inc.
Sofa, Fed., MA, ca. 1810-15, mah. w/ reeded tapering legs, slightly bowed frame, old surface w/ imper., 37½" H, 78" L $8,625.00

A-IA June 1998   Jackson's

Dresser, oak w/ mirror & frame, applied carvings, full serpentine front, 44" W, 82" H $402.50

A-IA June 1998   Jackson's

Left to Right

Hall Seat, walnut w/ beveled mirror, iron hooks & brass umbrella pan, 33" W, 82" H $885.50

Hall Stand, walnut w/ beveled glass mirror, marble top shelf & carved dec., 23" W, 87" H $632.50

A-IA June 1998   Jackson's

Secretary/Bookcase, w/ beveled mirror & applied carvings, 4 adjust. shelves, 71" H $603.75

A-IA June 1998   Jackson's

High Chest, oak w/ serpentine top drawer, 34" W, 66" H $258.75

A-IA June 1998   Jackson's

Left to Right

Hall Seat, oak w/ beveled mirror & bronzed hooks, 29" W, 82" H .$661.25

Hall Seat, walnut w/ beveled mirror & gilt hooks, 20" W, 77" H . . .$632.50

A-IA June 1998   Jackson's

Dresser, & matching commode, w/ towel bar, oak $345.00

A-IA June 1998   Jackson's

Bed & Dresser, oak, dresser w/ beveled mirror, applied carving $517.50

A-IA June 1998   Jackson's

Left to Right

File Cabinet, oak, stacking 4 section, paneled const., 24" W, 60" H .$287.00

Bookcase, oak, stacking, 4 section, claw feet, mkd. "Macey", 34" W, 60" H $747.00

A-IA June 1998   Jackson's

Secretary/Bookcase, oak w/ beveled mirror, drop front desk, adjust. shelves in bookcase, 40" W, 71" H $603.75

A-IA June 1998   Jackson's
Secretary, oak w/ beveled mirror, drop front desk w/ pigeon holes, 66" H $632.50

A-IA June 1998   Jackson's
Sideboard, oak w/ beveled mirror, carved crest & lamp shelves, 43" W, 68" H $920.00

A-IA June 1998   Jackson's
Sideboard, walnut w/ beveled glass & deep carved panels, 59" W, 79" H $833.75

A-IA June 1998   Jackson's
Dresser, Victorian, walnut w/ white marble, brass pulls & candle or lamp shelves, 43" W, 88" H $661.25

A-MA Oct. 1998   Skinner, Inc.
Sideboard, carved mah., ca. 1870 by Cincinnati Women's Wood Carving Movement w/ panels of fruit, vines, flowering trees, leaves, ferns & birds, 97" H, 58" W, 16¼" D $10,925.00

A-IA June 1998   Jackson's
Sideboard, oak w/ beveled mirror, claw feet, rich dk. patina, 57" W, 61" H $316.25

A-MA Oct. 1998   Skinner, Inc.
Armchairs, Rococo revival, laminated, mid/late 19th C., 43¼" H $6,037.50

A-IA June 1998   Jackson's
Chairs, Victorian, set of 4 w/ caned seats & incised dec. $230.00

A-IA June 1998   Jackson's

Left to Right

Desk, slant top writing w/ compartments, oak, 23" W, 32" H $143.75
Side Chair, Victorian, walnut w/ caned seat & back $51.75

A-MA Sept. 1998   Craftsman Auctions
Server, Lifetime, orig. finish, water stain, 40" x 38" x 19" $800.00

A-MA Sept. 1998   Craftsman Auctions
Table, Lifetime, dining, orig. finish w/ 5 leaves, insect damage to runners, 54" round $1,150.00

A-MA Sept. 1998   Craftsman Auctions
Table, Stickley Bros., 60" diam., fixed top, ref. $2,000.00

A-MA Sept. 1998   Craftsman Auctions
Dining Suite, Limbert Ebon, oak, w/ 56" dining table, 4 leaves, single door china cabinet, sideboard, server, 5 side chairs & 1 arm chair, all pcs. w/ orig. finish & branded signatures $47,500.00

A-MA Sept. 1998 .   Craftsman Auctions
Chairs, Lifetime, set of 6 side, 2 arm w/ orig. finish, sgn. $2,800.00

A-MA Sept. 1998   Craftsman Auctions
Sideboard, Lifetime, sgn. w/ orig. finish, some veneer lifting near edge, 44" x 60" x 22" $1,000.00

A-MA Sept. 1998   Craftsman Auctions
Sideboard, Gustav Stickley w/ exposed tenon const., orig. finish & mkd. w/ red decal & paper label, 48½" x 66" x 24" $6,500.00

A-MA Sept. 1998   Craftsman Auctions
Desk, drop front w/ paper label, Shop of the Crafters, 42" x 29" x 20" $1,450.00

AGATA GLASS was patented by Joseph Locke of the New England Glass Company of Cambridge, Massachusetts, in 1877. The application of a metallic stain left a mottled design characteristic of agata, hence the name.

AMBER GLASS is the name of any glassware having a yellowish-brown color. It became popular during the last quarter of the 19th century.

AMBERINA GLASS was patented by the New England Glass Company in 1833. It is generally recognized as a clear yellow glass shading to a deep red or fushcia at the top. When the colors are opposite, it is known as reverse amberina. It was machine-pressed into molds, free blown, cut and pattern molded. Almost every glass factory here and in Europe produced this ware, however, few pieces were ever marked.

AMETHYST GLASS — The term identifies any glassware made in the proper dark purple shade. It became popular after the Civil War.

ART GLASS is a general term given to various types of ornamental glass made to be decorative rather than functional. It dates primarily from the late Victorian period to the present day and, during the span of time, glassmakers have achieved fantastic effects of shape, color, pattern, texture and decoration.

AVENTURINE GLASS — The Venetians are credited with the discovery of aventurine during the 1860s. It was produced by various mixes of copper in yellow glass. When the finished pieces were broken, ground or crushed, they were used as decorative material by glassblowers. Therefore, a piece of aventurine glass consists of many tiny glittering particles on the body of the object, suggestive of sprinkled gold crumbs or dust. Other colors in aventurine are known to exist.

BACCARAT GLASS was first made in France in 1756 by La Compagnie des Cristelleries de Baccarat—until the firm went bankrupt. Production began for the second time during the 1820s and the firm is still in operation, producing fine glassware and paperweights. Baccarat is famous for its earlier paperweights made during the last half of the 19th century.

BOHEMIAN GLASS is named for its country of origin. It is ornate, overlay, or flashed glassware, popular during the Victorian era.

BRISTOL GLASS is a lightweight opaque glass, often having a light bluish tint, and decorated with enamels. The ware is a product of Bristol, England—a glass center since the 1700s.

BURMESE — Frederick Shirley developed this shaded art glass at the now-famous old Mt. Washington Glass Company in New Bedford, Massachusetts, and patented his discovery under the name of "Burmese" on December 15, 1885. The ware was also made in England by Thomas Webb & Sons. Burmese is a hand-blown glass with the exception of a few pieces that were pattern molded. The latter are either ribbed, hobnail or diamond quilted in design. This ware is found in two textures or finishes: the original glazed or shiny finish, and the dull, velvety, satin finish. It is a homogeneous glass (singlelayered) that was never lined, cased or plated. Although its color varies slightly, it always shades from a delicate yellow at the base to a lovely salmon-pink at the top. The blending of colors is so gradual that it is difficult to determine where one color ends and the other begins.

CAMBRIDGE glasswares were produced by the Cambridge Glass Company in Ohio from 1901 until the firm closed in 1954.

CAMEO GLASS can be defined as any glass in which the surface has been cut away to leave a design in relief. Cutting is accomplished by the use of hand-cutting tools, wheel cutting and hydrofluoric acid. This ware can be clear or colored glass of a single layer, or glass with multiple layers of clear or colored glass.

Although cameo glass has been produced for centuries, the majority available today dates from the late 1800s. It has been produced in England, France and other parts of Europe, as well as the United States. The most famous of the French masters of cameo wares was Emile Gallé.

CARNIVAL GLASS was an inexpensive, pressed iridescent glassware made from about 1900 through the 1920s. It was made in quantities by Northwood Glass Company, Fenton Art Glass Company and others, to compete with the expensive art glass of the period. Originally called "taffeta" glass during the 1920s when carnivals gave examples as premiums or prizes.

CONSOLIDATED LAMP & GLASS CO. of Coraopolis, PA, founded in 1894 and closed in 1967. The company made lamps, art glass and tablewares. Items made after 1925 are of the greatest interest to collectors.

CORALENE — The term coralene denotes a type of decoration rather than a kind of glass—consisting of many tiny beads, either of colored or transparent glass—decorating the surface. The most popular design used resembled coral or seaweed, hence the name.

CRACKLE GLASS — This type of art glass was an invention of the Venetians that spread rapidly to other countries. It is made by plunging red-hot glass into cold water, then reheating and reblowing it, thus producing an unusual outer surface which appears to be covered with a multitiude of tiny fractures, but is perfectly smooth to the touch.

CRANBERRY GLASS — The term "cranberrry glass" refers to color only, not to a particular type of glass. It is undoubtedly the most familiar colored glass known to collectors. This ware was blown or molded, and often decorated with enamels.

CROWN MILANO glass was made by Frederick Shirley at the Mt. Washington Glass Company, New Bedford, Massachusetts, from 1886–1888. It is ivory in color with a satin finish, and was embellished with floral sprays, scrolls and gold enamel.

CROWN TUSCAN glass has a pink-opaque body. It was originally produced in 1936 by A.J. Bennett, president of the Cambridge Glass Company of Cambridge, Ohio. The line was discontinued in 1954. Occasionally referred to as Royal Crown Tuscan, this ware was named for a scenic area in Italy, and it has been said that its color was taken from the flash-colored sky at sunrise. When transilluminated, examples do have all of the blaze of a sunrise—a characteristic that is even applied to new examples of the ware reproduced by Mrs. Elizabeth Degenhart of Crystal Art Glass, and Harold D. Bennett, Guernsey Glass Company of Cambridge, Ohio.

CUSTARD GLASS was manufactured in the United States for a period of about 30 years (1885-1915). Although Harry Northwood was the first and largest manufacturer of custard glass, it was also produced by the Heisey Glass Company, Diamond Glass Company, Fenton Art Glass Company and a number of others.

The name custard glass is derived from its "custard yellow" color which may shade light yellow to ivory to light green—glass that is opaque to opalescent. Most pieces have fiery opalescence when held to the light. Both the color and glow of this ware came from the use of uranium salts in the glass. It is generally a heavy type pressed glass made in a variety of different patterns.

CUT OVERLAY — The term identifies pieces of glassware usually having a milk-white exterior that have been cased with cranberry, blue or amber glass. Other type examples are deep blue, amber or cranberry on crystal glass, and the majority of pieces has been decorated with dainty flowers. Although Bohemian glass manufacturers produced some very choice pieces during the 19th century, fine examples were also made in America, as well as in France and England.

DAUM NANCY is the mark found on pieces of French cameo glass made by August and Antonin Daum after 1875.

DURAND ART GLASS was made by Victor Durand from 1879 to 1935 at the Durand Art Glass Works in Vineland, New Jersey. The glass resembles Tiffany in quality. Drawn white feather designs and thinly drawn glass threading (quite brittle) applied around the main body of the ware, are striking examples of Durand creations on an iridescent surface.

FLASHED WARES were popular during the late 19th century. They were made by partially coating the inner surface of an object with a thin plating of glass or another, more dominant color—usually red. These pieces can readily be identified by holding the object to the light and examining the rim, as it will show more than one layer of glass. Many pieces of "rubina crystal" (cranberry to clear), "blue amberina" (blue to amber), and "rubina verde" (cranberry to green), were manufactured in this way.

FINDLAY or ONYX art glass was manufactured about 1890 for only a short time by the Dalzell Gilmore Leighton Company of Findlay, Ohio.

FRANCISWARE is a hobnail glassware with frosted or clear glass hobs and stained amber rims and tops. It was produced during the late 1880s by Hobbs, Brockunier and Company.

FRY GLASS was made by the H.C. Fry Company, Rochester, Pennsylvania, from 1901, when the firm was organized, until 1934 when operations ceased. The firm specialized in the manufacturing of cut glassware. The production of their famous "foval" glass did not begin until the 1920s. The firm also produced a variety of glass specialties, oven wares and etched glass.

GALLÉ glass was made in Nancy, France, by Emile Gallé at the Gallé Factory founded in 1874. The firm produced both enameled and cameo glass, pottery, furniture and other art nouveau items. After Gallé's death in 1904, the factory continued operating until 1935.

GREENTOWN glass was made in Greentown, Indiana, by the Indiana Tumbler and Goblet Company from 1894 until 1903. The firm produced a variety of pressed glasswares in addition to milk and chocolate glass.

GUNDERSON peachblow is a more recent type art glass produced in 1952 by the Gunderson-Pairpoint Glass Works of New Bedford, Massachusetts, successors to the Mt. Washington Glass Company. Gunderson pieces have a soft satin finish shading from white at the base to a deep rose at the top.

HOBNAIL — The term hobnail identifies any glassware having "bumps"—flattened, rounded or pointed—over the outer surface of the glass. A variety of patterns exists. Many of the fine early examples were produced by Hobbs, Brockunier and Company, Wheeling, West Virginia, and the New England Glass Company.

HOLLY AMBER, originally known as "golden agate," is a pressed glass pattern which features holly berries and leaves over its glossy surface. Its color shades from golden brown tones to opalescent streaks. This ware was produced by the Indiana Tumbler and Goblet Company for only 6 months, from January 1 to June 13, 1903. Examples are rare and expensive.

IMPERIAL GLASS — The Imperial Glass Company of Bellaire, Ohio, was organized in 1901 by a group of prominent citizens of Wheeling, West Virginia. A variety of fine art glass, in addition to carnival glass, was produced by the firm. The two trademarks which identified the ware were issued in June 1914. One consisted of the firm's name, "Imperial," and the other included a cross formed by double-pointed arrows.

LATTICINO is the name given to articles of glass in which a network of tiny milk-white lines appear, crisscrossing between two walls of glass. It is a type of filigree glassware developed during the 16th century by the Venetians.

LEGRAS GLASS, cameo, acid cut and enameled glasswares were made by August J.F. Legras at Saint-Denis, France, from 1864-1914.

LOETZ GLASS was made in Austria just before the turn of the century. As Loetz worked in the Tiffany factory before returning to Austria, much of his glass is similar in appearance to Tiffany wares. Loetz glass is often marked "Loetz" or "Loetz-Austria."

LUTZ GLASS was made by Nicholas Lutz, a Frenchman, who worked at the Boston and Sandwich Glass Company from 1870 to 1888 when it closed. He also produced fine glass at the Mt. Washington Glass Company. Lutz is noted for two different types of glass—striped and threaded wares. Other glass houses also produced similar glass and these wares were known as Lutz-type.

MARY GREGORY was an artist for the Boston and Sandwich Glass Company during the last quarter of the 19th century. She decorated glassware with white enamel figures of young children engaged in playing, collecting butterflies, etc., in white on transparent glass, both clear and colored. Today the term "Mary Gregory" glass applies to any glassware that remotely resembles her work.

MERCURY GLASS is a double-walled glass that dates from the 1850s to about 1910. It was made in England as well as the United States during this period. Its interior, usually in the form of vases, is lined with flashing mercury, giving the items an all over silvery appearance. The entrance hole in the base of each piece was sealed over. Many pieces were decorated.

MILK GLASS is an opaque pressed glassware, usually of milk-white color, although green, amethyst, black, and shades of blue were made. Milk glass was produced in quantity in the United States during the 1880s, in a variety of patterns.

MILLEFIORI — This decorative glassware is considered to be a specialty of the Venetians. It is sometimes called "glass of a thousand flowers," and has been made for centuries. Very thin colored glass rods are arranged in bundles, then fused together with heat. When the piece of glass is sliced across, it has a design like that of many small flowers. These tiny wafer-thin slices are then embedded in larger masses of glass, enlarged and shaped.

MOSER GLASS was made by Ludwig Moser at Karlsbad. The ware is considered to be another type of art nouveau glass as it was produced during its heyday—during the early 1900s. Principal colors included amethyst, cranberry, green and blue, with fancy enameled decoration.

MOTHER-OF-PEARL, often abbreviated in descriptions as M.O.P., is glass composed of two or more layers, with a pattern showing through to the other surface. The pattern, caused by internal air traps, is created by expanding the inside layer of molten glass into molds with varying design. When another layer of glass is applied, this brings out the design. The final layer of glass is then acid dipped, and the result is mother-of-pearl satinware. Patterns are numerous. The most frequently found are the diamond quilted, raindrop and herringbone. This ware can be one solid color, a single color shading light to dark, two colors blended or a variety of colors which include the rainbow effect. In addition, many pieces are decorated with colorful enamels, coralene beading, and other applied glass decorations.

NAILSEA GLASS was first produced in England from 1788 to 1873. The characteristics that identify this ware are the "pulled" loopings and swirls of colored glass over the body of the object.

NEW ENGLAND PEACHBLOW was patented in 1886 by the New England Glass Company. It is a single-layered glass shading from opaque white at the base to deep rose-red or raspberry at the top. Some pieces have a glossy surface, but most were given an acid bath to produce a soft, matte finish.

NEW MARTINSVILLE PEACHBLOW GLASS was produced from 1901-1907 at New Martinsville, Pennsylvania.

OPALESCENT GLASS — The term refers to glasswares which have a milky white effect in the glass, usually on a colored ground. There are three basic types of this ware. Presently, the most popular includes pressed glass patterns found in table settings. Here the opalescence appears at the top rim, the base, or a combination of both. On blown or mold-blown glass, the pattern itself consists of this milky effect—such as Spanish lace. Another example is the opalescent points on some pieces of hobnail glass. These wares are lighter weight. The third group includes opalescent novelties, primarily of the pressed variety.

PEKING GLASS is a type of Chinese cameo glass produced from the 1700s, well into the 19th century.

PHOENIX GLASS — The firm was established in Beaver County, Pennsylvania, during the late 1800s, and produced a variety of commercial glasswares. During the 1930s the factory made a desirable sculptured gift-type glassware which has become very collectible in recent years. Vases, lamps, bowls, ginger jars, candlesticks, etc., were made until the 1950s in various colors with a satin finish.

PIGEON BLOOD is a bright reddish-orange glassware dating from the early 1900s.

POMONA GLASS was invented in 1884 by Joseph Locke at the New England Glass Company.

PRESSED GLASS was the inexpensive glassware produced in quantity to fill the increasing demand for tablewares when Americans moved away from the simple table utensils of pioneer times. During the 1820s, ingenious Yankees invented and perfected machinery for successfullly pressing glass. About 1865, manufacturers began to color their products. Literally hundreds of different patterns were produced.

QUEZAL is a very fine quality blown iridescent glassware produced by Martin Bach, in his factory in Brooklyn, New York, from 1901-1920. Named after the Central American bird, quezal glassware has an iridescent finish featuring contrasting colored glass threads. Green, white and gold colors are most often found.

ROSALINE GLASS is a product of the Steuben Glass Works of Corning, New York. The firm was founded by Frederick Carter and T.C. Hawkes, Sr. Rosaline is a rose-colored jade glass or colored alabaster. The firm is now owned by the Corning Glass Company, which is presently producing fine glass of exceptional quality.

ROYAL FLEMISH ART GLASS was made by the Mt. Washington Glass Works during the 1880s. It has an acid finish which may consist of one or more colors, decorated with raised gold enameled lines separating into sections. Fanciful painted enamel designs also decorate this ware. Royal Flemish glass is marked "RF," with the letter "R" reversed and backed to the letter "F," within a four-sided orange-red diamond mark.

RUBINA GLASS is a transparent blown glassware that shades from clear to red. One of the first to produce this crystal during the late 1800s was Hobbs, Brockunier and Company of Wheeling, West Virginia.

RUBINA VERDE is a blown art glass made by Hobbs, Brockunier and Company, during the late 1800s. It is a transparent glassware that shades from red to yellow-green.

SABINO GLASS originated in Paris, France, in the 1920s. The company was founded by Marius-Ernest Sabino, and was noted for art deco figures, vases, animals, nudes and animals in clear, opalescent and colored glass.

SANDWICH GLASS — One of the most interesting and enduring pages from America's past is Sandwich glass produced by the famous Boston and Sandwich Glass Company at Sandwich, Massachusetts. The firm began operations in 1825, and the glass flourished until 1888 when the factory closed. Despite the popularity of Sandwich Glass, little is known about its founder, Deming Jarvis.

The Sandwich Glass house turned out hundreds of designs in both plain and figured patterns, in colors and crystal, so that no one type could be considered entirely typical—but the best known is the "lacy" glass produced there. The variety and multitude of designs and patterns produced by the company over the years is a tribute to its greatness.

SILVER DEPOSIT GLASS was made during the late 19th and early 20th centuries. Silver was deposited on the glass surface by a chemical process so that a pattern appeared against a clear or colored ground. This ware is sometimes referred to as "silver overlay."

SLAG GLASS was originally known as "mosaic" and "marble glass" because of its streaked appearance. Production in the United States began about 1880. The largest producer of this ware was Challinor, Taylor and Company, The various slag mixtures are: purple, butterscotch, blue, orange, green and chocolate. A small quantity of pink slag was also produced in the inverted fan and feather pattern. Examples are rare and expensive.

SPANISH LACE is a Victorian glass pattern that is easily identified by its distinct opalescent flower and leaf pattern. It belongs to the shaded opalescent glass family.

STEUBEN — The Steuben Glass Works was founded in 1904 by Frederick Carter, an Englishman, and T.G. Hawkes, Sr., at Corning, New York. In 1918 the firm was purchased by the Corning Glass Company. However, Steuben remained with the firm, designing a bounty of fine art glass of exceptional quality.

STIEGEL-TYPE GLASS — Henry William Stiegel founded America's first flint glass factory during the 1760s at Manheim, Pennsylvania. Stiegel glass is flint or crystal glass; it is thin and clear, and has a bell-like ring when tapped. The ware is quite brittle and fragile. Designs were painted freehand on the glass—birds, animals and architectural motifs, surrounded by leaves and flowers. The engraved glass resulted from craftsmen etching the glass surface with a copper wheel, then cutting the desired patterns.

It is extremely difficult to identify, with certainty, a piece of original Stiegel glass. Part of the problem resulted from the lack of an identifying mark on the products. Additionally, many of the craftsmen moved to other areas after the Stiegel plant closed—producing a similar glass product. Therefore, when one is uncertain about the origin of this type ware, it is referred to as "Stiegel-type" glass.

TIFFANY GLASS was made by Louis Comfort Tiffany, one of America's outstanding glass designers of the art nouveau period, from about 1870 to the 1930s. Tiffany's designs included a variety of lamps, bronze work, silver, pottery and stained glass windows. Practically all items made were marked "L.C. Tiffany" or "L.C.T." in addition to the word Favrile".

TORTOISESHELL GLASS — As its name indicates, this type glassware resembles the color of tortoiseshell and has deep rich brown tones combined with amber and cream-colored shades. Tortoiseshell glass was originally produced in 1880 by Francis Pohl, a German chemist. It was also made in the United States by the Sandwich Glass Works and other glass houses during the late 1800s.

VAL ST. LAMBERT Cristalleries, located in Belgium, was founded in 1825 and the firm is still in operation.

VASA MURRHINA glassware was produced in quantity at the Vasa Murrhina Art Glass Company of Sandwich, Massachusetts, during the late 1900s. John C. DeVoy, assignor to the firm, registered a patent on July 1, 1884, for the process of decorating glassware with particles of mica flakes (coated with copper, gold, nickel or silver) sandwiched between an inner layer of clear or transparent colored glass. The ware was also produced by other American glass firms and in England.

VASELINE GLASS — The term "vaseline" refers to color only, as it resembles the greenish-yellow color typical of the oily petroleum jelly known as Vaseline. This ware has been produced in a variety of patterns both here and in Europe—from the late 1800s. It has been made in both clear and opaque yellow, vaseline combined with clear glass, and occasionally the two colors are combined in one piece.

VERLYS GLASS is a type of art glass produced in France after 1931. The Heisey Glass Company, Newark, Ohio, produced identical glass for a short time, after having obtained the rights and formula from the French factory. French-produced ware can be identified from the American product by the signature. The French is mold marked, whereas the American glass is etched script signed.

WAVECREST GLASS is an opaque white glassware made from the late 1890s by French factories and the Pairpoint Manufacturing Company at New Bedford, Massachusetts. Items were decorated by the C.F. Monroe Company of Meriden, Connecticut, with painted pastel enamels. The name wavecrest was used after 1898 with the initials for the company "C.F.M. Co." Operations ceased during World War II.

WEBB GLASS was made by Thomas Webb & Sons of Stourbridge, England, during the late Victorian period. The firm produced a variety of different types of art and cameo glass.

WHEELING PEACHBLOW — With its simple lines and delicate shadings, Wheeling Peachblow was produced soon after 1883 by J.H. Hobbs, Brockunier and Company at Wheeling, West Virginia. It is a two-layered glass lined or cased inside with an opaque, milk-white type of plated glassware. The outer layer shades from a bright yellow at the base to a mahogany red at the top. The majority of pieces produced are in the glossy finish.

A-OH July-Aug. 1998

Row 1, Left to Right

165-Vase, Imperial, pale iridized marigold ext., richer interior, 8½" H $175.00

190-Vase, Fr. Cameo, lifesize mandrian red poppies, gr. stems on textured red, gr. & mustard mottled ground, gold Art Deco on rim & base, 16" H $3,750.00

192-Vase, sgn. Quezal, irid. gold body dec. w/ gr. blue swirls & veins, double amber handles, 12' H $700.00

215-Vase, sgn. V. Durand, irid. gold w/ royal blue scattered leaves, gr. vine, amber base, 8" H $950.00

195-Urn, Royal Flemish, natural color ducks, yel. & frost raised gold ground w/ stars, annealing line on handle, 7" H $1,300.00

170-Vase, Steuben pomona gr., vertical ribbed body, knob stem, 11" H $225.00

22-Shakers, pr. Mt. Washington "tomato", both w/ almond ground w/ white enamel flowers, one w/ paper label, 1¾" H $150.00

168-Vase, Eng. Peachblow overlay, amber branch handles w/ 2 applied white spatter flowers & 4 amber leaves tinted w/ red or gr., crimped ruffled rim w/ amber trim 11" H $500.00

231-Lamp, irid. blk. shaft w/ amethyst hues, irid. gold pulled feathers on dec. base, overall 26" H, cloth shade, 12½" H $700.00

176-Pitcher, Webb crystal Cameo, red ruby acorns & leafy branches cover body, crystal handle, clear foot w/ cut daisy $1,400.00

202-Vase, Imperial freehand, reflective marigold w/ blue draped design, 10½" H $1,000.00

212-Vase, "sweet pea" sgn. Quezal, irid. gold int. floral form w/ pulled gr. leaf ext. on opal, 6¼" H $1,300.00

Row 2, Left to Right

200-Vase, Travaise opal & gold hooked design w/ 4 irid. gold leaf motif, 9¾" H $950.00

206-Vase, etched Schneider, purple rim shading to mottled yel., opal & cream, 6" H $650.00

219-Vase, trumpet form, sgn. Quezal, irid. gold w/ royal blue entwined vines & coiled designs, 6" H $1,200.00

214-Vase, gr. w/ dimpled shoulder, dk. irid. gold pulled leaf design, gold int. squared rim, attrib. to Durand, 8¾" H $900.00

166-Vase, irid. gold w/ scattered gr. leaves on vertical golden vines, sgn. L. C. Tiffany, Favrile $1,900.00

228-Vase, Fr. Cameo, sgn. Daum Nancy, red & purple cyclamen above gr. pod leaves, gilt on frost, pink & apple gr. ground, 8½" H ..$2,450.00

203-Vase, sgn. Quezal irid. blue w/ amber base, opal & swirl design $1,750.00

174-Compote, Steuben, topaz stem, pomona gr. bowl & base, 7" H $125.00

162-Vase, Northwood pull-up, greenish yel. satin swirl ground w/ radiated wine red pulled leaves, 9¼" H $2,300.00

211-Bud Vase, Cameo sgn. Legras, floral capsules in yel. & ora. w/ gr. fernery, pale pink to gr. textured ground, 9¼" H $225.00

Row 3, Left to Right

169-Candlesticks, pr. Steuben, clear & mica flecked stems w/ applied Pomona gr. fleur-de-lis, flanged ribbed pomona gr. cups & bases, 12" H $1,000.00

69-Shakers, trio of Mt. Washington "tomato" salt & peppers, one w/ gr. ivy on almond ground, other w/ pink & yel. trumpet flowers, peach color shoulder & burmese color w/ enamel asters, 1¾" H $90.00

218-Vase, Durand irid. gold w/ blue leaves scattered on entwined vines, 7½" H $650.00

177-Vase, red pink leafy vine w/ frosty ground, Cameo sgn. Gallé w/ star, 13¼" H $900.00

196-Bowl, Fr. Cameo apple gr., sgn. Gallé, textured ground w/ relief in natural enamel colors w/ gilt, disc base, 4" H, 8" diam. $2,000.00

193-Cologne, Fr. Cameo, amber & chocolate br. tones, scenic river, frosty sky w/ pink hues, frosty button stopper, sgn. Gallé, 4" H $1,100.00

189-Vase, Quezal, almond body w/ gr. & irid. gold pulled feathers, 12½" H $1,700.00

187-Vase, French Cameo, footed, purple Jack-in-Pulpit w/ foliage, purple shading to pale blue ground, sgn. Muller Fres Luneville, 11½" H $1,700.00

217-Vase, Durand irid. gold w/ bluish blk. vines w/ strewn leaves, 8½" H $700.00

181-Dresser Box, rainbow color opal, enamel floral wreaths & yel. scrolls, metal ormolu lion mask feet, brass ring handles, 5" H, 5" diam. $450.0

158-Vase, ribbed Amberina lily, w/ intense coloring to trefoil rim, 12" H $375.00

Row 4, Left to Right

171-Vase, Steuben pomona gr. ribbed, w/ fleur-de-lis mark, 6¼" H ...$225.00

205-Vase, Fr. Cameo, sgn. Mueller Frez Luneville, ebony landscape, olive gr. islands against yel. ora. & frosty sky, 5½" H $1,000.00

133-Vase, blue satin yel. Coralene, seaweed patt., 4" H $250.00

167-Vase, M.O.P. herringbone melon ribbed celery, rose pink to white, 6½" H $675.00

204-Vase, Fr. Cameo, sgn. deVez, plum color, canopy of floral vines against pale blue sky, 10" H ..$850.00

173-Compote, sgn. Steuben, ribbed celeste blue double knob stem, topaz swirl bowl & foot, 7" H $325.00

227-Gas Shades, pr., mkd. Steuben, opal w/ gr. pulled feathers w/ irid. gold tips, 4½" H $550.00

208-Vase, Fr. sgn. Schneider, footed conical, mottled ora., yel. to lilac & rose, 7" H $850.00

188-Vase, Eng. Cameo, white floral stalk w/ palm-like leaves on citron ground, 10½" H $1,300.00

175-Urn, acorn form covered, ribbed celeste blue, melon stem, 14" H $1,000.00

207-Vase, Fr. Cameo, sgn. Daum Nancy, ora. enamel bleeding hearts & fall color leaves, mottled ground, 6¾" H $1,800.00

165B-Gas Shades, three, sgn. Steuben, all tulip form, 2 pale yel. w/ pulled blue motif from ruffled rim, golden swirls, other shade same design only pulled gold on opal, firm's fleur-de-lis, 2¼" fitters, 5¼" H $1,050.00

198-Vase, Imperial, swirled cobalt & lt. blue, marigold int., 8¼" H .$375.00

Row 5, Left to Right

220-Vase, "sweet pea", sgn. Quezal & P, fine gr. pulled veins overlaid w/ irid. gold pulled leaves, trifold rim, irid. gold int. $1,500.00

223-Bud Vase, Loetz irid. gold tree bark w/ 3 golden applied pods, 5¼" H $350.00

163-Box, Fr. Cameo, dk. olive gr. orchids & maiden hair ferns on citron & pink blush ground, sgn. D'Argental, 2½" H, 5" diam. $1,000.00

216-Vase, sgn. L.C. Tiffany, Favrile, opal. Vaseline ribbed neck, pale wine red body, textured int., 8"H .$1,000.00

222-Nut Bowl, sgn. E. Gallé Nancy Pottery, oval shell form w/ vessels in mono. blue, gilt highlighted rim $250.00

194-Salt Tub, Cameo sgn. Daum Nancy, enamel dec. w/ blk. conifers, gilt rim, 1¼" H $850.00

225-Bowl, Loetz, metallic emerald gr., pink int., 4" H, 7½" diam. .$350.00

221-Baby Bird, Pate-de-Verre, frosty almond color w/ yel. feet on mottled gr. base, sgn. A. Walter Nancy & B, 4" H $1,000.00

213-Vase, Durand irid. marigold, cobalt blue leaves on gr. vines, amber base w/ bluish hues, 6" H ...$750.00

164-Bowl, acid Burmese w/ crimped rim, 1½" H, 4¾" diam. $175.00

209-Vase, sgn. Schneider, Fr. ovid w/ tri-pulled rim, ebony shoulder w/ applied ruby beads, 4¼" H ..$2,400.00

210-Atomizer, Fr., sgn. A. Docobu, lake scene w/ dk. foliaged trees $325.00

25-Shakers, pr. Mt. Washington "tomato", painted forget-me-nots on almond ground, one w/ blue & white enamel forget-me-nots on peach ground, 1¾" H $90.00

Row 1, Left to Right

614-Vase, irid. blue bronze w/ glossy finish, attrib. to Webb, 11½" H $325.00

611-Vase, Fr. Cameo, burgundy fox gloves w/ ebony leaves, mottled yel. ground, sgn. Daum Nancy, 21½" H $4,000.00

716-Lamp, hexagonal carmel slag shade w/ petal top rim, bronze textured base w/ figurines, overall 19" H, 12" diam. $1,750.00

718-Pitcher, glossy Wheeling Peachblow, amber handle, 8" H ..$1,000.00

61-Lamp, hexagonal shade, crown rim mkd. Handel, carmel slag panels overlaid w/ bronze fretwork, reeded bronze Handel base, 22½" H, 14" diam. $1,700.00

408-Muffineer, Amberina, tapered w/ inverted baby thumbprint, 5½" H $375.00

729-Vase, smokey amber sgn. Val St. Lambert, textured ground, emb. w/ 2 gilt metal peacock feathers, 10" H $900.00

662-Vase, Fr. Cameo, amber carmel nasturtiums & leaves w/ pink ground, translucent handles, one yel. & one pink, etched E. Gallé Nancy, 10¾" H $1,500.00

Row 2, Left to Right

664-Bowl, sgn. Quezal, uniform gr. pulled leaves w/ golden tips, opal ground, irid. gold int., 2¾" H, 4¾" diam. $600.00

601-Vase, Webb acid Peachblow, 13" H $325.00

666-Vase, Fr. Cameo, sgn. Richard, cobalt blue, holly & berry branches on crimson red ground, 4½" H ..$550.00

690-Vase, Loetz dimpled w/ ruffled rim, mottled emerald gr. w/ amber swirls, irid. blue oil spot surface, 15" H $900.00

627-Vase, Amberina ribbed, 12" H $325.00

600-Vase, New Eng. acid Peachblow w/ gold fern fronds, even coloring, 14½" H $1,650.00

701-Ewer, dec. w/ dk. & lt. blue flowers & leaves, yel. berries, outlined w/ raised gold dots on tan, chocolate br. handles, yel. neck, mkd. Karlsbad w/ horseshoe, 7¾" H $600.00

689-Vase, Loetz oversized w/ dimpled sides, ruffled rim, mottled red & citron pulled swirls, 12" H ...$650.00

736-Vase, mkd. St. Louis Cameo, textured frosty ground w/ cranberry passion flower & vine enhanced w/ gold, 11" H $950.00

Row 3, Left to Right

441-Pitcher, Amberina w/ squared rim, inverted thumbprint, amber reeded handle, 7" H $150.00

660-Vase, Fr. Cameo, etched LaVerre Francais, chocolate br. floral wreath, mottled yel. to rosy ground, 10" H $900.00

661-Vase, Fr. Cameo, sgn. Richard, mocha br. castle, citron ground, 13" H $1,000.00

721-Vase, sgn. R. Lalique, Fr., frosted w/ pale amber wreath of pod leaves tinted sparsely w/ blue, 6" H $1,300.00

717B-Vase, rustic amber w/ textured oxidized earthtone surface w/ applied dec., 16½" H $650.00

669-Bride's Bowl, Sandwich Peachblow satin swirl w/ hobnail & crimped rim w/ floral emb. silver holder & pierced double handles, 4¾" H, 10½" diam. $525.00

720-Vase, Imperial freehand w/ fastened tri-pulled loop rim, irid. cobalt blue w/ scattered opal leaves & vines, 8¼" H $1,200.00

667-Vase, Fr. Cameo footed, cobalt blue floral stalks on golden yel. ground, sgn. Richard, 6½" H $550.00

719-Vase, Wheeling w/ glossy finish, Peachblow, rich coloring, 6" H $425.00

Row 4, Left to Right

693-Vase, ribbed w/ ruffled rim, amethyst to clear, enamel dec. w/ pink or blue poppies w/ gr. foliage, attrib. to Mt. Joye, 9½" H, 10" diam. $500.00

409-Shakers, pr. w/ inverted baby thumbprint, 4" H $350.00

473-Bowl, English overlay cased, almond ext. w/ tooled rim, apricot int., attrib. to Steven's & Williams, 4" H, 8½" diam. $400.00

728-Vase, bronze garniture of rose garlands held by man, woman & child, maroon & yel. swirled vase, dec. pierced bronze base, 11" H .$1,700.00

681-Perfume, sgn. Steuben gr. jade w/ melon ribbed body, matching flame stopper, 4½" H $900.00

724-Bud Base, Fr. enameled, lady dressed in colorful & ruffled gown, floral path, some enamel missing, 5¼" H $425.00

Row 5, Left to Right

665-Creamer, sgn. Kew Blas, irid. gold pulled feathers, opal ground, applied irid. gold handles, 3" H $750.00

717-Boudoir Lamp, yel. slag leaded shade w/ amber "fig & diamond" rim patt., bronze base w/ reeded stem, 14¾" H, 7½" diam. $1,300.00

723-Syrup, Peachblow w/ glossy finish, pear form, applied crystal handle, hinged metal cap mkd. Pat. Oct. 31, 1891 ....$800.00

606-Mantle Clock, Tiffany gold Doré, dial mkd. Tiffany Studios, NY, wind-up clock mkd. Chelsea Clock Co., Boston, U.S.A., 9½" H, 11" W $1,250.00

702-Candlesticks, pr. Steuben gold ruby, swirl holder & base clear knob w/ prunts, 3½" H $300.00

722-Cruet, New Eng. Peachblow w/ glossy finish, almond handle & bulbous stopper, 6" H $820.00

730-Bowl, apricot D.Q. M.O.P. satin w/ ruffled rim, marked Pat., 2½" H $200.00

Row 5, Left to Right

714-Cologne, two pc., purple to clear, ribbed w/ intaglio tulip, sgn. Moser Karlsbad, cut diamond form, clear patt. stopper, 4¾" H $525.00

713-Cups & Saucers, Moser cranberry, 2 footed cups, 3" H & matching saucers, 5" diam., enameled rose swags, gold scrolls, cups w/ colorful enameled figures $475.00

715-Salt Cellars, pr. Smith Bros., almond melon ribbed w/ raised gold flowers, 1¼" H $150.00

680-Sherbet, Rosaline w/ alabaster stem, 3¾" H, undertray, 6" diam. $125.00

733-Punch Cups, pr. Amberina inverted thumbprint w/ amber handles, 3¼" H $60.00

731-Punch Cups, 3 fuchsia Amberina D.Q. w/ amber reeded handles, 2½" H $150.00

663-Plaque, Fr. Cameo, burgundy foliaged trees, sgn. Jaques Truber, w/ wood frame 7" x 13" $900.00

711-Demi-Cups & Saucers, 4 w/ gr. handles, 2½" H, saucers 4½" diam. all w/ mkd. sterling overlay, floral emb. rims $580.00

668-Tray, Pate-de-Verre circular, mkd. A. Dammouse, charcoal elephant w/ tan blanket, gr. floral vine, 4" diam. $850.00

696-Lamp, cranberry opal. swirl dome, 3½" H, resting on ornate brass base w/ cutout floral & jewel centers, 4¾" H $400.00

A-OH Oct. 1998   Early Auction Company

Row 1, Left to Right

588-Lily Vases, sgn. Steuben Ivorine 3 prong, 12" H $750.00

580-Plaque, porcelain, impressed K.P.M., hand dec. w/ sea nymph in blk. gr. ocean wave, royal blue sky, gr. velvet matt, gilt wood frame, 18" W, 27" H $5,000.00

589-Pitcher, Mt. Washington acid Burmese w/ glossy int., 5½" H . .N/S

552-Dresser Jar, Fr. cameo, amethyst w/ gilted leafy vine w/ red thistles, gold edge w/ repeated flower & vine, clear cut tab stopper, etched Daum Nancy, 3" H $1,350.00

579-Urn, crystal Steuben, script sgn., intaglio 1/2 eagle, designed by F. Carder .N/S

586-Vase, Fr. cameo, sgn. Daum Nancy, lemon yel. daisies w/ gr. foliage, mottled opal yellow & pink ground, 7¾" H $3,250.00

594-Lamp, leaded shade by Moran & Hastings Mfg. Co., 18" diam., designs of pr. of white lotus blossoms on gr. lily pods & stalk of br. cattail & gr. foliage, lt. gr. slag apron, carmel slag crown, bronze base, 23½" H overall $1,250.00

557-Vase, Loetz paperweight, waves of silvery blue w/ chartreuse, 5¼" H $900.00

564-Urn, Steuben irid. gold, sgn. Aurene, 9" H $650.00

466-Celery, New Eng. Peachblow w/ squared & scalloped rim, 6½" H $250.00

Row 2, Left to Right

593-Vase, mkd. Mont Joye, textured gr. cameo w/ gold flower & leafy stem, 8½" H $200.00

576-Vase, Fr. cameo tower, sgn. Daum Nancy, grayed opal sweet pea blossoms, base design in olive & gray greens, mottled marmalade ground w/ pale blue opal. at base, 28" H $6,500.00

554-Vase, Fr. cameo stemmed, gilt sgn. BS & Co., amethyst to frost w/ partial martele ground, 7" H $4,000.00

563-Vase, frosty textured, enamel sgn. Daum Nancy, cameo design of blk. & smoke colored floral branches, 7¾" H, 7" diam. $2,500.00

591-Vase, Loetz irid. gold w/ pitted surface, 4½" H . . . . .N/S

575-Vase, Imperial Freehand cobalt blue w/ infused opal leaves, 10¼" H $1,300.00

435-Lily Vase, Shiny Mt. Washington Burmese, 8" H $250.00

521-Vase, Monart corset form, teal & blk. mottled shoulder shading to ora. & yel. mottled body, bruised disc pontil, 9" H $350.00

416-Vase, Amberina D.Q. w/ dec. amber rigaree collar, 3¼" H . .$150.00

581-Vase, Fr. cameo, brick red lotus blossoms, opal yel. ground, etched Gallé, 22" H . . . . .N/S

484-Tazza, sgn. L.C.T., irid. gold w/ amethyst hues, 4" H, 3" diam. $825.00

488-Vase, Imperial emerald gr. w/ irid. marigold int., 8½" H $300.00

486-Vase, Imperial irid. marigold w/ flared rim . . . . .N/S

422-Lily Vase, Mt. Washington acid Burmese, 10" H $275.00

Row 3, Left to Right

421-Lily Vase, Mt. Washington acid Burmese, 8¼" H $150.00

508-Desk Lamp, 3 irid. gold lily shades sgn. L.C.T., 4½" H, bronze gold Doré base, mkd. Tiffany Studios NY, 8½" H $4,150.00

555-Vase, etched Vallerysthal olive gr., enamel dec. w/ purple, pink & yel. shaded dahlias w/ applied button cabochon centers, 9" H $1,100.00

570-Vase, crystal figural double "fish", etched E. Gallé Nancy, molded features, slightly opal. eyes, 6" H $800.00

567-Vase, Fr. cameo w/ gold wash base, burgundy thistle blossoms & textured rainbow ground, sgn. Daum Nancy, 5" H $900.00

553-Bud Vase, opal. white double gourd, w/ pulled handles, sgn. L.C.T., 3" H $400.00

571-Compote, Schneider, mottled white Cluthra style bowl, blk. amethyst columns on blk. wrt. iron tri-pedal base, 3 blue gr. glass berries, 8½" H, 9" diam. $950.00

446-Bowl, Steuben Ivory grotesque, 5½" H, 9½" diam. $200.00

558-Salt Tub, clear ribbed, gilt sgn. Daum Nancy, enamel dec. w/ blk. enamel pine trees around lake, gold floral spray on rev. $375.00

560-Toothpick Holder, Fr. cameo, enamel sgn. Daum Nancy, snowy woodland against mottled ora. & yel. sky, 2" H $1,050.00

423-Lily Vase, Mt. Washington acid Burmese, 16½" H $400.00

573-Vase, ribbed amber, etched Escalier de Cristal, Paris, blk. enameled leaves & gilt scrolled vines, 2 dec. raised bands w/ white enamel & gray & gold scrolls, 2 warriors battle below one spout, 7¼" H $1,500.00

559-Toothpick Holder, Fr. cameo, sgn. Daum Nancy, yel. red trumpet flowers, textured frosty yel. ground, 2" H $950.00

561-Toothpick Holder, pink textured w/ gilt highlighted daisies, sgn. Daum Nancy, 2" H $625.00

515-Desk Lamp, mkd. Tiffany Studios, NY, gilded base w/ abalone grape pods, 4 bent glass carmel slag panels, ...$4,250.00

569-Vase, Fr. cameo corset form, gilt sgn. Daum Nancy, textured amethyst w/ gold highlighted violets & leaves, clear base, 7" H $650.00

572-Bowl, almond basketweave pottery, sgn. E. Gallé Nancy, pale blue surface w/ royal blue floral int. & ext., gilt highlighted double handles, 3½" H, 11" diam. $250.00

Row 4, Left to Right

500-Place Setting, Steuben Aurene, 6 pcs., irid. gold, plate 8½" diam., sherbet 4" H, underplate 6" diam., stemware, 3½" H, goblet 6" H, wine 4¼" H, cordial 4¾" H $950.00

476-Bride's Bowl, Mt. Washington cameo, citron yel. griffins alt. w/ floral bouquets, plated handled frame 10" H, 9½" diam. $550.00

566-Vase, Fr. cameo, enamel sgn. Daum Nancy, snowy woodland against mottled burnt ora. sky, 2½" H $1,150.00

453-Vase, Eng. cameo, blue internal ribbed body, dec. w/ white morning glory vine, 5¼" H $650.00

568-Bowl, Fr. cameo sgn. Gallé, dk. autumn gr. branches w/ seed pods & chartreuse & frosty surface, 4" H, 11" L $900.00

514-Desk Set, gilded Tiffany, 8 pcs. w/ abalone grape pod & Art Deco design, letter holder 5½" H, 9½" L, desk pad ends, 2¼" H x 12¼" L, hinged covered stamp box 1¼" H, 4" L, ink blotter, 5¾" L, ink pen tray, 2½" W x 8¾" L, letter opener 10" L, ink well w/ hinged top & glass insert, 3", all mkd. Tiffany Studios, NY $4,250.00

Row 5, Left to Right

592-Vase, Loetz irid. opal w/ tooled rim, emerald gr. shoulder, 3¾" H .N/S

590-Vase, Webb acid Burmese, 5" H $600.00

551-Inkwell, sgn. Schneider, reddish ora. sq. body w/ mottled blk. burgundy attached tray, reddish ora. dome top w/ cobalt button finial covers glass insert $650.00

516-Vase, yel. pear form w/ irid. gold blue surface, rim w/ 4 jewels of ruby or turquoise . . . . .N/S

562-Match Holder, Fr. cameo amethyst, textured surface w/ gilt highlights, sgn. Daum Nancy, 2¾" H $250.00

582-Tray, circular Pate-de-verre, molded w/ colorful leaves, etched Despret, 5" diam. $275.00

577-Bowl, mkd. Wedgwood Eng., royal blue dragon covers rainbow M.O.P. center, gold highlights & floral designs, 2¼" H, 11" diam. . .$1,300.00

511-Cup, irid. gold footed w/ applied irid. bluish gold handle, sgn. L.C. Tiffany Favrile, 2½" H & saucer, 6¼" diam. . . . . .N/S

514-Desk Set, gilded Tiffany, 8 pcs. w/ abalone grape pod & Art Deco design, letter holder 5½" H, 9½" L, desk pad ends, 2¼" H x 12¼" L, hinged covered stamp box 1¼" H, 4" L, ink blotter, 5¾" L, ink pen tray, 2½" W x 8¾" L, letter opener 10" L, ink well w/ hinged top & glass insert, 3", all mkd. Tiffany Studios, NY $4,250.00

A-OH Oct. 1998   Early Auction Company

Row 1, Left to Right

146-Cracker Barrel
Pairpoint, paneled biscuit color ground, dec. w/ branch of iron red & pink wild roses, mkd. Pairpoint cover, 4½" H $225.00

114-Vase, white Cluthra, sgn. Steuben, bubbled design, firm's fleur-de-lis mark, 10" H $800.00

191-Cologne, Fr. Cameo, sgn. Daum Nancy, amethyst body w/ raised banner "a tout Seigneur tour honneur", gilt highlighted flowers, textured ground, clear tab stopper, 8¼" H $850.00

492-Lamp, rev. painted, 18" diam. shade, gr. & br. foliaged trees w/ blue waterway, aqua & yellowed sky, bronze color baluster form base, 24' H $2,350.00

176-Vase, Wheeling Peachblow acid finish double gourd, 7½" H . .$900.00

155-Vase, Fr. cameo, sgn. Gallé, lavender petunias on mottled pale yel. & frosty ground, 4¼" H $350.00

156-Cracker Barrel, Pairpoint, painted yel. body dec. w/ pink poppies & gr. foliage, raised floral & scroll base, dec. metal rim $225.00

188-Vase, Kimbal Cluthra trumpet form, mottled white w/ blk. base, sgn. K, 11½" H $275.00

174-Vase, sgn. V. Durand, pale yel. body w/ irid. gold & gr. leaves, marigold int., 8" H $1,050.00

152-Vase, Fr. cameo, sgn. Daum Nancy, gray gr. trees w/ pink tint against pale yel. & frosty sky, 9" H $1,000.00

102-**Vase,** Fr. stick, mottled gr. & cobalt blue, glossy acid mkd. Daum Nancy w/ Cross of Lorraine, 14½" H $275.00

101-**Vase,** Fr. stick, mottled acid finish of pink, yel. & opal glossy acid mkd. Daum Nancy w/ Cross of Lorraine, 14½" H $250.00

103-**Vase,** Fr. stick w/ tapered beehive body, mottled chartreuse into bluish-green, mkd. Daum Nancy w/ Cross of Lorraine, 14¼" H . . .$275.00

153-**Humidor,** Crown Milano dec. w/ raised gold fernery fonds on almond ground, 5" H $450.00

Row 2, Left to Right

104-**Vase,** Lalique, Fr., frosted w/ opal. birds in leafy vines, 5¾" H $375.00

185-**Lamp Base,** Eng. cameo footed, 3 color of white on pale cranberry against citron ground, 4½" H .$600.00

105-**Vase,** Steuben, alabaster ground & iris blossoms, rosaline cutout ground, 9¼" H $2,450.00

116-**Muffiner,** Wheeling Peachblow, glossy tapered surface / uniform shading, 5" H $1,000.00

133-**Cracker Barrel,** Mt. Washington, dec. w/ pastel thistle leaves & blossoms, outlined in raised gold, pink to yellowed ground, floral emb. silver rim & cover, 6" H $550.00

149-**Vase,** mini. footed w/ pinched double handles, opal. yel. sgn. L.C.T., paper label, 3¼" H $425.00

131-**Ewer,** rainbow M.O.P., camphor handle, 6½" H $650.00

127-**Atomizer,** glossy opalware perfume, pear form w/ swirl upper body dec. w/ flowers in natural colors, cobalt blue band w/ gilt buttons above cobalt blue base w/ gold outlining, 6½" H $225.00

168-**Vase,** irid. gold footed Durand w/ flared rim, 10½" H $400.00

190-**Vase,** Fr. cameo, sgn. deVez, harbor scene, emerald gr., yel. on opal ground, 7" H $1,300.00

150-**Cracker Barrel,** Mt. Washington, biscuit color ground, dec. w/ pink moss rose design w/ foliage, ornate rim, handle & cap mkd. M.W. . .$625.00

154-**Vase,** Fr. Cameo sgn. Gallé, paper label, golden br. trees, frosty coral sky $900.00

Row 3, Left to Right

145-**Cracker Barrel,** mkd. Smith Bros., almond body, dec. w/ raised gold floral branches, 6" H . . . . . .N/S

126-**Vase,** Mt. Washington, pulled & folded rin, tinted yel. int. edge, white swirled surface dec. w/ fall leaves, maroon branches w/ enameled blue berries, 3" H, 4" diam. $450.00

147-**Compote,** mkd. Pairpoint, footed, dec. w/ natural color grape pods w/ foliage, textured ext., yel. ground, sgn. J. Pailam, 4½" H, 8" diam. $450.00

172-**Pitcher,** Mt. Washington acid Burmese w/ pulled spout, applied handle, 6" H $600.00

173-**Tumblers,** 6 Mt. Washington acid Burmese $660.00

142-**Vase,** Mt. Washington Crown Milano, almond ground dec. w/ shadows of olive & yel. shields, overlaid w/ raised gold leaves w/ jeweled ruby flowers, 9" H $600.00

135-**Condiment Set,** Mt. Washington, pr. salt & pepper shakers, 4" H, white & yel. enamel flowers, mustard pot w/ pastel asters, silver spoon & hinged cap, pink to almond grounds, mkd. Pairpoint plated frame, 7½" H overall $1,200.00

171-**Creamer,** Wavecrest w/ plated spout & handle, 3¼" H, & plated covered sugar, 3" H, ea. w/ opal bodies enamel dec. w/ blue & white forget-me-nots $500.00

192-**Vase,** Fr. Cameo, golden red peonies, blk. mah. stems & leaves on yellowed frosty ground, sgn. Muller Fres Luneville, 5" H $1,300.00

118-**Vase,** Fr. cameo, carmel int., almond surface, dec. w/ mottled yel. & red honeysuckle blossoms, ivory color drip rim, sgn. Legras, 5½" H $1,000.00

181-**Lamp,** puffy shade mkd. Pairpoint, purple & pink floral border on yel. & white plaid frosty ground, 14" H overall, 8½" diam. $2,600.00

123-**Sweetmeat,** Mt. Washington, sprigs of gold wild roses w/ raised gold outlines & jeweled stamens, egg yel. alt. w/ white, metal cover, 4" H $450.00

Row 4, Left to Right

144-**Vase,** stamped Nakara, C.F.M. Co., portrait of Indian Chief w/ headdress, metal emb. rim, 5½" H $650.00

124-**Muffineer,** Mt. Washington "ostrich Egg", pansy sprays in natural colors, opal to yel. surface, 4" H, ...$275.00

132-**Pickle Castor,** Sandwich rose satin w/ D.Q. M.O.P., in ornate silver plated frame w/ rope handle, mkd. Middletown, bird foot tongs, 4¾" H $700.00

196-**Vase,** Fr. Cameo, butterfly motif, H. Muller Croismere, pres. Nancy, deep burgundy fuchsia blossoms & leafy vine, opal. blue ground mottled w/ burgundy, 10" H $750.00

186-**Syrup,** Findlay Onyx, thumblift metal hinged cap & spout, mkd. Pat. Applied for Aug. 28 '82, 6½" H $475.00

120-**Vase,** Steuben ribbed, sgn. Aurene $525.00

151-**Vase,** Royal Flemish w/ raised gold body in earth tone colors, neck has frosty leafy scrolls w/ raised gold outlines on purple br. ground, 11" H $3,100.00

125-**Cracker Barrel,** Mt. Washington Burmese, dec. w/ pink blossoms, gr. leafy branches, metal gold wash floral emb. rim, molded cover, 5½" H $500.00

143-**Vase,** Fr. Cameo, citron ground w/ burgundy fuchsia vine & leaves, Cameo sgn. Gallé, 4½" H $500.00

158-**Fairy Lamps,** Webb double acid Burmese, clear pressed Clarke's bases, brass wall mount holder, central Burmese insert w/ cone form vases w/ berry pontils & applied collars, 3¾" H, frame 11" H, 13½" W . . . . .N/S

189-**Vase,** Fr. cameo, sgn. D'Argental, deep burgundy orchids, citron ground, 8" H $475.00

137-**Vase,** Loetz, sgn. Austria w/ crossed arrows in circle, irid. silvery loops & swirls, golden ebony int., rich ruby glass, 4¼" H $1,200.00

Row 5, Left to Right

170-**Syrup,** Wavecrest Helmschmied swirl w/ hinged thumblift silver plated cover, spout & floral emb. handle, strewn violet sprays on pink to almond ground, 3" H $400.00

148-**Vase,** Pairpoint footed, natural color int. w/ grape pods & foliage on yellowed ground, frosty textured ext., sgn. Ambero below dec. base .$700.00

159-**Fairly Lamp,** Webb acid Burmese, dome shade 3½" H, pressed Clarke's Cricklite insert on acid Burmese petticoat base, 5½" H overall $650.00

130-**Muffineer,** mkd. Smith Bros., white enameled daisies w/ gr. foliaged stems on almond ground, silver floral emb. shaker top, 5" H $300.00

194-**Tray,** Fr. cameo clover form, gilt rim, textured emerald gr. to frost, clear gold outlined mistletoe branches, white enamel berries, sgn. Daum Nancy, 2" H, 5½" diam. $850.00

179-**Tumbler,** Amberina D.Q., colorful enamel wild flowers & foliage, 3½" H $130.00

187-**Spooner,** Findlay onyx, 4" H $275.00

112-**Sherbets,** 6 Steuben Oriental Poppy w/ opal. bases, swirl patt., 2¾" H $1,200.00

113-**Goblets,** 4 Steuben Oriental Poppy, swirl patt. bowls, opal. stems & bases, 2 mkd. w/ acid block letters, 5¾" H $1,000.00

193-**Vase,** Fr. Cameo, sgn. Daum Nancy, gold outlined apple blossom, ground shades frost, ora. to gr., 3¾" H $975.00

139-**Gas Shades,** 10 matching, 7 sgn. Quezal, opal bodies dec. w/ irid. gold & gr. leaves, 5¼" H, 2⅛" diam. $1,750.00

184-**Creamer,** N.E. Peachblow, gilt sgn. World's Fair 1893, 2½" H $200.00

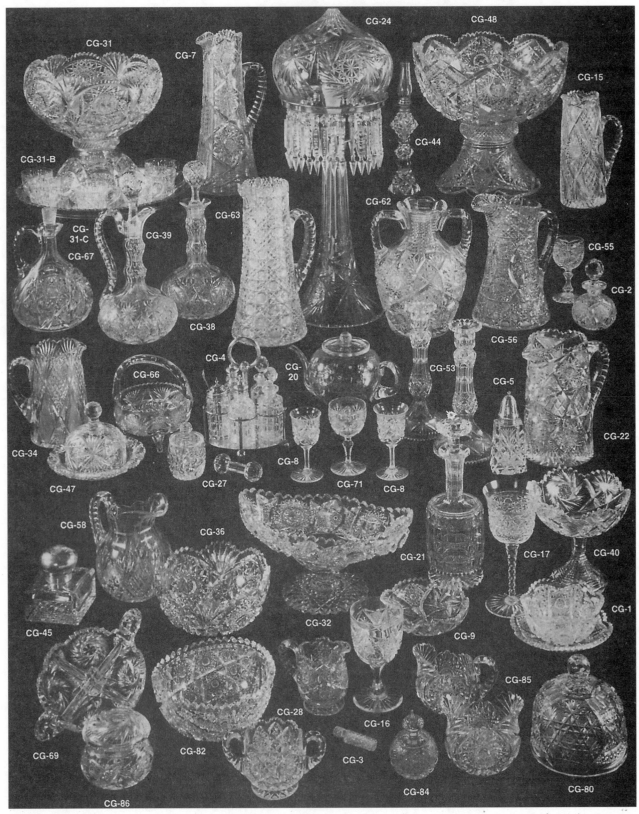

A-OH July-Aug. 1998   Early Auction Company

Cut Glass

Row 1, Left to Right

31-Punch Bowl, 2 part, vesicas w/ hobstars & nailhead, bars of bullseye below, central prism cutting, 11¾" H, 11½" diam. $950.00

31B-Punch Cups, matches punch bowl, in hobstars, fan & prism cutting, 2¼" H $300.00

31C-Mirror Tray, circular beveled tray w/ silver scrolled edge, 16" diam. $150.00

7-Pitcher, sgn. Libbey, hobstars w/ alt. cane & notched prism & fans, triple-cut handle, 14" H $275.00

24-Lamp, onion dome shade w/ matching base, stem w/ punty & notched flutes, prisms, 25" H .$700.00

44-Lamps, pr. w/ chimneys, hex knobs w/ all-over diamond cuts, 11¾" H $300.00

48-Punch Bowl, 2 part, shield w/ border of Russian variant w/ cross-cut buttons alt. w/ hobstars, glass ladle w/ notched handle, 13" H, 14" diam. $750.00

15-Pitcher, hobstars, cross-cut diamond fields, triple notched handle, 20 pt. hobstar base, 9½" H $200.00

Row 2, Left to Right

67-Decanter, flat sided, hobstars & fans, triple notched handle, faceted collar rim, stopper w/ relief diamond sides, 10" H $325.00

39-Decanter, w/ double faceted knob neck, triple-notched handle, patt. teardrop stopper, 14" H $400.00

38-Decanter, w/ double faceted knob neck, patt. teardrop stopper, 13" H $400.00

63-Tankard, all-over Harvard patt., double notched handle, 12" H. .$500.00

62-Vase, w/ triple notched handles, hobstars, cane & fan, step-cut neck, scalloped rim, 10" H $650.00

56-Pitcher, Harvard borders, vesicas w/ hobstars, step-cut spout, 10" H $275.00

55-Wines, six, hobstars alt. w/ shields of nailhead diamond & hobstars, teardrop fluted stem, 5" H . . .$240.00

2-Cologne, hobstars & cross-cut diamonds, faceted stopper, 5½" H $125.00

Row 3, Left to Right

34-Tankard, pineapple, fan & nailhead diamond patt., double-notched handle, 7¼" H $175.00

47-Butter, covered, hobstars & fans, faceted knob, 4½" H, tray w/ hobstar center, 7" diam. $150.00

66-Basket, tri-footed, hobstars, fan & hobnail, double notched handle, chippy feet, 7" H, 5½" diam. $80.00

27-Mustard, covered, hobstars & prism, faceted knob on cover & dumbbell knife rest, 4" H $80.00

4-Condiment Set, 5 bottles in cube cuttings, 2-5" H cruets w/ faceted stoppers; 2-5" H shakers w/ silver tops, 1-4½" H mustard w/ hinged sterling cap, mkd. sterling spoon, 5½" L, silver plated holder w/ ball feet . . .$170.00

8-Wines, 6, hobstars & fans, notched stem, rayed base, all sgn. Libbey, 5" H $180.00

20-Teapot, covered, wheel carved daisy stalks, applied handle & spout, patt. cover, 5" H $425.00

71-Wines, 4, hobstars, flashed fans & tri-leaves in cross hatched diamonds, faceted knob stem, 4¾" H $120.00

8-Wines, 6, hobstars & fans, notched stem, rayed base, all sgn. Libbey, 5" H $180.00

53-Candlesticks, pr., sawtooth flanged rims, cross-cut diamond bands, notched fluted stem, 9¾" H $325.00

5-Muffineer, diamonds & fans, hallmarked silver cap, 6" H $100.00

22-Pitcher, sgn. Libbey, hobstars & fans, bow tie relief diamond fields, triple notched handle, 8¾" H . .$300.00

Row 4, Left to Row

45-Inkwell, squared w/ hinged silver dome top, mkd. 800, cane button, 4½" H, 4" D $200.00

58-Pitcher, cross-cut diamond alt. w/ fans & hobstars, fluted neck, 7" H $125.00

36-Bowl, hobstars & fans, 8" diam. $90.00

32-Fruit Bowl, pedestaled, oblong bowl w/ hobstars, X split vesicas & cane, 6½" H, 12½" L $1,600.00

21-Decanter, cut panel body, cut & raised diamond bands, rayed star form base, patt. stopper, 12" H $200.00

9-Bowls, set of 5, 3 pinwheel leaves w/ ferns & hobstar center, alt. w/ Y triangulars w/ hobstars & cane, 1½" H, 6" diam. $100.00

17-Goblets, 8, Russian patt., honeycomb stems, rayed bases, 8¼" H $480.00

40-Compote, pinwheels, rayed stars & cane, horizontal step-cup base, 7" H $90.00

1-Mayo Set, hobstars w/ alt. cane, star center, 2½", 5½" diam., undertray 6¾" diam. $125.00

Row 5, Right Left

69-Tray, 4 sections, pinwheels w/ flashed hobstar center, sgn. Libbey w/ sword, 7" diam. $150.00

86-Hair Receiver, flashed fans on cover, pinwheels & dec. stars on base, 4" H $80.00

82-Bowl, 6 wedges of hobstars & X's, 3¾" H, 8" diam. $200.00

28-Sugar, pedestaled open, hobstars & stars, double notched handles, 3½" H & creamer, 4" H $70.00

16-Goblets, 8, hobstars, notched stems, rayed bases, 6¼" H . .240.00

3-Perfume, cylinder w/ relief diamonds, screw on cap, hallmarked floral, 3" H $110.00

84-Cologne, cane patt., hallmark silver dome cap w/ spring mech., 4" H $120.00

85-Creamer, w/ triple notched handle & open sugar bowl, each 4" H $325.00

80-Cheese Dome, 3 lrg. snowflakes alt. w/ hobnail bands, vertical & step-cut patt., faceted knob, 6½" H, 6" diam. $60.00

Photo on Following Page

A-OH July-Aug. 1998   Early Auction
                                Company

Row 1, Left to Right

324-Lamp, mini. G.W.T.W., pink satin beaded drape, glass chimney, 9½" H $275.00

331-Vase, Steuben gr. jade w/ alabaster foot, 5" H $175.00

361-Gas Shades, 3 irid. gold sgn. Steuben, w/ amethyst hues, puffy ribbed bodies w/ scalloped rims, ea. mkd. w/fleur-de-lis, 4¾" H, 2¼" fitter $405.00

335-Finger Bowl, New Eng. Amberina, faintly ribbed dish, strong fuchsia red to amber, 5¼" diam. $225.00

244-Vase, blue D.Q. M.O.P. oblong, 5½" H $175.00

150-Figural Lion, pottery, sgn. atop base Gallé Nancy, holding yel. & white tower draped w/ banner, maroon & blk. mane & fur, oval base molded w/ blue & yel. scrolls, 17" H . . . . . . .N/S

308-Pickle Castor, cranberry D.W. melon ribbed inserts, enamel dec. w/ pink floral sprigs, 4¾" H, ornate & dec. Aurora Victorian frame w/ canopy handle, 10½" H, tongs &

cover $650.00

178-Lamp, leaded shade, carmel slag lozenges w/ gr. slag diamonds, brass color base, mkd. Duffner & Kimberly Co., NY, 24" H, 19" diam. . .$4,000.00

242-Bowl, Webb Burmese glass five point petal top, deep coloration, matte finish, 2" H $350.00

259-Vases, pr., Webb satin Peachblow, dec. w/ spider web, flower & enameled birds, 11" H $650.00

CG-75-Decanter, amethyst cut to clear, star diamonds rows alt. w/

amethyst diamonds, patt. teardrop
stopper, 15" H $250.00
319-Vase, Webb acid Burmese crimp
petal top, 2½" H $175.00
Row 2, Left to Right
262-Lamp, mini., floral dec. top &
bottom w/ chimney shade . .$225.00

341-Vase, blue & white vertical
striped satin w/ yel. coralene seaweed
dec., 7" H $375.00
290-Vase, Steuben Rosaline w/
alabaster foot & handles w/ twisted
alabaster rings, 6" H, 4" diam. .$325.00

121-Lamp, dec. in Persian carpet
design, red iron ground w/ gr., yel. &
white design, mkd. Pairpoint Mfg. Co.,
23" H, 15" diam. . . . . .N/S
102-Lamp, mini. G.W.T.W., Rubina
crystal, 6" H $800.00

264-Vase, Verde Rubina Silveria-type w/ infused entwined threading, attrib. to Loetz, 10" H $225.00

329-Candlestick, Steuben blue & pink cintra, trimmed w/ blk. at rim, base & edge of boboche, 10" H $2,250.00

282-Vase, Mt. Washington Burmese lily, fine acid finish $400.00

246-Vase, M.O.P. raindrop patt., shading from pink to white, 13½" H $450.00

298-Vase, Steuben ribbed pomona gr. fan w/ amber connectors, 10" H, 9" diam. $200.00

269-Bowl, cranberry to clear Craqauelle w/ ruffled top edge, 9" diam. $275.00

240-Vase, glossy Webb Burmese, seven point petal top, deep coloration, 3½" H $225.00

233-Vase Steuben, ivory grotesque, 9¾" H $375.00

307-Sherbets, 12 Steuben gr. jade cone w/ alabaster bases, 2¾" H $720.00

306-Goblets, 9 Steuben gr. jade w/ half-twist alabaster stems, 7" H · $540.00

Row 3, Left to Right

99-Pickle Castor, 3¼" H, w/ resilvered Victorian holder, pierced fernery trim tons & emb. cover, 10½" H $500.00

265-Vase, shiny Rainbow swirled & ribbed, 13½" H $250.00

271-Vase, blue cut velvet satin, sq. top, 5½" H $125.00

197-Bowl, Fr. Cameo w/ silver pierced poppy floral, apricot & frosty ground, silver base mkd. V & S w/ ship, 5½" H, 8" diam. $1,750.00

267-Darner, New Eng., shiny Peachblow $100.00

315-Toothpick, irid. gold pinch sided, sgn. L.C.T. $275.00

243-Vase, pink D.Q. M.O.P. footed, ruffled top, 8" H $325.00

363-Vase
mini. Fr. Cameo, sgn. Gallé, tapered w/ chartreuse seed pod on leafy branch, 2½" H $450.00

30/Cruet, w/ clear hollow patt. stopper, cranberry to clear in cane patt., 10½" H $425.00

266-Pear, New Eng., shiny Peachblow $125.00

250-Vase, Peachblow ruffled top, satin finish w/ dec. enamel flowers, encrusted gr. leaves, 10½" H .$450.00

322-Punch Cup, pink slag inverted fan & feather, translucent, 2¼" H $125.00

272-Candlestick, Steuben faintly ribbed crystal w/ pink cintra handles, Matsu-no-ke dec, 10" H $350.00

311-Double Pickle Castor, cranberry inverted thumbprint w/ enameled blue asters bouquets, 4¾" H, ornate silver frame, 11" H, by Rogers, Smith, CT, 2 tongs & covers $1,000.00

261-Fairy Lamp, yel. overlay pineapple design, 5½" H $400.00

268-Vase, Northwood pull-up overlay w/ clear ruffled top, 10½" H $350.00

309-Pickle Castor, ribbed cranberry insert w/ white enamel daisy & blue forget-me-nots, 4½" H, resting in Homan silver plated frame, 11" H, tongs & cover $525.00

Row 4, Left to Right

260-Fairy Lamp, pink Nailsea, 4¾" H $175.00

C-1-Vase, sgn. Labino, w/ prunts, transparent cobalt blue, 1977, 8" H $175.00

C-45-Bud Vase, sgn. Lotton 1993, irid. gold shading to blue w/ pulled feather motif, 3¼" H $160.00

C-10-Paperweight, sgn. Labino, purple w/ multi-color inclusions, 1973, 2½" diam. $125.00

C-2-Ovoid Vase, sgn. Labino, w/ air sculptures, emerald gr., 1973, 5½" H $400.00

C-33-Perfume, sgn. Milropa, glossy almond blue w/ "windows" revealing encased cobalt & earthtone int., opal. stopper, 1975, 3¾" H $150.00

C-3-Vase, sgn. Labino, irid. w/ tooled surface, blue, amethyst & yel. essence, 1973, 7" H $200.00

C-5-Vase, signed. Labino, green w/ ribbed and tooled surface, 1972, 5" H $250.00

C-11-Vase, sgn. Labino, frosty irid. aqua w/ applied & connected pods, amber tinted bottom, 1970, 6" H $250.00

C-12-Bowl, sgn. Labino, chartreuse w/ 4 emerald gr. prunts, 1968, 2" H, 5¾" diam. $225.00

C-13-Vase, sgn. Orient & Flume, mottled iron red overlaid w/ 3 br. streaked trees supporting white flowers w/ emerald gr. centers, crystal encased, 4½" H $350.00

C-14-Vase, sgn. Richardson, irid. blue w/ cobalt blue pulled feathers, 1991, 3½" H $125.00

C-46-Vase, sgn. Mark Peiser, chartreuse w/ iridized residue surface, 1971, 3" H $160.00

C-17-Vase, sgn. Richardson, irid. cobalt blue w/ pulled feathers w/ amethyst hues, 1991, 4½" H . .$25.00

C-15-Vase, sgn. Richardson, turquoise w/ horizontal pulled waves of opal & silver, 1991, 4¼" H . . .$100.00

C-18-Vase, signed Richardson, irid. blue w/ opal leaves and vines, 1987, ...$125.00

122-Desk Lamp, cased irid. gold shade w/ pulled drape design, opal int., gold Doré harp base, mkd. Tiffany Studios, N.Y., 13" H, 7" diam. $2,500.00

C-19-Perfume, sgn. Richardson, crystal w/ band of gold foil inclusions, ruby flanged rim & encasement, clear teardrop stopper, 1994, 4¾" H .$150.00

C-23-Perfume, sgn. Lundberg, squatty stick, irid. blue, w/ mums & matching teardrop dauber, '82, 6" H . .$300.00

284-Vase, Mt. Washington Burmese Jack-in-Pulpit, strong color, 7" H $375.00

Row 5, Left to Right

318-Dresser Box, Wavecrest shield, w/ key, lt. blue petal form dec. w/ blue & pink floral clumps $550.00

C-28-Vase, sgn. Z, irid. amber w/ spiral & connected opal pulled feathers, 1988, 4½" H $100.00

C-29-Vase, sgn. Valerie Surian, mandrian red w/ flanged rim, silhouetted ACB red lily upon white, 1987 . . . .$150.00

C-30-Vase, crystal, sgn. Orrefors Graal , encased blk. outlined fish tinted pale gr. w/ aquatic plants, also sgn. Edward Hald, 5" H $775.00

C-31-Vase, sgn. Labino, amber opal. blown w/ pulled double handles, 1967, 6¾" H $325.00

C-39-Vase, sgn. Charles Lotton, 1976, emerald gr. w/ pink & opal flowers, irid. blue leaves & vines, 5" H $450.00

C-32-Paperweight, sgn. Bun Hean, lava style, rust, lt. & dk. blue spots against irid. silvery ground, 2½" H $70.00

C-35-Cologne, sgn. T. Buechner, frosty w/ amber red core, int., applied tiered leaves on sides, frost teardrop dauber, '83, 5" H $150.00

C-44-Bowl, sgn. Charles Lotton, frosty surface w/ irid. gold double pods w/ blue edges, 1989, 3" H $250.00

C-40-Cologne, sgn. Charles Lotton, w/ squatty teardrop stopper, cadmium ora. w/ long stalks of rust & opal flowers alt. w/ yel. double leaves w/ cobalt edges, 1985, 6½" H $275.00

C-43-Perfume, sgn. Trout Studios, w/ clear teardrop stopper, pale opal blue & irid. pink rev. swirl, 3½" H $110.00

364-Vase, sgn. Legras Fr. Cameo w/ maroon raspberry & leaf design, 5" H $175.00

104-Muffineer, spatter w/ brass cover, 4" H $250.00

317-Ewer, rainbow M.O.P. herringbone, tri-con rim, camphor handle, 6¾" H $700.00

Row 1, Left to Right

137-Candlestick, rosaline & alabaster, Steuben, 8½" H . . .$325.00

52-Vase, Fr. Cameo, Charder & Le Verre Francais, ora., copper & tangerine leaves w/ mottled opal ground, 19½" H $1,850.00

147-Vase, Fr. Cameo footed, enamel sgn. Daum Nancy, spring foliaged trees, reflective waterway, islands w/ trees against mottled opal, Prussian blue & chartreuse ground, 11" H $5,500.00

139-Vase, sgn. Muller Fres Luneville, Fr. Cameo, rose pink anemones w/ lavender tint above ebony leaves against almond & mottled yel. & royal blue ground, 4" H $3,500.0

90-Lamp, Pairpoint, artist sgn. H. Fisher, fall color court yard w/ royal blue sky & pastel clouds, silver double arm acanthus leaf fixture w/ bubble sphere, octagonal blk. marble base, double cornucopia finial, 26" H, 16" diam. $3,750.00

77-Toothpick, Holly Amber, beading intact, 2½" H $400.00

60-Vase, chartreuse M.O.P., overlaid w/ white Cameo rose upon leafy stems, ruffled rim, white int., 3 applied camphor branch feet, on w/ chips, 10" H $1,750.00

134-Vase, sgn. Steuben, irid. blue footed, 6" H $550.00

59-Lily Vase, Mt. Washington Burmese, 12¾" H $325.00

67-Vase, Loetz yel. "oil spot" lobed w/ graceful silver overlay vine w/ honeysuckle flowers, 4½" H $600.00

Row 2, Left to Right

138-Plates, pr. wisteria pastel, sgn. L. C. Tiffany Favrile, 8½" diam. $700.00

144-Creamer, Mt. Washington acid Peachblow, subtle form w/ applied handle, 3½" H $1,950.00

35-Vase, Steuben, ivory, 8½" H .$500.00

123-Vase, sgn. Steuben Aurene, 3 prong stump, irid. gold w/ amethyst hues, bluish cast on base, 6" H . .$800.00

120-Vase, Loetz irid. gold Jack-in-Pulpit, w/ vine coiled around stem w/ single leaf, tooled pod foot, 8" H $400.00

65-Cracker Barrel, mkd. Royal Flemish, dec. w/ roses in pink wash, raised gold & gilt leaves & thorny stems, frosty ground w/ raised gold segments, some w/ pale yel. scrolls, cover mkd. Pairpoint, 6" H $1,800.00

64-Vase, Durand irid. blue w/ opal "King Tut" design w/ traces of camel, 4" H $625.00

116-Goblet, Steuben, Oriental Poppy w/ Pomona gr. stem & base, 6¼" H $400.00

Row 3, Left to Right

CG26-Cut Glass Cornucopia Vase, all-over cane, faceted & notched fluted stem, patt. base, 14" H, 6¾" diam. $4,000.00

232-Shakers, pr., Findlay Onyx salt & pepper, floral & leaf in raspberry & amber, w/ irid. amethyst hues on creamy ground, 3" H $6,500.00

CG23-Cut Glass Vase, hobstar chain & fains, nailhead diamonds, wafer base w/ rays, 4½" H, 6½" diam. $200.00

55-Shade, acid Burmese dome, all dec. w/ meandering ivy vine, paper label, mkd. Thomas Webb & Sons, Queen's Burmese, 5¾" H . .$1,550.00

66-Cracker Barrel, Wavecrest, dec. w/ raised gold segments in rust, teal, lilac & almond w/ assort. patterns. Metal rim & bail w/ floral & scroll cover $1,600.00

118-Vase, sgn. V. Durand, irid. blue vase wrapped in fine threads, 6" H $500.00

81-Toothpick, New Eng. gr. opaque, strong mottling $1,200.00

49-Humidor, Wavecrest "cigar" box, puffy billow ware cover w/ bouquet of pink field clover & spray repeated on base w/ enamel highlights, ormolu shoulder trim, gold wash metal lid beneath cover, 5" H, 6½" D . .$625.00

136-Lamp, mkd. Pairpoint, rev. dec. w/ 4 seasons landscape, natural tones, silver trumpet form base molded w/ acanthus leaves, 15" H, 8" diam. $1,250.00

124-Vase, sgn. La Verre Francais, Fr. Cameo, mottled blue & red shoulder of leaves & berry pods against yel. ground, 4¾" H $450.00

Row 4, Left to Right

143-Cruet, Mt. Washington acid Burmese, ribbed body dec. w/ enamel white & yel. mums, handle & ribbed stopper w/ yellow-red trim, 6½" H $3,000.00

146-Vase, sgn. Legras, Fr. Cameo flare top w/ enamel dk. trees, reflective waterway, marmalade sky ground, 4½" H $600.00

140-Bowl, Fr. Cameo sgn. Daum Nancy, w/ quadrafold rim, plum color bell flowers, gr. foliage & clover against mottled pink & opal shading into spring gr. then cobalt blue, 2½" H, 5" diam. $1,600.00

114-Vase, N.E. Agata lily, tri-con rim, scattered blue oil spots, faint mottling, 6" H $500.00

141-Bowl, Eng. Cameo, red satin ground, surrounded by white irises & leaves, ornamental dental border trim, 2½" H $1,500.00

50-Dresser Box, almond satin baroque shell, mkd. Wavecrest w/ shield, white enamel daisies w/ mauve raised enamel scrolls, 3¾" H, 7" D $500.00

68-Inkwell, Loetz, textured irid. surface in gr. & amethyst hues, bronze hinged cover mkd. Sterling, 2½"H x 4½"D $375.00

51-Humidor, mkd. Handel Ware w/ shield, gr. & rust body, w/ white horse & beagle, sgn. Kelsey, metal rim, cover w/ figural pipe, 6½" H $650.00

109-Vase, Fr. Cameo, sgn. Gallé, blue flowers w/ purple foliage on frosty ground, 6" H $700.00

63-Vase, sgn. L. C. Tiffany, aqua opal. morning glory w/ ribbed body, clear distended stem, raised ribbed foot w/ opal. edge, 10¼" H $1,200.00

53-Vase, Burmese stamped Thomas Webb & Sons, Queen's Burmese w/ acid finish, 3½" H $225.00

142-Vase, Eng. Cameo, clump of white wild roses w/ lavender cast w/ thorn & leafy branches, acanthus leaf trim at rim, 5" H $1,300.00

Row 5, Left to Right

110-Tankard, Amberina D.Q. pitcher w/ applied amber handle, 5¼" H $400.00

54-Bowl, Burmese w/ lavender blue flowers, stamped Thomas Webb & Sons, Queen's Burmese, acid finish, 2" H, 4½" diam. $850.00

119-Nappie, sgn. L.C.T. Favrile, irid. gold w/ triangular rim, applied pinched handle, 2" H, 4½" diam. $725.00

56-Sweetmeat, sgn. Joe Webb, satin Peachblow, white enamel flowers w/ br. foliage, silver rim, bail & molded swirl cover, 2½" H $350.00

47-Shaker, Wheeling Peachblow, even coloring, 2½" H $400.00

145-Bowl, Fr. Cameo signed Legras, woodland w/ sparse crimson foliage against yel. sky mottled w/ blue clouds & emerald gr. distant foliage, 3" H, 3½" L $1,100.00

107-Wall Pocket, sgn. Emile Gallé, amethyst flowers w/ blue & yel. bird, insects & caterpillar, 12" L, 7½" W $900.00

A-IA July 1998   Jackson's

Row 1, Left to Right

671-Vase, enameled acid cut florals on mottled amber & red ground, sgn. "Daum Nancy Fr.", 9½" H . .$3,162.50

672-Lamp, mottled lavender, purple & gr. under satin finish, gilt-metal rams head mounts, sgn. "Mueller Fres, Luneville", 8" H $431.25

673-Vase, Fr. Cameo acid cut fern design in dk. & lt. gr. w/ white/amber satin ground, sgn. "Gallé", 4¾" H $800.00

674-Vase, Fr. Cameo, acid cut florals in amethyst, 14" H . . . . .N/S

675-Vase, Fr. Cameo, acid cut scenic design, in dk. & lt. gr. on satin mottled amber ground, sgn. "Daum Nancy" 18" H $3,335.00

676-Vase, Fr. Cameo, acid cut purple enameled florals on pink ground, sgn. "Legras", 15¾" H $1,600.00

677-Bowl, art glass, gold irid. oil spot finish, 6¾" diam. $115.00

678-Rose Bowl, scenic tree design on shaded purple ground, sgn. in cameo "Margot", 3¼" H $115.00

679-Ewer, w/ enameled florals, applied handle, sgn. "E. Gallé Nancy", 6½" H $2,200.00

Row 2, Left to Right

680-Vase, Fr. Cameo acid cut leaves & berries in amethyst on an ora. satin ground, sgn. "Delatte Nancy", 8" H $600.00

681-Vase, Leverre Francais Fr. Cameo, acid cut design, mottled ora., pink & gr. on mottled ora. "Chipped Ice" ground, 20¼" H $1,800.00

682-Vase, "Jack in the Pulpit", blue irid. on gr. glass, sgn. "Quezel", 6" H $690.00

683-Vase, Legras scenic enameled, 7" H $166.75

684-Vase, Gallé Fr. Cameo, fire polished florals on white opal. ground, 4¼" H $575.00

685-Boudoir Lamp, Fr. Cameo, acid cut florals in red, gr. & blue/gray on vitrified ground w/ mottled gr. & yel. shading to purple, sgn. "Daum Nancy" 13½" H $86.25

686-Vase, Trevaise art glass, swirled & pulled irid. colors on gr. glass, wafer pontil, hairline, 6½" H $115.00

687-Vase, Muller Fr. Cameo, fir trees on scenic ground, int. dec. sky scape in peach, azure, & gray, sgn. "Muller Fres Luneville", 9½" H $3,910.00

688-Pitcher, enameled cut florals & scene of cottage in forest on frosted ground, emerald green top shading to crystal, gold highlights, Daum Nancy sig. on base, 2½" H $1,955.00

689-Vase, enameled Cameo Vase in a winter scene, yel. ground, sgn. "Daum Nancy", 6" H $2,300.00

690-Vase, enameled Cameo of Bleeding Hearts/mottled vitrified glass, sgn. "Daum Nancy", 4½" H $1,600.00

691-Lamp, Puffy rev. painted, enameled scene of "Hummingbird & Roses", Stratford shade, bronzed base, mkd. "Pairpoint MFG Co.", 23¼" H, 16" diam. $9,775.00

692-Vase, Fr. Cameo, purple foliage, frosted ground w/ gr. shading, sgn. "Gallé", 3½" H $517.50

693-Vase, Fr. Cameo vitrified glass w/ design of leaves in br. & gr. on mottled & opal. ground w/ yel., 3 applied tadpoles, sgn. "Daum Nancy", 7" H $2,300.00

694-Vase, Fr. Cameo, acid cut design on swirled opal., lavender & amber ground, bronze pedestal, sgn. "Daum Nancy", 4¾" H $690.00

Row 3, Left to Right

695-Bowl, Fr. Cameo, fire polished design w/ 3 applied cabochons on white ground, sgn. "Gallé", 3¾" H, 8¾" diam. . . . . .N/S

696-Vase, Loetz art glass satin opal. glass w/ base of imbedded silver droppings below emerald snake, ground pontil, 5" H $230.00

697-Vase, Fr. Cameo, mottled br. & caramel leaves, chipped ice purple ground, 13" H $2,300.00

698-Vase, Fr. Cameo, butterscotch florals on satin ground, sgn. "DeVez", 6¼" H $230.00

699-Vase, Fr. Cameo, art deco design, pur, & ora. berries on mottled yel. ground, 2 applied handle, sgn. "LeVerre Francais", 5½" H $690.00

700-Vase, Loetz jack-in-the-pulpit", gr. iridescent glass w/ int. paneling, base overlaid w/ scrolled floral design in sterling silver, ground pontil, 7¼" H $431.25

701-Bowl, Fr. Cameo on pedestal, leaf design in gr. & purple w/ mottled yel. ground, sgn. "Daum Nancy", 6¼" H, 7½" diam. $2,587.50

702-Snuff Bottle, Peking glass, pink scrolled designs over white, no stopper, 2½" H $86.25

703-Salt Dip, Fr. Cameo, blk. enameled scene of trees & lake on frosted ground, sgn. "Daum Nancy", 1¾" diam. $690.00

704-Vase, Fr. Cameo, detailed mountain scene framed in magnolia blossoms in lavender & purple, sgn. "De Vez", 8¼" H $805.00

705-Vase, Fr. Cameo, acid cut floral, sgn. "Gallé", 17¼" H . . . . .N/S

706-Vase, Fr. Cameo, acid cut, white satin ground, sgn. "Gallé", 6" H . .N/S

707-Vase, Fr. Cameo, purple & gr. leaves, sgn. "Legras", 9½" H . . . .N/S

708-Vase, Gallé Fr. Cameo, acid cut berries & leaves on amber & cranberry ground, 3¾" H $460.00

Row 4, Left to Right

709-Vase, Fr. Cameo, acid cut design of pinecones & needles in br. over satin opal., sgn. "Gallé", 12¾" H . . . . .N/S

710-Vase, Loetz Art Glass two handled, gold irid. w/ emb. cracqulature design, ground pontil, 5" H . .$172.50

711-Vase, Loetz Art Glass, pinched rim w/ fine speckled irid. finish, ground pontil, 7½" H $143.75

712-Vase, Fr. Cameo, amethyst florals on faux frosted ground, gold highlights, gilt base, 8½" H $345.00

713-Vase, Legras Fr. enameled w/ trees & sailboat scene, 11 H .$310.50

714-Jar, covered, Fr. Cameo, multicolored enameled florals on frosted ground, emb. brass lid, 4" H .$172.50

715-Vase, Art Glass, fine gr. irid. oil spot finish, 9¾" H $172.50

716-Ewer, Daum Nancy Fr. Cameo, insect design in pink vitrified glass w/ yel. & gr. base, 8½" H $3,450.00

717-Vase, Fr. Cameo, blue trees w/ Spanish moss, sgn. "Michel de Nancy", 14" H . . . . .N/S

718-Vase, Durand Art Glass, blue hanging heart & vine over gold irid., 4½" H $203.75

719-Vase, Bohemian Art Glass, emb. craqulature & gr. irid., 7½" H .$86.25

720-Vase, Fr. Art Glass, int. dec. mottled colors in pink & ora. by D. Christian Meisenthal, partial signature, 10½" H $287.50

721-Vase, Fr. Cameo, acid cut designs w/ gr. splashes over a lt. powder blue glass, mkd. "Daum Nancy", 8" H $1,725.00

Row 5, Left to Right

722-Plate, Daum Fr. Pate sur Pate, ca. 1970 "Hiver" in blue depicting sculptured figures, orig. box, 10½" diam. $143.75

723-Mugs, Handleware set of 3 mini., two w/ monks, one of horse, artist sgn. "Gauer", 2½" H $115.00

724-Pintray & Jar, 2 pcs., pintray w/ bronze rim & int. dec. of dog, sgn. "Kelsey" and melon rib shaped jar, both mkd. Handleware, 5¾" diam. & 3¼" diam. $200.00

725-Sherbet, & underplate, Steuben, in gold over white opal., 4" H $172.50

726-Perfume, Bohemian Art Glass, swirled & pulled design in red & gold irid., possibly Loetz, 3" H $80.50

727-Cup & Saucer, Steuben gold aurene, internal hairline $40.25

728-Vase, Fr. enameled, design of br. leaves w/ blue berries over satin glass, signed, 14" H . . . . .N/S

729-Vase, Loetz, emerald gr. irid. glass w/ overall threading, applied handles w/ rosettes, ground pontil, 6" diam. $172.50

730-Vase, Italian art glass, ca. 1930, cobalt blue w/ 4 white applied handles, white rim, 4½" H $57.50

731-Tumblers, pr. matching Steuben, minor nick & scratch to one, both sgn. "Aurene-2361", 5¾" H $172.50

732-Compote, Quezal Art Glass, gold irid., sm. burst bubble on top, 7½" diam. $258.75

733-Perfume, Steuben, gold aurene, unsgn., 4½" H $230.00

734-Plate, Daum Fr. Pate su Pate, ca. 1969 in Amethyst "Automne", orig. box, 10½" diam. $172.50

A-IA July 1998   Jackson's

Row 1, Left to Right

735-Vase, Rubina enameled, cranberry shading to crystal w/ enameled pansies, gold dec. rim, ground pontil, 6½" H $316.25

736-Ewer, pink satin enameled, yel. florals, 10" H $143.75

737-Vase & Lustres, 3 pc., gr. opaque, floral enameled vase & pr. of matching lustres w/ cut glass prisms, 13" H & 7½" H $230.00

738-Vase, mini. cranberry w/ gold, white & blue enameled florals, 2½" H $103.50

739-Jar, pink satin clam shell enameled florals & scroll, 4½" diam. $40.25

740-Lamp, cranberry inverted thumbprint shade, pull down frame of grape vines, cut crystal prisms, 20" diam. $1,150.00

741-Bowl, Lutz Art Glass in cranberry w/ applied white threaded band & gr. petal feet, 5½" diam. $63.25

742-Vase, Bohemian art glass in white overlay, cut back to cranberry w/ gold dec., 11" H $161.00

743-Cruet, cranberry enameled, applied clear handle & stopper e/ bubble, gold, white & blue enameled florals, 11" H $235.75

744-Ewer, pink satin w/ applied handle & enameled florals, hairline, 9" H $69.00

745-Pitcher, pink satin in diamond quilted design w/ applied handle, rim flakes, 7½" H $51.75

Row 2, Left to Right

746-Celery, cranberry in opal. hobnail, fluted rim, ground pontil, damage, 6" H $86.25

747-Vase, blue opaque w/ emb. designs on ram's heads & scrolls, 8½" H $40.25

748-Cruet, cranberry w/ inverted thumbprint, cut crystal stopper & applied handle, ground pontil, 6½" H $138.00

749-Perfume, Czech blue crystal, stopper w/ dauber intact, 6¼" H $126.50

750-Vase, cranberry art glass in opal. hobnail fitted to a silver filigree frame, damage, 7" H $86.25

751-Lamp/Vase, Wavecrest enameled opaline glass, bronzed footed base w/ an int. candelabra socket, no cord, 6½" H $201.25

752-Pitcher, blue opal. coin spot, applied handle, 9½" H $86.25

753-Bride's Basket, cranberry, ribs w/ fluted white rim, ornate quad plate frame, ground pontil, 13" H . .$690.00

754-Vase, Bohemian art glass, blue cut to white w/ gold dec., applied ruby colored jewels, 10½" H $1,265.00

755-Vases, pr. matching, cranberry opal. w/ fluted vaseline rims, quad. plate pedestals, 7½" H $230.00

756-Ewer, blue satin enameled florals & applied pinched handle, 10" H $92.00

757-Vase, Smith Bros., enameled florals & buds, molded ring neck, 8" H $86.25

758-Salt & Pepper, pr., pink quilted, glossy finish, silver plated tops, 3¼" H $51.75

759-Biscuit Jar, Wavecrest emb. scrolled designs, enameled florals, quad. plate handle & lid, 7" H $201.25

Row 3, Left to Right

760-Biscuit Jar, pink satin quilted, minor flakes, 6½" H $201.25

761-Barber Bottle, white opal. on clear in "Stars & Stripes" patt., ground pontil, 7" H $230.00

762-Barber Bottle, cranberry opal. in "Stars & Stripes" patt., ground pontil, 7" H $258.75

763-Pitcher, M.O.P. satin, windows design in peach shading to white, 5¾" H $115.00

764-Bride's Basket, cranberry shading to white int., 2 transfer medallions, enameled florals, quad. plate w/ flowers, 10" H $460.00

765-Compote, blue opal. in a fan & fine cut patt., 5" H $40.25

766-Cracker Jar, Crown Milano, gold enameled florals on mottled peach & yel. ground, quad. plate lid mkd. "M.W...." $862.50

767-Jar, frosted Rubina w/ clear "Royal Oak" emb. patt., 3¾" H .$69.00

768-Pickle Castor, Rubina inverted baby thumbprint w/ gr. & blue enameled florals, quad. plate Derby frame, matching tongs, 11¾" H $546.25

769-Vase, M.O.P. in blue herringbone design, blown out melon ribs, minor bruise, 6" H $69.00

770-Biscuit Jar, dec. w/ finely enameled yel. florals & leaves, quad. plate lid, 7" H $517.50

771-Cruet, enameled in ice blue, int. ribs, enameled florals, cut crystal stopper, 7½" H $86.25

772-Butter Dish, Rubina shading to crystal inverted thumbprint top, 7" diam. $224.25

773-Vase, rose amber, inverted baby thumbprint patt., ground pontil, 4½" H $201.25

774-Tablesetting, 5 pc. in royal oak patt. consisting of syrup, cruet, satin salt & pepper & toothpick . .$517.50

775-Vase, cut velvet w/ applied blue lattice patt., 6¼" H $74.75

776-Vase, Smith Bros., enameled bird & florals, molded rings, 4¾" H . .$63.25

Row 4, Left to Right

777-Lamp, mini. in white opaque w/ enameled florals, 5½" H $34.50

778-Butter, covered, Cosmos, white opaque w/ polychromed florals, 8¼" diam. $69.00

779-Barber Bottle, in cranberry w/ opal. hobnails, damage, 7½" H $143.75

780-Cruet, cranberry opal., glossy paperweight finish, cut crystal stopper & applied handle, 6½" H $86.25

781-Beverage Set, 5 pc. M.O.P. in blue herringbone, melon ribbed pitcher, two tumblers, damage, 8½" H $143.75

782-Lamp, Mini. in ice blue, applied ring handle, P&A burner, 4" H .$51.75

783-Pickle Castor, cranberry w/ inverted thumbprint, enameled florals, orig. quad. plate frame, added lid, 9½" H $460.00

784-Biscuit Jar, satin dec. w/ multicolored shapes, lid mkd. Stevens, Woodman, 7" H $258.75

785-Cruet, in blue inverted thumbprint w/ applied amber handle & stopper, 8½" H $97.75

786-Pickle Castor, cranberry w/ int. ribs, enameled florals resting in 3 handled quad. plate frame, mkd. "Meriden", minor flakes, 9" H $575.00

787-Bride's Basket, in gr. satin shading to white, int. bowl enameled in florals & scrolls resting on quad. plate supported by winged cherubs, mkd. "Meriden", 12" H $460.00

788-Bud Vase, M.O.P. in cranberry, minute bruise, 7¼" H $97.75

789-Tablesetting, 5 pc. gr. Croesus w/ gold dec. incl. covered butter, cruet, covered sugar, spooner & toothpick, minor damage $431.25

Row 5, Left to Right

790-Vase, Verre de Soie, 2 prong thorn w/ applied flower & leaf, 7" H $230.00

791-Condiment Set, 3 pc., Rubina brilliant cut glass incl. vinegar, pepper & salt dip in "EPNS" frame, vinegar cracked $143.75

792-Dove, white latticino & pink twisted filigrano glass, applied beak & feet, mkd. "G.F. Murano", 7" H $172.50

793-Rose Bowl, blue opaline in satin finish, 4½" diam. $46.00

794-Dresser Box, Wavecrest enameled florals in a Helmschnied swirl mold, no lining, 7¼" diam. . .$402.50

795-Vase, blue cased w/ coralene dec. of flowers, 5" H $63.25

796-Cruet, blue opal. hobnail, clear stopper & applied handle, 6½" H $97.75

797-Shakers, pr. Mt. Washington, hand painted florals, 2½" H . . .$86.25

798-Cruet, cased glass w/ pink int., enameled florals, no stopper, 5" H $51.75

799-Vases, pr. Wavecrest, matching scroll mold one blue, one pink, mkd. w/ "Banner" mark, 9" H ...$431.25

800-Bowl, blue opal., emb. Greek keydesign, 8½" diam. $74.75

801-Epergne, center bowl yel. & white, interlocks in gr. glass frog, vaseline colored leaves & 3 yel. fruit w/ ora. spattering mounted on a mirrored plateau, repr. to stem, 10" H, 12" diam. ....N/S

802-Tumblers, pr. Art Glass, pink quilted satin & cranberry opal. windows, minor chip, 3¾" H $40.25

803-Serving Set, gr. Amberina, 7 pc. incl. footed tureen w/ lid & ladle, 6 cups, cranberry glass shading to gr., enameled florals, 8" H $1,035.00

804-Finger Bowl, frosted Rubina, hobnail, 5¾" diam. $34.50

805-Dresser Bottle, Bristol glass, applied pedestal, hand painted florals, 9" H $46.00

806-Pitcher, early 19th C., pink opaline w/ applied handle & lily pad design, 5" H $103.50

807-Toothpick, cased glass, pink int., ground pontil, 3½" H $69.00

Roseville Pottery

Row 1, Left to Right

808-Lamp, Consolidated "Cockatoo" in red w/ gr. crest, 13" H $345.00

809-Vase, Phoenix "Wild Geese", slate blue over milk glass, orig. paper label, 9½" H $230.00

810-Vase, "Dogwood" tri-color gr. highlighting on white, 11" H .$143.75

811-Vase, Phoenix "Dancing Girls", tri-color highlighting on custard satin, 11½" H $517.50

812-Vase, Consolidated "Dogwood", tri-color red highlighting on white satin, 11" H $402.50

813-Vase, Phoenix "Wild Geese", tan over pearlized milk glass, 9½" H $258.75

814-Lamp, Consolidated "Cockatoo" in gr. w/ red crest, 13" H $316.25

Row 2, Left to Right

815-Vase, Consolidated "Jonquil" w/ tri-color highlighting over custard satin, 6½" H $115.00

816-Vase, Consolidated "Dragonfly" in blue highlighting over white satin, 6" H $115.00

817-Vase, Consolidated "Owl" w/ br. owl & gr. reeds over custard satin, 6" H $115.00

818-Vase, Consolidated "Chickadee" w/ red birds on gr. leaves, 6½" H $143.75

819-Vases, pr. Consolidated "Floral" in blue over white satin, 9¼" H $172.50

820-Vase, Phoenix "Wild Roses" in slate blue over white, 10" H . .$488.75

821-Vase, Italian art glass in ruby shading to crystal w/ applied handles, controlled bubbles throughout, 9" H $92.00

822-Vase, Imperial art glass in ora. lustre over milk glass, ground pontil, 11" H 97.75

823-Jardiniere, Bohemian art glass in gr. irid. w/ pulled opal. art deco design, minor rim flakes, 8" diam. . . .$172.50

824-Vase, Imperial art glass, ora. lustre w/ blue pulled drapery patt. over milk glass, 10¾" H $747.50

Row 3, Left to Right

825-Epergne, Duncan Miller yel. opal., 9" H $195.50

826-Vase, art glass in cobalt blue, dec. w/ gold florals & sailing ships, sgn. "Jaryn '92...", 9½" H $80.50

827-Vase, art glass, irid. finish over amethyst glass, emb. "Imperial", minor chip, 5¼" H $86.25

828-Vase, Imperial art glass w/ blue hanging heart & vine over ora. lustre, 8½" H $575.00

829-Bird, Murano art glass, twisted purple & white ribbons between layers of gold leaf, 6" L $69.00

830-Ewer, Frederick Heckert enameled, dec. in blue scrolls w/ gold highlights, sgn. $86.25

831-Vase, art glass, int. dec. in blue, white & copper w/ vaseline ground, 4¾" H $74.25

832-Vase, Bohemian art glass w/ pulled wavy blue, white & red design in clear casing w/ irid. finish, 12" H $316.25

833-Vase, Imperial art glass, deep metallic hues of purple, gr. & blue w/ wavy opal. design, 8" H $120.75

834-Bird, Murano art glass, cranberry body, 4" H $40.25

835-Candlestick, Steuben in antique gr., unsgn., 9½" H $86.25

836-Vases, matching Bohemian glass, emerald gr. satin glass dec. w/ gold florals, ground pontil, 8" H $201.25

837-Novelty, blue patt. glass hand holding a button & daisy horn, 6" H $23.00

Row 4, Left to Right

838-Pitcher, Schneider art glass in yel. w/ suspended bubbles, ora. applied handle, ground pontil, 6" H $126.50

839-Vase, Murano art glass, cranberry cased glass w/ thumbprint design & silver leaf, 4" H $143.75

840-Plates, set of 4 Steuben in gr. jade, sgn. w/ Fluer de Lis, 8½" diam. $230.00

841-Wine, Bohemian glass, clear cut w/ ruby panels & gold dec., 4¼" H $40.25

842-Bowl, Murano glass, int. dec. w/ ribbons & latticino, 4¼" sq. . . .$40.25

843-Goblets, pr. Steuben in clear w/ gr. threading, unsgn., 7" H $92.00

844-Cup & Saucer, Bohemian in ruby red w/ enameled portrait, gold scrolling & floral swags $74.75

845-Vase, art glass, pulled designs on cobalt blue w/ aqua pedestal, sgn. "Vandermark", 11" H $201.25

846-Vase, art glass, cranberry w/ vaseline petals, 5" H $109.25

Row 5, Left to Right

847-Basket, Vasa Murhina, cranberry w/ opal. stripes & silver flecks, minor chip, 5½" H $28.75

848-Vase, Bohemian art glass, pink opaline w/ applied flowers, 6½" H $51.75

849-Bowl, art glass, pink cased glass w/ vaseline ribbon & applied feet, 4" H $51.75

850-Sweet Meat Basket, deep amethyst shading to white, petal form edge, 6½" diam. $34.50

851-Ash Tray, Murano, white paperweight finish w/ suspended gold bubbles, 6½" diam. $23.00

852-Misc. Bohemian, 5 pcs. glass in ruby red, intricate cut back designs, ...$172.50

853-Powder Jar, covered, Murano glass, purple w/ vaseline bulbous handle on lid, goldleaf, 4½" H $28.75

854-Misc. Murano, 3 pcs. glass, incl. mini. vase, swan dish & snail ashtray $40.25

855-Cups & Saucers, set of 4 Moser in emerald gr. w/ an overall filigree dec. in gold $258.75

856-Fruit, 3 pcs. of Murano glass, 4" H $97.75

857-Compote, blue opal. molded rib design, 8" diam. $34.50

Row 1, Left to Right

Pittsburgh Glass Jar, clear blown w/ applied blue rings, blue finial, chipped, possibly mismatch, 12¼" H $220.00

Pittsburgh Glass Candlestick, amber, pressed in one pc., chips & shallow flake, 9" H $55.00

Pittsburgh Glass Jar, clear blown w/ applied cobalt blue rings, clear finial, sm. flakes, 13⅝" H $220.00

Row 2, Left to Right

Christmas Lights, eight quilted pressed, two blue, red two amber, amethyst, clear & opaque white, chips, 3½" H . .$165.00

Christmas Lights, eight quilted pressed, two gr., cornstarch blue, amethyst, two amber, clear & opaque

white, chips, 3½" H $192.50

Christmas Lights, eight quilted pressed, two gr., cornstarch blue, amethyst, opaque white, cranberry, cobalt & amber, chips, 3½" H $247.50

Christmas Lights, eight quilted pressed, two gr., cornstarch blue, cobalt, two amethyst, clear & amber, chips, 3½" H $247.50

Christmas Lights, eight quilted pressed, three shades of amber, cobalt sapphire, peacock, puce & gr., chips, 3½" H $330.00

Christmas Lights, eight quilted pressed, amber, four shades of gr., cobalt, clear & amethyst, chips, 3½" H $357.50

A-OH Oct. 1998   Early Auction Company

Row 1, Left to Right

503-Compote, Durand, ext. w/ blue "King Tut" design over irid. gold, golden stem & base, irid. gold int., 6¾" H, 6" diam. $700.00

517-Lily Lamp, Tiffany's 6-lt., bronze weighted base, adjustable core on rod w/ 6 gooseneck supports, irid. gold shades, 4" H, ea. sgn. L.C.T., 21½" H $9,200.00

B142-Vase, K.T. & K. Lotus, dk. gr. pillow form w/ pierced scrolled handles, applied pale gr. & white meadow florals, firm's red mark, 8¼" H $1,300.00

B143-Vase, K.T. & K. Lotus, pale gr. pillow form w/ pierced scrolled handles, applied pale gr. & white meadow florals, firm's gr. mark, 8¼" H $1,300.00

499-Vase, sgn. Quezal Jack-in-Pulpit, base w/ emerald gr. pulled design w/. irid. gold pulled leaves, 9" diam. irid. gold flared rim , rev. of 8¾" diam. golden front dec. w/ emerald gr. swirl designs, 16" H $10,250.00

46-Vase, Federzeichnung teardrop form, mah. br., golden tracery & M.O.P. scrolled trailings, 12¾" H $1,750.00

578-Vase, Fr. cameo 4 color oviform, olive gr. leaf fronts, cranberry oleander floral clusters, yel. to frosty ground, sgn. Gallé, 14" H $6,750.00

Row 2, Left to Right

513-Vase, Fr. cameo, base etched Vallerysthal w/ orchid blossom, frosty body w/ mauve stems, maroon leaves, floral color spattered surface, 12½" H $3,500.00

463-Vase, Webb Eng. cameo, cased Peachblow body dec. w/ lifesize white geraniums w/ foliage & seed pod plants, 6¼" H $2,500.00

B145-Vase, K.T. & K. Lotusware, pink int., cream ext. w/ raised gold flowers, firm's gr. mark, 9" H .$800.00

471-Vase, 3 color cameo, acid stamped Thomas Webb & Sons, citron body w/ white over red foliaged stalks of daisies, 8" H $3,200.00

472-Vase, Eng. cameo double gourd, cased Peachblow body, dec. w/ white exotic flower buds & fringed leaves, acid stamped Thomas Webb & Sons, 7" H $2,750.00

498-Vase, irid. gold flower sgn. L.C.T., amethyst hues, translucent amber knob stem, 15" H $3,250.00

525-Vase, sgn. L.C. Tiffany, irid. gold vase, detailed veins & texture upon thin stems, 9" H $4,300.00

Row 3, Left to Right

464-Vase, Mt. Washington Lava w/ double reeded loop handles, colorful patches against reflective blk. surface, 8¾" H $2,750.00

504-Vase, irid. gold flower form, sgn. L.C. Tiffany Favrile, translucent amber stem on raised ribbed base, 13" H $5,300.00

468-Vase, Mt. Washington acid Burmese, w/ Queen's design, pastel enamel dotted flowers w/ raised gold berried stems, 11¾" H $2,300.00

470-Bowl, Eng. 3 color cameo, white over red flower & foliaged vine w/ coiled tendrils across frosty surface, 5" H $2,100.00

47-Bride's Bowl, mkd. Crown Milano, yel. scrolls & yel. red leaves & flowers overlaid w/ gold wild roses, 4½" H, 7" diam. ornate Pairpoint frame w/ floral emb. handle, 9" H $1,700.00

512-Candlesticks, pr. Tiffany, translucent red stems w/ gold Doré flanged cups, bases w/ enameled trim of mottled red & ora., ea. mkd. Louis C. Tiffany Furnaces, Inc. 12" H $4,750.00

Row 4, Left to Right

524-Compote, Quezal footed, irid. marigold bowl & knob stem, 4½" H, 5¼" diam. . . . . .N/S

462-Vase, Eng. cameo footed, white poppy blossoms, buds & foliage on rev., wild rose branches, prussian blue ground, 8½" H $2,800.00

509-Dresser Box, Loetz silver overlay, irid. blue covered w/ daisies & leafy stems, mkd. Sterling, 4" H, 5" diam. $1,250.00

478-Bowl, New Eng. plated Amberina, mah. ribs, 3½" H, 4½" diam. .$4,250.00

455-Vase, Mt. Washington acid Burmese, enamel dot dec. in Queen's design w/ raised gold berried stems, 5¼" H $1,850.00

B146-Rose Bowl, mkd. Ott & Brewer Belleek, cream body w/ golden clouds, matte br. stems w/ 2 gold pods w/ pink buds, cream insert w/ child's head finial, 6" H, 4" diam. $300.0

161-Candlestick, ivory cameo, pressed mkd. Thomas Webb & Sons, fern dec. urn form stem, acanthus leaves on base w/ beaded & cut edge, 5" H $900.00

510-Vase, silver overlay sgn. Loetz Austria, cobalt blue neck w/ mkd. Sterling lilies & leafy stems, irid. blue textured lower body, 5¾" H . . .$2,500.00

A-OH Jan. 1999   Garth's Auctions

Row 1, Left to Right

Kugel, cobalt blue, bunch of grapes, brass hanger, 5" L $495.00

Kugel, cobalt blue, bunch of grapes, brass hanger, 4" L $440.00

Kugel, red, brass hanger, 3¾" diam. $660.00

Kugel, cobalt blue, bunch of grapes, brass hanger, 4¼" L $495.00

Kugel, med. gr., bunch of grapes, brass hanger, 4¾" L $440.00

Row 2, Left to Right

Kugel, cobalt blue, unsilvered berry, brass hanger, 4¼" diam. $660.00

Kugel, med. gr., bunch of grapes, brass hanger, minor wear, 4¼" L $319.00

Kugel, lt. silvery gr., bunch of grapes, brass hanger, 4" L $440.00

Kugel, amber, bunch of grapes, brass hanger, 4¼" L $357.50

Kugel, amber, ribbed sphere, worn, 4" diam. $159.50

A-OH Sept. 1998   Garth's Auctions

All Clear Lacy Glass

Tea Plate, octagonal, Pittsburgh w/ side wheeler, chips, 6½" diam. $880.00

Plate, round, Pittsburgh w/ side wheeler, 5⅜" diam. $220.00

Tea Plate, octagonal, ship w/ union, sm. chips, 6⅝" diam. $962.50

Plates, two, "Victoria & Albert", 5⅛" diam., & "George Washington", 6" diam., sm. chips $192.50

Plate & Bowl, eagle plate, 7" diam., & nectarine bowl, 7⅜" diam., 1⅝" H, both have chips $165.00

Bowl, w/ rope rim & eight spoke center, minor chips, 6" diam. . . .$247.50

A-OH Sept. 1998   Garth's Auctions

Row 1, Left to Right

Candlesticks, pr., sq. stepped base w/ reeded stem, reeded & ribbed socket attached w/ wafer, chips & one w/ checks in socket, 6" H $440.00

Baccarat, two pcs., creamer, 4½" H, & oval dish, 8¾" L, both have minor chips $165.00

Baccarat, sugar bowl w/ lid, chips on rim 7¼" H $82.50

Row 2, Left to Right

Relish, peacock eye design, heavy glass, midwestern, chips, 7½" L .$55.00

Bowl, shallow, thistle & beehive, edge chips, 9¾" diam. $38.50

Relish, w/ scroll design, amethyst tint, edge chips, 9⅛" L $22.00

A-OH Oct. 1998   Early Auction Company

Row 1, Left to Right

21-Vases, pr., Prussian blue Mary Gregory, ea/ w. Victorian lady, cut scalloped rims, inverted ribbing, 18" H $700.00

92-Bride's Basket, Moser, swirl amethyst to crystal bowl w/ petal top rim, body dec. w/ gold flowers & leaves, gilt enhanced twig handled metal frame, 7" diam. $550.00

27-Vases, pr. Amberina swirl, amber serpent boils lower body towards gold morning glory vine, 10¼" H . .$200.00

183-Punch Cups, pr. Amberina, D.Q. w/ amber reeded handles, 2½" H $200.00

52-Vase, Mt. Washington acid Burmese, dec. w/ gr. maiden hair fernery w/ raised gold, 12" H $1,350.00

10-Pitcher, Amberina melon ribbed w/ herringbone patt., amber handle, 8½" H $300.00

157-Lamp, Pittsburg bent panel carmel slag shade, gilt double handled base w/ rose garlands 20" H .$700.00

9-Mugs, Three Amberina w/ swirl patt. amber handles, 3½" H . .$105.00

51-Vase, Cameo mkd. Mt. Joye, amethyst poppies, gold enhanced upon textured frosty amethyst ground, 10½" H $450.00

56-Vases, pr. footed, ea. mkd. Libby Amberina, 13½" H . . . . .N/S

Row 2, Left to Right

24-Vase, yel. cut velvet D.Q., applied camphor leaf w/ nut & stem forming handle, 7½" H $110.00

21-Vases, pr., Prussian blue Mary Gregory, ea/ w. Victorian lady, cut scalloped rims, inverted ribbing, 18" H $700.00

33-Vase, Steuben gold calcie footed morning glory, 8" H, 10" diam. $270.00

41-Punch Cup, glossy Wheeling Peachblow w/ applied amber handle, ground rim, 2½" H $300.00

43-Cracker Barrel, shiny Webb Peachblow, stamped Meriden Co., dec. w/ raised gold peacock on floral & foliage fine, rope handle, cover w/ melon ribbed finial $525.00

4-Punch Cups, 5 Amberina w/ inverted thumbprint & amber handles, 3" H $125.00

58-Vase, Webb acid Burmese w/ petal top rim, dec. w/ blue flowers, buds & gr. & br. foliage, 4" H $350.00

19-Ice Cream Trays, 2 Amberina Daisy & Button, 7" diam. $170.00

54-Bride's Bowl, cased pink D.Q. M.O.P., acid stamped Thomas Webb & Sons, dec. in enamel, white stork flying above br. tree limb w/ blue flowers, 5" H, 9" diam. $1,300.00

Row 3, Left to Right

29-Vase, Amberina corset form w/ squared rim, D.Q. netted design, 7¼" H $135.00

37-Cruet, Mt. Washington acid Burmese ribbed w/ melon stopper, pastel fernery w/ ora. enamel flowers $950.00

56-Vases, pr. footed, ea. mkd. Libby Amberina, 13½" H . . . . .N/S

25-Vase, rosy pink satin D.Q., M.O.P. w/ enamel wildflower bouquet design, 5½" H $200.00

Row 3, Left to Right

49-Cracker Barrel, mkd. Crown Milano, biscuit color ground, dec. w/ gold apple blossom, partial rope handle $475.00

17-Toothpick Holder, Amberina Daisy & Button tri-footed, 2¾" H $150.00

34-Vase, unique Wheeling Peachblow "drape", w/ fold down crimped rim w/ amber trim, 7½" H . . .$300.00

140-Lamp, rev. scenic shade, blue sky w/ ora. clouds, emerald gr. trees, mkd. Moe Bridges, 14" H, 8" diam. $750.00

195-Bowl, Fr. cameo w/ quadrafold rim, gilt sgn. Daum Nancy, textured opal. yel. w/ pale cranberry stripes, gilt highlighted & enamel tinted br., 3" H, 5" diam. $900.00

89-Fairy Lamp, acid Burmese, 3¾" H, dome shade dec. w/ gr. woodbine vine & red berries, clear pressed base w/ molded fairy, 5" H overall . . .$850.00

35-Lily Vase, ribbed Amberina, 8" H $215.00

45-Vase, Peachblow double gourd, gold & silver wild roses & leafy branches, stamped Thomas Webb & Sons $400.00

53-Vase, Mt. Washington acid Burmese, dec. w/ gr. maiden hair ferns w/ raised gold highlights, 9½" H $600.00

88-Fairy Lamp, 2¾" H, Burmese dome shade dec. w/ red floral vine, ceramic insert mkd. S. Clarkes Fairy Pyramid, clear pressed stemmed standard w/ cut glass patt., 9" H overall $550.00

136-Rose Bowl, Webb, crystal overlapped tooled petals, cranberry body, amber base, clear raspberry pontil, 4" H $450.00

48-Bride's Bowl, Mt. Washington acid Burmese, 4¾" H, 9" diam., crimson red leaves w/ enameled white berried vine w/ blue flowers, plated frame, floral emb. $1,000.00

160-Bowl, Webb acid Burmese w/ hex. rim, 3" H $125.00

44-Vase, Prussian blue cut velvet herringbone gourd w/ camphor handles & collar, 7½" H $350.00

59-Vase, Webb acid Burmese, lavender blue flowers, gr. & br. foliage, 2¾" H $450.00

Row 4, Left to Right

42-Pitcher, blue M.O.P. raindrop "coralene" w/ camphor trim, frosted reeded handle, mkd. Webb, 5" H $350.00

57-Vase, Webb acid Burmese w/ crimped petal top rim, 2¼" H .$275.00

14-Muffineer, Rubina crystal w/ inverted thumbprint gold wash helmet cap, 6" H $250.00

167-Bowl, Steuben irid. bluish gold w/ rainbow halo, sgn. Aurene, 2½" H, 10" diam. $300.00

1-Creamer, Amberina w/ amber reeded handle, 3 shell feet & 3 scrolled prunts on body, 4½" H . . . . .N/S

12-Celery, Amberina w/ inverted thumbprint, scalloped sq. rim, 6½" H $165.00

39-Creamer, Webb Burmese 2½" H & open sugar, 3" H, w/ hex. rims, red grape pods & gr. foliaged branches $900.00

20-Bowl, Amberina Daisy & Button oval, 4 curved tab handles, 8" x 11" L $350.00

Row 5, Left to Right

90-Vase, Webb satin finish Burmese, ivy design cascades from tri-fold rim, 3½" H $350.00

38-Rose Bowl, Mt. Washington acid Burmese, variegated gr. ivy vine, 3¼" H $325.00

138-Compote, mkd. Libbey Amberina, optic ribbed body w/ fuchsia Amberina edge, 3¼" H, 7¾" diam. $450.00

15-Canoe, Amberina Daisy & Button, 4¾" x 14" L $175.00

11-Basket, oval Amberina, amber handle partially gilt, swirl patt. body dec. w/ gold floral sprigs, 3½" H, 7¾" diam. $250.00

40-Juice, Webb Burmese barrel form, red berries & gr. foliage, 2¾" H $500.00

414-Pear, New Eng. Peachblow, translucent shading, 5" H $80.00

60-Fairy Lamp, dome shade 3½" H, dec. w/ ivy vine, clear pressed Clarkes insert & footed Burmese base, 5½" H $650.00

117-Tumbler, Amberina swirl, 3¾" H $60.00

36-Lily Vase, Mt. Washington acid Burmese, 6½" H $160.00

8-Cruet, Amberina chestnut form, inverted ribbing & 2 D.Q. bands, clear handle & hollow stopper $175.00

31-Punch Cups, 3 Amberina, 2 D.Q. & 1 inverted thumbprint, all w/ amber reeded handles, 2½" H $105.00

18-Butter, covered Amberina Daisy & Button, 5¼" diam., 4" H $425.00

A-OH Oct. 1998   Early Auction Company

Row 1, Left to Right

519-Pitcher, Wheeling Peachblow, clear reeded handle, 5¼" H . .$475.00

479-Vase, Steuben gr. jade w/ irid. gold threading, 10" H $1,500.00

497-Vase, irid. gold w/ greenish gold leaf tips at base, sgn. L.C. Tiffany Favrile, 18" H $1,500.00

475-Lily Vase, New Eng., Peachblow, 19" H $525.00

496-Vase, irid. gold flower form sgn. L.C. Tiffany Favrile, knob stem, 15" H $1,650.00

437-Epergne, Steuben Ivorine 3 prong lily, faint Steuben signature, 12" H $875.00

460-Bowl, Steuben, gr. jade to alabaster in "Matzu" patt., 7" H .$650.00

485-Vase, irid. gold footed sgn. L.C. Tiffany Favrile $800.0

439-Lamp, rev. scenic shade, lake & trees against amber evening sky, bronze base, mkd. w/ shield emblem, also has cloth label, 23" H overall, 16" diam. $2,200.00

505-Ewer, pink satin D.Q. M.O.P., melon ribbed body, crimp ruffled rim, camphor thorn handle, 11" H . .$450.00

493-Vase, sgn. L.C. Tiffany Favrile, irid. bluish gold w/ amethyst hues, 12" H $925.00

Row 2, Left to Right

523-Vase, irid. blue sgn. Durand, body wrapped in blue threading, 6½" H $700.00

474-Vase, Mt. Washington acid Burmese Jack-in-Pulpit w/ brass base supporting beveled mirror, 4¾" diam., 16½" H $350.00

451-Vase, Mt. Washington Peachblow, dec. w/ non-fired branch of white flowers, 8" H $2,300.00

426-Vase, Steuben Ivory grotesque footed, 12" H $250.00

518-Vase, Steuben Aurene irid. blue, 8" H $900.00

428-Vase, Steuben Ivory w/ Nubian blk. foot, 8¾" H $325.00

495-Bowl, Steuben irid. blue w/ 8 loops at rim, sgn. Aurene, 10½" diam., 3½" H $1,900.00

Row 3, Left to Right

465-Vase, New Eng. Peachblow lily, 10" H $300.00

415-Vase, Stevens & Wms. M.O.P. swirl w/ citron shading to white, 4¾" H $325.00

585-Lamp, mkd. Pairpoint shade, 10" diam., inter. dec. w/ vibrant purple pods on variegated gr. leaves, butterscotch & almond patch ground, frosted ext. w/ blk. enamel outline, 4 panel metal base w/ red heart leaves & gr. vine, 16" overall $2,500.00

444-Tazza, Steuben, topaz swirl bowl & foot connected w/ celeste blue mica stem, 8" H, 8" diam. $575.00

459-Vase, Steuben ACB cylindrical w/ bowl form rim, frosty "Mansard" patt., firm's acid cut fleur-de-lis mark, 9½" H $700.00

454-Vase, New Eng. agata lily, 7" H $700.00

461-Vase, Steuben, irid. blue w/ silvery pulled feather design, 4½" H N/S

429-Fairy Lamp, Webb acid Burmese, 13" diam., 16" H overall N/S

483-Toothpick, Webb cameo, white holly & berried branches, snowy chartreuse ground, 2½" H $1,500.00

481-Rose Bowl, Webb 3 color cameo, almond to apricot flower & leafy vine one chartreuse w/ butterfly on rev., 1¾" H $950.00

520-Cologne, Daum Nancy, textured opal. body enamel dec. w/ blk. windmills & harbor scene, flat cut ebony stopper, gilt sgn. Daum, 3¼" H $650.00

456-Vase, Mt. Washington acid Burmese gourd, 12" H . . . . .N/S

430-Vases, pr., Eng. double handled, cobalt blue carved to white, dec. & repeated palm leaf shoulder, 9" H $1,350.00

Row 4, Left to Right

526-Vase, Steuben alabaster w/ irid. gold vines & leaves, 6" H . . . . . .N/S

490-Vase, Durand w/ blue pulled feathers w/ golden tips, irid. opal shoulder, golden threads . .$1,300.00

482-Rose Bowl, Webb cameo, white wild rose, rosa red ground, 2½" H $1,200.00

436-Vase, Mt. Washington acid Burmese Jack-in-Pulpit, 14½" H $450.00

469-Vase, Mt. Washington acid Burmese petticoat form, pastel daisies & leaves edged w/ gold enamel dots, sponged gold ground, 10" H . .$2,800.00

487-Vase, Imperial Freehand, irid. opal surface w/ lt. gr. vines & leaves, irid. marigold int., 10½" H . .$1,200.00

447-Vase, Steuben ivory fan form w/ nubian blk. foot, 6¼" H, 8½" W $500.00

507-Dresser Box, Wavecrest Helmschmied swirl, pastel fern fronds w/ enamel highlights, red floral spray against satin opal & yel. tinted ground $400.00

489-Vase, Eng. cameo, white morning glory blossom on chartreuse body, 9¼" H $600.00

494-Vase, Fuchsia Amberina, sgn. Libbey, 11" H $650.00

473-Vase, Mt. Washington acid Burmese, thin double handles, 10" H $350.00

Row 5, Left to Right

411-Tumbler, Mt. Washington acid Burmese, 3¾" H $60.00

458-Vase, Steuben irid. gold 3 prong, sgn. Aurene, 6" H $575.00

413-Vase, Mt Washington acid Burmese, 5¾" H $215.00

452-Vase, Eng. cameo, acid stamped Stevens & Wms., white leafy vines w/ fuchsia or floral clusters on rose pink ground, bruise & chip on base, 4¼" H . . . . .N/S

432-Vase, Acid Burmese petal top, mkd. Queen's Burmese Thomas Webb & Sons, 3¼" H $225.00

448-Vase, Steuben Ivorine Jack-in-Pulpit, w/ ribbed throat, etched Steuben sig., 6½" H $450.00

449-Vase, Steuben Ivorine Jack-in-Pulpit w/ ribbed throat, etched Steuben signature $450.00

522-Vase, glossy plum to yel. surface enamel dec. w/ portrait framed in raised gold., silver lustre accents at base, 3" H $325.00

431-Vase, mkd. Smith Brothers, pastel blue pansies, ivory surface, enamel dotted rim, 4" H $200.00

506-Glove Box, mkd. Wavecrest, pink wild roses & white enamel daisy w/ foliage, raised scrolls w/ mauve enameling, chartreuse ribbed body, 3" H, 8½" L $1,250.00

407-Vase, Steuben Ivory w/ waisted body & flared rim, 6" H $200.00

477-Lava Vase, Mt. Washington, 5" H $800.00

A-OH Sept. 1998   Garth's Auctions

Flask, Nailsea, clear cased in white w/ loops of red & blue, 8¾" L . . .$192.50

Paperweight, clear dome top w/ white sulfide dog on a cranberry ground, ...$275.00

Flask, Nailsea, clear w/ white & pink loops, 8¾" L $220.00

Flask, Nailsea, clear w/ white & pink loops, 7¾" L $192.50

Flasks, two, one opaque white w/ blue spatter, 7⅝" L & one clear w/ fiery opal. ribs, 6¾" L $275.00

A-OH Oct. 1998   Early Auction Company

Row 1, Left to Right

658-Gas Shades, 5 ribbed irid. opal bell form w/ golden interior, 5" H, sgn. Quezal, 2¼" fitters $500.00

656-Frame, perpetual fountain ornate brass, 2 cranberry globes, cranberry bowl mounted on top of frame, 20" H $1,000.00

624-Desk Lamp, cased irid. gold shade, 7" diam., sgn. L.C.T., mounted on Zodiac harp base, mkd. Tiffany Studios, NY, 13" H $2,000.00

633-Pickle Castor, cased pink "cone" insert, ornate pierced frame, tongs & cover, 10" H $400.00

663-Vase, Marjorelle, golden ora. mottled w/ tangerine & cobalt blue, wrt. iron frame, etched Degue, 13" H . . . . .N/S

643-Vase, royal blue Durand by Larson, opal pulled leaves & blue swags, 8½" H $600.00

584-Lamp, Tiffany's leaded "Acorn" shade, 16" diam., gr. acorns, 9 rows in shades of textured reddish amber, amethyst, opal & yel., fully ribbed base w/ tri-arm support, mkd. Tiffany Studios, NY, 22" H $5,500.00

635-Pickle Castor, cranberry opal. swirl insert, ornate frame, tongs & cover, 9" H $600.00

651-Vase, irid. gold border, pulled gr. & chartreuse petals against golden opal, irid. gold raised foot w/ opal edge, 13" H $250.00

664-Vase, Steuben flared rim Bristol D.Q. w/ blk. threading, faint fleur-de-lis , 7" H, 7" diam. $500.00

Row 2, Left to Right

635-Pickle Castor, frosty & wood textured barrel form, molded blue wild rose wreath, plated frame, tongs & cover, 11" H $450.00

660-Floor Lamp
calcite shade w/ pulled gr. ruffled rim, irid. gold trim, gold int., 5¾" H, 7½" diam., bronze color reeded base, 56" H $440.00

655-Vase, Moser amber spangled w/ enamel gr. lizard among multi-color flowers, partial paper label, 5¼" H $350.00

652-Ewer, Webb Peachblow w/ amber thorn handle, 12½" H .$200.00

647-Vase, Steuben irid. gold footed, sgn. Steuben Aurene, 10" H . .$850.00

654-Vase, Moser pillow form, raised gold scrolls surround multi-color enamel butterflies & stylized flowers, gold rigaree side trim, 6½" H .$650.00

678-Vase, Steuben oriental poppy, 7" H $300.00

638-Pickle Castor, Rubina crystal ribbed, gilt design, ornate Reed & Barton frame, shell tongs, cover w/ floral finial, 14" H $1,150.00

662-Gas Shade, irid. gold bell form, opal pulled & swirl designs, sgn. L.C.T., 4" H, 2" fitter $250.00

649-Vase, Steuben gr. jade ribbed fan w/ alabaster knob stem & base, 10½" H $300.00

467-Vase, Mt. Washington acid Burmese double gourd, 8" H .$225.00

653-Vases, pr. sgn. Moser, entire cranberry surface w/ lush gold foliage, 13½" H $700.00

Row 3, Left to Right

556-Chandelier, Handel sgn. globe, ext. dec. w/ fall foliaged trees, irid. gold ground, metal ceiling mount, metal tassel, 6" diam., 20" L .$3,100.00

637-Pickle Castor, yel. ora. mottled w/ opal gray body, ornate frame, tong & floral emb. cover, 10" H . . .$600.00

648-Compote, Steuben gold calcite, 10" diam., 8¾" H $500.00

667-Cologne, cameo, cranberry floral vines on frosty leaf surface, clear faceted stopper, 7¾" H $225.00

634-Pickle Castor, Royal Flemish frosty insert, dec. w/ yel. & white enamel mums, gilt highlights, orange gold Pairpoint frame, tongs & emb. cover, 10" H $2,000.00

650-Vase, sgn. Nash, golden br. pulled design from base mingled w/ chartreuse & opal pulled motif, 11" H $600.00

631-Pickle Castor, cased insert, red rose bud bouquet on white, red int., ornate frame w/ fork & cover, 11" H $350.00

661-Gas Shades, 2 gas, sgn. Quezel, reddish irid. gold ribbed, 4" H, 2⅛" fitters $220.00

600-Lamp, shade mkd. Pairpoint, 10" diam., ext. dec. w/ textured grove of fall foliaged trees, colorful floral meadow, slender stem on step base, 15" H $2,500.00

668-Basket, Malachite, w/ molded cherubs on sides, 6" H $70.00

672-Vase, pink M.O.P. peacock feather, 8" H $250.00

Row 4, Left to Right

665-Vase, Steuben w/ ribbed pear shape topaz bowl on Pomona gr. footed base, 6¼" H, 4½" diam. $200.00

632-Pickle Castor, cranberry inverted thumbprint, enamel yel. or blue flowers & gr. foliage, w/ tongs & cover, 11½" H $700.00

434-Bowl, Mt. Washington ruffle top, 2¾" H, 6" diam. $120.00

544-Desk Set, six pcs., Tiffany, gilded w/ abalone grape pods, includes covered sq. ink well w/ clear insert 3" H, stamp box 2¼" H x 4" L, pen tray 2½" H x 8½" L, blotter ends 2¼" x 12¼" L, letter holder 5½" H, 9¼" L, all mkd. Tiffany Studios, NY $2,150.00

674-Marmalade, Steuben Cyprian w/ celeste blue trim, double yel. & red pear handles, 5" H, matching saucer, 6¼" diam. $450.00

636-Pickle Castor, cranberry inverted thumbprint, wreath of white & blue enamel flowers & gr. foliage, ornate frame, tongs & cover, 11½" H $900.00

669-Perfume, w/ stopper, 4 tapered sides have molded scrolls & flowers, 5½" H $200.00

657-Gas Shades, 5 ribbed morning glory, sgn. Quezal, 6" H, irid. opal w/ golden pulled leaves & tips, 2¼" fitters $1,000.00

670-Cologne, w/ atomizer, Malachite, molded roses, 6" H $150.00

574-Gas Shades, 3 Fostoria, irid. gold leaves & vertical vines on opal, irid. gold int., 4¾" H, 2¼" fitters $525.00

412-Vase, Mt. Washington acid Burmese 3¼" H, 5¼" diam. .$1,160.00

640-Pickle Castor, Daisy & Button canoe, amber & clear, resting in Homan wheeled frame w/ butterfly & crescent handle w/ 2 owls, 8" L $350.00

671-Ewer, M.O.P. herringbone rainbow w/ trefoil rim, champhor handle, 6½" H $700.00

666-Vase, clear ovoid w/ air trap, sgn. V. Durand, ca. 1995, 4" H, 4" diam. $155.00

A-OH Sept. 1998   Garth's Auctions

Jar, Pittsburgh clear blown, applied foot, hollow stem, sm. rim flake, 18¾" H $275.00

Lamp, brass, mkd. "Pat. Oct. 28, '79", oil burner w/ wick advance knob, dent in font & soldered reprs., 15½" H $220.00

A-OH Oct. 1998   Early Auction Company

Row 1, Left to Right

610-Candlestick, irid. gold w/ twist stem & flared rim, sgn. Aurene, button pontil, 4¾" H $250.00

615-Vase, Fr. cameo, sgn. Gallé, ebony trees along serene lake, slightly hammered cinnamon sky, 18" H $750.00

547-Arabian Lamp, Tiffany, conical shade, lime gr. design w/ irid. gold zipper patt., sgn., 14" H overall . . . .N/S

533-Charger, Mettlach, portrait or woman w/ long lt. br. hair, dusty pink lilies, 18" diam. . . . . .N/S

595-Vase, Steuben alabaster w/ irid. gold vines, 6¼" H $675.00

607-Vase, Fr. cameo, deep purple conifers, pale blue mountainscape, chartreuse & frosty sky, sgn. Gallé $3,000.00

618-Vase, Imperial Freehand, reflective cobalt surface, 11¼" H . . . . .N/S

527-Vase, Fr. cameo mold blown, cameo sgn. Gallé, pale blue rose hips among golden br. leaves on citron ground, amethyst base, 9½" H $7,000.00

545-Lamp, rev. scenic shade sgn. Handel, fall foliaged trees against cloudy blue sky, bronze base, 23" H, 18" diam. $6,250.00

608-Vase, irid. opal amber w/ infused pulled leaf wreath on shoulder, pinkish tint festoons at base w/ yellowed opal foot, sgn. L.C. Tiffany, Favrile, 9¾" H $1,900.00

Row 2, Left to Right

616-Vases, pr. white enamel dandelion w/ gold highlights, pale gr. enamel leaves, 19¾" H, 20¾" H . . . . . .N/S

609-Claret, glossy Wheeling Peachblow, flat-sided, amber rope handle & faceted stopper, 9" H $1,500.00

546-Vase, Mt. Washington acid Burmese, lavender blue floral stems, enamel beaded rim, 12" H .$1,500.00

605-Vase, Fr. cameo flat-sided, sgn. Gallé w/ star, fuchsia red leafy branches w/ berry pods, frosty ground, 12¼" H $2,250.00

550-Cologne, Fr., sgn. Daum Nancy, enamel citron floral clusters on amethyst leafy stems w/ gr. & yel. leaves, frosty ground, silver pear form cap reveals clear stopper, 6" H $400.00

528-Vase, Fr. marquetry de Verre, purple leaves, reddish amber bud, blue gray ground, 5" H . . . . .N/S

625-Vase, Fr. cameo, sgn. Gallé, cranberry leafy vines w/ berries against frosty ground, 13½" H $850.00

602-Vase, Fr. cameo, sgn. Gallé, frosty flat-sided stick form dec. w/ honey amber & lavender leaves, 13¼" H $3,600.00

534-Vase, Rookwood, ca. 1955, cluster of blue plums w/ lt. br. branches, tan ground, 6¼" H $1,100.00

626-Vase, Fr. cameo trumpet form, etched Le Verre Francais, lilac floral blossoms, deep purple foliaged stems, mottled pink ground, 13¾" H $1,100.00

596-Vases, pr., pearlized gray lustre Jack-in-Pulpit, ivory color woman, 12" H $675.00

Row 3, Left to Right

548-Vase, Quezal, pulled gr. leaves w/ amethyst gold veins, irid. gold threading on neck, 5 irid. bluish gold reeded pods, 6¼" H $3,500.00

529-Lamp, Pate-de-Verre shade molded w/ 3 Fr. blue "mums" against frosty ground, 7½" H . . . . .N/S

535-Stein, Rookwood unglazed, nude toddlers under banner encised Cinn. Coop. Co., rev. w/ 3 seated & drinking at table, 7½" H $500.00

614-Vase, irid. gold trumpet form, raised ribbed base, sgn. L.C. Tiffany-Favrile, 3" line in base $300.00

611-Vase, rose pink, D.Q. cut velvet, 6" H $135.00

536-Vase, Rookwood wax matt, initials Wihelmine Rehm, blue & lilac stylized flowers w/ tan & gr. leaves, pink ground, 5" H $550.00

531-Lamp, shade sgn. Handel, tranquil rev. Peachblow sunset & reflective waterway w/ dk. gr. trees, ebony base, 14" H $2,750.00

530-Vase, Fr. cameo, etched atop dk. pitted foot, Daum Nancy, emerald gr. foliage, saffron yel. ground, 10"H N/S

604-Lamp, pr. dec. Quezal, 4 lrg. emerald gr. leaves w/ pulled tips w/ irid. golden veins & amethyst hues, almond shoulders, irid. citron or gold pulled feather motifs, 12" H $2,000.00

627-Vase, irid. gold trumpet form, etched sgn. Steuben $300.00

Row 4, Left to Right

532-Vase, smokey amber, enamel sgn. Emile Gallé, enamel stylized flowers, raised gold stems w/ blue berries & russet leaves, 8¾" H $500.00

538-Vase, Rookwood vellum, pink & lt. blue iris blossoms w/ gray gr. leaves, blue ground, ca. 1930, 13½" H $4,100.00

613-Urn, Meissen w/ natural color raised nudes & children w/ goat, hand repr., 6" H $950.00

598-Vase, Moser, emerald gr. to clear body, enamel dec. w/ pink, plum, & salmon exotic flowers, yel. web leaves, 9" H $400.00

537-Candleholders, pr. pink "lotus", 3¾" H $225.00

599-Celery, glossy Wheeling w/ ruffled rim, 6¼" H $650.00

628-Vase, Fr. cameo teardrop form, citron yel. ground w/ chocolate br. vines, grape pods, cameo sgn. Gallé, 9¼" H $650.00

617-Vase, Loetz, pulled & swirl patt. in amethyst blue & irid. gold hues, hollow stem, 8¾" H $600.00

Row 5, Left to Right

549-Salt Tubs, six clear cut panel, ea. sgn. Daum Nancy, all dec. w/ blk. enamel, gilt rims, 1½" H, embedded w/ fitted silk lined hinged box, 5" H, x 8" L . . . . .N/S

601-Cruet, New Eng., agata, almond stopper, base mottled $475.00

629-Dresser Box, Wavecrest Helmschmied swirl, white enamel floral bouquets against gray gr., 3½" H, 5½" diam. $300.00

612-Vase, Webb acid Burmese, 4¼" H . . . . .N/S

603-Dresser Box, Steuben irid. blue covered, sgn. Aurene, 3½" H .$750.00

630-Vase, Fr. cameo, red flowers & leaves, ribbed & textured ground, etched Cristaberie de Panun, 4½" H $400.00

597-Bowl, Teplitz style, pr. gargoyle birds astride pierced & ruffled pink rim, blue body w/ cobalt & raised gold flowers, molded purple br. base, 7" H, 8½" L $325.00

A-OH Sept. 1998   Garth's Auctions

Row 1, Left to Right

Kugel, cranberry, brass hanger, 3¼" diam. $220.00

Kugels, four, silver & amber pear shaped, 3⅝" H, & gold & lt. gr., w/ wear, round, 2¾" diam., all have brass hangers $220.00

Kugels, three w/ brass hangers, granny apple gr., 4½" diam., lt. teal gr., 4½" diam., & gold, 6" diam., all have wear $247.50

Row 2, Left to Right

Kugel, cobalt blue w/ brass hanger, 5¾" diam. $302.50

Kugels, four in various shades of gr., brass hangers, all have wear, 3¾" & 5½" diam. $275.00

A-MA Oct. 1998   Skinner, Inc.

Cut Glass – Brilliant Period

Left to Right

Vase, Am., center star cut, applied handles, scalloped edge base, 10¼" H $1,380.00
Lamp, Am., fan & hobstar shaft w/ scalloped & notched base, shade w/ hobstar & fan cuts, cut glass prisms, minor chips, 29½" H, 11½" diam. $3,680.00
Vase, Am. brilliant cut glass, star & fan motifs on trumpet shaped vase w/ ruffled notched edges on rim, rim chips, 14¼" H $460.00
Lamp, Am. brilliant cut glass, shade & base w/ "chair bottom", patt., w/ prisms, chips to base, 27" H . .$1,150.00

A-MD Sept. 1998   Richard Opfer
                          Auctioneering, Inc.

Row 1, Left to Right

Rainbow Vase, swirl ribbing, 8½" H $175.00
Vase, N. Eng. peach blow, floral enamel dec. 11½" H $325.00
Vase, jack-in-the-pulpit, N. Eng., peach blow, bruise in lip, 7¼" H $55.00

Row 2, Left to Right

Vase, Amberina footed, possibly Libbey, bruise at foot, 6" H . .$160.00
Vase, Federzeichnung, pinched ruffled top, slight wear on gold rim, 6" H $1,150.00

A-MD Sept. 1998   Richard Opfer
                          Auctioneering, Inc.

Left, Top to Bottom

Perfumes, lot of 2, one painted floral porcelain, brass cap & chain, chipped, 3½" H, one blue glass horn shaped, enameled dec., brass hinged top & cap w/ chain, has stopper, 3" H $230.00

Center, Top to Bottom

Perfumes, lot of 2, Italian red, white & blue swirl, no stopper, minor chip, 2" H, & one Posey holder, cranberry glass vase, pin w/ gold enameling, 2½" H $130.00

Right, Top to Bottom

Perfumes, lot of 2, floral enameled, gr. to clear w/ unmkd. hinged top, no stopper, 2 minor flakes on bottom, 3" H, one w/ gr. glass w/ enameled cherries, brass hinged top & ring, has stopper, 3" H $160.00

A-MD Sept. 1998   Richard Opfer
                          Auctioneering, Inc.

Row 1, Left to Right

Vase, Tiffany Favrile, partial paper label, 8" H $625.00
Compote, Tiffany Favrile, bright color, 8" diam. $525.00
Vase, Durand, 5½" H $525.00

Row 2, Left to Right

Compote, Tiffany Favrile, bright color, 3½" H $650.00
Vase, silver overlay, rainbow colors, 5" H $300.00
Vase, Steuben Aurene, brilliant color, paneled, paper label, 5" H . . .$475.00

A-MD Sept. 1998   Richard Opfer
                          Auctioneering, Inc.

Row 1, Left to Right

Perfume, enameled & transfer vignette of cherub on red glass; hinged brass cap w/ ring, has stopper, 3" H $180.00
Perfume, sterling silver w/ enameled inset flowers, screw on cap, 3¼" H $375.00
Perfumes, lot of two, one multi-color Venetian type glass paneled perfume, hinged jeweled brass top, stopper recessed, 2¾" H, one multi-color foil glass, jeweled hinged brass top, 3" H $350.00

Row 2, Left to Right

Perfumes, lot of two, one enameled vignette of courting scene on porcelain, brass hinged top w/ ring, has stopper, 2½" H, one floral enameled gr. glass, possibly Moser, brass hinged top w/ ring, has stopper, 3' H . . .$375.00

A-MD Sept. 1998   Richard Opfer
                          Auctioneering, Inc.

Row 1, Left to Right

Perfumes, lot of 2, painted enamel over lass, no stopper, blue perfume has base chip, 2" H $150.00
Perfumes, lot of 2, painted enamel over glass, both have stopper, 2" H $185.00

Row 2, Left to Right

Bottle Vinaigrettes, lot of 2, ruby is silver topped, ½" H & 2" H . . .$360.00
Perfumes, lot of 2, both porcelain, both have stoppers, floral perfume has hairline, 2¼" H $250.00

A-OH Sept. 1998 Garth's Auctions

Left to Right

Mold Bowl, emerald gr. w/ applied foot, ground pontil & cut design at top of ea. rib, 4⅜" H $1,100.00
Tumbler, yel. gr. w/ applied handle, diamond smocked design, wear & sm. chips, 4" H $165.00
Five Pieces, tumbler, amethyst, 4" H, pan w/ folded lip, amethyst, 6" diam., tumbler w/ nine panels in peacock blue, 2½" H, jigger w/ ten panels in apple gr., 2" H, & footed cup, teal blue, 3⅝" H, most w/ chips $220.00

A-OH Sept. 1998 Garth's Auctions

Left to Right

Vases, pr., amethyst, hexagonal w/ ellipse & circle bowl & ruffled rim, chips on base, 8¾" H $825.00
Candlesticks, two canary w/ petal detail, not a pr., both damaged, 6⅞" & 7⅜" $99.00
Candlestick, Pittsburgh canary w/ opal. socket, round base, hex. stem & socket, pewter insert missing, chips & crack in socket, 9¼" H $110.00

A-MD Sept. 1998 Richard Opfer Auctioneering, Inc.

Row 1

Kugels, lot of 3, blue, gr. & gold, largest 4¾" diam. $310.00

Row 2

Kugels, two, grape, largest 4½" L $575.00

A-OH Sept. 1998 Garth's Auctions

Row 1, Left to Right

Candlestick, grass gr., hex. Pittsburgh, chips & check in socket, 9⅜" H $55.00
Candlestick, canary hex. w/ wafer, good color, sm. chips 7⅝" H .$110.00
Lamp, clear Pittsburgh, sq. base, wafer stem & font w/ cut roundels & fans, brass collar, chips, 7⅛" H $286.00
Bowl, clear blown w/ applied sapphire blue rim, 5⅝" diam., 3¾" H $110.00
Candlestick, canary hex. w/ flaring base & wafer, broken blister inside socket, 7½" H $137.50

Row 2, Left to Right

Candlestick, clear, stepped pressed base & clear hollow socket w/ two knop stem, pewter insert, chips on base, 9⅛" H $110.00
Candlesticks, pr., clear, pressed base & blown hollow socket w/ baluster stem, checks in base, no inserts, 8⅛" H $357.50
Canister, clear blown w/ two applied sapphire rings, lid has matching ring & clear finial, 9½" H $907.50
Candlesticks, two clear flint, hex. w/ wafer, one plain, 9¼" H, one acanthus, 9¼" H, pinpoint flakes $192.50

A-MA Oct. 1998 Skinner, Inc.
Lustres, white overlay gr. glass, ca. 1880-1900 w/ circular foot painted w/ multicolored foliage & gilt scrolls, faceted prisms, 12½" H $2,300.00

A-MD Sept. 1998 Richard Opfer Auctioneering, Inc.

Row 1, Left to Right

Cruet, N. Eng. peach blow, enameled floral & dragon fly dec., missing stopper, 5½" H $600.00
Syrup, Mt. Washington, enamel dec., plated top, hairline, 5½" H . . .$225.00
Pickle Jar, Amberina, painted floral dec., plated top, 6" H $350.00

Row 2, Left to Right

Biscuit Jar, peach blow, gold enamel floral & butterfly dec., plated top & brass swing handle, 7" H $575.00
Perfume Bottles, pr., peachblow, gold enamel floral & butterfly dec., sm. flake on lip of one bottle, 5½" H $850.00

A-MD Sept. 1998 Richard Opfer Auctioneering, Inc.

Row 1, Left to Right

Bowl, Gallé, fern dec. on gr., 2¼" H $425.00
Bud Vase, Gallé, lavender & gr. floral design on pink, 6¼" H $425.00
Inkwell, cameo glass, blue & white floral design, Gorham sterling mono. lid, 3½" H $950.00

Row 2, Left to Right

Bud Vase, Gallé, red floral design on amber ground, 5¼" H $500.00
Bud Vase, Gallé, red berry & leaf design, chip on lip, 5¼" H . . .$225.00
Bud Vase, Gallé, purple grapes cameo, flaw or crack, 4" H . .$200.00

A-OH Sept. 1998　　　　Garth's Auctions

Shaker Bottles

Row 1, Left to Right

Three, "Shaker Digestive Cordial", 5¾" H, aqua "Shaker Anodyne" 4" H & amber "The Shaker Family Pills, stain, 2¼" H $132.00

Six, aqua "Shaker Fluid, Extract Valerian", stain & sm. chips, 3½" to 3¾" H $192.50

Three, aqua, two "Shaker Digestive Cordial", 6¾" & 5¾" H, one "Shaker Fluid, Extract Valerian", 3⅝" H, stains $148.50

Row 2, Left to Right

Pickle Jars, two, clear w/ worn paper label "Shaker Pickles", stain, 9¾" H, & aqua "Shaker Pickles", 6⅞" H $412.50

Four, aqua, "Shaker Syrup", 8' H, "Shaker Digestive Cordial", 5¾" H, "Shaker Cherry Pectoral Syrup", 5½" H, & "Shaker Fluid, Extract Valerian", 3⅝" H, stains $220.00

Four, aqua "Shaker Fluid, Extract Valerian", 3⅝" H, aqua "Shaker Anodyne", 3¾" H, "Shaker Digestive Cordial", 5⅝" H, & amber "Shaker Hair Restorer", 7¾" H, stain $225.50

A-MA Aug. 1998　Robert C. Eldred Co., Inc.

Am. Smelling or Scent Bottles

Seahorse-Type, clear w/ blue & white ribbon dec. & applied clear rigaree, 2½" L $121.00

Seahorse-Type, clear w/ white ribbon dec. & applied rigaree, 2¾" L $77.00

Seahorse-Type, clear w/ white ribbon dec. & applied blue rigaree, 2¼" L $132.00

Seahorse-Type, blue w/ applied white rigaree, 3" L $165.00

Seahorse-Type, clear w/ applied rigaree, 2½" L $55.00

A-MA Oct. 1998　　　　Skinner, Inc.

Left to Right

Bowl, English cameo glass, amber body overlaid in ora. & white, carved & etched lattice design, frosted glass feet, 3½" H, 4½" diam. $1,092.50

Vase, Webb cameo glass, tricolor orchid, lt. amber body overlaid in red & opal, etched & carved floral, gold ground, sgn. "Thomas Webb & Sons, Gem Cameo", 5¾" H $5,175.00

Pitcher, English cameo glass, attrib. to Thomas Webb, bright red body overlaid in white cameo, butterfly at rev., w/ applied foliate dec. handle, 3½" H $1,150.00

Perfume, English cameo glass, attrib. to Thomas Webb, ruby red overlaid in opal, butterfly in flight, sterling screw cap stamped "Gorham", int. stain, 10½" L $2,645.00

Vase, cameo glass, body of red diamond quilted satin glass overlaid in opaque white, base mkd. Webb, 8" H $575.00

Perfume, English cameo glass, turquoise blue body w/ raised rim, overlaid in bright white, gilt cap set w/ red & blue stones, hallmarks, w/ orig. fitted box, 4½" H $1,955.00

A-MA Oct. 1998　　　　Skinner, Inc.

Left to Right

Cruet Stand, George II, London, 1765 w/ 5 later cut glass bottles, 2 w/ stoppers, 3 w/ metal mounts, 9" H $747.50

Cruet Stand, George III, London, 1797, mkd. "C C", w/ 7 cut glass bottles, 4 w/ cut glass stoppers, 6 w/ hallmarked silver mounts, 10¼" H $1,036.00

A-OH Sept. 1998　　　　Garth's Auctions

Lacy Sandwich Glass

Row 1, Left to Right

Salt, gr., 3⅝" L $82.50
Salt, clear, 3¼" L $60.50
Salt, med. gr., chips, 3" L . . .$192.50
Salt, clear, chips, 3" L $104.50
Salt, amber, crack, 3⅛" L . . .$104.50

Row 2, Left to Right

Salt, pr clear, 3½" L chip $93.50
Salts, two clear, chips $27.50

Row 3, Left to Right

Lacy Glass, 6 pcs. 2 salts, 3" L, one damaged & missing feet, plate "T & J Robinson, Pittsbg.", 5¾" diam., sauce, stippled dish w/ ellipses, 4½" diam., & dish 4⅞" diam., chips $192.50

Salts, 2, clear, 3¼" L, chips . .$33.00

Row 4, Left to Right

Cup Plates, three, one lt. gr., 3⅝" diam., one peacock blue, 3⅜" diam., & one fiery opal. w/ minor chips, 3½" diam. .$412.50

A-MA Mar. 1999　　　　Skinner, Inc.

Cut Glass - Brilliant Period

Left to Right

Vase, Am., late 19th C., attrib. to Hawkes, 13½" H . . . . .N/S

Table Lamp, Am., dome shaped shade w/ leaves & daisies, w/ prisms, 25" H, 12" diam. $1,150.00

Jug, Am., flared form in colorless glass, notched & scalloped rim, hobstar & fan patt., 11½" H $805.00

Tray, Am., hobstar border, scalloped rim, central star, 1½" H, 21" L . . .N/S

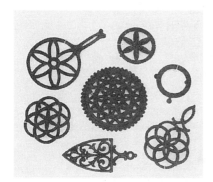

A-PA Mar. 1999   Horst Auctioneers

Clockwise

Lrg. Cast Iron Trivet, w/ handle, 3 legs, 7½" diam. $140.00
Sm. Cast Iron Trivet, w/ six lobed star design, 5½" diam. $120.00
Hand Wrt. Iron Trivet, w/ incised sawtooth & dot designs, penny-like feet, 4½" diam. $200.00
Round Rivet, cast iron w/ six lobed designs & handle, 6½" diam. . .$80.00
Shield-shaped Trivet, w/ int. scrolled designs, footed, 9½" L . .$50.00
Round Cast Iron Trivet, w/ six lobes & notched designs on top surface, 6½" diam. $80.00

Center Trivet

Lrg. Cast Iron Round Trivet, w/ six-lobed radial or star design in center surrounded by sawtooth-like bands, 9" diam. $50.00

A-PA Mar. 1999   Horst Auctioneers
Coffeepot, punched tin, mid-19th C., Lancaster Co., PA, w/ lrg. punched urn of floral design on both sides of pot, gooseneck spout, 11½" H $3,200.00

A-PA Mar. 1999   Horst Auctioneers
Utensil Set, four pcs., wrt. iron & brass w/ dec. handles, brass bowls . .$3,200.00

A-OH Jan. 1999   Garth's Auctions

Candy Mold, heart shape, pine w/ old patina, carved house like design, 6" H $137.50
Butterprint, rectangular, stylized flowers w/ "H.M." in cross hatched design, carved date "1823", pine w/ old patina, 2⅝" x 4" $165.00
Dipper, ash burl w/ varnish finish, figured bowl & plain handle, 11¾" L $715.00
Dish, burl, carved animal handle, good wear & old finish, 4⅜" diam., 1½" H $742.50
Butterprint, primitive tulip & ;eaves, poplar w/ old blk. finish, dated "1796", PA, 4½" x 5" $550.00
Butterprint, round, four hearts w/ cross hatching, hardwood w/ old patina, sq. self handle, 4¾" x 4⅞" $440.00
Butter Paddle, burl maple w/ old finish, chamfered handle, 10½" L $165.00
Butterprint, eagle w/ star, hardwood w/ old patina, age crack, 4" diam. $302.50
Paddle, burl ref. oak, filled worm holes, 8¾" L $38.50
Tongs, wrt. iron pipe, may have been shortened, 11½" L $137.50

A-MA Aug. 1998   Robert C. Eldred Co., Inc.
Butter Churn, Davis No. 4, swing-type, painted yel., 41" H, 48" W $275.00
Jug, stoneware w/ cobalt blue bird dec., 2 gal. $143.00
Butter Churn, w/ four bands & plunger, 17" H $176.00
Crock, stoneware w/ cobalt blue floral dec., ...$143.00

A-ME July 1998   Cyr Auction Co. Inc.
Chopping Bowl, blue painted & carved, 20" x 11½" $2,500.00

A-PA Mar. 1999   Horst Auctioneers

Row 1, Left to Right

Lantern, w/ pierced tin dec., mid 19th C., 16½" H $270.00
Kettle, tin w/ cover, late 19th C., 7" H $20.00
Teapot, tin, 19th C., w/ surface rust, 6½" H $55.00
Milk Pail, tin, late 19th C., w/ surface rust, 7½" H $55.00

Row 2, Left to Right

Chocolate Mold, tin, 2 pc., fisherman, mkd. "Made in Holland", 1 clamp, 6½" H $30.00
Chocolate Mold, tin, 2 pc., Girl on Swing, mkd. "Made in Ger.", 4¼" H $45.00
Tin Horn, w/ loop for hanging, 17½" L $40.00
Tea Kettle, tin w/ removeable cover, 19th C., 7½" H, 10" diam. $80.00
Oil Lamp, w/ triple spout, 19th C., wear, denting & surface rust, 11½" H $90.00
Pudding Mold, Graniteware, gray agate, early 20th C., 9½" diam., 3½" H $35.00

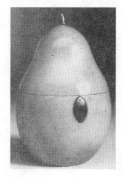

A-MA Feb. 1999   Skinner, Inc.
Tea Caddy, fruitwood, Eng., late 18th C., 6¼" H $5,750.00

A-PA Mar. 1999   Horst Auctioneers

Tinware, 19th C.

Row 1, Left to Right

Basin, late 19th C., w/ handles, 15½" diam. $70.00
Mush Pan, late 19th C., w/ rolled rim, pierced, 15½" diam.
. . . .$40.00

Row 2, Left to Right

Lamp Filler, w/ lid & handle on back, 5" H $170.00
Strainer, 2 pc., 4 sm. feet, 10" L w/ handles $75.00
Foot Warmer, w/ oval ends & rounded sides, hinged hasp
& catch, 14" L $55.00

Row 3, Left to Right

Bucket, w/ footed-like base, fitted wire bail handle w/
wooden grip, 6½" H $95.00
Pitcher & Cup, one of two pcs., one covered cup 3½" H,
one pitcher w/ rolled rim & long spout, 3½" H $100.00
Cheese Strainer, w/ round gallery-like foot, pierced bot-
tom, 4" H $50.00
Baby Bottle, w/ hinged lid w/ pewter end, arched tapered
ribbon handle on back, int. tube, 3⅞" H $230.00
Cookie Cutters, one of three, lrg. chicken w/ sq. back & 3
sm. holes 6½" W, one hex. shape w/ inset tulips & diamond
shaped leaves, crimped rim, one heart-shaped w/ inset
tulips $370.00
Covered Kettle, w/ applied arched handles, 7½" diam.,
6½" H, ex. lid $130.00

Row 4, Left to Right

Shaker & Measure, one of two, one sugar or flour shaker
w/ pierced top, 5¼" H, one long-handled measure, cylindrical shape w/ broad rounded spout, w/ handle $200.00
Nutmeg Graters, one of two, one Pat. Nov. 18, 1897 w/
sm. wood knob on top, 5¼" L, one Pat'd. Sept. 3, 1867,
maple w/ paddle-shaped wheel, 4" L $525.00
Baby Rattle, drum shape, whistle handle, 5½" L . . .$240.00
Cup & Pitcher, one of two pcs., one covered cup w/
tapered ribbon handle on side & hinged lid, 3½" H, one
pitcher w/ straight sides, tapered spout, 3½" H . . .$100.00

A-PA Mar. 1999   Horst Auctioneers

Row 1, Left to Right

Storage Jar, Redware w/ cover, chips, 8½" H $50.00
Mixing Bowl, Redware, PA or Shenandoah Valley w/ ear
shaped handles on sides, int. flaking, chips, 6¼" H, 15½"
diam. $550.00
Plate, Redware, PA or Shenandoah Valley w/ coggle dec.
rim, crack, 10½" diam. $140.00

Row 2, Left to Right

Pie Plates, two Redware, one w/ orange-brown ground, 6½"
diam., one w/ int. glazing resulting in a dk. br. ground w/ mica
flecks, 8¼" diam. $120.00

Row 3, Left to Right

Crock, stoneware w/ dk. br. glazed ground, war, 5¼" H,
7¼" diam. $25.00
Washboard, Redware in wooden frame, nailed const., w/ 5⅝"
sq. Redware panel, 7½" W, 13½" L $550.00
Soap Dish, Redware w/ coggle rim dec., rim chip, 6" x 4"
x 1¼" $550.00

A-OH Nov. 1998   Garth's Auctions

Left to Right

Box, Shaker oval, old natural finish w/ gray sawtooth borders & découpage flowers, finger constructions w/ copper
tacks, age crack in lid, damage, 5⅜" L $143.00
Box, oval, old worn lt. blue repaint, MA, finger const. w/
copper tacks, 4⅝" L $302.50
Box, bentwood, worn orig. polychrome floral dec.,
3¼" L $104.50
Two Pieces, ink well w/ gold stenciled dec. on sponged br.
ground, "S. Sillman...CT", 3½" diam., & a sander w/ yel.
varnish, 2⅞" H $220.00

A-PA Sept. 1998   York Town Auction Inc.

Row 1, Left to Right

Pail, blue & white Graniteware pail w/ matching lid, sm.
swirl, blk. rim, blk. tab ears, wood bale, matching lid int.,
white pail int., some chips, 7½" H, 7" diam. $130.00
Dinner Carrier, white Graniteware, 5 stack, cobalt rims,
metal frame w/ wood handle, minor lid rim flake . .$85.00

Row 2, Left to Right

Pan, Graniteware, multi-colored swirl in lighter tone, cobalt
rim, white int., 12" x 7½" x 2⅛" deep $400.00
Berry Pail, red & white Graniteware, sm. swirl w/
white int., wood bale handle & flat ears, 6⅛" diam., 4¾" H,
chips $2,200.00
Milk Can, emerald gr. Graniteware w/ matching cover, lg.
swirl w/ wood bale handle, enameled wire ears, blk. rim,
white int., base chip, 9¼" H, 4¾" diam. $1,250.00

A-OH Jan. 1999   Garth's Auctions
Baker's Lamp, tin, added wooden handle, two spout whale oil burner, lt. rust, 13" L overall $165.00
Mold, bronze two pc. for pewter spoons, dk. patina, 8¾" L . . .$110.00
Mold, redware fish shaped, br. glaze, hairline, 12¼" L $220.00
Mold, pottery heart shaped, clear glaze is cream colored w/ br. slip initials & date "1853", hairlines, 7¾" L $440.00
Dipper, curly maple paddle, round bowl, worn finish, 10" L $93.50
Dough Scrapers, two wrt. iron, 2½" & 4¼" W $71.50
Ember Tongs, wrt. iron, spring loaded w/ good detail & attached pipe tamper, 17¼" L $550.00
Treen Spoon, mah. w/ chip carved detail & worn patina, 13¾" L ....N/S
Dipper, hardwood w/ natural burl growth bowl, lt. natural finish w/ some curl in handle, 12½" L .$148.50
Butterprint, cow & tree, hardwood w/ weathered finish & age cracks, turned one pc. handle, 4¼" L .$132.00

A-OH Jan. 1999   Garth's Auctions

Row 1, Left to Right

Two Pieces, blue & white graniteware, bowl 6¾" diam., container w/ wire bale, chips & no lid, 3¼" diam. $99.00
Mustard, w/ spoon & lid, graniteware, br. & white w/ blk. mkd. "G.B.N.", minor chips, 3½" H .$220.00
Coffee Pot, sm. mauve & white w/ nickel plated lid, wooden handle, chips, 5¼" H $192.50
Chamberstick, blue & white graniteware, chips, 5¼" diam. $192.50
Bowls, two blue & white graniteware, 6" diam., 2¾" H $77.00

Row 2, Left to Right

Bowl, blk. & white graniteware, wear & pitting, 10¼" diam., 4½" H . .$55.00
Bowls, three blue & white graniteware of various sizes, chips, 5¼", 5¾" & 7¼" diam. $137.50
Washbowl, blue & white graniteware, chips, 11½" diam., 3¼" H .$55.00

A-OH Nov. 1998   Garth's Auctions
Utensil Rack, wrt. iron w/ scrolled detail, 26" L $247.50

Left to Right

Utensils, three, wrt. iron & brass mkd. "F.B.S. Canton", skimmer & two dippers $220.00
Utensils, four wrt. iron & brass, two dippers, skimmer & spatula, not matching, 10¾" to 15" L $220.00
Utensils, four wrt. iron & brass, two dippers, skimmer & sm. dipper, not matching, 11¾" to 18½" L . . .$192.50
Utensils, four wrt. iron & brass, spatula, dipper & two sm. bowl dippers, not matching, 14" to 18" L . . .$198.00
Utensils, four wrt. iron & brass, spatula, dipper, skimmer & sm. bowl dipper, not matching, 15" to 18¾" L $220.00

A-OH Jan. 1999   Garth's Auctions

Row 1, Left to Right

Mortar & Pestle, burl, ref., pestle has brass tip, 4⅛" H $121.00
Lamps, one Skater's lamp w/ brass base & mismatched tin top, blue globe cracked, repr., 7" H, one hanging lamp w/ wire frame, tin shade, clear glass font & chimney, brass kerosene burner, repr., 16" H $192.50
Compote, burl, ash w/ good figure, old shellac finish, 9" diam., 4¼" H $797.50
Candlestick, wrt. iron spiral, tripod base w/ penny feet, push up missing, crooked, 6½" H $121.00
Mortar & Pestle, sm. turned, hardwood w/ old worn finish, 4⅜" H $110.00

Row 2, Left to Right

Two Pieces, burl mortar w/ old soft finish & age cracks, 5½" H, & a treen funnel w/ old finish, 6½" H . .$110.00
Bowl, burl, ref. ash, filled & repr. crack, 12" diam., 5¼" H $330.00
Two Pieces, cylindrical treen canteen w/ old red, 7" H, & redware mortar w/ spotted brownish amber glaze wear, 4½" H $55.00

A-OH Nov. 1998   Garth's Auctions
Dry Sink, hutch top, poplar w/ worn olive over cream over blue over blk. paint, repl. latches, drawers from reused wood, 54¼" W, 22¼" D, 54" H $2,035.00
Knife Box, poplar w/ orig. red & gr. paint, scalloped edges & cut out handle in divider, 9" x 13" $330.00
Knife Box, pine w/ old red repaint, cut out handle in divider, 8½" x 15½" $110.00
Knife Box, walnut & poplar w/ gr. repaint, 7¼" x 12½" $82.50
Sugar Bucket, wooden stave const., bluish gray paint, copper tacks & swivel handle, lid rim loose, 12" diam., 11¾" H $330.00
Box, gray paint over gr., lapped seams w/ rusted nails, 8" diam. $220.00
Bowl, wooden, bluish gr. stain on ext., int. has honest wear, 16" diam., 5½" H $247.50
Sugar Bucket, wooden stave const., old gray repaint, copper tacks & swivel handle, 9½" diam., 10" H . .$247.50
Box, round, old gray repaint, lapped seams, lid branded "H. Steele", 6¾" diam. $302.50
Jug, ovoid stoneware, strap handle & impr. label "Lyons", cobalt blue brushed flower & "2", 15½" H .$82.50

A-OH Nov. 1998   Garth's Auctions

Row 1, Left to Right

Pease Jars, three, old varnish, one has chips on lid, 2⅛" to 2¾" H$605.00
Treen Jars, three, two are Pease, old varnish, 2½" to 3⅞" H $330.00

Row 2, Left to Right

Pease Jars, two, old varnish, 3¾" to 4½" H $660.00
Treen Jar, pear shaped, old blk. paint w/ gilded foliage, 4¾" H $192.50
Two Pieces, treen pear w/ hinged lid, 5¾" H, & Pease sewing caddy w/ compartments & repl. pincushion, 5¾" H $990.00

A-MA Oct. 1998   Skinner, Inc.
Lamp, Handel Obverse painted daffodil, glass shade handpainted w/ gr. & yel. blossoms, mkd. "Handel 5648", three-socket gilt-metal tripartite base, old repaint on metal base, 23½" H, 18" Diam. $10,350.00

A-MA Oct. 1998   Skinner, Inc.
Table Lamp, leaded glass, shade of lapped marquise motifs in white & amber slag glass, geometric shaped border in gr. & cream, patinated metal floral & foliate base, 25½" H, 17¾" Diam. $460.00

A-MA Oct. 1998   Skinner, Inc.
Candlestick, Tiffany Favrile three-part electrolier, swirled rib gold irid. holder fitted w/ gilt-metal & Favrile glass candle supporting gold irid. shade, both inscribed "L.C.T. Favrile", 12' H $1,150.00

A-MA Oct. 1998   Skinner, Inc.
Table Lamp, leaded glass, attrib. to Charles Lamb, ca. 1920, shade ground of caramel & cream slag glass segments w/ borders of pink slag glass blossoms & gr. leaves, base of dk. patinated metal, 22" H, 18" Diam. $1,725.00

A-MA Oct. 1998   Skinner, Inc.
Table Lamp, Art Nouveau, eight ribbed glass panels w/ floral motif in red & amber, patinated metal base, impr. "Bradley & Hubbard Mfg.", 24" H, 17" Diam. $517.50

A-MA Oct. 1998   Skinner, Inc.
Table Lamp, Tiffany, spun bronze tobacco leaf & ribbed base w/ inserted electrified oil-lamp sgn. "Tiffany Studios 25907", peacock feather leaded glass shade, 18½" H $6,325.00

A-MA Oct. 1998   Skinner, Inc.
Table Lamp, leaded glass, shade w/ twelve panels of streaked pink, blue, & gr., slag glass w/ border band of pink & gr. rectangles, stepped base of patinated metal, cracks, 22" H, 16½" Diam. $690.00

A-MA Oct. 1998   Skinner, Inc.
Desk Lamp, Tiffany Favrile glass & bronze desk lamp, gilt bronze base w/ Zodiac patt., adjust. swing-socket frame for gold Favrile domed shade, stamped "Tiffany Studios NY 661', chip under rim, 13' H, 6" Diam. $3,220.00

A-MA Oct. 1998   Skinner, Inc.
Table Lamp, Dirk Van Erp, copper & mica, orig. med. patina, shade panels set in riveted hammered copper frame w/ rolled edge, four curving arms riveted to neck, impr. windmill in rectangle, "D'Arcy Gaw" over "Dirk Van Erp", dent to shade cap, 16½" H, 16½" Diam. $20,700.00

A-MA Mar. 1999   Skinner, Inc.
Table Lamp, rev. painted, attrib to Pairpoint, dec. w/ floral & urn motifs on tan ground, metal urn form standard, chips to top rim, 23½" H, 17" diam. $2,300.00

A-MA Sept. 1998   Craftsman Auctions
Table Lamp, Roycroft, w/ Steuben shade, sgn., 14" x 8" w/ hammered copper base $9,000.00

A-MA Sept. 1998   Craftsman Auctions
Table Lamp, Handel, slag glass shade w/ overlay leaf border, 24" x 18" diam. $4,400.00

A-MA Mar. 1999   Skinner, Inc.
Boudoir Lamp, Pairpoint, domed shade flaring to rim, dec. w/ autumn leafed trees amid grass, flowers & butterflies on frosted glass ground, 14½" H, 9¾" diam. $1,265.00

A-MA Sept. 1998   Craftsman Auctions
Table Lamp, Handel, w/ Hampshire base, shade sgn., 21" x 17" diam. $3,750.00

A-MA Sept. 1998   Craftsman Auctions
Table Lamp, w/ swirling leaf shade, sgn. Tiffany, base has heat cracks, ...$6,500.00

A-MA Mar. 1999   Skinner, Inc.
Boudoir Lamp, Pairpoint "Roses", Portsmouth shade, reverse-painted roses on pale yel. & white ground, blk. enamel outline on ext., bronzed metal base, shade mkd. "The Pairpoint Corp'n,", 14" H $2,070.00

A-MA Sept. 1998   Craftsman Auctions
Table Lamp, Miller, slag glass shade w/ overlay of morning glories, 24" x 18" diam. $1,000.00

A-MA Sept. 1998   Craftsman Auctions
Table Lamp, w/ fiery dichrotitic glass shade, one cracked panel, sgn. Tiffany $9,200.00

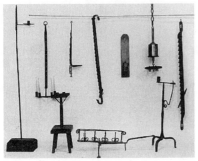

A-OH Jan. 1999   Garth's Auctions

Lighting Stand, wrt. iron, rush lt. holder w/ candle holder counter weight, wooden base, 48" H .$770.00
Candelabra, wrt. iron, hanging four candle sockets w/ adjustable trammel, adjusts from 27" L $1,760.00
Hanging Lamp, wrt. iron on adjustable sawtooth trammel, grease lamp has pear shaped pan, adjusts from 20" L $495.00
Sawtooth Trammel, wrt. iron, adjusts from 32" L $137.50
Candle Sconce, pine w/ worn patina, sq. nails hold socket to back, 15¾" H $159.50
Brass Clock Jack, cast iron wheel w/ hooks for roasting meat, has key, 16" H $275.00
Sawtooth Trammel, wrt. iron, old dk. patina, adjusts from 39" L $522.50
Lighting Stand, pine base w/ red branded "B. Hoyt", tin top w/ two candle sockets, repr., 19½" H . . .$330.00
Toaster, wrt. iron, penny feet, tooled detail w/ twisting & scrolled work, repr., 16½" W, 19" L $330.00
Lighting Stand, wrt. iron, tripod base, tooled stem w/ candle socket & spring clamp, 24" H $577.50

A-MD Sept. 1998   Richard Opfer Auctioneering, Inc.

Lithophane Lamp, 5 colored panes, all w/ people, amethyst to clear font on brass column & marble base, 16" H $950.00

A-OH Sept. 1998   Garth's Auctions

Row 1, Left to Right

Betty Lamp, wrt. iron w/ chicken finial, hanger & pick, pitted, 7¼" H $660.00
Betty Lamp, wrt. iron w/ cast chicken finial, hanger & pick, pitted, 6½" H $605.00
Betty Lamp, wrt. iron, no pick, 4¼" H $55.00
Betty Lamp, wrt. iron w/ brass chicken finial, pitted lid & finial replacements, arm brazed, no pick, 4" H $192.50

Row 2, Left to RightLeawood BoldItalic

Student Lamp, brass mini. soldered repr., 12¼" H $440.00
Candle Holders, two similar wrt. iron w/ spiral push ups, turned wooden bases have age cracks, 10" & 10½" H $412.50
Goffering Iron & Pan, wrt. & cast iron goffering iron w/ holder, not a matched set, 14" L, & wrt. iron ember pan, wooden handle damaged, 13" L $82.50
Rush Light Holder, wrt. iron w/ candle socket counterweight, repl. wooden base, 13" H $71.50

A-MA Sept. 1998   Craftsman Auctions

Lamp, by Gustav Stickley, hammered copper w/ wicker shade, 23" x 18" $4,000.00

A-OH July 1998   Garth's Auctions

Row 1, Left to Right

Peg Lamp, tin petti-coat w/ dk. br. japanning, 6" H, plus whale oil burner $88.00
Inkwell, wooden w/ worn orig. br. sponging w/ gold stenciled eagle, paper label "...Chester, Con.", two glass inserts, one loose, 4¾" diam. $165.00
Chamber Lamp, tin, font has center wick support, 7" H $165.00
Chamber Lamp, brass, whale oil burner w/ hinged snuffer, 6½" H $137.50
Lighting, four pcs., tin conical factory torch w/ cast iron handle, 6" H, cast iron miner's lamp w/ chicken finial, no hanger, 6¼" H, & two wrt. iron grease lamps, pans have four spouts, 3¾" & 6" H plus hanger $357.50

Row 2, Left to Right

Lamp, w/ drum shaped font, brass collar & burner, mismatched tin chimney w/ mica window, repr., 11½" H $137.50
Lamps, two primitive hanging, tin, 7¾" H plus hanger & wrt. iron, 2½" H plus twisted hanger $247.50
Lamp, Fr. brass w/ single spout wick advance knob, 5⅜" H plus burner, 10¾" overall $93.50
Lamp, tin kerosene w/ side chimney, no burner lt. rust & slightly battered, 9½" H $82.50
Lantern, brass w/ kerosene burner, pressed glass globe mkd. "H.B. & H", tin bottom has sm. holes & bottom edge of globe is chipped, 9½" H $192.50

A-MA Aug. 1998   Robert C. Eldred Co., Inc.

Table Lamp, white-cut-to-clear, electrified, gilt dec. w/ brass & marble stepped base, 25" H $935.00

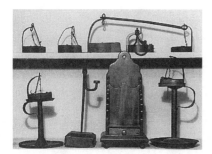

A-OH Jan. 1999   Garth's Auctions

Row 1, Left to Right

Betty Lamp, wrt. iron, hinged lid, wick support missing, chain wick pick, 4" H plus hanger 137.50
Betty Lamp, wrt. iron, hinged lid, chain wick pick, 4" H, plus repl. hanger $137.50
Betty Lamp, wrt. iron, hinged lid, rusted, hanger & wick pick missing, 5¼" H $49.50
Betty Lamp, cast & wrt. iron, brass heart finial & hinged lid w/ heart thumb latch, chain wick pic, 4" H plus hanger $385.00
Betty Lamp, wrt. iron, hinged lid, chain wick pick, 4" H plus long one hook hanger $165.00

Row 2, Left to Right

Betty Lamp, tin plus stand w/ crimped edge on saucer base & shelf, hinged lid, twisted wire hanger & chain wick pick, dk. finish, 10½" H plus hanger $198.00
Rush Light Holder, wrt. iron, wooden base has worm holes & age crack, 13" H $165.00
Writing Box, mah. w/ old finish, turned feet, cut outs for holding quills, sm. dovetailed drawer in base, pine secondary wood, KY, reprs., 14" H .$495.00
Betty Lamp, & stand, tin, hinged lid, hanger & wick pick, some rust, sm. hole, repr., 13" H $385.00

A-MD Sept. 1998   Richard Opfer
Auctioneering, Inc.

Left to Right

Lithophane Lamp, 5 various scenes, cut ruby enamel to clear font on milk glass base, 16" H $925.00
Lithophane Lamp, 6 portraits of woman, stamped brass marquee, ruby flashed font, brass column & marble base, 18" H $950.00

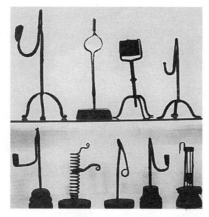

A-MD Sept. 1998   Richard Opfer
Auctioneering, Inc.

Row 1, Left to Right

Lighting Devices, lot of 2, early wrt. iron rush or candle holder, slight rust, 14¼" H, & W wrt. iron squeeze-type rush holder, 13" H $300.00
Lighting Devices, lot of 2, early wrt. iron elevating & pivoting candle holder, penny feet, 10" H, & wrt. iron rush holder, penny footed, 10" H . .$475.00

Row 2, Left to Right

Lighting Devices, lot of 2, early twisted wrt. iron rush & candleholder, 10½" H, & wrt. iron spring-type candleholder w/ twist to elevate candle, 8½" H $325.00
Lighting Devices, lot of 3, early wrt. iron rush holder, 9" H, one twisted wrt. iron rush & candle holder, 9½" H, & one tin elevating candleholder, 8½" H $400.00

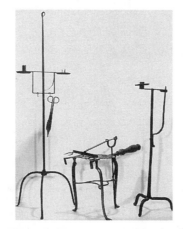

A-MD Sept. 1998   Richard Opfer
Auctioneering, Inc.

Left to Right

Lighting Device, early wrt. iron floor candlestick & rush lt., penny feet, stamped S. L. R., 40" H $1,150.00
Pot Stand & Roaster, brass & wrt. iron, apple wood handle, open work pot stand, slipper feet, 19" L .$525.00
Candlestick, floor, wrt. iron, 27" H $250.00

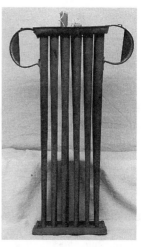

A-PA Mar. 1999   Horst Auctioneers
Candlemold, made for molding 12 tall church candles, 21¼" H . .$650.00

A-NH Aug. 1998   Northeast Auctions

Left to Right

Lighting Device, wrt. iron & brass, two lt. stand on tripod base w/ penny feet, 52" H $2,500.00
Candle Holder, Am., wooden two-light, 37" H $900.00

A-MA Sept. 1998   Craftsman Auctions
Lamp, Grueby, w/ sgn. Bigelow-Kinnard Shade, Grueby paper label, 3 minor lines in glass, 23" x 16" $6,250.00

A-MD Sept. 1998   Richard Opfer Auctioneering, Inc.

Left to Right

Oil Lamp, mini., cobalt, stamped "Fire Fly", w/ stars, 6¼" H $400

Oil Lamp, mini., milk glass & clear alt. star & chevron design, base of shade broken, 6" H $170.00

Oil Lamp, milk glass & clear, stamped "Little Jim" $220.00

Oil Lamp, mini., lt. blue & clear, burner needs re-cementing, 6¾" H $275.00

Oil Lamp, mini., lt. blue & clear, alt. star & chevron design, 6½" H $350.00

Oil Lamp, mini., lt. blue & clear, no burner or shade, 4½" H $210.00

A-MA Feb. 1999   Skinner, Inc.

Lanterns

Row 1, Left to Right

Fixed Globe, w/ pierced tin frame, 19th C., 11½" H $115.00

Bulging Lighthouse-form, w/ fixed globe, pierced tin frame, Am., mid-19th C., 10" H $632.50

Globe Onion Lantern, one of two w/ pierced tin frames, Am., mid-19th C., w/ fixed metal fonts, 9½" H $920.00

Nautical Lantern, w/ fixed globe in brass frame, mid-19th C., mkd. "Wm. Porter Maker", brass font, minor imper., 13" H $517.50

Row 2, Left to Right

Dark Room Lamp, w/ hanger & wire, one of three, painted blk. w/ stenciled dec., burner mkd. "Deitz Convex", 8½"H $258.75

Globe Onion Lantern, w/ fixed globe & pierced tin frame, 9½" H $920.00

Tin Lanterns, 19th C., "beaver hat" campaign torch w/ brass spout & two painted candle lanterns, one shown, w/ cutout star lens $690.00

A-MA Feb. 1999   Skinner, Inc.

Lanterns

Row 1, Left to Right

Pear-Shaped Globe Lantern, fixed, w/ pierced brass frame & wire guards, Am., mid-19th C., base lacking font, 12" H $345.00

Bulging Lighthouse-form, w/ fixed globe in painted pierced tin frame, Am., mid-19th C., minor paint loss, 9½" H $488.75

Vertical Ribbed Lantern, w/ fixed globe in pierced tin frame, Am., mid-19th C., mkd. "H & J Sangster Pat. June 1841", wire guards missing, 10" H $690.00

Thumbprint Patt. Globe, w/ pierced brass frame, late 19th C., minor imper., 13½" H $1,035.00

Lighthouse-form Globe, fixed w/ two panels in pierced tin frame, one of two, paint loss, 9½" H $632.50

Row 2, Left to Right

Shoulder Lantern, painted tin & glass, mid-19th C., w/ spout burner, 6" H $230.00

Lamp Jugs, 1 of 5, emb. glass & tin kerosene oil lamp jugs, late 19th C., 2 w/ gr. paint, 3 colorless w/ corrosion, 11½" H $862.50

Onion Globe Lanterns, pr. fixed w/ pierced tin frames, one font missing burner, corrosion, 8" H $805.00

Lunch Box Lantern, tin, mid-19th C., mkd. "Pat. Oct. 3, 1871 & Dec. 18, 1877", res., 10½" H $315.00

Lighthouse Form, w/ fixed globe, 1 of 2, 19th C., pierced tin frame, 9½" H $632.50

A-MA Feb. 1999   Skinner, Inc.

Left to Right

Nautical Lanterns, port & starboard, pr. w/ fixed globes, Am., 19th C., port lantern painted blk., globe mkd. Perkins 8, brass font; starboard lantern w/ mold blown globe & brass font, mkd. "The National Marine Lamp Co.", paint loss & minor corrosion, 13½" & 14¼" H $805.00

Canal Boat Bow Lantern, tin, mid-19th C., mkd. "Sherwoods Ltd., BHAM", 20" H; accompanying lantern is a tin steersman's horn, 43" L $1,150.00

Barn Lantern, painted tin, 19th C., no reflector, hanging loop missing, corrosion, paint loss, 19" H $345.00

A-PA Sept. 1998　　　　　　　　　　　　　Pook & Pook Inc.

Row 1, Left to Right

Porringers, one pewter double handled, reprs., 9¾" diam., together w/ 2nd porringer w/ Boardman type handle, 7" diam. $125.00

Coffee Pots, two pewter, one w/ touch of James Putnam, MA, 7½" H, one unmkd., 11¾" H, both w/ reprs. . .$175.00

Plates, pewter one w/ eagle touch of Blakslee Barnes, PA, 7⅞" diam. & one w/ eagle touch of Thomas Danforth, PA, 7¾" diam. $400.00

Plates, one pewter w/ touch of Gershom Jones, RI, 8¼" diam., w/ five other pewter plates, 8" diam. $275.00

Pitchers, pewter lidded, one syrup w/ touch of Homan & Co., CI, mid 19th C., 6¼" H, together 9½" H $200.00

Porringers, pewter, one w/ eagle touch of Samuel Hamlin, RI, sm. crack, together w/ 2 others impr. 'IG' $650.00

Teapot, pewter pear-shaped by Eben Smith, MA, retains label "Orig. John B. Kerfoot Collection" $1,300.00

Row 2, Left to Right

Coffee Pot, pewter by Rufus Dunham, MA, ca. 1761, 11½" H $900.00

Misc., open salt pewter, late 18th C., w/ pewter whale oil lamp, 6" H, 2 beakers, 2¾" H & sm. measure $250.00

Lamp, pewter attrib. to Roswell Gleason, MA $500.00

Coffee Pot, touch of Roswell Gleason, 11½" H . . .$325.00

Tankard, pewter lidded, late 19th C., 7½" H $300.00

Candlesticks, pr. pewter, touch of Henry Hopper, NY, mid 19th C., w/ removable bobeches, 10" H $900.00

Coffee Pot, pewter, bearing touch of Allen Porter, MA, 10½" H $300.00

A-MA Oct. 1998　　　　　　　　　　　　　　　Skinner, Inc.

Toby Jug, w/ Eng. hallmark Chester 1903, 3⅜" H . .$287.50

Bottle Labels, group of seven, four shown, Eng. & Am., silver $460.00

A-NH Aug. 1998　　　　　　　　　　　　　Northeast Auctions

Plates, two, CT, pewter, touchmark of John & William Danforth, 8" diam. $400.00

Porringers, pr., Boston pewter, Crown-handle, w/ I.C. mark w/ larger example w/ S.G. mark $450.00

A-NH Aug. 1998　　　　　　　　　　　　　Northeast Auctions

Left to Right

Andirons, pr. Am. bronze & iron, Dachshunds, 14" H . . .$900.00

Andirons, pr. of cast-iron Owls, 15" H $300.00

Andirons, pr. of George Washington cast-iron, 21" H . . .$300.00

Andirons, pr. Am. cast-iron brownies, mkd. C. Freihofer, 16" H $1,000.00

A-PA Feb. 1999　　　　　　　　　　　　　Pook & Pook Inc.

Row 1, Left to Right

Coffee Pot, PA, tin toleware, ca. 1830, hinged lid, dec. w/ red, gr. & blue & yel. floral & leaf motifs on blk. ground, 10½" H $1,800.00

Container, tin toleware, ca. 1830, hinged lid & wire handle, dec. w/ red & yel. flowers & gr. leaves on blk. ground, 6" H, 9" W $225.00

Document Box, PA, tin toleware, dec. ca. 1830 w/ red & yel. on blk. reserve, 4½" H, 8⅛" W $200.00

Warmer, tin toleware, ca. 1860, 9¼" H $475.00

Coffee Pot, tin toleware dec. ca. 1825, 10¾" H $1,200.00

Coffee Pot, PA, tin toleware, ca. 1825, dec. in red, yel. & gr. floral on blk. ground, 8¾" H $950.00

A-MA Oct. 1998　　　　　　　　　　　　　　　Skinner, Inc.

Copper Molds, 12, Euro., 19th C., assorted sizes$1,495.00

A-IA July 1998   Jackson's

Row 1, Left to Right

945-Candle Lamp, tin, 19th C., emb. #2, missing socket & one pane, 12" H $33.00

946-Tea Kettle, dovetailed copper, early 19th C., swivel handle & wood lid finial, mkd. "W. Heyser Chambersburg", 7" H $99.00

947-Coffee Boiler, copper, 19th C., folded seams, brass bail handle, 13" H $132.00

948-Coffee Pot, granite & pewter in gray, hinged lid w/ wood finial, 10" H $121.00

949-Coffee Boiler, granite, blk. & white fine mottled, granite lid w/ bail handle, minor bruises, 11" H . .$44.00

950-Lantern, Paul Revere, ca. 1820, pierced tin w/ hinged door, 15" H $88.00

951-Whale Oil Lamp, 19th C., orig. burner, chip on base, 10½" H .$88.00

952-Candle Holder, early brass refractory, double lt., spring loaded, mkd. "F.A. Walker & Co., Boston", 11" H $93.50

953-Whale Oil Lamps, pr., 1-3 thumbprint & block, hexagonal, one w/ wheelcut designs, 10" H . .$165.00

Row 2, Left to Right

954-Betty Lamp, 19th C., copper & tin, on T base, 9" H $99.00

955-Coffee Pot, copper, 19th C., wood handle & finial, 8" H . . .$55.00

956-Candle Lantern, tin, 19th C., "Universal Lantern, PA", 14" H .$82.50

957-Candle Lantern, tin, early 19th C., 4 glass panes, 11" H $110.00

958-Pot, brass, 19th C., wrt. iron handle, 12" diam. $44.00

959-Whale Oil Lamp, brass, early 19th C., turned brass, 9" H . . .$110.00

960-Lantern, Paul Revere, ca. 1800 w/ pierced wheel & star designs, 13" H $121.00

961-Candle Holders, pr. brass, spring loaded w/ shade fitters, zinc bottom 11" H $132.00

962-Sauce Pan, dovetailed copper, 19th C., copper handle, 6½" diam. $83.50

963-Tallgrass Lamp, wrt. iron, early 19th C., tripod base, adjustable pan w/ pick, 22" H $231.00

Row 3, Left to Right

964-Kerosene Lamp, amber swirled stem & base w/ opal. ribbed font, 9" H $275.00

965-Sauce Pan, copper, dovetailed, 19th C. w/ copper handle plus later copper skillet, 6" diam. 433.00

966-Spout Lamp, early pewter, hinged lid, flared base & ring handle, 9" H $104.50

967-Coffee Pot, copper, brass lid w/ pewter finial, pewter spout & wood handle, mkd. "Hanning Bowman", 7" H $49.50

968-Spout Lamp, early pewter, hinged lit w/ pick, flared base & ring handle, 9" H $121.00

969-Pan, dovetailed copper, early 19th C., copper handle, 10" diam. $82.50

970-Pan, dovetailed copper, early 19th C., copper handle, 10" diam. $71.50

971-Fuel Mix Can, Maytag, tin w/ litho trademark, 8" H $71.50

972-Saucepan, early copper, lidded, dovetailed w/ wrt. iron handles, 6" diam. $60.50

973-Candle Stand, brass, 19th C., spring loaded w/ shade fitter, sand weighted base, 10" H $38.50

974-Bucket, granite ware covered, tin lid & finial, bail handle, 5" H $49.50

975-Work Lamp, kerosene, 10" H $38.50

976-Lamp, mini. milk glass w/ emb. florals, 4"H $16.50

Row 4, Left to Right

977-Candle Stand, brass, iron weighted with pierced base, 8" H $82.50

978-Samavar, Russian brass, 7½" H $16.50

979-Chamber Stick, pewter push-up, 19th C., rich dk. patina, mkd. "EWN", 4" H $38.50

980-Railroad Lantern, tin, "Chicago & North Western Railway" by Adlake, 9" H $77.00

981-Chamber Stick, early tin w/ porcelain socket, 7" L $38.50

982-Angle Lamp, hanging, double burner, nickel plate emb. brass, orig. shades, early elec. conversion, 18" H $247.50

983-Tea Kettle, granite & pewter, br. & white, fine mottle w/ pewter trim & copper base, 7" H $165.00

984-Tea Kettle, granite & pewter, gray, medium mottle w/ pewter trim, bruises, mkd. "Granite Ironware", 7" H $165.00

985-Match Holder, tin advertising for "Earlville Hatchery", IA, 5" H $16.50

986-Chimney Heater, tin lamp, 19th C., for warming liquids, 9½" H .$49.50

987-Spout Lamp, early brass, 19th C., cone shape pedestal, brass pick, 10½" H $88.00

988-Grease Lamp, early cast brass w/ drip pan, 7" H $77.00

989-Candle Mold, 5 tin, 19th C., 10½" H $55.00

990-Spout Lamp, early pewter, 19th C., hinged lid, wrt. iron pick, 6" H $132.00

991-Betty Lamp, early copper & iron, hinged lid, wrt. iron hanger & pick, 5" H $137.50

992-Miner's Lamp, brass carbide, "The Baldwin Lamp", 4" H $44.00

993-Miner's Lamp, brass carbide, "Guys Dropper", adjust. flame, by Shanklin Mfg. Co., 4" H $33.00

Row 5, Left to Right

994-Bed Warmer, brass, 19th C., pierced box & hinged lid, 20" L $110.00

995-Bed Warmer, early wood & tin, ca. 1830, pierced tin in hickory frame work, bail handle, 9" L $165.00

996-Candle Stick, turned brass, w/ beaded drip pan, 6" H, plus two 3 lt. brass candelabra w/ lion stems, not pictured $16.50

997-Mining lamps, pr. wrt. iron, "Stickers", for candles, 19th C., impr. "Varney", 9" L $77.00

998-Spice Mill, iron & brass, "Kenrick & Sons", 6" H $165.00

999-Fire Stand, wrt. iron, 19th C., 3 legged, 8½" diam. $44.00

1000-Betty Lamp, fine iron, early 19th C., w/ hanger, brass rooster finial, 9" H $231.00

1001-Candle Sticks, pr. brass, 19th C., w/ twisted stems, 8" H $88.00

1002-Match Holder, cast iron, 19th C., wall mount w/ grape & scroll dec., 9" H $88.00

1003-Pan Lamp, early brass, 19th C., w/ iron trammel, plus hanger, 6" H $154.00

1004-Clockwork Spit, brass, 19th C., impr. Salter & Co., 13" L . .$77.00

1005-Match Holder, tin advertising for "Farmers Co-op", Anita, IA, blue enamel, 6" H $33.00

1006-Pot Stand, wrt. iron, swivel grate top on handle, 24" L $44.00

1007-Candle Stick, bronze, 19th C., of a winged lion, finely detailed w/ gilt remnants, 10" H $99.00

1008-Betty Lamp, iron, early 19th C., wrt. iron bail & hook, 7" H .$33.00

1009-Sad Iron, cast, 19th C., emb. mono. & shield, 6½" L $33.00

A-MA Oct. 1998   Skinner, Inc.

Candlesticks, Pricket, brass, late 17th early 18th C., possibly Dutch, dents & reprs., 15" H $805.00
Basin, on pedestal, brass, 7¾" H, 10¼" diam. $488.75

A-MA Aug. 1998   Robert C. Eldred Co., Inc.

Tavern Measures, pewter , assembled set of 6, Eng. $247.50

A-MA Aug. 1998   Robert C. Eldred Co., Inc.

Pewter

Coffee Pot, w/ horizontal banding, mkd. "F. Porter No. I Westbrook", Freeman Porter, MA, 1835-1860's, 11" H $154.00
Coffee Pot, w/ banded dec., mark of Roswell Gleason of Dorchester MA, 1822-1871, 11" H $352.00
Coffee Pot, w/ banded dec., unmkd., 10½" H $132.00
Coffee Pot, w/ banded dec., unmkd., 11" $121.00
Coffee Pot, banded w/ engr. dec., attrib. to Israel Trask, Beverly MA, ca. 1852, 11" H $220.00

A-MA Aug. 1998   Robert C. Eldred Co., Inc.

American Pewter

Candlesticks, w/ push-up, unmkd., 8½" H $319.00
Teapot, conical-form, mkd. Morey & Ober, 2 Boston, 7" H $110.00
Candlesticks, in baluster form, 10" H $231.00
Teapot, mkd. Morey & Ober, Boston, ca. 1852, 7½" H $88.00
Candlesticks, w/ push-up in baluster form, 8" H .$308.00

A-MA Aug. 1998   Robert C. Eldred Co., Inc.

Pewter Whale Oil Lamps

Lamp, w/ double wick burner, mark of Smith & Co., 6" H $77.00
Chamberstick, w/ double wick burner, mark of Smith & Co., 7½" H $187.00
Lamp, w/ double wick burner, mark of Samuel Rust, NYC, 1837-1845, 6¾" H $154.00
Lamp, w/ double wick burner, 8" H $165.00
Lamp, gimbaled, 7½" H $145.00
Lamps, two w/ double wick burners, mark of Smith & Co., 6" & 5½" H $154.00
Chamberstick, gimbaled w/ double wick burner, 4" H $110.00

A-MA Aug. 1998   Robert C. Eldred Co., Inc.

Pewter

Whale Oil Lamp, by Roswell Gleason, 9¼" H $187.00
Inkwell, Eng. w/ glass insert, 6¾" H $77.00
Norman Flagon, w/ fleur-de-lis on lid & base, twin acorn thumb-piece, 7½" H $66.00
Funnel, 6½" H $55.00
Porringer, Am., 6" L $44.00
Candlestick, w/ beaded dec. & push-up, 10" H . .$132.00

A-MA Aug. 1998   Robert C. Eldred Co., Inc.

American Pewter

Whale Oil Lamps, pr., mark of Roswell Gleason, 6" H $297.00
Teapot, mark of William Calder, Providence, RI, 1817-1856, 9" H $467.50
Candlesticks, in baluster form, 7" H $330.00
Teapot, mark of J.W. Cahill, 7" H $121.00
Teapot, mark of Boardman & Co., NYC, ca. 1825-1827, 7" H $451.00
Teapot, unmkd., pear-form, 7" H $110.00
Porringer, unmkd., 5" diam. $77.00
Porringer, w/ pierced handle, 8" L $187.00
Porringer, mkd. "L.S." w/ crown handle, 6" L $77.00

A-MA Oct. 1998   Skinner, Inc.

Row 1
Thimbles, four stone-top, two J.S. & S. Birmingham, Eng. $143.75
Rows 2 & 3
Thimbles, 15 Champleve & Cloisonné enameled, nine floral & six figural incl. heads of birds $57.50
Rows 4 & 5
Thimbles, 12 sterling silver, various hallmarks & inscriptions, some damage $287.50

A-MA Oct. 1998   Skinner, Inc.

Rows 1 & 2
Thimbles, 10 gold, 3 Simon Bros. Co., 1 French, many monogrammed, some damaged $258.75
Rows 3 & 4
Thimbles, 11 glass, 2 w/ paperweight tops, 6 colorless glass w/ applied dec., 1 figural boot, 2 opaque . . .$115.00

A-MA Oct. 1998   Skinner, Inc.

Row 1
Thimbles, 3 sterling silver, all w/ cherub motif incl. a Gabler, W. Ger. . . .$109.25

Row 2
Thimbles, seven w/ animal & insect motif $57.50

Row 3
Bodkins, set of five, sterling silver, floral motif $258.75

A-MA Oct. 1998   Skinner, Inc.

Row 1, Left to Right
Thimbles, five gold, two scenic, two floral, one dated 1866 ......$230.00

Thimbles, five gold, bird & floral, three scenic & one plain $517.50

Row 2
Thimbles, ten sterling, Wait, Thresher Co., Katcham & McDougall,

Simons Bros. Co., etc., each w/ applied gold bands $488.75

Row 3
Thimbles, five gold, scenic, floral & plain $258.75

A-MA Oct. 1998   Skinner, Inc.

Row 1
Thimbles, 11 sterling & coin silver, ten Mexican, one sgn. "Taxco", one

set w/ turquoise, one souvenir, etc., & one made in Portugal w/ enameled house & heart motif $115.00

Rows 2 & 3
Thimbles, 16, eleven sterling or coin, five plated $57.50

A-MA Oct. 1998 — Skinner, Inc.

Row 1, Left to Right

Thimble, Vermeil "Washington", Simon Bros. Co., re-issue 1891, the Capitol & the White House . . .$115.00
Thimble, sterling silver w/ applied reserve "Mount Vernon" $80.50
Thimbles, two porcelain, Spode w/ cupids & Irish Belleek w/ blue bells . . . . .N/S

Thimble, modern Plique & Jour enameled $11.50

Row 2, Left to Right

Thimble, brass "Peeps", "Golf: Fashion for Sportswomen," Eng. - No. 187 . . . .$149.50
Thimble, Simons Bros. Co. sterling silver, "A Stitch in Time Saves Nine." $316.25

Thimble, Katcham & McDougall sterling silver, three birds & foliage, faceted rim, "Pat. Sep.20.81," $172.50
Thimble, Gabler silver, applied cherub face & six stars $316.25
Thimbles, Simons Bros. Co. sterling silver, "Chicago World's Columbian Exposition" $230.00
Thimbles, Katcham & McDougall sterling silver, "Souvenir of St. Augustine, Florida $143.75

Row 3, Left to Right

Thimbles, 13 sterling silver, many Stern Bros., one dated 1909, incl. floral scenic & paneled bands . . . . .N/S
Thimble, sterling silver, Lilies of the Valley, mkd. in apex "B.N.Co." $120.75
Thimble, Simons Bros. Co. sterling silver, "Grape" $92.00
Thimble, sterling silver, w/ cabbage rose & leaf band, sgn. w/"S" .$109.25
Thimbles, Waite, Thresher Co., sterling silver, bluebird motif $253.00
Thimbles, Simons Bros. Co. sterling silver, three views of Washington D.C. $402.50

Row 4, Left to Right

Thimble, Simons Bros. Co., "Golden Spike", mkd. "St. Louis World's Fair, 1904" $747.50
Thimble, Waite, Thresher Co. sterling silver, birds in foliage $230.00
Thimbles, Stern Bros. sterling silver, femme-fleur-swimmer $603.75
Thimble, enameled sterling silver, David Anderson, Oslo, ca. 1930, bas relief basse-taille white lilies w/ gr. leaves, moonstone top $285.75
Thimble, Georg Jensen-type sterling silver, Denmark, amethyst tone top $230.00

Row 5, Left to Right

Sewing Kit, Basse-taille enameled sterling silver, royal blue w/ a yellow-green stone top . . . . .N/S
Thimbles, gold in maroon leather case, mid-19th C., alt. plain & scrolled panels, mkd. "M.T." $287.50

A-MA Oct. 1998 — Skinner, Inc.
Thimbles, 12 misc., vermeil Art Nouveau head, six pointed star, scenic band, half-moon band, two silver-plated, one brass $201.25

A-PA Aug. 1998   Hunt Auctions Inc.
Jersey, 1939 Carl Hubbel NY Giants, Spalding cream colored shirt in orig. condition, "39" chain stitched in red on back of jersey tail, few sm. usage holes & some age toning . . .$10,450.00

A-PA Aug. 1998   Hunt Auctions Inc.
Jersey, Willie Mays 1972 SF Giants, Spalding jersey & pants w/ all proper taggings incl. name, year, & sizes, also incl. belt & socks which are unmkd., lt. overall usage   . .$7,700.00

A-PA Aug. 1998   Hunt Auctions Inc.

Left to Right
Hat, Skeeter Webb game worn Cleveland Indians, ca. 1938-39, retains orig. tag & chain stitched name $209.00
Hat, Cleveland Indians prof. model, ca. 1965-68, shows little if any game usage, retains orig. label $55.00
Hat, Houston Colt 45's game worn hat, ca. 1962-64, navy blue w/ ora. trim hat, retains orig. McAullife label $220.00

A-PA Aug. 1998   Hunt Auctions Inc.
Jersey, Lou Gehrig NY Yankees road jersey, ca. 1927-1928, used by Gehrig during height of Yankee dynasty, Spalding grey flannel jersey retains orig. collar tag next to which "Gehrig" is chain stitched, no. "46" chain stitched at bottom of front of jersey, button repl. & fading due to age $88,000.00

A-PA Aug. 1998   Hunt Auctions Inc.
Jersey, "Brooklyn Aces" baseball, ca. 1930-40's, white flannel shirt w/ royal blue satin lettering & numbers, "Circle Athletic Co." tag inside collar .$522.50

A-PA Aug. 1998   Hunt Auctions Inc.
Helmet & Jersey, Chuck Conerly game used, ca. 1960, w/ photo of Horace & Tom McMahon, helmet made by Riddell & is mkd. Kra-Lite on back, orig. int. leather pads & strapping w/ "NY" & "42" decals, jersey is road version, tagged Wilson size 48 . . . .$9,350.00

A-PA Aug. 1998   Hunt Auctions Inc.
Jacket, PA Phillies warm-up, ca. 1948-51, Wilson model, lightweight gray jacket w/ red trim & logo patch $1,925.00

A-PA Aug. 1998   Hunt Auctions Inc.
Jersey, Stan Musial 1963 home uniform, mellow cream color w/ orig. embroidery, buttons & tagging, tag on tail is chain stitched "Musial 63" $11,550.00

A-PA Aug. 1998   Hunt Auctions Inc.
Jersey, Michael Jordan game worn, 1984 ACC Charity All-Star game, blue w/ white lining, 100% Nylon knot jersey, made by Merrygarden Athletic Wear $20,900.00

A-PA Aug. 1998   Hunt Auctions Inc.

Glove, Brooks Robinson game used glove, ca. 1963-64, Rawlings Stan Musial model, orig. tag., wear, fully broken in pocket, autographed four times on back of finger pockets $7,700.00

A-PA Aug. 1998   Hunt Auctions Inc.

Left to Right

Glove, crescent pad fielder's glove, ca. 1890-1900 by Victor, RHT, nice orig. surface $522.50
Mitt, crescent pad baseman's, ca. 1890, RHT, loose grommet back $412.50

A-PA Aug. 1998   Hunt Auctions Inc.

Glove, D&M fielder's glove in its' orig. box, ca. 1920's, RHT, lt. overall usage, orig. tag & button $412.50
Mitt, Goldsmith model baseman's, ca. 1910, unused glove, retains orig. tag, buckle back, & all int. markings $660.00

A-PA Aug. 1998   Hunt Auctions Inc.

Left to Right

Mitt, Paddy Livingston game used, ca. 1910, autographed on int. $1,100.00
Glove, James M. Burns game used full web workman's style, ca. 1888-1891, retains orig. button back strap patch & button $1,210.00

A-PA Aug. 1998   Hunt Auctions Inc.

Left to Right

Baseball, 1941 NY Yankees team autographed, 28 sig. incl. DiMaggio, Dickey, Ruffling, Rizzuto, Gomez, on Reach "Lively League" ball, clear coated $605.00
Baseball, Honus Wagner single sig. ca. 1947, sgn. "To Tom from J. Honus Wagner Pirates 47", Amateur League baseball, lt. soiling, fading .$1,100.00

A-PA Aug. 1998   Hunt Auctions Inc.

Row 1, Left to Right

Baseball, Babe Ruth single sig., ca. 1925-27, blk. & red stitched " J&G Official League" ball $2,860.00
Baseball, 1929 Chicago White Sox team autographed w/ Babe Ruth & Lou Gehrig & 18 other players, Barnard A.L. ball w/ lt. toning $1,375.00

A-PA Aug. 1998   Hunt Auctions Inc.

Left to Right

Baseball, 1956 N.Y. Giants team autographed, 27 sig. on a clear coated Harridge A.L. ball $110.00
Baseball, Hall of Famer autographed, ca. 1960's, Cronin A.L., has lt. toning, sgn. by 11 players incl. Foxx, Sisler, Hornsby, Jackie Robinson, Grove, Feller, Cronin, slight stains .$2,530.00
Baseball, Hall of Famer/Old Timer autographed, ca. 1960's, Cronin A.L., sgn. by 20 players incl. Foxx, DiMaggio, Grove, Medwick, L. Waner, Terry, age toning $209.00

A-PA Aug. 1998   Hunt Auctions Inc.

Left to Right

Baseball, 1955 Chicago White Sox team autographed, Harridge A.L., clear coated, sgn. by 31 players incl. Fox, Minoso, Kell, has lt. stampings $88.00
Baseball, 1956 N.Y. Yankees & Brooklyn Dodgers team ball lot, incl. one ball from each of the teams who traded World's Championships from 1955 to 1956, Harridge A.L. ball w/ clear coated & sgn. by 21 players incl. Robinson, Campanella, Hodges, Alston, Reese $1,265.00

A-PA Aug. 1998   Hunt Auctions Inc.

Baseball, Babe Ruth & Lou Gehrig auto. home run baseball, ca. 1924-1927, clear coated $2,090.00

A-PA Aug. 1998   Hunt Auctions Inc.

Baseball, Babe Ruth single signature w/ Ruth autographed picture ca. 1934, ball is a Spading "Official League" red & blue stitched ball that is lt. cream color $9,350.00

A-PA Aug. 1998   Hunt Auctions Inc.
Golf Balls, lot of 14, incl. 1899 Spalding "White" & "Baby Dimple" $385.00

A-PA Aug. 1998   Hunt Auctions Inc.
Footballs, lot of three, team autographed, ca. 1960's, N.Y. Giants w/ 27 ink sigs, N.Y. Giants w/ 29 ink sigs, & 1964 Syracuse Univ. team ball, w/ numerous sigs $77.00

A-PA Aug. 1998   Hunt Auctions Inc.
Bat, Eddie Collins decal, ca. 1915, L. Slugger 40 E.C. model, -1/4" cut off barrel end, is 31¾" L 242.00

A-PA Aug. 1998   Hunt Auctions Inc.
Bat, Brooks Robinson game used bat autographed by the 1964 Orioles, wear incl. handle crack, 34½" L $1,045.00
Bat, Gene Woodling game used bat autographed by the 1962 Orioles, 36" L $319.00

A-PA Aug. 1998   Hunt Auctions Inc.
Bat, Bob Boyd game used bat, ca. 1956-60, cracked $313.50
Bat, Rocky Colavito game used bat, ca. 1955-59, 35" L $962.50

A-PA Aug. 1998   Hunt Auctions Inc.
Bat, Joe Ginsberg game used bat, ca. 1956-60, cracked, measure 34½" L $231.00

A-PA Aug. 1998   Hunt Auctions Inc.
Bat, Boog Powell game used bat, ca. 1961-67, w/ handle crack, 35" L $495.00
Bat, Brooks Robinson game used bat, ca. 1955-60, bold markings & autographed by Brooks, 34" L . .$1,595.00

A-PA Aug. 1998   Hunt Auctions Inc.
Bats, lot of two, St. Louis Cardinals, unused, ca. 1964, mkd. New Era on int. band $321.00

A-PA Aug. 1998   Hunt Auctions Inc.
Bat, Stan Musial game used, ca. 1961-64, slender handled 34½" $2,920.00

A-PA Aug. 1998   Hunt Auctions Inc.
Turnstile, Shibe Park, orig. cast iron revolving gate retaining several period coats of paint, overall wear incl. paint chipping, rusting, 40" H x 30" W $3,960.00

A-PA Aug. 1998   Hunt Auctions Inc.
Stadium Chair, "Smoke Piedmont" ad, ca. 1910, cobalt blue double sided enamel sign w/ emb. white lettering, 30" H $275.00

A-PA Aug. 1998   Hunt Auctions Inc.
Metal Sign, Shibe Park w/ admission pricing w/ yel. lettering on a gr. ground, paint chipping & crazing, 18" x 51" $110.00
Metal Sign, Shibe Park football "reserved seats", yel. lettering on gr. ground, retains 70% of orig. paint, 18" x 60" $110.00

A-PA Aug. 1998   Hunt Auctions Inc.
Matchsafe, baseball figural, ca. 1890-1900, retains orig. silver plating, 2¾" H $1,650.00

A-PA Aug. 1998   Hunt Auctions Inc.
Photograph, 1934 tour of Japan Am. All-Star team, team in uniform seated & standing incl. Ruth (Mgr.), Gehrig, Foxx, Berg, Gomez, orig. frame, 6" x 9" $5,500.00

A-PA Aug. 1998   Hunt Auctions Inc.
Stadium Seats, pr., Polo Grounds, vintage iron & wood, retain a portion of their orig. paint, dryness to wooden seat planks $1,072.50

A-PA Aug. 1998   Hunt Auctions Inc.
Baseball Rack, metal A-frame, ca. 1939, hods six bats on each side, retains orig. framework & metal ad. sign at top which has 95% of orig. paint $1,870.00

A-PA Aug. 1998   Hunt Auctions Inc.
Patch & Tag, Cincinnati Reds, ca. 1939, patch is blue w/ applied red logo & lettering $187.00
Ticket Stubs, log of four 1940 World Series ticket stubs, one each for Game #'s 1, 2, 6 & 7 at Cincinnati, all have rain check stub $385.00

A-PA Aug. 1998   Hunt Auctions Inc.
Top to Bottom
Pennant, PA Phillies ca 1940's $660.00
Pennants, lot of two, PA Phillies, ca. 1950's $357.50
Pennant, PA Athletics, ca. 1930's, purple w/ yel. lettering, matted & framed, overall wear $319.00

A-PA Aug. 1998   Hunt Auctions Inc.
Top to Bottom
Pennant, 1958 World Series, clean blue w/ players names on banners, faint center crease $154.00
Pennant, 1967 St. Louis Cardinals, N.L. Champions w/ Roger Maris $165.00
Pennant, 1966 A.L. Champions Baltimore Orioles, bold ora. & blk. color, age holes $88.00
Pennant, 1959 Chicago White Sox A.L. Champs $143.00

A-PA Aug. 1998   Hunt Auctions Inc.
Top to Bottom
Pennant, St. Louis Browns, ca. 1930-40's $49.50
Pennant, Brooklyn Dodgers "Ebbets Field" ca. 1930-40's, sm. portion of point missing $143.00
Pennant, 1940's Washington Nationals $143.00

A-PA Aug. 1998   Hunt Auctions Inc.
Top to Bottom
Pennant, Baltimore Orioles, ca. 1950-60's $66.00
Pennant, 1956 World Series Dodgers vs. Yankees, color fading & frayed point $154.00
Pennant, 1955 World Series Dodgers World Championship year, good color, tassels intact $907.50

A-PA Aug. 1998   Hunt Auctions Inc.
Baseball Pins, lot of five, incl. Phila. Blue Jays & Babe Ruth $275.00

A-PA Aug. 1998   Hunt Auctions Inc.

Row 1, Top to Bottom

Baseball Pins, shield shape ca. 1890-1910, positional designations in blk. print, missing pin posts, 1¾" W $407.00

Row 2, Top to Bottom

Babe Ruth Pieces, lot of 3, celluloid counter, celluloid scorer w/ color lithographic baseball scene & 1/2" pin, ca. 1900, 3" H . .$1,485.00

A-PA Aug. 1998   Hunt Auctions Inc.

Row 1, Left to Right

Nodder, 1960's Baltimore Orioles , gold base, fresh color & gloss, sm. chip $55.00

Milk Jar, Bechtel's, ca. 1960 w/ baseball graphic, clear glass w/ red lettering, retains orig. cardboard lid 5" H $49.50

Row 2, Left to Right

Milk Jar, Collin's, ca. 1950 w/ baseball graphic, amber glass w/white detail, 9" H $93.50

Stein, porcelain, unmkd. stein w/ relief dec. body picturing baseball scene, figural handle & lid finial ca. 1970-80's, 9" H $77.00

A-PA Aug. 1998   Hunt Auctions Inc.

Row 1, Left to Right

Press Pins, lot of two World Series, 1949 NY Yankees & 1951 NY Yankees both by Dieges & Clust $352.00

Press Pin, 1952 Brooklyn Dodgers World Series, enameled Bum retains orig. paper backing, by Dieges & Clust $319.00

Row 2, Left to Right

Press Pins, lot of two, Brooklyn Dodgers World Series, incl. 1956 tie bar pin, 1956 pin has some scratching $550.00

A-PA Aug. 1998   Hunt Auctions Inc.

Row 1, Left to Right

Pin, Am. League, sterling silver w/ A.L. symbol on front, by Dieges & Clust $165.00

Press Pin, 1939 NY Yankees World Series, from ex-player Stan Baumgartner, slight chipping .$264.00

Press Pin, 1938 NY Yankees World Series, red, white & blue enamel, by Dieges & Clust $253.00

Row 2, Left to Right

Press Pins, pr., 1936 World Series, one Yankee & one Giant, both by Dieges & Clust $467.50

Press Pin, 1926 NY Yankees World Series, red, white & blue enamel, by Dieges & Clust $495.00

A-PA Aug. 1998   Hunt Auctions Inc.

Award Pendant, 1924 Washington Senators World Series, presented to Joe Martina (Oyster Joe) . . .$5,885.00

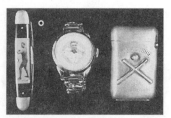

A-PA Aug. 1998   Hunt Auctions Inc.

Row 1, Left to Right

Pen Knife, ca. 1900, pictures Jess Williard in boxing stance, kids pic on verso, 3¼" L $209.00

Wristwatch, Babe Ruth by Exacta Time Co., top condition, 100% orig. incl. metal band, group of four watches $440.00

Matchsafe, 1891, silverplated pc. w/ emb. bats & ball & enameled Princeton flag on rev. $687.50

A-PA Aug. 1998   Hunt Auctions Inc.

Left to Right

Display, Kessler's Whiskey football player ad statue, ca. 1960's, compo. player in early football suit, repr. crack in base, 47" H $264.00

Statue, cigar store hand carved baseball player, ca. 1960-70, early style batsman, age cracking, 58" H $605.00

A-PA Aug. 1998   Hunt Auctions Inc.

Mickey Mantle Misc., incl. 1962 sports champ. record, auto. 1956 Sport Mag., 1958 Sports Council folder & pamphlets & 1962 Baseball board game $253.00

A-PA Aug. 1998　　　Hunt Auctions Inc.
Poster, 1911 Goldsmith Ad, pictures 10 of the era's greatest players endorsing products, incl. Honus Wagner, Lajoie, Mathewson, Johnson, Collins & Ty Cobb, 12" x 19" $1,155.00

A-PA Aug. 1998　　　Hunt Auctions Inc.
Poster, Milt Neil artwork from Cincinnati Classic baseball card show, auto. by all of the pictured players, 27 total sig. incl. DiMaggio, Mantle, B. Martin, Rose, Dandridge, Durocher, Conland & Muhammad Ali . .$852.50

A-PA Aug. 1998　　　Hunt Auctions Inc.
Baseball Card, 1908, Christy Mathewson, well centered w/ vibrant colors, slight wear to each corner $440.00

A-PA Aug. 1998　　　Hunt Auctions Inc.
Row 1, Left to Right
Baseball Card, 1908, Eddie Collins $99.00
Baseball Card, 1908, John Evers $99.00
Baseball Card, 1908, Chief Bender $121.00

A-PA Aug. 1998　　　Hunt Auctions Inc.
Row 1, Left to Right
Baseball Card, 1954 Bowman Mickey Mantle #65 . . . .$302.50
Baseball Card, 1954 Ted Williams #66, well centered w/ lt. wear to each corner, good color, faint blemish to back $1,045.00

Row 2
Baseball Card, 1955 Topps Sandy Koufax rookie #123, well centered w/ orig. gloss & colors $522.50

A-PA Aug. 1998　　　Hunt Auctions Inc.
Row 1, Left to Right
Baseball Card, 1941 Play Ball, Jimmie Foxx #13 . . . .$110.00
Baseball Card, 1941 Play Ball, Carl Hubbell #6 . . . .$132.00

A-PA Aug. 1998　　　Hunt Auctions Inc.
Baseball Card, 1941 Play Ball, Ted Williams #14, w/ bold colors, clean back, centered to left $385.00
Baseball Card, 1941 Play Ball, Hank Greenberg #18 . . . .$99.00

A-PA Aug. 1998　　　Hunt Auctions Inc.
Ad, Dizzy Dean on cardboard stock, promoting Sat. Daily News, 10¾" x 13¾" $132.00
Ad, Tom Lasorda pictured in Montreal uniform in Montreal newspaper on cardboard stock, 11" x 17" . . .$110.00

A-PA Aug. 1998　　　Hunt Auctions Inc.
Row 1
Baseball Card, 1912 T-202, Mathewson/Fletcher $110.00

Row 2, Left to Right
Baseball Card, 1912 T-207 John McGraw $121.00
Baseball Card, 1911 Sporting Life M116, Fred Clarke $82.50

A-PA Aug. 1998   Hunt Auctions Inc.

Row 1, Left to Right

Baseball Cards, lot of 3, 1911 T-205 HOF'ers: McGraw, Wallace & Speaker $143.00

Row 2, Left to Right

Baseball Card, 1909-11, T-206 Fred Clark, off center, Piedmont back $99.00
Baseball Card, 1909-11, T-206 Cy Young, Sw. Cap. back $187.00
Baseball Card, 1909-11, T-206 John McGraw, Piedmont back $176.00

A-PA Aug. 1998   Hunt Auctions Inc.

Left to Right

Baseball Card, 1940 Play Ball, Jimmie Foxx #133 . .$88.00
Baseball Card, 1940 Play Ball, "Shoeless Joe" Jackson #225 . . . . .N/S
Baseball Card, 1940 Play Ball, Christy Mathewson #175 . . . .$143.00

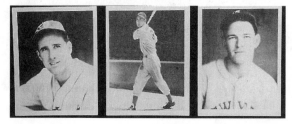

A-PA Aug. 1998   Hunt Auctions Inc.

Left to Right

Baseball Card, 1939 Play Ball, Hank Greenberg #56 . . . .$99.00
Baseball Card, 1939 Ted Williams rookie #92, his first Play Ball card, slight wear to corners, clean back $687.50
Baseball Card, 1939 Play Ball, Mell Ott #51, fairly sharp corners, perfect photo registry, clean back $143.00

A-PA Aug. 1998   Hunt Auctions Inc.

Row 1, Left to Right

Baseball Card, 1909-11, T-206 Rube Waddell, Piedmont back $110.00
Baseball Card, 1909-11, T-206 Christy Mathewson, Piedmont back $374.00
Baseball Card, 1909-11, T-206 Roger Breshahan, Piedmont back $60.50

Row 2, Left to Right

Baseball Card, 1909-11, T-206 Miller Huggins, Piedmont back $88.00
Baseball Card, 1909-11, T-206 Rube Marquard, Piedmont back $176.00
Baseball Card, 1909-11, T-206 Ty Cobb, Sw. Cap. back, two line creases $352.00

A-PA Aug. 1998   Hunt Auctions Inc.

Left to Right

Baseball Card, 1909-11, T-206 Christy Mathewson, Piedmont back, surface wrinkle $176.00
Baseball Cards, lot of 3, 1909-11, T-206 HOF'er portrait variation cards, Lajoie, Brown & Wallace, all have Piedmont backs $165.00

A-PA Aug. 1998   Hunt Auctions Inc.

Left to Right

Baseball Card, 1909-11, T-206 Willie Keeler, Piedmont back $220.00

Baseball Card, 1909-11, T-206 Ty Cobb, Piedmont back, well centered, orig. color $990.00

Baseball Card, 1909-11, T-206 Ty Cobb, Piedmont back, slight wrinkling $797.50

Baseball Card, 1909-11, T-206 Joe Tinker, Sw. Cap. back $176.00

A-PA Aug. 1998   Hunt Auctions Inc.

Baseball Cards, lot of ten 1909-11 T-206, minor league, incl. McGinnity, Donlin, Lentz, Pelty, all have Old Mill or Piedmont backs $165.00

A-PA Aug. 1998   Hunt Auctions Inc.

Baseball Cards, lot of 32, 1909-11 T-206, fine condition grades, incl. Jacklitsch, Carrigan, Bates, Lipe, Piedmont backs $715.00

A-PA Aug. 1998   Hunt Auctions Inc.

Baseball Cards, lot of 32, 1909-11 T-206, fine condition grades, incl. Beckely (2), Jimmy Collins, Bill Hart, Jimmy Hart, McGinnity, Piedmont backs $1,017.50

A-PA Aug. 1998   Hunt Auctions Inc.

Baseball Card, near complete set of 1909 PA Caramel E95 cards, missing only Eddie Collins, incl. Cobb, Wagner, Mathewson, condition varies $2,200.00

A-PA Aug. 1998   Hunt Auctions Inc.

Sign, John a. Andrews folk art cigar store ad, ca. 1880-90, oil on canvas w/ polychrome dec. and lettering on a white ground, 20" x 49" canvas mounted on orig. pine frame, repairs $7,700.00

Tour of Japan Poster, Broadside of George Kelly 1931, large orig. photograph, overall size 18" x 32" . . .$1,100.00

A-OH Sept. 1998   Garth's Auctions
Coverlet, jacquard two pc. single weave, corners labeled "Samuel Slaybaugh...OH, 1849", red, gr., blue & natural white, minor damage, 76" x 85" $550.00

A-OH Sept. 1998   Garth's Auctions
Quilt, pieced, mosaic w/ pinwheel stars in shades of blue, blk., gr. & yel. on lavender ground, fish scale quilted border, PA, overall wear & some stains & color loss, machine sewn border, 67" x 80" $220.00

A-OH July 1998   Garth's Auctions
Coverlet, jacquard single weave, one pc., floral design w/ star center, deer corners & capital bldg. borders, sewn on fringe loose, minor wear, 66" x 78" $275.00

A-OH Sept. 1998   Garth's Auctions
Quilt, pieced, pinetree, made by Mrs. Mose Miller, OH, shades of blue, gr., blk., br., lavender, etc., worn & faded, sm. tears, machine sewn binding, 72" x 72" $302.50

A-OH July 1998   Garth's Auctions
Coverlet, jacquard double weave two pc., peacock feeding young & Christian & heathen border, dated "1846", blue & natural white, overall edge wear, 68" x 84" $385.00

A-OH July 1998   Garth's Auctions
Quilt, pieced, stars in solid red & gr. calico on white ground, overall age stains w/ some dk. stains, 84" x 84" $1,210.00

A-OH July 1998   Garth's Auctions
Quilt, pieced, bear paw in pink & gr. calico, good color, 90" x 90" .$440.00

A-OH July 1998   Garth's Auctions
Coverlet, jacquard double weave two pc., four rose patt., navy blue & natural white, wear, stains, rebound, 78" x 88" $192.50

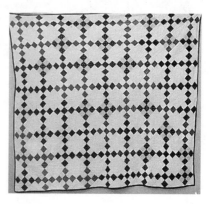

A-OH July 1998   Garth's Auctions
Quilt, pieced, nine patch in blue & white calico, overall wear & some stains, 76" x 84" $247.50

A-ME July 1998   Cyr Auction Co. Inc.
Hooked Rug, w/ Boston Terrier & geo. ground, 23" x 36" $2,250.00

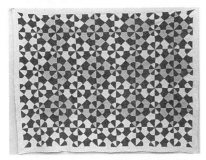

A-OH Sept. 1998   Garth's Auctions
Quilt, pieced, figure ground reversal patt. in yel., blk. & ora., wear, minor stains & sm. holes, 65" x 86" .$165.00

A-PA Mar. 1999   Horst Auctioneers
Coverlets, matched pr., date 1847, sign. John Kachel, wool & linen, woven in dk. blue, red, gr. & natural w/ center seam & rolled hem across top, mint, 82" W x 96" L . . .$6,300.00

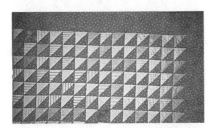

A-PA Mar. 1999   Horst Auctioneers
Quilt, late 19th or early 20th C., Lancaster Co., PA, "Mosaic" patt., red fabric w/ sm. floral pint w/ assorted plain br. striped fabric patches, backing of br. & white fabric w/ sm. pink & white flowers, 7 stitches per inch, 76" W, 82" L, minor stain mark . .$230.00

A-MA Oct. 1998   Skinner, Inc.
Needlework, silk memorial, Am., early 19th C., worked in silk & chenille threads on painted silk ground, dated 1780, unframed, toning, staining & minor fabric loss, 27" x 14½" $1,380.00

A-MA Oct. 1998   Skinner, Inc.
Needlework, family register, MA, early 19th C., chart of family names & dates w/ verses, minor toning & staining, 16 x 16¼" $2,415.00

A-MA Mar. 1999   Davies Auctions
Coverlet, blue & white w/ birds, willow trees & compotes of flowers, eagle corner block mkd. DELHI (NY) dated 1841 . . . .$2,860.00

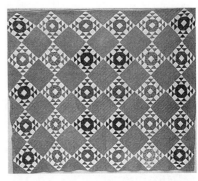

A-OH Aug. 1998   Garth's Auctions
Quilt, crown of thorns patt. in blue & blk. calico on white w/ alt. sq. of olive gr. calico, overall wear, repr. & stains, 74" x 88" $220.00

A-PA Dec. 1998   Pook & Pook Inc.

Row 1, Left to Right

Hooked Rug, pictorial, ca. 1900, 2 roosters, 3' x 1'6" $1,700.00

Hooked Rug, pictorial, ca. 1900, dog w/ colorful floral border, 3'1" x 1'9" $1,300.00

Row 2, Left to Right

Hooked Rug, pictorial, ca. 1900, 2 horse heads, on in bright red, staining, 3' x 1'11" $300.00
Hooked Rug, pictorial, ca. 1900, horse w/ mauve & gr. chain border, 3'1½" x 2'7" $700.00

Row 3, Left to Right

Hooked Rug, folk art, ca. 1900 w/ 2 converging hearts w/ heart border, 3'2½" x 2'1" $900.00
Hooked Rug, pictorial w/ lrg. blk. & br. cat, reprs. & losses, 2'9¼" x 1'7" $200.00

A-OH July 1998   Garth's Auctions
Quilt, pieced, Irish chain in blue white & red calico, wear, rebound, 82" x 82" $220.00

A-OH Sept. 1998   Garth's Auctions
Quilt, applique, stylized floral medallions & swag & flower border in solid red & gr. print, overall wear, some bleached spots in gr., 83" x 86" $495.00

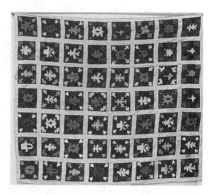

A-OH Aug. 1998   Garth's Auctions
Quilt, pieced blk. & blue wool in goldenrod cotton grid w/ appliqued designs in various fabrics & colors, machine sewn & quilted, applique hand sewn, wear, 66" x 76" . . .$330.00

A-OH Sept. 1998   Garth's Auctions
Rag Rug, hooked, star design in shades of blue, red, gray, blk., gr. & pink, reprs., 17" x 32" $1,155.00

A-OH Sept. 1998   Garth's Auctions
Amish Quilt, sunshine & shadow in multi-colored design in wool, crepe, knit, etc., purple border, made in 1930, moth damage w/ sm. holes in wool & border is fading, 80" x 80" . . .$357.50

A-OH Aug. 1998   Garth's Auctions
Quilt, pieced, lone star patt. in red, med. blue, goldenrod & white, sm. blk. stains & aging, machine sewn binding, 80" x 82" $385.00

A-OH Sept. 1998   Garth's Auctions
Quilt, pieced, blue & white, well quilted, wear, some loose seams & blues vary slightly, 84" x 84" $412.50

A-OH Aug. 1998   Garth's Auctions
Quilt, applique, stylized floral medallions in teal blue, red & burnt ora., minor stains, 86" x 90" $687.50

A-OH Sept. 1998   Garth's Auctions
Quilt, pieced, Fence 'round a field, Holmes County, OH, gr. & goldenrod w/ br. center, minor stains & overall wear, 81" x 82" $302.50

A-MA Feb. 1999   James D. Julia Inc.

Row 1, Left to Right

95-Snuff Mull, Scottish, fine horn, silver top w/ raised thistle motif, lrg. inset cut crystal, 4½" L $650.00

101-Snuff Mull, double Scottish horn, 19th C., brass mounted, 4⅝" L $350.00

97-Snuff Mull, Scottish horn, silver top w/ raised thistle motif & inset cut crystal, 4⅞" L $300.00

102-Snuff Mull, double Scottish horn, 19th C., brass mounted, sm. plaque w/ initials, 5" L $300.00

103-Snuff Mull, Scottish horn, carved animal head w/ inlayed eyes, silver mounted plaque, inscribed "James McDuff Cireff 1844", 3¾" L $700.00

104-Snuff Mull, Scottish horn, carved animal head w/ inlayed eyes, silver mounted, 4½" L $650.00

Row 2, Left to Right

99-Snuff Mull, Scottish horn, brass mounted horn top, 4½" L $125.00

100-Snuff Mull, Scottish horn, 19th C., carved animal head w/ bone or ivory teeth, silver mounted top w/ inlayed pink agate stone, motto "Hold Fast...", 5¾" L $1,050.00

96-Snuff Mull, Scottish horn, silver top w/ raised thistle motif & inset crystal, silver plaque w/ coat of arms, 3¾" L $400.00

98-Snuff Mull, Scottish horn, top w/ silver thistle & crown dec., silver collar inscribed "Sawney Lent the Man his Mull...1815", 5¾" L $375.00

105-Snuff Mull, Scottish horn, silver mounted horn top, plaque w/ owners initials, 5¼" L $400.00

106-Snuff Mull, Scottish horn, silver mounted horn top, plaque w/ owners initials, 4" L $425.00

107-Snuff Mull, Scottish or English horn, late 18th early 19th C., silver mounted w/ initials, 3" L $200.00

Row 3, Left to Right

108-Snuff Mull, three Scottish or English, late 18th or early 19th C., two horn, one pewter, 3" - 3½" L .$275.00

112-Donation Box, Euro. iron multi lock, 18th C., embellished shapes to latches, locks, handle, moldings & turn finials, 11¾" H x 6" L x 6" W $600.00

113-Donation Box, Euro. iron coin, 17th or 18th C., shaped iron strapping w/ similar motifs on top, 11¾" H, 8" diam. $200.00

114-Cigar Mold, Am. wooden, late 19th or early 20th C., 11⅞" L x 4⅞" W $75.00

Row 4, Left to Right

109-Tobacconist Shop Sign, carved wood, in form of pipe, old polychrome dec. over earlier gilding, 68" L $2,000.00

111-Tobacco Store Sign, Euro. tin, paint dec. w/ pipes, playing cards & word "Tobac", iron mounting bracket, 25½" L $1,300.00

110-Tobacco Store Sign, Am. or Euro., tin, old red paint, 31½" L$50.00

115-Snuff Jars, pr., Eng. stoneware w/ tin tops, late 18th C., raised figure of woman, grapevine dec., 9¾" H, 6⅜" diam. $1,000.00

Row 5, Left to Right

116-Brass Box, Middle Eastern, 20th C., 7⅜" x 3⅞" W x 3" H $25.00

117-Box, brass & iron mounted, Asian, prob. Euro. market, 17th-18th C., two drawers under lift top, raised animal & flower dec. on front in brass, iron handle & locking mech., 11" L x 7½" W, 6¼" H $75.00

A-MA Feb. 1999   James D. Julia Inc.

Tobacco Box, German, stamped brass & copper, monarch on top, 18th C., 6¼" L, 2" W $275.00

Tobacco Box, Dutch, brass, engr. w/ animal motifs, 18th C., 6⅛" L, 1¾" W $900.00

Tobacco Box, Dutch, multi metals, engr. on top, dates 1712, 6¼" L x 2" W $725.00

Tobacco Box, Dutch, copper, engr. coach w/ horses, 18th C., 6½" L x 2" W $800.00

Tobacco Box, Dutch, brass & copper, engr. w/ biblical scenes, 18th C., 6⅞" L x 1¾" W $750.00

A-MA Feb. 1999   James D. Julia Inc.

Row 1, Left to Right

Tobacco Box, Dutch, oval, brass, engr. biblical scenes, 18th C., 5" L x 3" W $750.00

Tobacco Box, Dutch, copper & brass, engr. w/ figures & architecture, 18th C., 5" L x 1¾" W $375.00

Tobacco Box, Dutch, oval, brass, engraved w/ domestic scenes, 18th C., 4¾" L x 2¾" W $500.00

Row 2, Left to Right

Tobacco Box, Dutch, oval, brass, engr. biblical scenes, 18th C., 4½" L x 2½" W $300.00

Tobacco Box, Dutch, oval, brass, engr. w/ domestic scenes, 18th C., 5" L x 2¾" W $500.00

A-MA Feb. 1999   James D. Julia Inc.

Tobacco Box, prob. Middle Eastern, brass w/ all over engraving, int. w/ 12 compartments, early 19th C., 6¾" L x 2⅞" W $10.00

A-MA Feb. 1999   James D. Julia Inc.

Row 1, Left to Right

Tobacco Box, Dutch, oval, brass, domestic scenes on top & tobacco theme, 18th C., 5⅛" L x 3" W $1,100.00

Tobacco Box, Dutch, oval, brass, engr. & reticulated domestic scene, removable panel inside top w/ engr. dec., 18th C., 5½" L x 3" W . .$200.00

Row 2, Left to Right

Tobacco Box, Dutch, silver & brass, engr. w/ floral motif & human figures, slide const., 18th C., 5⅛" L x 2¼" W $2,925.00

Tobacco Box, Dutch, oval, brass, repose monarchs on top & cipher, worn banner, dated 1740, 5" L x 3¼" W $150.00

A-MA Feb. 1999   James D. Julia Inc.

Tobacco Strongbox, 17th C., elaborate locking mech., engr. panels, 5¾" W x 3¾" D x 3⅞" H $800.00

A-MA Feb. 1999   James D. Julia Inc.

Tobacco Box, brass w/ hinged top, wire dec., bail handles, 3 compartment int., 2 w/ hinged tops, 19th C., 5" L x 2½" D x 2½" H $20.00

A-MA Feb. 1999   James D. Julia Inc.

Left to Right

Tobacco Box, Dutch, brass & copper, engr. w/ animal motifs, 18th C., 6¼" L x 1⅞" W $450.00

Tobacco Box, English, round, brass, engr. coat of arms on top w/ "Jacob Zeberrer", bottom w/ elephant motif dated 1707, 3¾" diam. $2,000.00

Tobacco Box, Dutch, octagonal, brass, engr. domestic scene, 18th C., 4" L x 3¾" W $600.00

A-MA Feb. 1999   James D. Julia Inc.

Row 1, Left to Right

Snuff Box, Dutch, silver, 19th C., 1⅜" x 1⅝" W $275.00

Snuff Box, English, pewter, 19th C., in form of pistol, 4½" L $300.00

Row 2, Left to Right

Snuff Boxes, English, three cast pewter, 19th C., floral dec., inside labels, 2" to 3" L $70.00

A-MA Feb. 1999   James D. Julia Inc.

Left to Right

Snuff Box, English, cast dec., in form of watch case, floral motifs, 2½" diam. $125.00

Snuff Boxes, English, pr. of oval, pewter, early 19th C., cast dec. on sides, 2½" L $25.00

A-MA Feb. 1999   James D. Julia Inc.

Snuff Box, Euro. paper mache, 19th C., transfer dec., 3¾" diam. . . .$65.00

A-MA Feb. 1999   James D. Julia Inc.

Tobacco Box, Dutch brass & copper, 19th C., w/ engr. railroad engine & tender on lid, 7" L x 2½" $250.00

A-MA Feb. 1999   James D. Julia Inc.

Row 1

Snuff Box, English, cast dec. pewter, floral dec. 2⅞" L x 1½" W . . .$100.00

Row 2

Snuff Boxes, English, lot of 4, cast dec. pewter, round, 19th C., 1⅝" to 2" diam. $100.00

Row 1, Left to Right

Snuff Box, English, pewter, oval cast dec., 19th C., dec. w/ boy w/ dog surrounded w/ foliage, 2" L x 1¼" W $95.00

Snuff Box, English, three, pewter, 19th C., two w/ engr. dec., 2¾" to 2½" L $125.00

Row 2, Left to Right

Snuff Box, English, pewter cast dec., 19th C., reeded top & molded sides, 3½" x 1½" W $120.00

Snuff Box, English, four, pewter cast dec., 19th C., one dated 1836, one engr. "F Stapleton", one w/ horse & chariot dec., 2⅜" to 3" L $125.00

Row 1

Snuff Boxes, English, pr., cast dec. boat shaped, 19th C., floral motifs, 2¾" L x 1⅝" W $50.00

Row 2, Left to Right

Snuff Box, English, pewter cast dec. 19th C., w/ dispensing mech., floral motifs, 3¾" L x 1⅝" W $150.00

Snuff Box, English, round cast dec., portrait of "The Right Honorable Lord Byron", 3⅛" diam. $200.00

Tobacco Box, Dutch brass & copper, 18th C., w/ engr. agri. scenes, 6½" L x 2¼" $250.00

Row 1, Left to Right

Snuff Box, English, cast dec., 19th C., dec. w/ man on horseback on top w/ floral dec., 3⅛" L x 2" W $75.00

Snuff Box, English, cast dec., 19th C., dec. w/ man on horseback w/ floral dec., 2¾" L x 1⅕" W $20.00

Row 2

Snuff Boxes, English, three, cast, 19th C., 3¼" - 2⅝" L $150.00

Row 1, Left to Right

Snuff Box, English, cast dec. pewter, floral dec. 2⅞" L x 1½" W . . .$100.00

Snuff Box, English, cast dec. pewter, 19th C., foliate dec. 3⅛" L x 1½" W $125.00

Row 2, Left to Right

Snuff Boxes, English, two, pewter, 19th C., form of pocket watches, 2¼" diam. $100.00

Snuff Box, English, cast dec., 19th C., foliate dec., 3" L x 1½" W . . .$120.00

Row 1, Left to Right

Brass Snuff Boxes, four Eng., 19th C., three made w/ coins, one a portrait of man, "Keep Your Temper", 1" to 2" diam. $75.00

Snuff Boxes, English, four, pewter, 19th C., two w/ cast dec., 2½" to 3¼" L $95.00

Snuff Boxes, English, four, pewter cast dec., 19th C., 3" to 3½" L .$60.00

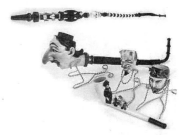

Pipe Stem, early 19th C., ebony horn & carved ivory, numerous inlays & carved applied ornaments, 26" L $475.00

Porcelain Pipe, humorous 19th C., wood stem w/ flexible fabric upper & horn mouthpiece, bowl approx. 2½" H, 10¼" L $475.00

China Pipe, 19th C., glazed polychrome china pipe, humorous, man polishing lady's high boots, bowl 2¼" H, 5¼" L $65.00

China Pipe, two 19th C., glazed polychrome, bearded man w/ gr. cloth hat & Satan w/ horns, both mkd. "Goedwaage", bowl 1¾" H, pipe 5" & 6" L $65.00

Top to Bottom

Opium Pipe, early brass, bow w/ twisted rib design, bowl½" H, 2" diam., overall 11½" L $70.00

Opium Pipe, bowl & mouthpiece brass, iron stem, bowl½" H, 5½" L $15.00

Pipes, two, one early steel pipe, prob. Dutch, 18th C., 1½" H, 13" L, one sm. brass African figural pipe w/ steel stem w/ animal head on bowl, 1¼" H, 6" L $25.00

A-MA Feb. 1999   James D. Julia Inc.

Row 1, Left to Right

Smoking Set, 19th C., mini. carved wood, boar splits to reveal 2 sm. wooden carved boar's heads w/ glass eyes, lrg. boar, 4" L $200.00
Match Safes, lot of five, one depicts baby, one silver or nickel-plated cello, brass combo match safe & cigar nipper, one copper colored in form of owl, one brass zither shaped case, 2½" L to 3" L $625.00

Row 2

Match Safes, lot of 10, most Victorian or turn of c., approx. size, 2½" L $450.00

A-MA Feb. 1999   James D. Julia Inc.

Cigar Holders, two carved meerschaum & amber, one w/ star & crescent moon, 5" L, other in shape of bramble twig, 4½" L $200.00
Cigarette Holder, fine cased ivory, amber & gold, late 19th or early 20th C., 4" L $20.00
Cigar Holder, fine ivory amber & gold color, inlaid wire & gold colored inserts, 3½" L $35.00
Cigarette Holder, carved 19th C., ivory Eskimo, carved in form if sm. totem, approx. 4" L $150.00

A-MA Feb. 1999   James D. Julia Inc.

Pipe Tampers, three Eng. brass, 19th C., one w/ reversible silhouette, one Shakespeare, & one portly figure, 2" to 2¾" L $200.00

A-MA Feb. 1999   James D. Julia Inc.

Left

Lady's Snuff Box, early 19th C., shaped like lady's boot, tiny tack inlays, 3" L $200.00
Box, early 19th C., veneer birdseye maple w/ bronze insert, dated 1780, 5" L x 3½" W $250.00

Right

Card Cases, 2 of five, 19th C., M.O.P., approx. 3½" L to 4" L $155.00

A-MA Feb. 1999   James D. Julia Inc.

Row 1

Card Cases, two 19th C., smaller w/ elaborate relief & dec., inscribed "E.A. Brown", 3" L, other w/ heavy high relief Tibetan or Indian silver, 4" L $300.00

Row 2, Left to Right

Card Cases, lot of two, one in pressed tortoise shell w/ cathedrals & mkd. "York Minster", 3¾" L, one mounted w/ ivory w/ fine gold tacks, 3¾" L $250.00
Calabash, cast iron, shaped in form of pipe, 6" L $20.00

A-MA Feb. 1999   James D. Julia Inc.

Left to Right

Snuff Boxes, two, 19th C., transfer printed dec., 2¼" diam. $65.00
Snuff Box, Euro. paper mache, 19th C., transfer dec., 3½" diam. . . .$25.00
Box, laquered, Russian, early 20th C., monarch on lid, 4¾" L x 3¼" W $50.00

A-MA Feb. 1999   James D. Julia Inc.

Row 1, Left to Right

Misc. Boxes, one of six, 18th to 20th C., 2¾" L to 4½" L $45.00
Snuff Box, Eng. paper mache, 19th C., transfer dec. inscribed top, 2⅞" diam. $85.00
Snuff Box, Fr. paper mache, 19th C., transfer dec. of Bataille de Leuipsic en 1813, 3½" diam. $25.00

Row 2, Left to Right

Tobacco & Pipe Box, Eng. tin, 19th C., stamped dec., human figures spell out "Tobacco", 5" L $75.00
Snuff Box, Eng. turned wood, 19th C., 3½" diam. $35.00

A-MA Feb. 1999   James D. Julia Inc.

Row 1, Left to Right

Snuff Box, Eng. brass, 19th C., stamped portrait, 3" diam. $75.00
Boxes, one of four, Euro. brass & copper, 18th & early 19th C., 3" to 4¾" $250.00

Row 2, Left to Right

Tobacco Boxes, two Eng. brass, 18th C., engr. dec., 3¾" diam. $750.00
Snuff Boxes, 19th C., dial locking system on lids, two are 3½" L & one 2¾" diam. $50.00

A-MA Feb. 1999   James D. Julia Inc.

Snuff Box, Euro. brass & copper, 19th C., reposse top w/ gardening motif, gilded bottom & silvered top, 3¼" L x 2" W $175.00

A-MA Feb. 1999   James D. Julia Inc.

Row 1, *Left to Right*

Snuff Boxes, one of two Eng. paper mache shell shaped, 4" L x 2" W .$50.00
Snuff Box, Eng. brass & hoof tin, 19th C., 4⅞" L $50.00

Row 2, *Left to Right*

Silver Box, Euro., late 18th C., raised rococo dec., 4¼" H $200.00
Snuff Box, Euro. shell & pewter, 3¼" L $200.00
Snuff Box, Eng. 19th C., pen work dec. of ice-skaters, 3⅛" L x 2" W $200.00

A-MA Feb. 1999   James D. Julia Inc.

Row 1, *Left to Right*

Snuff Bottle, Eng. stoneware & pewter, 19th C., raised molded dec. 3½" H $50.00
Writing Case, Eng. brass, early 19th C., 4" L $150.00

Row 2, *Left to Right*

Trinket Box, Euro. slide top, 19th C., silver w/ inlayed dec., 2¾" L x 1¾" W x 1¼" H $50.00
Pipe Tamper, Eng. silvered copper, in shape of Victorian gentleman, 2¾" H $45.00
Misc. Silver, five of eight objects, 19th & 20th C. $450.00

A-MA Feb. 1999   James D. Julia Inc.
Pipes, three clay, 19th C., various dec., 7" L to 9" L $50.00

A-MA Feb. 1999   James D. Julia Inc.

Row 1, *Left to Right*

Match Safe, & lighter, 2nd half of 19th C., both w/ eagle & shield motif, safe 2¾" L, lighter 2" L $200.00
Snuff Box, Ger. brass, late 19th C., stamped view of city of "Koln", 3¼" diam. $55.00

Row 2, *Left to Right*

Snuff Box, Eng. boat shaped brass, 19th C., triple door const., stamped figure of "Paul Pry", 2⅛" L $25.00
Snuff Box, Eng. brass shell shaped, 19th C., engr. "Isaac Briggs's", 3¼" L $35.00
Snuff Box, Eng. brass, 19th C., stamped brass portrait of "M Stowe", 2⅝" L x 2" W $25.00

A-MA Feb. 1999   James D. Julia Inc.

Row 1, *Left to Right*

Snuff Box, Euro. wood, 19th C., pen work of hunting scene on lid, 3⅜" L x 2" W $50.00
Misc. Boxes, three of six Euro. metal & wood, 1" L to 2⅜" L $200.00

Row 2, *Left to Right*

Box, brass, Euro. 19th C., four pivoting compartments, initials "L D", 2½" L $125.00
Containers, three misc. brass, 19th C., one Japanese & two Asian, 2¼" L to 2½" L $55.00

A-MA Feb. 1999   James D. Julia Inc.
Cigar Boxes, two Eng. brass, stamped dec. on top, "... Christmas 1914", 5" L x 3¼" W $40.00

A-MA Feb. 1999   James D. Julia Inc.

Row 1, *Left to Right*

Pipe, 19th C., clay, w/ head of man, 6½" L $105.00
Pipes, lot of four, clay, one of military officer, one of Turks head, a Queen's head, etc., all white clay, some w/ labels, 3½" L to 5" L $35.00

Row 2, *Left to Right*

Pipe Bowls, five figural clay, all are white & never used, largest 3" H $250.00
Pipes, four sm. clay, one has coiled pipe, one w/ fish bowl, one w/ figural head, & one of reclining man, two br., not used, approx. 4" L $175.00

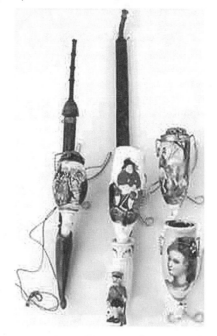

A-MA Feb. 1999   James D. Julia Inc.

Left to Right

Pipe, 19th C. porcelain Bavarian, polychrome scene, titled "Wallensteins Lager", stem is ebony & mouthpiece carved horn, bowl 3½", 12½" L . .$25.00
Pipe, 19th C. porcelain, Staffordshire w/ Ger. figures, bowl w/ polychrome relief, bowl 4" H, 15½" L $50.00
Pipe Bowls, two 19th C. porcelain, one w/o lid depicts woman wearing pearl, one w/ gentleman & two maids in woods, approx. 4" H $50.00

A-IA July 1998   Jackson's

Row 1, Left to Right

819-Toy Stove, child's cast iron & sheet metal, by Kenton, w/ oven and 5 utensils, orig. silver & blue, 12" x 14" T $550.00

820-Boy Doll, jointed hips, br. felt LederHosen, gr. felt shoes, mkd. Kathe Kruse, sm. purse w/ Bavarian crest, sm. blemish on nose, 18" H . .$825.00

821-Princess Diana, bride doll, Danbury Mint, mint in box . . .$77.00

822-Doll Dresser, 2 drawer painted pine w/ mirror, 17" H, 12" W . .$38.50

Row 2, Left to Right

823-Doll, Ger. bisque head, Russian costume, jointed wooden body, leather boots, beaded dress & head-dress, 12" T $148.50

824-Doll, Ger. bisque head, Russian peasant child, wooden jointed body, 8" T $137.50

825-Doll, Ger. Bisque head, Russian costume, leather boots, jointed wood body, beaded headdress $302.50

826-Doll, Ger. bisque head on old kid leather w/ new bisque legs & arms, sleep eye head mkd. "Floradora..." 19" H $66.00

827-Salesman Sample Range, cast iron, Buck's Stove & Range Co. Buck's junior, chrome finish w/ reservoir, minor damage, 19" H, 19" L, 12" W $1,155.00

828-Doll, Ger. bisque head on soft replm. body, sleep eyes, mkd. "Made in Ger.", 24" T $60.50

829-Teddy Bear, gold mohair plush pads on feet & hands, embroidered mouth & nose, button eyes, mohair loss, homemade sweater, 13½" H $93.50

Row 3, Left to Right

830-Doll, Ger. tin head, kid body w/ porcelain forearms to shoulder, head has good paint, 23" H $38.50

831-Hutch, doll size pine, 2 doors below painted gr. & cream, 12" W, 15" H $38.50

832-Doll Heads, Nippon bisque, 3 heads, ca. 1922 . . . .$16.50

833-Doll, Kewpie Nippon bisque, wearing molded sword, kepi & rifle $44.50

834-Dolls, Kewpie Nippon bisque, 2 babies in night shifts, w/ moveable arms, 3½" T $49.50

835-Dolls, Kewpie Nippon all bisque, 2 w/ moveable arms, 4" T $33.00

836-Doll, Kewpie Nippon all bisque, mkd. "baby bud", 4½" T $49.50

837-Doll, Kewpie Nippon all bisque, w/ moveable arms, 6" T $22.00

838-Chein Popeye, in barrel windup, some rust, not working, 5" T $126.50

839-Diorama, Navajo weaver, woman works loom, baby on cradle board, 12" H, 6" W $22.00

840-Doll, Ger. bisque, kid body w/ bisque arms, mkd. "A.M.", w/ sleep eyes & open mouth, 13" H . . .$82.50

841-Pony Bank, cast iron, gold paint, 4½" H $49.50

842-Barbie Doll, w/ blk. trunk & accessories, 3 other pcs. of clothing, ...$550.00

Row 4, Left to Right

843-Doll, Ger. bisque head, gauze dress & hat, papier-mâché body, 9" H $60.50

844-Still Bank, cast iron, "Royal Safe Deposit", brass combination picture of child on 2 sides, orig. paint, 6" H, 5¼" x 4¼" $110.00

845-Kewpie Doll, bisque, moveable arms, blue wing, 7" T $104.50

846-Sewing Machine, child's Singer "Sew Handy", in orig. box, clamp & instruction book, ca. 1955 . . .$115.50

847-Sewing Machine, child's Necchi plastic "Supernova", spool holder missing $44.00

848-Advertising Tops, wood & metal "pluto physic" & "Des Moines Jobbers & Mfg." $11.00

849-Candy Container, automatic, glass w/ tin lid, contains orig. red hots, paint worn, mkd. w/ mfg. names $60.50

850-Sewing Machine, child's Stitchwell, cast iron in original wood-en box with instructions, dec. designs, ...$550.00

851-Candy Container, glass & tin lantern, w/ bail handle 4" T . .$38.50

852-Dolls, Nippon bisque, one fully jointed, one partial jointed, 4½" $22.00

853-Sewing Machine, child's Singer, in orig. box w/ instruction book, ca. 1948 & clamp $192.50

854-Teddy Bear, mohair w/ embroi-dered nose, mouth, toes & hands, felt pads, bead eyes, jointed arms & legs, some mohair missing $412.50

855-Sewing Machine, child's "Baby", cast iron w/ chrome, handle pat. date 1894 . . . .$165.00

856-Plate & Cup, Disney child's featuring 3 little pigs, mkd. Patriot Cinaco $38.50

857-Noisemakers, "Buster Br. Shoes", two, Harris Emery Co., Des Moines, IA $27.50

858-Sewing Machine, child's painted tin, working hand powered $104.50

Row 5, Left to Right

859-Doll, Japanese bisque, flapper type w/ moveable arms, 8" T .$22.00

860-Stove, child's cast iron tin, Kenton Royal, blk. w/ chrome, 6" W, 3½" H $38.50

861-Toy Sad Iron, child's w/ trivet, removable handle $38.50

862-Comb & Brush, child's set in orig. box $11.00

863-Stove, child's cast iron "Baby", 2½" x 3" $16.50

864-Bicycle Bell, chrome plated iron & chromed cyclist's folding cup $825.00

865-Doll, china head, new dress & undergarments, pearl necklace, new legs, 7" H $33.00

866-Beaded Purse, w/ drawstring, closure linen lined w/ heart designs $71.50

867-Hose Box, "Buster Brown", dec. w/ picture, Gold Medal award from Lewis & Clark Centennial Expo. Portland, 1905, 9" x 4" $33.00

868-Doll, China head, new clothing & new legs, old shoulder head, wear-ing necklace, 4½" H $44.00

869-Beaded Bag, silver plated frame & clasp, gr. & red flowers on blue carnival ground, chain miss-ing $71.50

870-Toy Store, child's cast iron & tin, "Eagle", 4 lids, coal bucket, pan, lid lifter & shovel, Hubley, 3½" x 4½" $33.00

871-Mesh Bag, by Whiting Davis Co., enameled w/ wire handled chased gold plated frame $55.00

872-Still Bank, cast iron, U.S. Mail in red on silver, lift lid to deposit coin, ...$44.00

873-Glass Bank, in shape of house, adv. Pittsburgh Paints, "Natures colors ... Save w/ ..., Smooth as glass" $27.50

874-Doll, Ger. tin head, kid body, bisque arms, old clothing, 17" T $16.50

875-Washboard, tin & wood for doll clothes, 6" H $22.00

876-Doll, Nippon all bisque, fully jointed w/ wig & dress, 5½" H $27.50

877-Child's Drum, tin litho w/ animals in parade, bright colors, 6" diam. $33.00

878-Sad Iron, child's w/ trivet, some damage $33.00

A-NH July 1998   Richard W. Withington, Inc.

Row 1, Left to Right

Doll, early compo. body, mkd. Greiner's Improved Pat. Heads, pat. Mar. 30th, 19" H \$525.00

Doll, all wood spring jointed mkd. Schoenhut boy, 21" H \$175.00

Doll, bisque head, blue eyes, open mouth w/ teeth, orig. wig, pierced ears, chipped, jointed compo. body, 22" H \$500.00

Doll, all wood spring jointed mkd. Schoenhut girl, 21" H \$225.00

Doll, all cloth, all orig., unmkd. Lenci type girl, 17" H \$120.00

Row 2, Left to Right

Doll, Parian shoulder head, unmkd., painted/molded short blonde curly hairdo, blk. bow & features, cloth body, parian lower limbs, chips, pitting & discoloration, 17½" H \$120.00

Doll, bisque head, incised "Heubach Koppelsdorf... Ger.", 2 upper teeth, compo. toddler body, 12" H \$650.00

Doll, wax shoulder head doll, unmkd., 19" H \$225.00

Doll, all cloth girl, unmkd., 18" H \$80.00

Doll, parian shoulder head, unmkd., painted molded blonde hairdo, features & shirt, cloth body, bisque lower arms, new bisque lower legs, 17½" H \$175.00

A-NH July 1998   Richard W. Withington, Inc.

Row 1, Left to Right

Doll, Jumeau Madaille D'Or Paris w/ bisque head, bluish-gray glass eyes, pierced ears, jointed compo. straight wrist body, 17" H \$4,700.00

Doll, bisque head, blue glass eyes, pierced ears, jointed compo. straight wrist body, chipped, 20" H \$2,800.00

Doll, bisque head, blue glass eyes, pierced-in ears, jointed compo. straight wrist body, wear & repr., 18½" H .\$650.00

Doll, bisque head, blue glass eyes, jointed compo. straight wrist body, wear, chipped, 15" H \$2,850.00

Row 2, Left to Right

Doll, bisque shoulder & head br. eyes, wig, pierced ears, cloth body, compo. lower limbs, wear, 16" H \$500.00

Doll, bisque head, blue eyes, w/ 2 upper teeth, wig, jointed compo. straight wrist body, cracked, wear, 13½" H \$1,250.00

Doll, bisque head, blue eyes, molded w/ 2 molded upper teeth, wig, jointed compo. body, wear, chipped, 12½" H \$300.00

Doll, all wood, spring jointed carved hair, mkd. Schoenhut Boy, 16½" H \$300.00

A-NH July 1998   Richard W. Withington, Inc.

Row 1, Left to Right

Doll, bisque head, unmkd., blue glass eyes, closed mouth, wig, pierced ears, jointed compo. straight wrist body, chipped, wear, 18" H \$1,900.00

Doll, bisque shoulder head, blue glass eyes, pierced ears, swivel neck, kid body, bisque lower arms, compo. lower legs, wear, chipped, 18" H \$6,400.00

Doll, Depose Jumeau w/ bisque head, br. glass eyes, orig. wig, jointed compo. straight wrist body, needs stringing, agelines, chipped ear, orig. clothes 19" H \$9,400.00

Doll, Simon & Halbig w/ bisque head, sleeping blue eyes, jointed compo. toddler body, wear, 18½" H \$4,000.00

Row 2, Left to Right

Doll, bisque shoulder, pale blue glass eyes, pierced ears, swivel neck, kid body, bisque lower arms, 15" H .\$2,100.00

Doll, Jumeau Medaille D'Or Paris w/ bisque head, br. glass eyes, pierced ears, jointed compo. straight wrist body, chipped, needs stringing, wear, 15" H \$10,100.00

Doll, K & W w/ bisque head, gray glass eyes, 2 upper teeth, jointed compo. toddler body, 15" H \$725.00

Doll, bisque head, sleeping blue eyes, closed mouth, wig, jointed compo. body, wear, 16" H \$2,000.00

A-MA Jan. 1999   Skinner, Inc.

Schoenhut Dolls

Left to Right

Girl, all wood, blue intaglio eyes, blonde mohair wig, orig. suit, 15" H .$488.75
Character Girl, molded & painted face, orig. ash blonde mohair wig, paint loss, orig. cotton suit, 19" H $1,035.00
Character Boy, paint hair, molded & painted features, jointed at shoulders & hips, orig. decals, cotton Russian-style suit, paint wear, 17¼" H $517.50

A-MA Jan. 1999   Skinner, Inc.

Left to Right

Character Boy, Kammer & Reinhardt, bisque head "Hans", ca. 1909, painted intaglio eyes, blonde mohair wig, fully jointed compo. body, some paint chipping on limbs, 19½" H, blue cotton sailor suit $5,175.00
Doll, Bru bisque swivel shoulder head, ca. 1879, blue paperweight eyes, tiny flakes, pierced ears, orig. lt. br. mohair wig, cork pate, kid body & legs, left hand damaged, 17" H $6,612.50

A-MA Jan. 1999   Skinner, Inc.

Left to Right

Doll, Fr. bisque swivel shoulder head, ca. 1870's, blue paperweight eyes, pierced ears, lambskin wig, kid body, bisque hands 14" H $862.50
Doll, bisque shoulder head, blue paperweight eyes, solid pate, wig missing, jointed kid body, bisque hands, 15" H $345.00
Doll, Fr. bisque swivel shoulder head, blue paperweight eyes, shoulders res., orig. blonde mohair wig, cotton body & legs, 21½" H, blue wool two-piece suit $1,265.00
Doll, Belton-type bisque head, late 19th C., gray glass eyes, closed mouth, three holed flat-top closed pate, wig missing, straight wrist compo. body, paint wear, 12½" H $460.00
Doll, bisque socket shoulder head, ca. 1880, molded elaborate blonde hairdo w/ ribbon, stationary blue glass eyes, cloth body, bisque hands & legs missing, 13" H $690.00

A-MA Jan. 1999   Skinner, Inc.
Girl w/ Cart, two wheel automation, ca. 1900, Simon & Halbig bisque head w/ stationary blue glass eyes, dk. blonde mohair wig, cardboard body, compo. legs, bisque hands, clockworks in body, key, wooden stake cart, 14" L $1,092.50

A-MA Jan. 1999   Skinner, Inc.
Doll, lrg. Jumeau porcelain, ca. 1900, blue paperweight eyes, red stamped Tete Juneau mark, dk. blonde Chereox naturals hair wig, straight wrist, compo. body, Bebe Jumeau stamp, damage & restoration, 28"H $3,450.00

A-MD Sept. 1998   Richard Opfer Auctioneering, Inc.

Left to Right

Bru Bisque Doll, circle dot, bisque shoulder plate, kid body & legs, 14" H $8,700.00
Jumeau Bisque Doll, Tete Jumeau #6, jointed body, sm. filled hole, 15" H $3,300.00

A-MA Jan. 1999   Skinner, Inc.
Doll House, lrg., ca. 1900, yel. w/ white trim, two rooms on all 3 floors, glass windows, paneled int. doors, paint wear, slight shingle damage, some glass missing, 60" H, incl. porch 51" W, 23" D $1,610.00

A-NH July 1998   Richard W. Withington, Inc.

Row 1, Left to Right
Doll, "Ger. 3800..." w/ bisque head, br. eyes, w/ teeth, orig. wig, jointed compo. body, wear, 23" H $425.00
Doll, Schoenhut girl, all wood spring jointed, 22" H $275.00
Doll, Ger. Heinrich...Simon & Halbig w/ bisque head, blue eyes, w/ teeth, pierced ears, jointed compo. body, wear, 24" H $400.00
Doll, bisque head, incised "Made in Ger.", br. eyes, w/ teeth, jointed compo. body, wear, 23" H $625.00
Doll, Depose Tete Jumeau w/ bisque head, br. glass eyes, molded mouth, pierced ears, jointed compo. straight wrist body, 18½" H $2,100.00

Row 2, Left to Right
Doll, bisque head, incised "Made in Ger.", br. glass eyes, 2 upper teeth, jointed compo. straight wrist body, 9" H $350.00
Doll, Ger. Handwerck w/ bisque head, incised br. eyes, w/ teeth, orig. wig, pierced ears, jointed compo. body, 17" H $350.00
Doll, Ger. Heinrich...Simon w/ bisque head, br. eyes, w/ teeth, pierced ears, jointed compo. body, 18" H . . .$300.00
Doll, JDK w/ bisque head, incised"Made in Ger.", br. flirty eyes, w/ teeth, jointed compo. body, 18" H $675.00
Doll, bisque head, painted/molded tufts of hair, blue eyes to right, crude compo. toddler body, 10" H $2,300.00

A-MA July 1998   Skinner, Inc.

Left to Right
Doll, Kestner w/ bisque shoulder head, br. paperweight eyes, crazed, orig. blonde mohair wig, kid body & arms, bisque hands, cloth lower legs, 16½" H $517.50
Doll, Kammer & Reinhardt w/ bisque head "Marie", ca. 1909, painted features, impr. K star R 101 mark, orig. blonde mohair wig, fully jointed compo. body, 10" H, w/ orig. costume $1,150.00
Oriental Doll, Simon & Halbig w/ bisque head, br. glass eyes, stuck open, remnants of blk. human hair queue, fully jointed compo. body, needs restringing, 17" H, dressed in silk boy's outfit $1,840.00
Doll, bisque swivel shoulder head, blue paperweight eyes, sm. lot of mostly white garments, remnants of skin wig, new cloth body & legs, bisque hands missing, 15¼" H $4,945.00
Doll, Kestner w/ bisque turned shoulder head, blue glass eyes, orig. blonde mohair wig, jointed kid body, bisque hands, 17¼" H, period pink silk costume, Fr. kid shoes, missing heels $805.00

A-MA July 1998   Skinner, Inc.

Left to Right
Doll, Ideal compo. & cloth, ca. 1933, gr. sleeping & flirting steel eyes, cloth body, traces of rubber skin, rubber arms & hands, compo. legs, rubber polymerized on arms, 22½" H $230.00
Shirley Temple Doll, Ideal, compo., mid-1930's, sleeping eyes, crazed, orig. mohair wig, body jointed at shoulders & hips, paint crazed, 13" H, orig. plaid outfit from "Bright Eyes", orig. pin & paper tag $546.25
Shirley Temple Doll, Ideal, compo., mid-1930's, hazel sleeping eyes, orig. blonde mohair wig, body jointed at shoulder & hips, paint damage, shoe soles missing, 14½" H $488.75
Dolls, three compo. & cloth, 1920's, two shoulder heads, one swivel shoulder head, all have steel sleeping eyes, two have wigs, two unmkd., one Madame Hendren, neck damage, 20" H, 20" H & 28" H $460.00
Dolls, two compo., Ideal, Shirley Temple, hazel eyes, orig. mohair wig, body jointed at shoulder & hips, fine overall paint crazing, orig. outfit, 13" H, & Cameo "Joy", by Kallus, molded head & body, fully jointed limbs, decal on chest, paint crazing on head & body, needs restringing, 13¾" H $517.50
Shirley Temple Doll, Ideal, compo., mid-1930's, sleeping/flirty eyes, one crazed, body jointed at shoulders & hips, paint cracked, orig. sailor suit, hat & pin missing, fabric soiled, 27" H $747.50
Washington Dolls, Effanbee, George & Martha, compo., ca. 1932, w/ br. & blue painted eyes, jointed at neck, shoulders & hips, orig. off-white mohair wigs, both have Geo. Washington buttons, 9" H, orig. felt & cotton outfits, needs restringing $230.00
Kewpie Doll, Cameo compo., 1920's, jointed at shoulders & hips, fine paint crazing, 13" H, orig. cotton sunsuit, shoes & socks, paper label $143.75

A-MA Jan. 1999   Skinner, Inc.

Left to Right

Character Doll, Jean Orsini all bisque, "VIVI" ca. 1919, 5"
H . . . . .N/S
Doll, sm. all bisque, stationary blue glass eyes, closed
mouth, orig. blonde mohair wig, body jointed at shoulders
& hips, 5½" H $517.50
Character Girl, French-type sm. all bisque, socket head,
blue paperweight eyes, orig. blonde mohair wig, kid lined
leg joints, 8⅝" H $1,840.00
Doll, tiny all bisque, br. glass eyes, all-in-one head & body,
jointed at shoulders & hips, 3½" H $103.50
Native Girl, Schoenau & Hoffmeister br. painted, br. glass
eyes, impr. "Hanna", blk. mohair wig, color loss, br. compo.
body jointed at shoulders & hips, 7¼" H $97.75
Doll, Kestner bisque head, br. glass eyes, orig. blonde
mohair wig, needs repr., fully jointed body, 32" H . .$805.00

A-MA July 1998   Skinner, Inc.

Left to Right

Doll, Simon & Halbig bisque head, br. glass eyes, orig.
blonde mohair wig, metal body w/ music box, jointed
compo. arms & legs, 22" H $1,150.00
Doll, bisque turned shoulder head, stationary blue glass
eyes, open mouth, impr. "...Ger. #11", orig. blonde mohair
wig, kid body, damage, 24" H $257.50
Doll, Kestner bisque head, br. glass eyes, blonde human
hair wig, fully jointed compo. body, wear, 18½" H $1,840.00

A-MA Jan. 1999   Skinner, Inc.

Left to Right

Shirley Temple, Ideal compo., ca. 1934, sleeping hazel
eyes, crazed, orig. blonde mohair wig, jointed at shoulders
& hips, minor paint checks, 18" H, orig. outfit $632.50
Dolls, two hand-crafted "Shakespeare" artist dolls, mid
20th C. . . . . .N/S
Doll, Mary Hoyer plastic girl, 1950s, blue eyes, lt. red
mohair wig, jointed at head, shoulders & hips, hand knit
suit, 14" H $258.75
"Baby Snooks", Ideal flexy doll, ca. 1938, compo. head,
hands & torso, flexible metal cable arms & legs, wooden
feet, paint wear, 12¾" H $143.75
"Jiggs", Schoenhut all wood, ca. 1924, jointed at head,
shoulders & hips, 7" H, orig. felt shirt & trousers . .$373.75

A-MA July 1998   Skinner, Inc.

Left to Right

All-Felt Doll, Lenci girl, Italy, 1930's, br. painted eyes,
blonde mohair hair w/ coral & gray dress, cape & hat costume, fiber loss & fading, no labels, 12" H . . . . .N/S
Dutch Girl, Stiff, ca. 1913, either Hellen or Helma, center
face seam, blk. steel eyes, lt. br. hair, orig. costume, fabric
fading, back of left sabot damaged, button missing,
13¾" H $1,150.00
Kathe Kruse Boy, ca. 1916, lt. br. painted hair, gray painted eyes, jointed at shoulders & hips, separate sewn-on
thumb, sgn., handmade cloths, dressed in wool coat, some
staining & fiber loss to clothes, 17" H $2,875.00
All-Felt Doll, Lenci-type, 1930's, young girl w/ blonde hair,
molded & painted features, dressed in a felt & velveteen
Bavarian costume, some fading & moth damage,
12" H $115.00
Martha Chase Doll, early 20th C., yel. hair, blue eyes, cotton sateen body w/ trademark, paint wear, little finger
missing on both hands, 25" H $287.50

A-MA July 1998   Skinner, Inc.

Left to Right
Baby Dolls, lot of three, early 20th C., two all bisque w/ br. glass eyes, swivel neck, orig. blonde mohair wigs, 6¼" H & 5" H, one Armand Marseille painted bisque, blue glass eyes, compo. body jointed at shoulder & hips, right hand missing, 5" H $1,092.50
Twin Dolls, Kestner all bisque, br. glass eyes, swivel necks, jointed at shoulder & hips, boy has lt. br. mohair wig, girl has traces of blonde mohair wig, bent limb legs, moth damage to clothing & missing bootie, 5" H $1,035.00

A-MA Jan. 1999   Skinner, Inc.
Schoenhut Dollhouse, "Daggle" two-story, ca. 1923, wood & fiberboard, emb. faux gray stone siding, 8 int. rooms plus attic, rooms finished in litho. papers to represent woodwork, doors, & fancy wall papers, wear, 27⅝" H, 25½" W, 23⅝" D $2,415.00

A-MD Sept. 1998   Richard Opfer Auctioneering, Inc.
Dionne Quintuplets, Madame Alexander, jointed compo. toddlers, orig. tagged outfits & pins w/ extra set of tagged dresses & bonnets, hairline on one face, & slight crazing on one head, 7½" H $1,350.00

A-NH July 1998   Richard W. Withington, Inc.

Row 1, Left to Right
Doll, all compo., mkd. Ideal Doll, in orig. dress, 20" H $190.00
Doll, bisque head incised "My Dearie Ger.", sleeping br. eyes, open mouth w/ teeth, wig, jointed compo. body, wear, 25" H $325.00
Doll, early compo, mkd. Greiner's Pat. Doll Heads, 28" H $500.00
Doll, "Simon & Halbig" w/ bisque head, incised , blue eyes, w/ teeth, jointed compo. body, dressed, 27" H $400.00
Doll, "Ger. Heinrich Handwerck Simon & Halbig...", w/ bisque head, br. glass eyes, open mouth w/ teeth, pierced ears, jointed compo. body, wear, chipped $200.00

Row 2, Left to Right
Doll, all compo., all orig. boy, mkd. Petite "Puggy", 13" H $350.00
Doll, bisque head, incised "XI", blue eyes, orig. wig, jointed compo. straight wrist body, wear, 16½" H $2,600.00
Doll, bisque head, unmkd., br. eyes, wig, pierced ears, jointed compo. body, chipped, 24" H $750.00
Doll, Jumeau Depose w/ bisque head, blue glass eyes, wig, pierced ears, jointed compo. body, speckling, wear, rim chipped, 19" H $2,950.00
Doll, bisque head incised "Germany...", sleeping blue eyes, open mouth w/ 2 upper teeth, dressed, compo. toddler body, 14" H $250.00

A-MA July 1998   Skinner, Inc.
Dollhouse, painted wood, possibly MA, late 19th C., white ext., blk. roof & carved trim, dk. gr. window & door surrounds, dk. red doors & steps, single pane glass windows, two rooms on all three floors, painted sim. parquet floors, wall papers appear to be orig., four white int. doors, rooms finished w/ assort. of early 20th-mid 20th C. furniture & accessories, some Tyne-Toy pcs., chimney missing, reprs., paint wear, 46" H, 29" W, 25" D $2,760.00

A-MA July 1998   Skinner, Inc.

Snow & No Snow Babies, group of 39, Ger., Am., Japan, early 20th C., to present, mostly bisque, four metal, two compo., one plaster, children, babies, Santas, animals; some imper., 1 - 2¾" H $1,380.00

A-MA July 1998   Skinner, Inc.

Left to Right

Doll Carriage, tin mini., w/ painted bisque doll & two parasols, pink & cream vehicle, silk hood, 8" L, jointed baby w/ "An East Coast Studio Doll" label on back, 3" H, ivorene handled parasol w/ printed silk cover, 13⅜" L, wooden handled parasol w/ cream cotton cover, 22¾" L $4,025.00
Musical Toy, bisque head flower girl, early 20th C., blue glass eyes, impr. II, orig. blonde mohair wig, compo. limbs, orig. costume, music activates w/ base is squeezed, some discoloration on base fabric, 9" H, w/ accompanying photo of orig. owner $1,050.00

A-MA July 1998   Skinner, Inc.

Doll Bedroom Set, Renaissance Revival, 1870's, walnut & walnut burl veneer, white porcelain knobs, bed 23" L, drop well bureau, 23½" H, commode, 10" H, side table, 7½" H, some trim missing, table legs damaged $862.50

A-MA July 1998   Skinner, Inc.

Left to Right

Kestner bisque head, blue glass eyes, orig. blonde mohair wig, fully jointed compo. body, paint loss & reprs., needs restringing, 19" H, w/ handmade clothes & roller skates $747.50
Kestner bisque turned shoulder head, blue glass eyes, impr. N, made in Ger., cloth body & limbs, kid hands, repl. wig, 23" H $488.75
Kestner bisque head, br. glass eyes, orig. blonde mohair wig, full jointed compo. body, 25" H $1,035.00
Kestner bisque turned shoulder head, blue glass eyes, impr. P, made in Ger. mark, orig. blonde mohair wig, repl. cloth body & legs, 30" H . . . . .N/S
Kestner bisque head, br. glass eyes, orig. blonde mohair wig, fully jointed compo. body, paint wear & chip by left eye, 17" H, period red wool crepe dress & additional clothing $1,495.00
Steiner bisque head crying/moving, late 19th C., blue glass eyes, orig. blonde mohair wig, papier mache body, kid lower body & upper legs, compo. arms & legs, arms restored, heat crack, 23½" H $977.50

A-MA July 1998   Skinner, Inc.

Left to Right

Kewpie Doll, bisque sitting soldier, 1913 & on, blk., red, & gold Ger. helmet, jointed at shoulders, 3½" H .$1,150.00
Kewpie Doll, bisque w/ broom & dust bin, impr. O'Neil, broom broken, 3½" H $230.00
Kewpie Doll, bisque, sitting in wicker armchair, 1913 & on, 3½" H $345.00
Kewpie Doll, O'Neil, bisque, farmer, 1913 & on, wooden rake, tines missing, paper label on back, 5½" H $517.50
Kewpie Doll, bisque, guitar player, paper label on back, red & navy cloth ribbons on guitar, 3⅝" H $402.50
Kewpie Doll, bisque, traveler w/ valise & umbrella, paper tag on chest, tiny nick on right wing, 3½" H $201.25
Kewpie Doll, bisque, sitting w/ blk. cat, paper label on back, 3¼" H $575.00

A-MA Jan. 1999   Skinner, Inc.

Left to Right

Teddy Bear, Steiff ginger mohair center-seam, ca. 1905, fully jointed, blk. steel eyes, embroidered nose, mouth & claws, excelsior stuffing, fur & fiber loss on muzzle & ears, slight overall fur loss, 19" H $8,050.00
Teddy Bear, Steiff ginger mohair, ca. 1905, fully jointed, blk. steel eyes, embroidered nose & mouth & claws, felt pads, excelsior stuffing, fur wear, 23" H $14,950.00
Teddy Bear, Steiff blonde mohair center seam, ca. 1905, fully jointed, blk. steel eyes, embroidered nose, mouth & claws, excelsior stuffing, felt pads, fur loss, button missing, 20" H $11,500.00
Teddy Bear, Ideal, gold mohair, ca. 1919, fully jointed, glass eyes, embroidered nose, mouth & claws, excelsior stuffing, beige felt pads, minor fur loss, 25" H $546.25

A-MA July 1998   Skinner, Inc.

Left to Right

Ideal, yel. mohair, late teens to early 1920's, repl. shoe-button eyes, blk. embroidered nose, mouth & claws, fully jointed, excelsior stuffing, tan felt pads, short limbs, fur loss, moth damage, 15" H $230.00
Ideal, ginger mohair, ca. 1919, fully jointed, blk. shoe-button eyes, blk. embroidered nose, mouth & claws, excelsior stuffing, felt pads, some pad damage, slight fur loss, 20" H $460.00
Steiff, ginger mohair, ca. 1905, fully jointed, blk. steel eyes, blk. embroidered features & claws, needs stuffing, pads replace, fur loss, fabric damage, 12" H $287.50
Steiff, golden mohair, ca. 1905, blk. steel eyes, fully jointed, blk. embroidered nose, mouth & claws, felt pads, excelsior stuffing ear button, growler, moth damage, 17" H $2,990.00
Steiff, two, ca. 1905, blonde mohair, blk. steel eyes, lt. br. embroidered features & claws, fur, fiber & stuffing loss, larger one has ear button, 9⅞" H & 15½" H $575.00
Steiff, early, golden mohair, ca. 1905, blk. steel eyes, fully jointed, br. embroidered nose, mouth, & claws, felt pads, excelsior stuffing, button missing, soppy fur & fiber loss, need repr., 16" H $1,955.00
Steiff, golden mohair, ca. 1904-09, blank button, blk. steel eyes, fully jointed, blk. embroidered features, felt pads, excelsior stuffing, spotty fur loss, 14" H $1,380.00

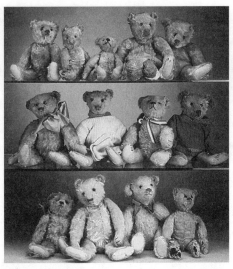

A-MA Jan. 1999   Skinner, Inc.

Row 1, Left to Right

Teddy Bear, Steiff golden mohair, fully jointed, shoe button eyes, blk. embroidered nose, mouth & claws, excelsior stuffing, felt pads, fur wear, 10" H $1,035.00
Teddy Bears, two sm. mohair, possibly Steiff, lt. yel., fully jointed, blk. steel eyes, embroidered nose, mouth & claws, felt pads, excelsior stuffing, 7½" H, both have wear & fiber loss $517.50
Teddy Bears, two Steiff mohair, ca. 1905, both fully jointed, excelsior stuffed, blk. steel eyes, embroidered nose, mouth & claws, felt pads, blonde has blank button, 13"H, yel. w/ button missing, 12" H, both have extensive fur loss $977.50
Teddy Bear, Steiff light gold mohair, ca. 1905, fully jointed blk. shoe button eyes, embroidered nose, mouth & claws, tan feet pads, some fur loss, 12½" H $1,725.00

Row 2, Left to Right

Teddy Bear, Steiff gold mohair, ca. 1905, fully jointed, blk. steel eyes, embroidered nose, mouth & claws, button missing, repl. pads, fur loss, 12" H $690.00
Teddy Bear, Steiff blonde mohair, ca. 1905, fully jointed, blk. shoe button eyes, embroidered nose, mouth & claws, excelsior & kapok stuffing, beige felt pads, extensive fur loss, 12" H $690.00
Teddy Bear, blonde mohair Steiff, ca. 1910, fully jointed, glass eyes, embroidered nose, mouth & claws, excelsior stuffing, 11" H $402.50
Teddy Bear, Steiff lt. yel. mohair, ca. 1905, fully jointed, blk. steel eyes, embroidered nose, mouth & claws, excelsior stuffing, felt pads, blank button, fur & pad loss, 12½" H $1,265.00

Row 3, Left to Right

Teddy Bear, Steiff lt. yel. mohair, ca. 1905, fully jointed, blank button, blk. steel eyes, embroidered nose, mouth & claws, felt pads, spotty fur loss, 10" H $1,265.00
Teddy Bear, Steiff blonde mohair, ca. 1905, fully jointed, blk. steel eyes, embroidered nose, mouth & claws, excelsior stuffing, some seam reprs., fur & fiber loss, button missing, 13" H $460.00
Teddy Bear, lt. yel. mohair, possibly Aetna, fully jointed, blk. shoe button eyes, embroidered nose, mouth & claws, beige felt pads, fiber loss, 12" H $345.00
Teddy Bear, Steiff blonde mohair, ca. 1905, fully jointed, blk. steel eyes, well loved, remnants of embroidered nose, mouth & claws, fur & fiber damage, 10" H $345.00

A-MA Jan. 1999   Skinner, Inc.

Left to Right

Teddy Bear, Ideal light gold mohair, ca. 1905 . . . . . . .N/S
Teddy Bear, Steiff gold mohair, ca. 1905, fully jointed, blk. steel eyes, embroidered nose, mouth & claws, excelsior stuffing, button missing, some fur & fiber loss, moth damage, 16" H $2,415.00
Teddy Bears, two mohair, ca 1920's, possibly Fadup, golden yel. w/ blk. embroidered nose & mouth, yel. felt pads, 16¾" H, one lt. yel. w/ embroidered nose, 20" H, both w/ glass eyes, excelsior stuffing, fully jointed, larger bear damaged at neck & has repl. pads & fiber loss, both have fur loss $230.00
Teddy Bear, Ideal, gold mohair, ca. 1919, fully jointed glass eyes, applied twill nose, embroidered mouth & claws, excelsior stuffing, beige felt pads, minor fur loss, 20" H $575.00
Teddy Bear, pink mohair, possibly Stevans Mfg. Co., 1920s, fully jointed, glass eyes, embroidered nose, mouth, & claws, excelsior stuffing, felt pads, two pads repl., some fading & spotty fur loss, 20" H $431.25

A-MA July 1998   Skinner, Inc.

Left to Right

Twin Teddy Bears, Steiff, lt. yel. mohair, ca. 1905, fully jointed, blk. steel eyes, excelsior stuffing, tan embroidered nose, mouth, claws, cream pads, moth damage, fur loss, ear buttons missing, 10" H $2,530.00
Teddy Bear, Steiff, blonde mohair, blank ear button, fully jointed, blk. steel eyes, br. embroidered noise, mouth & claws, felt pad, overall fur loss, slight fiber loss, autographed "J.R. Junginger" $862.50
Teddy Bear, Steiff, blonde mohair, ca. 1907, fully jointed, blk. steel eyes, yel. felt pads, embroidered claws, moth damage, fiber loss, button missing, 12" H $287.50
Bears, two sm. mohair, one w/ ginger fur, fully jointed, blk. shoe-button eyes, blk. embroidered nose, mouth, & claws, ginger felt pads, spotty fur loss, fiber wear, 10" H, one w/ saffron fur, fully jointed, embroidered nose & mouth, beige felt pads, glass eyes, one missing, spotty fur loss, 11" H $258.75

A-MA July 1998   Skinner, Inc.

Left to Right

Animals, two, one Ideal gold mohair plush bear, 1920's, fully jointed, embroidered nose & mouth, some fur loss, 14½" H, & one Steiff 1910 blk. mohair Puss-in-Boots, (not shown) glass eyes, felt ears, one missing, pink embroidered nose, mouth & claws, cloth boots, jointed head, limbs & tail, minor fur loss, moth damage, button missing, 10" H $488.75
Teddy Bear, Ideal blonde mohair, ca. 1919, glass eyes, fully jointed, rust embroidered nose, mouth, & claws, possibly restitched, excelsior stuffing, beige felt pads, some pad damage & slight fur loss, 34" H $2,530.00
Teddy Bear, by American-made Stuffed Toy Co., NY, red, white & blue mohair electric-eye, arms jointed, well loved, fur & fabric loss, mech. missing, 19" H $115.00
Teddy Bear, beige mohair, possibly Bruin, fully jointed, blk. shoe-button eyes, blk. embroidered nose, mouth, & claws, beige felt pads, excelsior stuffing, spotty fur loss, some fiber loss at neck, 24" H $345.00
Teddy Bear, Steiff, lt. yel. mohair, 1920's, "Heins" glass eyes, fully jointed, blk. embroidered nose, mouth & claws, excelsior stuffing, ear button, fiber loss, pads repl., 24" H $2,760.00
Bear, by American-made Stuffed Toy Co., pink mohair electric eye, ca. 1907, jointed at shoulders & head, fabric nose, embroidered mouth, light-bulb eyes, switch on left ear, repr. on neck joint, fur loss, pad damage, 23" H . . . . .N/S

A-MA Jan. 1999   Skinner, Inc.

Left to Right

Bear, Steiff ginger mohair, ca. 1905, fully jointed, blk. steel eyes, excelsior stuffing, embroidered nose, mouth & claws, tan pads, button missing, fur worn, 24" H $5,750.00
Teddy Bear, lrg. Steiff curly blonde mohair, ca. 1905, blk. steel eyes, blank ear button, tan embroidered noise, mouth & claws, blonde felt pads, excelsior stuffing, fur loss & spotty moth damage, 20" H $9,200.00
Teddy Bear, Ideal gold mohair, ca. 1920, fully jointed, excelsior stuffing, blk. steel eyes, embroidered nose & mouth, beige felt pads, extensive fur loss, 23" H . . . . .N/S
Teddy Bear, early Steiff blonde mohair, ca. 1910, fully jointed, blank button, glass eyes, excelsior stuffing, re-embroidered nose, mouth, & claws, felt pads, well loved, button missing, fur & fiber loss, 21" H $805.00

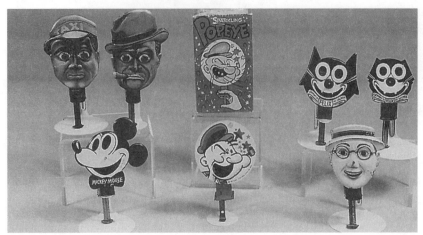

A-NJ Oct. 1998   Bill Bertoia Auctions
Hook & Ladder Wagon, Ives, cast iron, ornate cast, two open bench seats w/ drivers, two horses w/ center wheel, 26½" L $1,100.00

A-NJ Oct. 1998   Bill Bertoia Auctions

Sparklers

Amos-N-Andy, Ger., litho. tin, hand held, both w/ glass eyes, 6¼" to 6½" $715.00
Mickey Mouse, Copy, Walt Disney, tin litho., 5½" H $462.00

Popeye, Chein, litho. tin, hand held push lever activates spark, incl. orig. box $385.00
Felix, two, Copr. Pat Sullivan, two sized, both in tin litho., one made in Ger., 5" to 5¼" H $880.00
Harold Lloyd, Ger., litho. tin, hand held, 5½" H $275.00

A-NJ Oct. 1998   Bill Bertoia Auctions
Fire Patrol Wagon, Carpenter, cast iron, hand painted in blue w/ yel. lanterns mounted on sides, incl. four fireman figures, 16½" L $1,210.00

A-NJ Oct. 1998   Bill Bertoia Auctions

Left to Right

Popeye Walker, Chein, litho. tin, clockwork activated, incl. orig. box, 6" H $1,210.00
Popeye Drummer, Chein, King Features Synd., litho. tin, Popeye w/ parade drum w/ sticks, hand squeezed clockwork mech., 7" H $2,750.00
Popeye, in barrel, Chein, litho. tin, clockwork action, 7" H $770.00

Barnacle Bill, w/ punching bag, Chein, litho. tin, metal base, celluloid punching bag, clockwork activated, 7½" H $715.00
Barnacle Bill, in barrel, Chein, litho. tin, clockwork mech., 7" H . .$605.00
Barnacle Bill, Chein, litho. tin, colorful attire, clockwork mech., minor scratches, 6" H $418.00
Popeye Sparkler, King features Synd., litho. tin, hand held, colorful, 6" H $825.00

A-NJ Oct. 1998   Bill Bertoia Auctions
Hook & Ladder Wagon, Carpenter, cast iron, blk. overall w/ red frame & ladder, two open bench seats, two horses w/ center wheels, 26" L $880.00

A-NJ Oct. 1998   Bill Bertoia Auctions
Fire Pumper, horse drawn, Dent, cast iron, white overall w/ gold trimmed boiler, drive seated on open bench, red spoke wheels, 20" L $770.00

A-NJ Oct. 1998   Bill Bertoia Auctions
Fire Pumper, Dent, cast iron, red w/ silver & gold boiler, 22" L . . .$462.00

A-NJ Oct. 1998   Bill Bertoia Auctions
Fire Pumper, Hubley, cast iron, red overall, nickel boiler, 21½" L $550.00

A-NJ Oct. 1998   Bill Bertoia Auctions
Hook & Ladder Truck, Hubley, cast iron, white overall w/ red trim, red hitch frame & spoke wheels, three horses & two figures, 27" L overall $605.00

A-MA Jan. 1999   Skinner, Inc.

Row 1, Left to Right

Tamany Bank, by J. & E. Stevens, w/ blk. jacket & gray trouser, chipping, 5½" H $690.00
Two Frogs Bank, mech., by J. & E. Stevens, remnants of paint, lacking baby frog's leg, 8½" L $920.00
Still Banks, Aunt Jemimah w/ spoon by A. C. Williams, 5¾" H, & sharecropper w/ toes visible on left foot by Williams, 5¼" H $316.25

Row 2, Left to Right

General Butler Bank, still, by J. & E. Stevens, lacking trap, paint loss, 6¾" H $3,795.00
Mammy & Child, mech. by Kyser & Rex Co., lacking trap & spoon, chipping, 7½" H $9,200.00
Owl Bank, mech., by J. & E. Stevens Co., w/ turning head mech., paint worn, 7½" H $287.50
Pig in Highchair Bank, by J. & E. Stevens Co., nickeled & cast w/ floral & foliate motifs, lacking trap, 6" H .$1,380.00
Pay Phone Bank, by J. & E. Stevens, finished in maroon, blk. & silver, w/ 5, 10 & 25 cent slots, handle operated bell, chipping, 7¼" H $3,220.00

Row 3, Left to Right

Humpty Dumpty Bank, by Shepard Hardware Co., multicolored, chipping, 7½" H $1,265.00
Stump Speaker Bank, by Shepard Hardware Co., paint loss, 9½" H $3,105.00
Monkey & Coconut Bank, mech., by J. & E. Stevens, lacking trap, paint loss, 8¼" H $2,990.00
Uncle Sam Bank, by Shepard Hardware Co., paint loss, 11½" H $1,610.00

A-MA Jan. 1999   Skinner, Inc.

Row 1, Left to Right

Reclining Chinaman Bank, mech., by J. & E. Stevens Co., lacking trap, arm inoperative, chipping, 8¼" L . .$10,350.00
Trick Pony Bank, by Shepard Hardware Co., paint worn & chipped, lacking trap, 7" W .N/S
Trick Dog Bank, mech. by Hubley, 8¾" W $690.00

Row 2, Left to Right

Leap-Frog Bank, by Shepard Hardware Co., considerable chipping especially to figures, 7½" W $2,645.00
Acrobat Bank, by J. & E. Stevens, w/ blue base, some chipping, 7¼" L $6,325.00
Organ w/ Monkey Bank, Kyser & Rex Co., in form of barrel organ, w/ hand-turned mech., paint loss, lacking trap, 6½" H $1,035.00
Organ Bank, w/ boy & girl, cast iron in form of barrel organ, slight chipping to figures, 7¾" H $2,990.00

Row 3, Left to Right

Clown on Globe Bank, mech. by J. & E. Stevens, w/ turning & flipping mech., red & ora. outfit, blue sphere & tan base, lacking trap, unextended 9" H $26,450.00
Shoot the Chute Bank, by J. & E. Stevens Co., nickel plated w/ Buster Br. & Tige in boat, lacking trap, extension repl., 9¾" W $5,462.50
Boy on Trapeze Bank, by J. Barton & Smith Co., w/ red shirt & blue trouser, damage to base top, 9½" H .$1,495.00

A-MA Jan. 1999   Skinner, Inc.

Row 1, Left to Right

'Spise a Mule' Bank, mech., by John Harper & Co., Ltd., Eng., 10" W . . . . .N/S
Artillery Bank, by J. & E. Stevens Co., lacking trap, 8" W $3,795.00
Hen & Chick Bank, mech., by J. & E. Stevens Co., lacking trap, 9¾" W $4,600.00

Chief Big Moon Bank, mech., by J. & E. Stevens, remnants of gold stripe, lacking fish & trap, 10" L . . .$1,035.00

Row 2, Left to Right

New Creedmoor Bank, by J. & E. Stevens Co., lacking trap, paint worn, 10" W $690.00
Paddy & Pig Bank, mech., by J. & E. Stevens, w/ dk. blue jacket, moving mouth & eyes, lacking pig's leg, lever & base, 8" H $1,150.00
William Tell Bank, by J. & E. Stevens Co., lacking trap, paint loss & staining, 10½" H $690.00
Squirrel & Tree Stump Bank, by Mech. Novelty Works, underside possibly repl., 7" W $862.50

Row 3, Left to Right

Teddy & Bear Bank, mech. by J. & E. Stevens Co., w/ br. tree, lacking trap, 10¼" W $2,760.00
Lion & Monkeys Bank, mech., by Kyser & Rex Co., lacking baby monkey & trap, paint loss, 9" W $632.50
Indian & Bear Bank, mech., by J. & E. Stevens Co., paint wear & chipping, 10¼" H $1,380.00

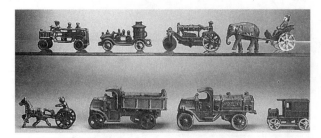

A-MA Jan. 1999   Skinner, Inc.

Row 1, Left to Right

Cast Toys, five, red road roller w/ wood roller, 5½" L, ora. patrol wagon, 4¾" L, red tractor w/ silver details & wood wheels, a white "Milk Truck" w/ four wood cars & a Hubley "Navy Fighter" w/ folding wings & landing gear   ..$488.75
Various Toys, red cast iron fire pumper, 5" L, a cast iron motor van, damaged, a tinplate duck, a tinplate "Clucking Hen", a Masutoku tinplate vintage car & other toys   ..$201.25
Cast Toys, five, red road roller w/ wood roller, 5½" L, ora. patrol wagon, 4¾" L, red tractor w/ silver details & wood wheels, a white "Milk Truck" w/ four wood cars & a Hubley "Navy Fighter" w/ folding wings & landing gear   ..$488.75
Chariot, Kenton elephant & clown, elephant w/ remnants of silver paint & red blanket, chariot w/ yel. spoked wheels & detachable clown, wear & chips, 6¼" L $126.50

Row 2, Left to Right

Sulky & Driver, Kenton, nickeled cast iron w/ red spoked wheels, 5" L................................$115.00
Dump Truck, cast iron, possibly by Dent, finished in green-gray w/ red spoked wheels, spring-operated bed & swinging tailgate, paint loss, 7" L...................$316.25
"Gasoline" Truck, blue painted cast iron w/ 12-spoke nickeled wheels, paint loss, 7¼" L............$402.50
Various Toys, red cast iron fire pumper, 5" L, a cast iron motor van, damaged, a tinplate duck, a tinplate "Clucking Hen", a Masutoku tinplate vintage car & other toys   ..$201.25

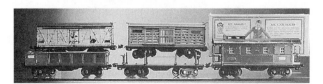

A-MA Jan. 1999   Skinner, Inc.

Freight Cars, five Lionel 500 series, incl. 511 D flat in dk. gr., 512 gondola, 513 B cattle in ora. & gr., 514 R refrigerator in ivory & 517 B caboose in gr. & red, boxed, paint wear $316.25

A-MA Jan. 1999   Skinner, Inc.

Freight Cars, Am. Flyer standard gauge, incl. 4022 stake in ora. & gray, 4020 cattle in gray & blue, 4017 gondola in gr. & caboose in red w/ internal lt., pain loss $402.50

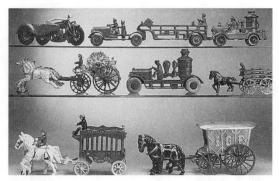

A-MA Jan. 1999   Skinner, Inc.

Row 1, Left to Right

Motorcycle & Side Car, Hubley red cast iron "Indian", w/ cast aluminum handlebars, rubber tires, & sprung steel noise-maker, paint & decal loss, 9" L...........$862.50
Fire Trailer Truck, Arcade, red w/ blue firemen, detachable trailer, hose reel & ladder turntable, lacking ladders & hose, paint loss, 16" L......................$316.25
Fire Pumper, red cast iron w/ helmeted driver, nickeled spoked wheels, boiler w/ gold colored top, 7¾" L .$172.50

Row 2, Left to Right

Hose Reel, Kent cast iron, three white horses, white carriage & reel, paint poor, horses repainted, 13¾" L .$431.25
Fire Pumper, Kenton, painted in red w/ gold boiler top & lamps w/ driver & white tires, chipping, 10¼" L   ..$230.00
Horse & Dray, cast iron w/ red wagon & driver, yel. spoked wheels & yellow-brown horse, chipping, 8½" L .. N/S

Row 3, Left to Right

"Overland Circus", Kenton, cage wagon in red w/ yel. wheels & white horses, 14" L.................$402.50
"Ice Wagon", double-team cast iron, blk. horses w/ gold harnesses, nickeled wagon & red spoke wheels, rust to roof, lacking driver, 15" L....................$373.75

A-MA Jan. 1999   Skinner, Inc.

Passenger Set, Lionel standard gauge, incl. No. 8 locomotive, 337 Pullman & 338 observation cars, all in red, & mkd. Lionel Lines, wear & possible retouching $373.75

A-MA Jan. 1999   Skinner, Inc.

Left to Right

Motor Car, Lehmann, white-suited driver w/ horn, bellows & coil spring, paint loss & rust, 6½" L..........$632.50
Milk Cart, litho. tinplate w/ clockwork motor, 10" L.....
$345.00
Lehmann, "Walking Down Broad-way", litho. w/ pug dog, rack & pinion flywheel driver, 6¼" H..........$1,840.00

A-OH July 1998 Garth's Auctions

Row 1, Left to Right

Teddy Bear, worn gold mohair & button eyes, paw pads repl., 19" H $220.00
Tiger, "Steiff", "Molly Jungtiger", 19" L $165.00

Row 2, Left to Right

Leopard, "Steiff", "Snobby Schnee-leopard", 24" L $110.00
Dog, silver mohair & button eyes, wear & added ribbon, 12" L . .$93.50

A-OH Nov. 1998 Garth's Auctions

Teddy Bear, worn gold mohair, articulated limbs, glass eyes & felt paw pads, damage & repr., 23½" L $220.00
Teddy Bear, worn gold mohair, front legs articulated, felt paw pads, ears resewn $220.00
Hand Warmer, w/ teddy bear, gold mohair, glass eyes, 11½" H . .$467.50
Hand Warmer, w/ bear head, worn white mohair, glass eyes, 6" L .$27.50
Teddy Bear, worn gold mohair, articulated limbs & bead eyes, head & tail move together, paw pads very worn, 10" L $1,045.00

A-OH Sept. 1998 Garth's Auctions

Race Car, soap box derby, laminated pine w/ blk. stenciled signage, red metal wheels w/ rubber treads, 77" L $440.00

A-OH Sept. 1998 Garth's Auctions

Tandem, pedal car, sheet metal & wood w/ steel fittings, orig. blk. paint w/ red & yel. striping, decals "...Toledo, Ohio", wear but good color, wooden steering wheel loose, 64" L $2,090.00

A-OH July 1998 Garth's Auctions

Toys, five stuffed blk. cats w/ embroidered features, in various fabrics, felt, velvet, silk, satin & oil cloth, some wear & fading, 7' to 12½" . . .$302.50
Rag Dolls, three, girl, 12½" H, woman w/ blk. yarn hair, 14" H, & woman w/ blk. painted hair, blue glass beads & plaid pant suit, 16½" H $110.00

A-NJ Oct. 1998 Bill Bertoia Auctions

Toy Stove, the "Dainty", cast iron w/ nickeled emb. stove door, polished, pots & pans, 12½" x 22" H . . .$770.00

A-NJ Oct. 1998 Bill Bertoia Auctions

Left to Right

Toy Stove, the "Eagle", nickeled cast iron, four removable lids, 12¼" H x 13½" W $550.00
Toy Stove, the "Pet", nickeled cast iron, pressed steel body, five removable lids, door hinge missing, 11" W, 11¼" H $275.00
Toy Stove, the "Bess", nickeled cast iron, heavy const., four removable lids, front opening doors, 6¼" H x 10¼" W $242.09

A-NJ Oct. 1998 Bill Bertoia Auctions

Toy Stove, the "Royal", nickeled cast iron, five removable lids, pots, pans & dump bucket, 11½" H x 12½" W $825.00

A-NJ Oct. 1998 Bill Bertoia Auctions

Toy Stove, Ger., pressed steel w/ nickeled edge molding, inter. alcohol burner tube, pots & teapots, 9½" W x 9½" H $330.00

A-OH Jan. 1999 Garth's Auctions
Rocking Horse, wood & composition w/ br. mohair covering, glass eyes, hide mane & horse tail, wooden base w/ old worn red paint, white striping & gold trim, wear, head loose, 39" H $385.00

A-ME Sept. 1998 Cyr Auction Co. Inc.
Pedal Tractor, w/ heart shaped steering wheel, 32" L, 25" T . .$225.00

A-MD Sept. 1998 Richard Opfer Auctioneering, Inc.

Left to Right
Doll House, paper litho inside & out, some staining & damage, 20½" H $1,100.00
Roly Poly Clown, compo. w/ bells, some restoration, 15' H $100.00

A-IA June 1998 Jackson's
Left to Right
Doll Buggy, wicker w/ orig. unpainted finish & corduroy upholstery, 34" H $230.00
Child's Rocker, oak $51.75

A-PA Sept. 1998 York Town Auction Inc.

Left to Right
Pedal Car, Steelcraft 1928 Cadillac, red, ora., blk. & silver, res. .$1,800.00
Child's Carriage, attrib. to Lancaster Co., PA, Amish, dovetailed pine body w/ canvas covered top & side curtains, wood & iron wheels .$1,500.00

A-NH Aug. 1998 Northeast Auctions
Horse, pull-toy, hide covered w/ iron wheels on red painted rockers, 59" L $500.00

A-ME July 1998 Cyr Auction Co. Inc.
Circus Wagon, w/ lion, carved & painted, 30" L $2,750.00

A-MA Jan. 1999 Skinner, Inc.
Locomotive, tinplate, possibly by Fallows, clockwork motor, cast wheels, old repaint, 10" L . . .$460.00

A-MA Jan. 1999 Skinner, Inc.
Locomotive, tinplate "Victory", w/ red boiler, blk. & gilt stack, one wheel damaged, 4¾" L $977.50

A-MD Sept. 1998 Richard Opfer Auctioneering, Inc.

Row 1, Left to Right
Squeak Duck, painted compo., wear, chipped, 4½" H $65.00
Squeak Dogs, two, one w/ compo. flocked & painted, 4¾" H, one painted compo., wear, 5¼" H $90.00

Row 2, Left to Right
Squeak Dog, painted compo., working, wear, 5½" H $350.00
Squeak Hen, on nest, painted compo., tear in fabric, not working, paint wear, 5" H $110.00
Squeak Parrot, painted compo., not working, crack, 5¾" H $80.00

A-NJ Oct. 1998   Bill Bertoia Auctions

Left to Right

Popeye, riding horse toy, Fischer Price Toys, paper litho over wood, articulated action, 10" L $528.00

Jeep Doll, jointed body, KFS, 1936, wood, painted yel. overall w/ red nose, chest stenciled "Jeep", 4¼" H $352.00

Jeep Doll, 1935, King features, wood w/ jointed arms, comp. head, painted yel. overall w/ red nose, decal on body, crazing, 8¼" H $715.00

Jeep Doll, 1935, King features Synd., wood compo. w/ wood tail, arms, legs & head move, yel. overall w/ red nose, decal on body, stain to face, 13" H $990.00

Popeye, jointed wood figure, Chein, King Features, 1932, wood body, hand painted overall, decals, cloth bag, 8" H $495.00

A-OH July 1998   Garth's Auctions

Row 1

Bank, cast iron steamboat by "Arcade", traces of gold, 7½" L $220.00

"Overland Circus", cast iron, by Kenton, unused condition in orig. box, two horses w/ outriders, wagon w/ polar bear & driver, 14" L . . .$605.00

Row 2

"Handsom Cab", cast iron, by Kenton, unused condition in orig. box, one horse, driver & passenger, 15¾" L $220.00

Row 3

Windup Toy, tin, fireman climbing ladder, wear & rust, added wooden base, 21¼" H $220.00

"Covered Wagon", cast iron, by Kenton, unused condition in orig. box, two horses & driver, cloth top in envelope, 14¾" L $220.00

A-NJ Oct. 1998   Bill Bertoia Auctions

Popeye Holster Set, six shooter, J. Halpern Co., incl. two six shooters in leather holsters, orig. litho. cardboard pkg. w/ pic. of Popeye, 12" H $242.00

A-OH Sept. 1998   Garth's Auctions

Velocipede, w/ two horses, wood w/ steel frame, orig. red, blk. & white paint, horses move when pedaled, mkd. "Galloppede, Patented", 43½" L $935.00

A-NJ Oct. 1998   Bill Bertoia Auctions

Popeye, pencil items, incl. boxed oversized pencil w/ colorful graphics, & pencil box, 10¾" L $88.00

A-OH Jan. 1999   Garth's Auctions

Baby Carriage, w/ horse, wood wicker & steel, horse has old dapple gray paint w/ worn harness, wood frame has old cream colored paint w/ red & blk. striping & wicker has old yel. paint w/ gr. trim, wire wheels, 70" L $605.00

A-NJ Oct. 1998   Bill Bertoia Auctions

Garden Pails, assort. Walt Disney made by Ohio Art, all litho. tin, various images, ca. 1938, 3" to 7" H $1,430.00

A-NJ Oct. 1998   Bill Bertoia Auctions

Child's China Set, assorted pcs., incl. dishes, platters, cups, terrine & tea service, floral design decal patt., incl. bottom slotted box, missing two sm. pcs., some crazing, box measures 9½" x 13", no lid $83.00

A-MA Jan. 1999   Skinner, Inc.

Left to Right

Two-Seater Tourer, tinplate Penny Toy, litho. in red, yel., & cream, w/ driver & fly-wheel driver, 3" L $402.50
Delivery Carriage, tinplate Penny Toy, litho. in blk. red, yel. & pink w/ flywheel driver, 4¼" L $143.75
Beetle, Lehmann/Adam, early model w/ trademark, spring motor, leg detached $230.00
Toys, two, Lehmann Beetle w/ crawling mech. & cast iron horse w/ remnants of white paint $172.50
"Autin", Lehmann, coil-spring motor, litho. car & blue jacketed box, 3¾" L $287.50
"Joko" Dog Cart, Stock, w/ monkey driver, coil spring, staining, 6½" L $431.25

A-MA Jan. 1999   Skinner, Inc.

Row 1, Left to Right

Felix the Cat, by Schoenhut w/ label, stringing loose, approx. 8½" H $207.00
Mr. Peanut, painted jointed wood ad. figure, 8½" H .$201.25
Popeye, & three toys, walking Popeye, 8¼" H, a Popeye Pencil in box, 10¼" L, a Tricky Taxi in box, & a tinplate three-wheel cart driven by flapper, litho. in red, blue & yel. w/ clockwork motor $517.50
"Charlie McCarthy Benzine Buggy", by Marx, litho. in blk., cream & red w/ clockwork motor, wear $373.75
Charlie Chaplin Bell Toy, w/ flat cast iron Chaplin pivoting in center, res., 6" L .N/S

Row 2, Left to Right

Felix the Cat, w/ spring motor, ora. cart w/ gr. wheels, & blk. Felix, 7" L $690.00
"Dick Tracy Squad Car", Marx, w/ battery-operated motor & light, litho. in gr.,11¼" L $172.50
Donald Duck, & nephews, Linemar, Japan w/ clockwork motor, 11¼" L $373.75
Toys, cartoon characters "Sandy", tinplate in ora., blk. & cream w/ clockwork motor, 5" L, & a painted cast iron Popeye figure mkd. 1929, 3¼" H $258.75

A-MA Jan. 1999   Skinner, Inc.

Row 1, Left to Right

Toys, various comprising a Marx "Smokey Joe" a Japanese friction-drive trolley by Kanto, a pressed dump truck, a "Security Safe Deposit" bank, & a "Mercury Eight" bank, plus three sm. cars $258.75
Whistling Spooky Kooky Tree, by Marx, battery-operated tinplate w/ moving eyes, mouth & plastic arms & top, some wear, 14½" H $690.00
Official Mr. Magoo Car", Hubley, battery-operated, tinplate & plastic in yel. & gr., removable top, scratching, 9" L $115.00
Popeye, & three toys, walking Popeye, 8¼" H, a Popeye Pencil in box, 10¼" L, a Tricky Taxi in box, & a tinplate three-wheel cart driven by flapper, litho. in red, blue & yel. w/ clockwork motor $517.50

Row 2, Left to Right

"Merrymakers" Band, Marx, ...$575.00
"Humphrey Mobile", Wyandotte, litho. tinplate w/ fixed steering, clockwork motor, some scratching, 9" L .$345.00
Jazzbo-Jim, dancing figure, on log cabin dec. w/ caricature figures, coil-spring motor, some rust, 9½" H $257.75
Jazzbo-Jim, Strauss, clockwork litho. tinplate w/ banjo player in plaid jacket, in maker's box, 10¼" H $488.75

A-MA Jan. 1999   Skinner, Inc.

Left to Right

Bears, two Ger. mohair, Schuco off-white windup roller skater, fully jointed, glass eyes, embroidered features, key missing, 8½".H, & yel. muzzled bear on all fours pull-toy, red leatherette muzzle & collar, 8" L $575.00
Wind-up Bears, ten assort. & one bear figure, various countries & makers, tan, yel. or lt. br. mohair furs, four-piece band, others dancing or walking, nine have glass eyes, one eye missing, & one has steel eyes, one key, some lot wear, 4 to 6⅞" H $546.25

A-MA Jan. 1999   Skinner, Inc.

Row 1

Truck, "Machinery Moving" Marx, pressed steel in blk., red, yel. & silver, w/ traversing crane, plastic motor, & two wooden crates, in maker's box, rust & discolored, box taped & water stained, 22" L $172.50

Row 2

Trucks, two Marx, a U.S. Army transport, gr. w/ canvas top & plastic canon, scratches, tow hook broken, 19" L, & a "Sand-Gravel Hauling Contractors" dump truck in red, white & blk., w/ hinged back & shute, scratches & surface rust, 12" L $258.75

Row 3, Left to Right

Delivery Truck, Marx "Railway Express Agency", ca. 1950's finished in gr. w/ yel. details, silver roof, operating tailgate, Wyandotte tires & access., few scratches & scuffs, 20" L $373.75

Truck, Marx "Lumar Wrecker Service", multicolored pressed steel w/ rear winch, scratches & staining, 16" L $201.25

A-MA Jan. 1999   Skinner, Inc.

Row 1

Steam Shovel, Buddy L, finished in blk. w/ red corrugated roof & base, cast wheels, boiler, surface rust, crazing to roof, 14" H $115.00

Row 2

Dump Truck, Buddy L, finished in blk. w/ red chassis & wheels, hinged tailgate, lacks chain to winch, scratches, 25" L $1,150.00

Row 3

Lincoln Sedan, Turner, pressed steel w/ gray body, blk. roof & lines, gr. int., red wheels & rubber tires, paint loss & surface rust. 26½" L $1,840.00

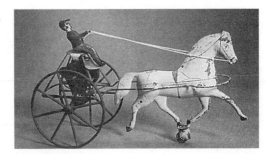

A-MA July 1998   Skinner, Inc.

White Horse Gig, Stevens & Br. clockwork, ca. 1870, jockey has blk. hat, red jacket & yel. trousers, paint wear on rider, horse & gig, wagon repr., 13½" L $4,140.00

A-MA July 1998   Skinner, Inc.

Train Outfit, Marklin, "0" gauge, clockwork engine & tender, blk. w/ red & gr. striping, 1817 gr. open coal w/ bake box, 1816 two br. open coal cars, 1812 gray petroleum tank, 1803 br. guard's van w/o doors, 1804 dk. gr. guard's van w/ sliding doors, 1805 two passenger cars, two 816 pea gr. stake body cars, extra coal car, 1045 Good's station, 2621 covered platform, 2064 E railroad crossing, 2367 ticket collector's stand, 2062 three-part railroad foot bridge, 2037 Linekeepers house w/ semaphore, 2375 three-part railroad bridge, 2472 clockwork signal bell, two 1049 semaphore signals, crane car, two 2018 semaphore signals, six 2054 telephone poles, two 2052 non-lighting arclamps, six similar loco. headlights, plus additional accessories, paint wear, damage & some parts missing $8,050.00

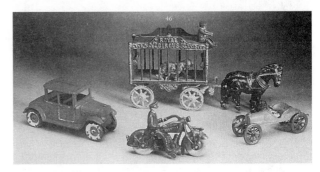

A-MA July 1998   Skinner, Inc.

Row 1

Circus Wagon, Hubley cast iron, ca. 1920, blk. horses, gold & rust tack, dk. gr. wagon w/ gold accents, one tiger, cage door off, 15½" L $1,265.00

Row 2, Left to Right

Car, Hubley red cast iron coupe, ca. 1928, cream & gold accents, white tires, paint chips, & paint loss, rust on tires, spare tire & driver missing, 8¾" L $1,380.00

Motorcycle, Hubley cast iron Champion, blue paint, rubber tires, rubber polymerized, 7¼" L $345.00

Car, Hubley cast iron Roadster, ca. 1920, mustard yel. w/ red spoke wheels, paint darkened, driver missing, 7½" L $258.75

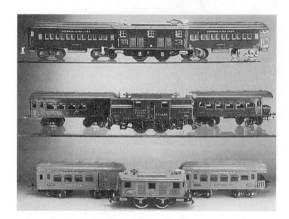

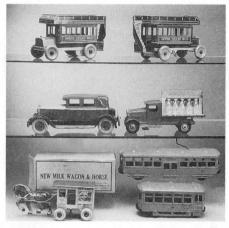

A-MA Jan. 1999　　　　　　　　　　Skinner, Inc.

Row 1

Passenger Set, Am. Flyer standard gauge, incl. 4644 0-4-0 electric locomotive in red & gray, 4151 Eagle, 4152 Eagle observation cars in red w/ litho. features, the observation w/ rear platform, all three in maker's cartons w/ track, slight wear $920.00

Row 2

Passenger Set, Ives standard gauge, incl. 3241 NYC & HR electric locomotive, 184 Buffet, & 186 observation cars finished in gr., car roofs repainted $287.50

Row 3

Passenger Set, Ives standard gauge, incl. motor 3236 locomotive in gr., 184 Pullman club, & 186 observation cars both in tan, chips & scratches $575.00

A-MA Jan. 1999　　　　　　　　　　Skinner, Inc.

Passenger Set, Ives standard gauge, incl. NYC & HR 3243 elec. locomotive w/ leading & trailing trucks, 187-1 buffet, 188-1 parlor, & 189-1 observation cars, all in ora. w/ gr. window frames, cars w/ pierced vaulted roofs, scratching & chipping $920.00

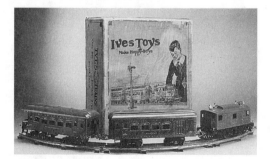

A-MA Jan. 1999　　　　　　　　　　Skinner, Inc.

Passenger Set, Ives set 690 standard gauge, incl. 3235 0-4-0 elec. locomotive, 171 buffet & 173 observation cars, all finished in gr. for NYC & HR w/ track in maker's box, flaking paint & few scratches $402.50

A-MA Jan. 1999　　　　　　　　　　Skinner, Inc.

Row 1, Left to Right

"Inter-State Bus", Straus tinplate, litho. in ora. & yel. w/ clockwork motor, right hand driver, open top deck, scratches, 10½" L $805.00
"Inter-State Bus", Strauss, litho. in gr. & yel. w/ clockwork motor, open top-deck, rear stairs, scratches & some rust, tin bent, 10½" L $373.75

Row 2, Left to Right

Kingsbury Sedan, w/ clockwork motor, front steering, rubber tires, gr. roof & body, yel. hood, repaint, damage, paint loss, 12¾" L $1,150.00
"Coca Cola Truck", Metalcraft, 1931-32 model w/ red cab & chassis, yel. rear w/ ten bottles, paint & decal wear, 10¾" L $402.50

Row 3, Left to Right

"New Milk Wagon & Horse", w/ clockwork motor, litho. finish w/ legends, in maker's box, slight wear, 10¼" L $488.75
Streetcar, Kingsbury, finished in ora. w/ blk. bumpers w/ clockwork motor, fixed turning & bell, chips to roof & front, 14" L $143.75
Streetcar, Kingsbury, finished in ora. w/ blk. bumpers, some scratching & chipping, 9¼" L $201.25

A-MA Jan. 1999　　　　　　　　　　Skinner, Inc.

Row 1, Left to Right

Locomotive & Tender, Lionel, Standard Gauge 2-4-0, w/ gr. lining, some retouching to tender top rail $632.50
Station, Lionel, w/ two ext. & one int. lt., gray base & two card arrivals signs, one repl. $287.50

Row 2, Left to Right

Passenger Set, Am. Flyer standard gauge, incl. 4644 0-4-0 electric locomotive in gr. & two Am. cars in gr. w/ litho. details, one w/ rear platform $402.50

A-NJ Oct. 1998   Bill Bertoia Auctions
Plane, Schiebles, pressed steel, blue fuselage w/ creme wings, paper litho. images, 27½" wingspan $660.00

A-NJ Oct. 1998   Bill Bertoia Auctions
Army Bomber, pressed steel, silver fuselage w/ litho. images of pilot & crew, bi-wings in red, 25" wingspan $413.00

A-NJ Oct. 1998   Bill Bertoia Auctions
US Mail Plane, Steelcraft, pressed steel, painted gray overall w/ red tail fin, rubber tires, 22½" wingspan $358.00

A-NJ Oct. 1998   Bill Bertoia Auctions
Airplane, Keystone "Rapid Fire", pressed steel, olive gr. fuselage w/ red wings & tail fin, blk. motors, 24" wingspan $1,760.00

A-NJ Oct. 1998   Bill Bertoia Auctions
Airplane, Steelcraft, pressed steel painted gray overall w/ red tail fin, blk. motor, 22½" wingspan . .$605.00

A-NJ Oct. 1998   Bill Bertoia Auctions
US Mail Plane, Keystone tri-motor, pressed steel, olive gr. fuselage w/ red wings, blk. motors, 24" wingspan $660.00

A-NJ Oct. 1998   Bill Bertoia Auctions
Air Mail, Keystone, pressed steel, painted olive gr. overall, nickel plated single propeller, 24" wingspan $385.00

A-NJ Oct. 1998   Bill Bertoia Auctions
Spirit of St. Louis, Am. National, pressed steel monocoupe, painted silver fuselage w/ red wing, rubber tires, nickeled disc wheel on back, decal, 24" wingspan $10,450.00

A-NJ Oct. 1998   Bill Bertoia Auctions
Popeye Holster Set, six shooter, J. Halpern Co., incl. two six shooters in leather holsters, orig. litho. cardboard pkg. w/ pic. of Popeye, 12" H $242.00

A-NJ Oct. 1998   Bill Bertoia Auctions
Sand Pails, assorted lot of litho. tin, colorful graphic images of asst. scenery, sizes vary & many contain wood & tin shovels, 2½" to 8¼" H $440.00

A-NJ Oct. 1998   Bill Bertoia Auctions
Sand Pails, WDP & Walt Disney Ent., Ohio Art Co., assort. litho. tin, w/ Mickey Mouse & many famous friends, ca. 1938 to 1940, 5" to 9" w/ handles $1,320.00

A-NJ Oct. 1998   Bill Bertoia Auctions
Disney Toys, assorted, all litho. tin, grouping incl. early beach sand sifter, Mickey Tool Chest and snow shovel, missing wooden handle, & Three Little Pigs play pan, 6¾" diam., to 11" L $770.00

A-PA Sept. 1998   Pook & Pook Inc.

Chest, PA, Sheraton painted walnut, ca. 1810, dec. in faux mah. graining, bold ora. & yel. faux tiger maple painted surface, 38" H, 29½" W $3,750.00

Fireplace Mantle, PA, painted, early 19th C., retaining orig. yel. painted surface, 54½" H, 48" W $950.00

Armchair, CT sackback painted Windsor, ca. 1790, retains old red painted surface $2,500.00

Settee, PA, dec. mini., retains orig. blk., yel. pinstripe & floral dec. surfaces on gr. reserve, 17" H, 24½" L, together w/ mini. plank seat chair $3,500.00

Charger, N. Eng. redware, early 19th C., inscribed in yel. slip "Charles Murvin", 13½" diam. $1,500.00

Trade Sign, Optician's in form of gilded zinc spectacles, mid 19th C., lens painted w/ blue eyes, 18¼" L ..$3,250.00

Coverlet, blue, gr. & red jacquard by G. Renner & P. Leidig, 1838, w/ floral patt. $900.00

Drawing, PA, plumed bird on tree, sgn. "Eliza A. Wirl, Cedar Hill Cemetery, ca. 1833", 14½" x 11½" $425.00

Crock, rare blue dec. stoneware by Geddes NY, waterbug dec. flanked by #2, 11" H ....N/S

Crock, 3-gal. PA stoneware w/ blue dec., 10½" H .$275.00

Butter Churn, wooden, mid 19th C., retaining the orig. blue & yel. pinstripe dec., 38" H $1,100.00

Bellows, 19th C., w/ polychrome fruit & floral dec., damaged $175.00

Hooked Rug, N. Eng., late 19th C., in overall block design, red, blue & yel. oak leaves, 5'2" x 3'3" $1,000.00

A-ME July 1998   Cyr Auction Co. Inc.

Tavern Table, Hepplewhitew/ drawer, pine, birch & oak, splayleg two board breadboard top, top 27½" x 36", 27½" T $950.00

Chair, Windsor brace back in old dk. br. paint, 37" T $800.00

Side Chair, Windsor fanback w/ carved ears in old finish, 36¾" T $1,250.00

Crock, 6-gal. stoneware w/ cobalt dec., "New York Stoneware Co. Fort Edward, NY" $350.00

Crock, 5-gal. stoneware w/ cobalt bird on branch, "Bangor Stoneware Co., Bangor, Me." $225.00

Box, wallpaper covered dometop pine in red & gr., 22½" x 13" x 10¾" $200.00

Ovoid Jug, mkd. "Goodwin & Webster, 11" H $175.00

A-PA June 1998   Pook & Pook Inc.

Pembroke Table, PA, Chippendale walnut, ca. 1790, w/ drop-leaf top, single drawer & sq. tapering legs, blocks repl., 28½" H, 18" W, 31¾" L $850.00

Side Chairs, two similar N. Eng. Q.A. maple , ca. 1750 w/ yoke backs, rush seats & Spanish feet, together w/ country Chippendale birch side chair $1,000.00

Tea Service, silver plated $175.00

Plates, porcelain, group of 8, late 19th C. $650.00

Banjo Clock, Boston, ca. 1830, w/ mah. throat & base panels, 29¾" L $750.00

Mirror Clock, NH, by Benjamin Morril, ca. 1815, w/ rev. painted upper panel, half column gilt & grain dec. frame, 30¼" H, 14" W $3,000.00

Barometer, Georgian mah. banjo form, made by "A. Solca, Tunbridge Wells" $450.00

A-ME Jan. 1999   Cyr Auction Co. Inc.

Chairs, pr. of banister back, 43" x 16" $800.00

Weathervane, steer, fully body, painted red sheet metal, 34" x 24½" $900.00

Washstand, grain painted drawer & top, 36" x 17" x 32" $400.00

Rocking Horse, carved & painted $950.00

Quilt, appliqué, 72" sq. $250.00

A-OH Sept. 1998 Garth's Auctions

Shaker Grain Shovel, wooden w/ some curl, impr. "GMW", old patina & rusted tin edge repr. on blade, 44" L $385.00

Pump, wooden, old grayish paint, one pin at joint repl., 24" H . .$187.00

Shaker Apple Peeler, w/ table clamp, Canterbury, NH, hard & soft wood w/ old patina, 17" H . .$522.50

Shaker Buck Saw, old patina, Union Village, OH, 26" L $330.00

Broilers, two wrt. iron, rotary w/ wheel like grill, 11" diam., 22" L & "rectangular, 12" x 14¾", w/ 10½" handle $192.50

Beetle & Grain Measure, heavy wood beetle w/ age cracks, 24½" L, & bentwood grain measure w/ bentwood handles, insect damage, 8½" diam., 6½" H $82.50

Balance Scale, cast & wrt. iron frame, worn & rusted tin pan has old repr., wooden weight pan has damage, 55½" H $192.50

Double Grain Measure, stave const., old gray repaint, top band is missing, mkd. "C & D, Philadelphia", 12½" H $55.00

Bushel Basket, splint stave, wire & wood rim handles, old patina, 22½" diam., 15½" H $192.50

Decoys, three w/ old working repaint, some damage, 13½", 15" & 16" L $110.00

A-NH Aug. 1998 Northeast Auctions

Coverlet, Am appliquéd & quilted w/ repeated blocks of floral motifs in red, gr. & yel. on white, 74" x 66" .$800.00

A-PA Sept. 1998 Pook & Pook Inc.

Row 1, Left to Right

Document Box, PA, early 19th C., w/ domed lid & front dec. w/ gr. & red flowers on blk. ground, 7½" H, 9¾" W, 6½" D $650.00

Coffee Pot, PA, tole dec., early 19th C., floral dec. on a blk. ground, 10" H $900.00

Tea Caddy, red tole dec., early 19th C. w/ red tulip & blk. & yel. leaves, 5¼" H $125.00

Document Box, PA, early 19th C., tole dec. w/ floral & swag, 4" H, 8½" W, 3¾" D $200.00

Tray, red tole dec. w/ overall floral & fruit dec. & gilt highlights, 12" L, together w/ tray w/ red, yel. & gr. dec. on blk. reserve, 12¼" L $200.00

Row 2, Left to Right

Bowl, PA redware slip dec. in gr., yel. & blk., early 19th C., 10¾" diam. .$13,000.00

Bowl, PA slip dec. redware, early 19th C., w/ yel. parrot, 12" diam. .$100.00

Ring Bottle, earthenware, w/ overall gr. & br. splash dec. on yel. ground, 10½" H $450.00

A-MA Oct. 1998 Skinner, Inc.

Shaker Items

Left to Right

Revolving Stool, New Lebanon, NY, 1860-70, gr. painted seat, 17" H $1,150.00

Armed Rocker, MA Community, 1840-50, early surface, imper. $12,650.00

Revolving Stool, New Lebanon, NY, 1860, imper., 17¼" H $1,150.00

Revolving Stool, New Lebanon, NY, 1860-70, old surface, 30" H .$6,324.00

Revolving Stool, New Lebanon, NY, 1860-70, old surface, minor imper. $6,325.00

A-PA Sept. 1998 Pook & Pook Inc.

Powder Horn, Am. carved in manner of Timothy Tansel of Indiana, one side dated 1841 w/ religious pictorial, other side w/ seal of U.S. & running deer & swag dec. borders . .$7,500.00

A-OH Sept. 1998 Garth's Auctions

Shaker Items

Shaker Cupboard, Enfield, NH, pine w/ old worn white repaint on ext. & orangish orig. paint on int. w/ old pumpkins repaint on inside of doors, repl. latches, 21¼" W, 7½" D, 80" H $5,280.00

Hay Rake, all wood w/ four tines, 64½" L $275.00

Hay Rake, all wood w/ four tines, 68½" L $220.00

Side Chairs, set of seven similar low-back, six have old gr. repaint, one had dk. gr. paint partially removed, woven rope seats, two have older seats covered in cloth $605.00

Shaker Child's Cloak, blue wool, machine sewn, minor moth damage, some wear & soiling, 25" L . .$267.50

A-OH Sept. 1998   Garth's Auctions

Row 1, Left to Right

Bowl, turned wooden, ext. has old worn lt. blue paint, int. has wear from much use, 16¾" x 17½", 5¾" H $357.50

Rooster Weathervane, cast zinc & sheet steel w/ old blk. paint, overall 51" H $1,127.50

Basket, round woven splint for herb drying, open rim handles, good patina, 21" diam., 6¼" H $247.50

Row 2, Left to Right

Bench, pine w/ worn red repaint, top has wear & age crack, 10½" x 72½" L $357.50

Fruit Basket, woven splint, open rim handles, good patina, 16½" diam., 11" H $231.00

Shaker Chip Carrier, poplar w/ old finish, painted initials "R.C.", dovetailed, bentwood handle is split at one end, 9¾" x 16", 9" H $247.50

Basket, oblong woven splint, open handles on one side w/ wooden handle on the other, good patina, 13" x 19", 8" H $192.50

Row 3, Left to Right

Box, round bentwood, swivel handle, old varnish finish w/ stains, minor edge damage, 11½" diam., 6½" H $82.50

Basket, woven splint & cane buttocks, Eye of God design at bentwood handle, 16" x 20", 8" H $192.50

Box, round bentwood, old varnish finish, lapped seams w/ copper tacks, age crack in lid, 11½" diam., 6" H $110.00

A-ME Sept. 1998   Cyr Auction Co. Inc.

"The Graphophone", disc record player w/ wooden horn, 12" x 12" oak case $3,500.00

A-OH Sept. 1998   Garth's Auctions

Lighting Stand, wrt. iron, tripod base w/ penny feet, pole w/ four hooks for lamps, pitted, 56½" H $357.50

Whirligig, male figure w/ swivel arms, vanes missing, worn & weathered surface w/ traces of red, white & blue paint, overall 44" H $605.00

Weathervane, carved wooden fish w/ good folky detail, 20th C., w/ weathered gray finish & age cracks, top fin missing, wire nails hold other fins, 40" L, 56" H $605.00

Plate Warmer, Euro., wrt. iron, old gr. repaint, 35½" H $121.00

Lighting Stand, wrt. iron, tripod base w/ penny feet, adjustable rush lt. holder w/ candle socket counter balance, twisted detail & acorn finial, 43½" H $385.00

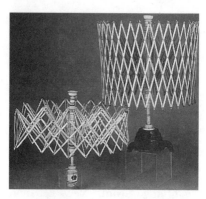

A-MA Oct. 1998   Skinner, Inc.

Left to Right

Double Swift, whalebone & whale ivory, 19th C., scribed staves, inlaid w/ coin silver plaque & rings, minor losses, 16" L $1,840.00

Swift, whalebone & whale ivory "Clothespin", 19th C., turned mah. base, minor losses, excluding base 19½" H $3,450.00

A-PA Feb. 1999   Pook & Pook Inc.

Cupboard, pine & maple, ca. 1825, 59" H, 56½" W, 22½" D . . . . .N/S

Top, Left to Right

Jug, 3 gal. ovoid stoneware, ca. 1830, extensive blue floral dec., 14" H $600.00

Jug, 2 gal. stoneware, ca. 1850 w/ vibrant blue floral dec., 13¼" H, w/ ovoid form redware jar, 10" H $650.00

Crock, 5 gal. double-handled stoneware, ca. 1840, blue bird dec., 11¼" H $425.00

Crock, 2 handled stoneware, ca. 1840, dec. w/ cobalt tulips on bulbous body, 10¾" H $275.00

Bottom, Left to Right

Water Cooler, PA, 5 gal. stoneware, attrib. to Richard Remmey of PA, ca. 1870, w/ bold blue floral & leaf dec., 15¾" L $175.00

Crock, 4 gal. stoneware, mkd. "Evan R. Jones, Pittston, PA", ca 1840, blue floral dec., 11½" H $425.00

A-MA Oct. 1998   Skinner, Inc.

Drum, Civil War Snare, manuf. by A.H. White, Boston, 2nd qtr. 19th C., wooden rim, metal body, engr. w/ star dec., & MA State Seal, heads missing, 12½" H, 17" diam. $977.50

A-MA Oct. 1998   Skinner, Inc.

Left to Right

Presentation Cane, Narwhal, carved whalebone w/ silver top, pre 1836, 37½" L $2,530.00
Cane, whale ivory & whalebone, 19th C., four baleen spacers, age cracks, 36¾" L $402.50
Cane, sectional carved whale ivory & whalebone, 19th C., hoof handle w/ baleen inlay, age cracks, 36" L . . .$287.50
Cane, carved whale ivory & whalebone, 19th C., L-shaped two-part handle, dec. in jockey motif of cap, repr., missing spacer, 38" L $345.00
Cane, carved whale ivory & whalebone, 19th C., handle carved in form of eagle's head, one eye missing, minor age cracks, 34¾" L . .$2,530.00
Cane, carved whale ivory & whalebone, late 19th early 20th C., brass tip, age crack, 34¼" L $862.50

A-IA June 1998   Jackson's

Left to Right

Commode, Eng. w/ mottled rose marble top & backsplash, 36" W, 49" H $230.00
Commode, Eng., walnut w/ marble top & tile backsplash, 34" W, 41" H $316.25

A-IA June 1998   Jackson's
Commode, Eng. w/ white carrera marble, bracketed back splash, 47" L, 23" H $230.00

A-MA Oct. 1998   Skinner, Inc.

Left to Right

Cane, carved whale ivory & whalebone, 19th C., traces of red sealing wax, top w/ M.O.P. inlaid disk, damage to spacers, tip end of shaft missing, 31¼" L $747.50
Cane, carved walrus tusk & whalebone, 19th C., octagonal cane w/ ebony spacer, w/ sailor's knots, ring turnings & diamond points, age cracks, 35½" L $2,645.00
Cane, carved whale ivory & whalebone, 19th C., having a Turk's-head knot handle, inset baleen spacers, minor cracks, 35¼" L $1,092.50
Cane, carved whalebone & whale ivory, 19th C, w/ Turk's-head knot handle, dec. w/ ivory woven ring & single baleen spacer, slight warping, 34½" L $2,645.00
Cane, carved whale ivory & whalebone, 19th C., have polyhedron handle inlaid w/ ebony dots, ebony & metal spacers, crack beneath knob, 34¾" L . .$1092.50
Cane, carved walrus tusk & whalebone, 19th C., two inset baleen spacers, slight warping, minor age cracks, 34¾" L $920.00

A-ME Sept. 1998   Cyr Auction Co. Inc.
"Reginaphone", mah. case, 15" disc music box, 21" x 19" x 12½" T $6,000.00

A-ME July 1998   Cyr Auction Co. Inc.
Backgammon Board, red, blk. & yel., 18½" x 21½" $650.00
Gameboard, w/ Parcheesi on back, red, gr. & blk., 18" x 25" $300.00
Lanterns, pr., tin w/ red glass, 10½" T $350.00
Basket, splint w/ gr., blue, yel. & red paint dec., 12" diam., 10" T . .$400.00
Chest, Sheraton, ME, four drawer in tiger maple w/ red painted case, top 18" x 38", 39" H $750.00

A-MA Oct. 1998   Skinner, Inc.

Left to Right

Child's Sled, painted wood, late 19th C., "Kelly", solid wood frame w/ iron runners, dk. gr., mustard & red paint, blk. letters & highlights, paint losses, 34" L, 11½" W $805.00
Sleds, two painted wood, late 19th C., an olive gr. child's push sled w/ gold, blk. & yel. striping, & a red toy sled w/ metal runners & dec. w/ lilies of the valley, 24" L, w/o handle 15" L $1,725.00

A-ME Jan. 1999   Cyr Auction Co. Inc.

Crib Quilt, appliqué, 42" sq. \$325.00
Chair, Sheraton grain painted & dec., 33" x 17" ..\$175.00
Sewing Table, Fed. birdseye, top 16" x 19", 28" T \$1,750.00
Box, grain painted w/ brass handle, 9" x 15" x 6" T \$150.00

A-ME Jan. 1999   Cyr Auction Co. Inc.

Pewter Hutch, red open top, 20" x 49" x 84" ...\$3,750.00
Work Table, Sheraton, 2 drawer birch w/ birdseye fronts & mah. banding, 18½" x 21" x 28¾" \$650.00
Hat Rack, gr., 33" x 46" \$325.00
Cupboard, molded panel in red, 16" x 44" x 67" ..\$750.00

A-ME Jan. 1999   Cyr Auction Co. Inc.

Cupboard, grain painted glazed door, stepback, 24" x 7' x 36" \$1,000.00
Box, blk. & gr. pin-striped, 6" x 16" x 7½" \$150.00
Box, blk. pin-striped, 10½" x 18" x 6" \$150.00
Sailboat, pond model, 34" L \$800.00
Wall Cupboard, red painted w/ molded paneled door, 10" x 28½" x 42½" \$1,500.00
Weathervane, full body zinc, 20" \$1,250.00
Box, tole dec. dome top, 6" x 9½" x 7½" \$500.00
Butterstamp, carved pineapple design \$150.00
Whirligig, figure, 10" T \$675.00
Tap Table, blue tapered leg, 24" x 24", top 29" T .\$550.00
Bootjack Footstool, red & blk. grained, 6½" x 13½" x 8 ....\$200.00
Squirrel Cage, gr. painted, 12" x 28" x 15½" \$75.00
Pitcher, blue & white Spongeware, 9" \$150.00
Wooden Dividers, 43" H \$75.00
Cupboard, blue painted two door chimney, 14" x 30" x 6' T \$750.00
Box, grain painted, mustard & blk., 12" x 24" x 10" .\$75.00
Hooked Rugs, two, 54" x 60" x 36" x 70" \$900.00

A-ME Jan. 1999   Cyr Auction Co. Inc.

Redware

Ovoid Jug, gr. spotted dec., 7½" T \$450.00
Ovoid Jug, dk. br., 5½" T \$220.00
Stew Pot, beige w/ gr. spots, 7¼" T \$125.00
Ovoid Jug, br. striping w/ gr. spots, polished glaze, 5" T \$225.00
Cup, gr. & br. glaze, 3" T \$100.00
Mug, br. glaze, 3½" T \$275.00
Chest of Drawers, 6¾" T x 7" W x 3¼" D \$170.00
Mold, hand formed, br. glaze, impr. w/ childs handprint \$325.00
Jar, gr. glaze w/ ora. spots, 8¾" T \$500.00
Ovoid Jug, gr. glaze w/ ora. spots, 7½" T \$750.00
Dye Pot, gr. glaze w/ ora. spots, 6" T \$350.00

A-ME Jan. 1999   Cyr Auction Co. Inc.

Shelf, hanging, 36" x 46" . .$2,700.00
Box, grain painted $175.00
Blanket Chest, w/ bracket base, red & blk. orig. dec., 19" x 44" x 24" $650.00
Weathervane, horse $185.00

Weathervane, cow $250.00
Horse Toys, pr. $200.00
Shelf, hanging $300.00
Box, tole dec. $120.00
Child's Rocker, Boston, w/ stencil dec. $125.00
Chest of Drawers, w/ red wash $850.00

A-PA Sept. 1998   Pook & Pook Inc.
Dutch Cupboard, PA, pine, ca. 1790, upper section w/ a molded cornice over two 6-lt. doors, shelved int. w/ spoon racks, 86½" H, 60" W $2,800.00
Measures, set of 7 Fr. graduated pewter, late 19th C. $375.00
Charger, pewter w/ raised coat of arms, dated 1670, 14¾" diam., together w/ a pr. of pewter candle-sticks $250.00
Needlework, silk on silk, picture of parrot perched on floral branches, mid 18th C., 9" x 7½" $375.00
Kettle, Eng. copper, early 19th C., w/ wrt. iron trivet, 13½" H $275.00
Pot, lrg. copper lidded w/ wrt. iron swing handle $350.00

A-ME Sept. 1998   Cyr Auction Co. Inc.
Music Box, Regina "Sublima piano & mandolin orchestra", upright paper roll music box in oak case, 41" x 64" x 20½" $2,750.00

A-ME Sept. 1998   Cyr Auction Co. Inc.
Nickelodeon, oak case leaded glass door, "Kelley Automatic Music Co. Albany, NY", 11¼" paper roll, "Seeburg Piano Co., Chicago USA" . .$3,500.00

A-ME Sept. 1998   Cyr Auction Co. Inc.
High Wheel Bicycle, 54" front wheel, 19" back wheel $1,900.00

A-ME Jan. 1999   Cyr Auction Co. Inc.
Sailor Valentine, mah. case, swags of pink w/ dense clusters in star & heart design, 13" x 13" $4,000.00

A-ME Jan. 1999   Cyr Auction Co. Inc.
Sailor Valentine, mah. case, tight compartmentalized clusters, 9" x 13" $2,750.00

A-ME Jan. 1999   Cyr Auction Co. Inc.
Sailor Valentine, mah. case w/ dense cluster in star designs, 13" x 13" $4,000.00

A-PA Feb. 1999   Pook & Pook Inc.

Pewter Cupboard, N. Eng., pine canted-back, ca. 1735, tall cut-out Q.A. feet, retains old dk. surface, 74" H, 49½" W $2,900.00

Row 1, Left to Right

Misc. Pewter
nine pc. lot, shown here is 2 pewter casters & an inkwell, lot also includes two spirit lamps, 19th C., 11" H, 3 modern pewter salts, & porringer $250.00

Row 2, Left to Right

Charger, pewter, ca. 1800, mkd. "BMS", 13⅜" diam., together w/ Ger. pewter plate mkd. "IHP", 12" diam. & four plates w/ scalloped rims $600.00

Misc. Pewter
nine pc. lot, shown here is porringer, lot also includes two spirit lamps, 19th C., 11" H, together w/ 2 pewter casters, an inkwell, & 3 modern pewter salts $250.00

Plates, four w/ scalloped rims, together w/ pewter charger, ca. 1800, mkd. "BMS", 13⅜" diam., together w/ Ger. pewter plate mkd. "IHP", 12" diam. $600.00

Row 3, Left to Right

Vintners Bowl, Ger. pewter, dated 1763, w/ fully engr. drinking scene, w/ pewter charger & 4 pewter plates & a basin $600.00

Misc. Pewter
nine pc. lot, shown here is 3 modern pewter salts, 19th C., 11" H, lot also includes two spirit lamps & an inkwell, 2 pewter casters, & porringer $250.00

Eng. Measure, lrg. pewter, late 18th C., mkd. "Bulls Head Strand Gr.", 8½" H $550.00

Misc. Pewter
nine pc. lot, shown here is one of two spirit lamps, 19th C., 11" H, lot also includes 3 modern pewter salts & an inkwell, 2 pewter casters, & porringer $250.00

Plates, four pewter, included in lot is Vintners Bowl, Ger. pewter, dated 1763, w/ fully engr. drinking scene, w/ pewter charger & a basin $600.00

Row 4, Left to Right

Cast Iron, shown, lot also incl. pr., Swedish candelabra, early 19th C., w/ Dutch brass emb. & engr. candlestick w/ spiral shaft, 6½" H, & brass iron $350.00

Charger, pewter, included in lot is Vintners Bowl, Ger. pewter, dated 1763, w/ fully engr. drinking scene, also four pewter plates & basin $600.00

Candelabra, pr., Swedish, early 19th C., together w/ Dutch brass emb. & engr. candlestick w/ spiral shaft, 6½" H, & Scottish cast iron & brass iron $350.00

Charger, London pewter by William Cooke, dated 1707, 13½" diam., together w/ 18th C., London charger, 15" diam. $275.00

Candelabra, pr., Swedish, early 19th C., together w/ Dutch brass emb. & engr. candlestick w/ spiral shaft, 6½" H, & Scottish cast iron & brass iron $350.00

Floor Charger, lrg. pewter, ca. 1800, mkd. "CTM", 20" diam. $750.00

Charger, London pewter by William Cooke, dated 1707, 13½" diam., together w/ 18th C., London charger, 15" diam. $275.00

Tankard, lrg. baluster form pewter, dated 1775 w/ initials "MBH" on lid, 13½" H $650.00

Pitcher, lrg. Eng. pewter, ca. 1800, mkd. "H.L. Sun Romford", 11¼" H $750.00

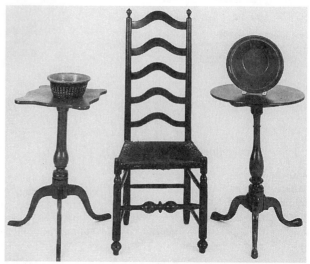

A-PA June 1998   Pook & Pook Inc.

Candlestand, N. Eng. birch, ca. 1790, retains orig. red stained surface, 28¼" H, 16" sq. $450.00

Candlestand, PA, Q.A. walnut, ca. 1790, w/ circular tilting top, 28½" H, 19¾" diam. $375.00

Side Chair, PA, Chester Co. ladderback, ca. 1780 w/ ball & ring turned stretcher $750.00

Bowl, PA, slip dec., early 19th C., w/ yel. band, 4" H, 11½" diam., together w/ another slip dec. bowl $325.00

A-PA June 1998   Pook & Pook Inc.

Side Chair, fine Windsor bowback, ca. 1780, w/ carved seat, retains blk. painted surface w/ gilt highlights . . .$850.00

Armchair, PA, Windsor combback, ca. 1775, w/ carved ear crest rail, D-shaped seat, res. feet tips $3,600.00

Settee, PA, painted child's highback, ca. 1830, retains old red painted surface, 40½" H, 25" W $3,000.00

Pitcher, stoneware, 19th C., w/ profuse blue floral dec., repr., 10½" H $600.00

Crock, "Cowden & Wilcox, Harrisburg, PA", stoneware, 19th C., w/ blue dec. of horse, 13" H $18,000.00

Pitcher, stoneware, 19th C., w/ blue dec. initials & floral design, 14" H $275.00

Owl Decoy, late 19th early 20th C., retaining orig. white & br. painted surface, horn repr., 19" H $650.00

Painting, Viola E. Weed, Am. 19th C., oil on panel, house & trees, 16" x 10" $500.00

Hooked Rug, Am. pictorial depicting a Model T in a village, 17½" x 37½" $1,700.00

A-PA Dec. 1998   Pook & Pook Inc.

Blanket Chest, PA, York Co., dec. ca. 1830 w/ ochre & red oak leaf dec., 22" x 34½" $1,100.00

End Table, Hepplewhite pine, ca. 1830 w/ overall gr. surface w/ blk. pinstriping & floral dec. top & drawer, 29" H, 19" W $350.00

Cedar Mask, NW Coast Tlingit, mid 20th C., applied feathers & horse hair above painted face, 13½" x 10½" .$100.00

Pottery Bowl, Hopi Pueblo, sgn. "Patricia Honie" 8¼" diam. $300.00

Olla Bowl, Santo Domingo Pueblo, sgn. "Paulet Pachico", w/ blk. & cream colored geo. patt., 7" H, 6½" diam. $300.00

Indian Basket, MA, round lidded splint, ca. 1900 w/ shades of ora., yel. & blue, 12" H, 17½" W $250.00

Indian Basket, MA, open splint, ca. 1900 w/ sq. base & dec. of alt. blk. & red stripes, 10" H, 16" diam. $75.00

Basket Bowl, Hopi Walipi w/ tight weave, 10¼" diam. . .$35.00

Eskimo Basket, lidded, w/ blk. & red seal gut dec., 12½" H, 10" diam. $75.00

Indian Basket, MA, rectangular open, late 19th C., w/ blk. banding, diamonds & stylized branches, initialed "MH", minor losses $300.00

Canoe, Mic Mac birch bark, early 20th C., w/ moose & floral dec., 36" L $425.00

Canoe, Mic Mac birch bark, mid 20th C., dec. w/ hearts & shamrocks, 28" L $325.00

Serapi, Saltillo, ca. 1800 w/ fringed border, 90" x 48" .N/S

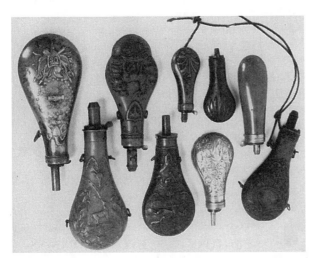

A-ME Jan. 1999   Cyr Auction Co. Inc.

Left to Right

Peace Flask, two-sided, 4" x 9" $200.00

Flask, w/ stag & oak garland, two-sided, 3½" x 9" $100.00

Flask, w/ stag in woods, 3¼" x 8¼" $95.00

Flask, w/ stag & dogs, two-sided, 3½" x 7½" $100.00

Flask, w/ acanthus dec., two-sided, 2" x 4½" $55.00

Flask, plated, w/ neptune design, 2¾" x 6" $150.00

Flask, w/ open leaf design, two-sided, 2" x 5" $75.00

Flask, plain, 2" x 6" $60.00

Flask, acanthus dec., two-sided, 3½" x 7½" $100.00

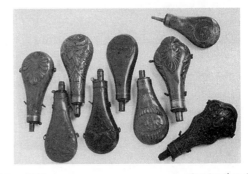

A-ME Jan. 1999   Cyr Auction Co. Inc.

Left to Right

Flask, w/ acanthus design, 3½" x 8", two-sided . . .$45.00.

Flask, w/ deer design, 3½" x 7½", two-sided $50.00

Flask, w/ oakleaf design, 3½" x 8" $70.00

Flask, w/ standing dog design, 3¼" x 7¾" $80.00

Flask, w/ pointing dogs, 3¼" x 7¼" $85.00

Flask, w/ dog, 3½" x 8", two-sided $70.00

Flask, w/ acanthus, two-sided, 3½" x 7½" $60.00

Flask, tin w/ geese, two-sided, 3" x 7" $45.00

Flask, Baroque, two-sided, 3½" x 8" $95.00

A-MA Jan. 1998   Skinner, Inc.
Knife Urns, George III w/ checker inlay & crossbanded, early 19th C., fitted int. & carved finial, 25½" H $4,600.00

A-MA Aug. 1998   Skinner, Inc.
Spice Chest, PA, 1780-1800, walnut, 11 sm. int. drawers w/ brass pulls, old surface, minor imper., 18¼" H, 15½" W, 11" D $14,950.00

A-MA Aug. 1998   Rafael Osona Auctioneer
                              & Appraiser
Barometer, gimbaled stick, walnut, mid-19th C., 36" H $1,400.00

A-PA Dec. 1998   Pook & Pook Inc.
Corner Cupboard, PA, Bucks Co., folk art relief carved mini., const. by itinerant carver, made for Elinora Frey, ca. 1885, polychrome cornice w/ blk. painted feet, 34" H, 18" W ..$2,200.00
Blanket Chest, PA, Sheraton dec., ca. 1840, overall red & yel. grain dec., 21½" H, 36" W $700.00
Storage Box, N. Eng. dome lidded, early 19th C., w/ polychromed scene, framed by yel. stripes on lid, 7½" H, 15' W, 9½" D $1,500.00
Box, PA, dec. lift lid, mid 19th C., w/ Mahantongo type dec. w/ yel. & red stenciling on blue ground, paint loss, 9½" H, 19½" W, 11" D $850.00
Fire Wagon, folk art mech. carving, retains orig. red & yel. painted surface, figure retains orig. linen uniform, 12½" L $500.00
Pincushion, tole dec. in form of an iron, 19th C., w/ red & gilt pinstriping w/ blk. tole pail w/ gr. yel. & red floral dec. $300.00
Pitcher, Remmey type 2-gal., stoneware w/ profuse blue dec., hairline, 13½" H $375.00
Bellows, PA, tole dec., early 19th C., w/ gilt basket on red ground .$350.00
Paper Cutout, PA, mid 19th C., eagle astride heart etc. all surrounded by moon & floral dec., 9¾" x 7½"$1,100.00
Hooked Rug, pictorial, swan w/ arrow on shaded blue ground, 2'11" x 1'11½" $650.00
Hooked Rug, ca. 1900, w/ central floral cartouche w/ braided border, 3'7¼" x 1'10½" $1,800.00

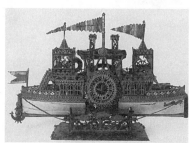

A-PA Dec. 1998   Pook & Pook Inc.
Side-Wheeler Model, trampwork ca. 1890 w/ tin flags & elaborate deck work w/ oars etc., 17" H, 25" L $10,000

A-PA Dec. 1998   Pook & Pook Inc.
Tall Case Clock, Pa, Chippendale walnut, ca. 1790, 8-day painted dial works, narrow waist w/ highly figured door, reeded fluted quarter columns, 7'9" H $4,750.00
Chest of Drawers, MA, Chippendale mah. block front, ca. 1770 w/ thumb molded edge top, drawers retaining orig. brasses, 29½" H, 32" W ..$10,000.00
Mirror, Chippendale mah., ca. 1790, 43½" H $800.00
Platter, Historical blue, early 19th C., w/ conch shell & foliate border, 18½" L, together w/ transfer dec. cup & saucer $1,500.00
Mug & Tea Caddy, blue & white mug, both ca. 1800, Nanking tea caddy, hairline, ...$750.00
Canton Dish, scalloped, ca. 1800, 8½" L, together w/ shell form dish, 4½" L $350.00

A-PA Sept. 1998   Pook & Pook Inc.

Left to Right

Hanging Cupboard, PA, walnut ca. 1790, cornice res., 43½" H, 25" W $1,300.00
Blanket Chest, N. Eng. Q.A., ca. 1780, lift lid, retains orig. vibrant blk. & red feather graining, 21½" H, 42½" W $600.00
Weathervane, copper horse, ca. 1890, full bodied running horse & sheet sulky & rider, 24" H, 46" L $4,750.00

A-PA Oct. 1998   York Town Auction Inc.
Weathervane, gilded & molded copper & zinc horse & rider, attrib. to A.L. Jewell Co., MA, w/ partial coat of old yel., ca. 1870-1890's, 24½" H, 26" L $10,500.00

A-PA Oct. 1998   York Town Auction Inc.
Weathervane, gilded & molded copper dove, retaining orig. gilding & verde gris surface, ca. 1880-1890's, 21" H, 25" L $4,500.00

A-PA Oct. 1998   York Town Auction Inc.
Weathervane, molded copper horse & sulky, w/ orig. directionals, overpainted w/ minor old reprs., ca. 1890-1910, 44" L, 25" H $5,500

A-NH Aug. 1998   Northeast Auctions
Left to Right
Weathervane, horse & sulky, Cushing, on rod & stand, 32" L $6,500.00
Weathervane, Jewell full-bodied copper running horse, on rod & stand, 26½" L $3,750.00
Weathervane, Harris & Co., Boston lrg. horse in form of "Goldsmith Maid", on stand, 37" L $5,000.00

A-NH Aug. 1998   Northeast Auctions
Carousel Horse, Charles J.D. Looff carved & polychrome painted & "jeweled" w/ blk. mane & horse-hair tail, cream body w/ eagle carved saddle, 57" H overall, approx. 65" L $14,000.00

A-NH Aug. 1998   Northeast Auctions
Figure, Am. carved & blk. painted wooden full-size Retriever, 50½" L $10,500.00

A-PA Sept. 1998   Pook & Pook Inc.
Spoon Rack, PA, Lancaster Co., pine, ca. 1770, w/ tulip crest, retains old stained surface, 21" H $1,000.00
Blanket Chest, PA, Sheraton mini., dec., w/ thumbmolded lift lid & turned feet, retains orig. overall mottled & stripe dec. w/ central gr. circle, 9¼" H, 14½" W, 7¼" D $3,100.00
Deer, pr. of PA chalkware, early 19th C., resting on blk. plinths, 10½" H, 8" L $2,200.00
Poodle, PA, chalkware, early 19th C., w/ red, yel. & blk. polychrome surface, 7½" H, 6" L $700.00
Ram & Ewe, PA chalkware figures, early 19th C., w/ red, gr. & yel. dec., 3½" H, 4" L $1,800.00
Cat, PA, chalkware, early 19th C., w/ yel. & blk. highlights, 5½" H .$700.00

A-PA Feb. 1999   Pook & Pook Inc.
Watercolor, on paper by Hattie K. Bruner, snow scene w/ horse-drawn sleigh, Am., 1890-1982, 10½" x 14½" $1,100.00

A-PA Feb. 1999   Pook & Pook Inc.
Watercolor, on paper by Hattie K. Bruner, landscape & covered bridge, etc., Am., 1890-1982, 10¾" x 13¾" $2,700.00

A-PA Feb. 1999   Pook & Pook Inc.
Watercolor, on paper by Hattie K. Bruner, snow scene w/ covered bridge & horse-drawn sleigh, Am., 1890-1982, 10¾" x 14" $2,600.00

A-MA Oct. 1998   Skinner, Inc.
Theorem, unsgn. watercolor on velvet, in yel. period frame, Am. School, 19th C., minor toning & facing, 16¼" x 14½" $4,025.00

A-ME Sept. 1998   Cyr Auction Co. Inc.
Arcade Machine, Simplex Electric Shock, 5 Cents, oak base w/ iron top, 57" T $29,000.00

A-ME Sept. 1998   Cyr Auction Co. Inc.
Strength Machine, "The Caille Tug of War", painted cast iron w/ litho face, 25-1000 lbs. 57" T . . .$19,000.00

A-ME Sept. 1998   Cyr Auction Co. Inc.
Mutoscope, "Am. Mutoscope & Biograph Co. NY", painted iron, 65" x 17" x 15" $3,250.00

A-ME Sept. 1998   Cyr Auction Co. Inc.
Lighthouse, "Grip Test Muscle Developer", oak case w/ iron feet, 7' x 14" x 14" $5,500.00

A-NH Aug. 1998   Northeast Auctions
Child's Sleigh, Am. in orig. red & blue paint w/ white striping, w/ companion carriage wheels, hinged hood & additional handle, buggy w/ blue velvet tufted int. $2,000.00

A-PA Mar. 1999   Horst Auctioneers
Hanging Cupboard, PA, early 19th C., dovetailed const., solid ends, ref., 28" H, 24" W, 12" D $7,400.00
Chair, Windsor, bowback w/ "H" stretcher, ref. $650.00
Table, w/ splay legs, PA, late 18th or early 19th C., softwood painted red, top w/ res., runners repl., 28" H, top 29" x 20" $650.00
Chair, Windsor, bowback w/ "H" stretcher, ref., legs cut down & res. $150.00

A-ME Sept. 1998   Cyr Auction Co. Inc.
Grip Tester, one cent, "D. Gottlieb & Co.", 13" T $275.00

A-IA June 1998   Jackson's
Folding Screen, Chinese, dec. w/ figures & horseman w/ colored hardstone, bone & ivory, 72" H . . .$402.50

A-PA Sept. 1998   Pook & Pook, Inc.

Left to Right

Hooded Cradle, tiger maple, late 18th C., w/ heart cutouts $950.00
Blanket Chest, Q.A., Chester Co. PA, tiger maple, late 18th C., 20½" H, 41½" L $2,000.00

A-PA Mar. 1999   Horst Auctioneers
Hanging Corner Cupboard, early 19th C., tiger maple w/ early br. paint, minor wood loss to corners, 41" W, 22" D, 29¼" H $9,900.00
Dough Box, late 18th or early 19th C., w/ br. paint, dovetailed const., some wood loss to top edge of trough on 1 side, 29" H, 41" W, 22" D $800.00

A-MA Aug. 1998   Rafael Osona Auctioneer
                              & Appraiser
Dinner Service, Limoges, 19th C., 127 pcs. w/ gilded fine on gr. border $2,000.00
Cupboard, Welsh, oak, 18th C., in 2 parts, 83½" W, 87" H $5,000.00
Fire Fender, brass, 19th C., 47½" W, 9" H $650.00

A-PA June 1998   Pook & Pook, Inc.

Left to Right

Armchair, N. Eng., Windsor bowback, ca. 1790 . . . .$550.00
Blanket Chest, NY, ca. 1810, w/ blk. trailing vine dec., 18" H, 42" W, 17½" D $4,500.00
Weathervane, copper hollow body running horse w/ cast iron head & directionals, 31" L $350.00
Armchair, N. Eng., Windsor sackback, ca. 1790, ends of arms res. $600.00

A-IA June 1998   Jackson's

Left to Right

Child's Rocker, oak & maple w/ arm rests $86.25
Table, gate leg, walnut, mini. .$86.25

A-MA Aug. 1998   Rafael Osona Auctioneer
                              & Appraiser
Candle Sconces, Georgian, 18th C., brass w/ blown glass smoke bell over a glass hurricane w/ brass drop finial, 21½" H $1,000.00
Theorem, Am., yarn, NY, ca. 1870, woven floral arrangement in vase, fruits & vegetables around base, on gr. felt ground, 20½" x 22¼" $3,000.00
Side Chairs, four Windsor fan back, early 19th C., w/ yel. paint, br. trim, 34½" H $1,700.00
Basket, Nantucket w/ swing handle, ca. 1900, hinged to brass ears, 9½" D, 4½" H $1,400.00
Platter, Canton, 17th C., w/ rain & cloud border, 13" L, 10¾" W .$300.00
Tea Table, Q.A., tiger maple, ca. 1750, 24½" diam., 31¼" W, 26½" H $1,700.00

A-MA Aug. 1998   Rafael Osona Auctioneer
                              & Appraiser
Terrestrial Globe, by W. & A.K. Johnston, Eng., 1897 w/ iron stand, globe 18" diam., overall 45" $2,900.00

A-MA Oct. 1998   Skinner, Inc.

Left to Right

Windmill Weight, painted cast iron, late 19th/early 20th C., paint losses, 15½" H, 16½" W $747.50

Windmill Weight, cast iron, late 19th/early 20th C., w/ traces of red paint, 19" H, 17" W $1,380.00

A-PA Dec. 1998   Pook & Pook Inc.

Tall Case Clock, PA, Wm. and Mary, Lancaster Co., cherry, ca. 1760, w/ flat top bonnet & blind fret frieze, 8-day brass face works, name plated inscribed, feet of later date, 87½" H . . .$16,000.00

Chest, VA diminutive, ca. 1760 w/ 2 short drawers over 3 long drawers, orig. bold plate brasses, feet res., 34¾" H, 33¼" W $4,000.00

Mirror, Q.A. mah., ca. 1750 w/ orange crest & ears, retains orig. beveled glass & fine old patina, 36" H, 19½" W $2,500.00

Paper Cut-out, pinwheel valentine, inscribed "Peggy Blauvelt 1709", w/ verse & hearts, 12½" diam. . .$2,100.00

Candlestick, bell metal, late 17th C., 14½" H, together w/ sm. pr. of brass fluid lamps & pewter candlestick . .N/S

A-IA June 1998   Jackson's

Kitchen Cupboard, oak w/ frosted glass doors, spice drawers & flower bin, ca. 1910, 70" H $345.00

A-PA Dec. 1998   Pook & Pook Inc.

Dutch Cupboard, PA, pine, ca. 1800, upper section w/ two 6-lt. doors resting on base, 2 drawers over 2 paneled doors, 83" H, 54½" W $5,250.00

Theorem, Ellinger, Am. 20th C., oil on velvet, fruit & vines w/ bird, etc., sgn., 14¼" x 16" $1,500.00

Chalkware Deer, PA, late 19th C., w/ overall br. painted surface together w/ chalkware mounted head of stag $375.00

Chalkware Animals, group of PA, 19th C., incl. stag w/ overall striped dec., squirrel, rabbit & horse, some losses $750.00

Pitcher, Remmey type stoneware, 2-gal., 19th C. w/ blue floral dec., 14" H, hairline, together w/ another 2-gal. stoneware pitcher $500.00

Hooked Rug, w/ 2 central cornucopias w/ multicolor scalloped border, 6'1" x 2'11" $1,100.00

A-PA Dec. 1998   Pook & Pook Inc.

Walnut Vargueno, late 17th C., upper section w/ hinged M.O.P. inlaid cornice, multiple line inlaid drawers & doors centering on an arched recess, res., 59½" H, 43½" W $1,700.00

A-PA Sept. 1998   Pook & Pook Inc.

Pewter Cupboard, Welsh oak, ca. 1740, 79½" H, 63½" L $4,750.00

Crock, stoneware, 6 gal. w/ blue dec., mkd. "New York Stoneware Co., Fort Edward, NY", crack $850.00

A-PA Sept. 1998   York Town Auction Inc.

High Chair, ladderback, PA, ca. 1780-1800 . . . .$2,600.00

Weathervane, gilded copper cow, 19" H, 27" L $5,750.00

Crock, stoneware, Cowden & Wilcox, 5 gal. w/ cobalt blue tulip dec. $900.00

Blanket Chest, Chippendale, dovetailed case w/ painted dec., PA, ca. 1840-50 . . . .$5,000.00

A-PA Sept. 1998 — Pook & Pook Inc.

Farm Table, Fr. provincial fruitwood, early 19th C., w/ 3-board bread-board top, scalloped skirt w/ single drawer, 30" H, 29¼" W, 66" L $4,250.00

Chairs, assembled set of 5 Windsor birdcage rodback, w/ 1 armchair & 4 side chairs, minor damage to one chair $1,600.00

Charger, Eng. pewter bearing touchmark of Henry Little, London, 1740-70, 20¼" diam. $350.00

Charger, lrg. continental pewter, 18th C., 17¼" diam. $175.00

Squirrel Cup, Continental silver drinking cup in form of squirrel holding nut & perched $2,300.00

Burl Bowl, massive Am., 19¼" diam. $900.00

A-PA Oct. 1998 — Pook & Pook, Inc.

Candlestand, PA, Q.A., mah., ca. 1780 w/ birdcage, pad feet, repr. to one, 20" diam., 27½" H $6,000.00

Chairs, pr., PA, Chester County, 18th C., old dk. finish $7,250.00

A-MA May 1999 — New England Auctions of Brookfield

Side Chair, w/ pillow back, grain & stencil dec., N. Eng., 1st qtr. 19th C., sgn. J.D. Pratt, split in seat $375.00

Dressing Table, Fed. w/ orig. grain paint & stencil, Am., 4th qtr. 18th C $5,500.00

A-ME July 1998 — Cyr Auction Co. Inc.

Side Chairs, set of six, tiger maple saddleback, saber leg w/ caned seats, 32" T $1,800.00

Table, Sheraton figured birch, drop-leaf w/ reeded legs, 43" x 42", 28¾" T $450.00

A-ME July 1998 — Cyr Auction Co. Inc.

Stand, Sheraton one drawer w/ grain painting, 15½" sq. top, 28" H $750.00

Candlestand, rustic, carved from tree formation & grain painted, top 12" diam., 22" H $250.00

Tap Table, Hepplewhite, w/ drawer, blue painted top, 23" x 34", 28¾" H $1,600.00

Chair Table, 18th C., shoefoot, natural finish, top 38" x 49", 28" H $3,000.00

A-MA Oct. 1998 — Skinner, Inc.

Dining Table, Limbert oak w/ 2 leaves, branded mark, ref., 47" diam. $862.50

Dining Chairs, Limbert oak w/ branded mark, set of 6 . . . .$1,840.00

A-NH Aug. 1998   Northeast Auctions

Left to Right

Highchair, Am. country ladderback, 38½" H $400.00
Firkins, three painted, ea. w/ lid & sing handle, one blk., gray, & blue-gray, mkd. "C & A Wilder, Hingham, MA", 9", 11" & 12" H $200.00
Armchair, Wallace Nutting, Windsor comb-back, H-stretcher $2,100.00
Firkins, three painted, drum-form, two of tapering form, smallest yel., 10", 12" & 14" H $300.00
Side Chair, sausage-turned ladderback, turned frontal stretcher $500.00

A-PA Sept. 1998   Pook & Pook Inc.
Blanket Chest, PA, ca. 1830, paint dec., w/ lift lid & red & blk. grained, 26" H, 50" W $2,500.00
Staffordshire Spaniels, pr., early 19th C., 9½" H . .$1,500
Staffordshire Spaniel, carrying basket of flowers, 8½" H, sm. chip w/ 2 other Staffordshire spaniels $1,000.00
Staffordshire Spaniel, lrg. blk. & white, 19th C., 13" H $225.00
Spaniels, pr. stoneware, one mkd. "W.H. Farrar & Co." Geddes, NY, ca. 1850, 9¼" H, together w/ a Bennington spaniel, 7¾" H $1,600.00
Staffordshire Hounds, pr., early 19th C., w/ mottled high-lights, 11½" H $1,700.00
Gaudy Dutch Plate, in War Bonnet patt., 9½" diam. $1,000.00
Gaudy Ironstone Platter, 19th C., overall floral patt. on a fish eye reserve 21" L $700.00
Dresser Box, ca. 1830, red papered surface w/ brass & steel appliques, 7½" H, 10¼" L $850.00

A-PA Dec. 1998   Pook & Pook Inc.
Dining Table, Eng. Sheraton, ca. 1810 w/ 2 oblong ends w/ rounded corners, brass casters, 2 leaves, 30" H, 80" L extended $550.00
Mirror, Fed. w/ gilt inlay, ca. 1880, res., 60" H, 24" W . . .$950.00
Mirror, PA, ca. 1790, may be replm., 58" H, 28¼" W . .$2,800.00
Barometer, Georgian banjo form mah., engr. "G. Soldini & Co...", conch shell inlaid ovals, 28½" H $1,200.00
Plate, scalloped edge porcelain, late 18th C., w/ armorial surrounded by floral border, 9¼" diam., together w/ pr. of floral dec. export plates, 18th C., 9" diam. & shallow bowl, 10½" diam. $200.00
Vegetable Dish, porcelain lidded, late 18th C., scalloped oval form w/ pomegranate gilt finial, 11½", together w/ another covered vegetable dish $400.00
Vases, pr. Japanese Satsuma, late 19th C., depicting seated men on gold reserve, 8¼" H $300.00
Cache Pots, famille rose, ca. 1900 w/ overall garden dec. w/ cockbirds & scalloped edges, 9" H $1,500.00

A-PA Sept. 1998   Pook & Pook Inc.
Side Chair, Windsor, ca. 1800, w/ fanback, old blk. paint-ed surface $1,700.00
Side Chair, Windsor, prob. Frederick, MD, ca. 1800, retains fine mellow surface, Am. Windsor Chairs $4,250.00
Candlestand, PA, Sellersville type, walnut, ca. 1790, retains old period surface, 26" H, 26½" diam. . . .$1,600.00
Tea Kettle, mini. Am. copper, ca. 1800 , 5" H $150.00
Tea Kettle, PA Lancaster Co., copper, ca. 1800 w/ swing handle, 13" H $900.00
Tea Kettle, PA, copper, ca. 1800 w/ swing handle $300.00
Tea Kettle, PA, copper, ca. 1800 w/ swing handle, impr. "A. Sheriff" $750.00
Tea Kettle, PA, copper, ca. 1800 w/ swing handle, inscribed "G. Tyron" $900.00
Hooked Rug, Am. late 19th C., in overall vibrant red, blue & gr. striped dec., 37" x 16¾" $1,200.00

A-PA Feb. 1999   Pook & Pook Inc.

Corner Cupboard, child's PA, softwood, one pc., ca. 1900 w/ molded cornice over a 6 lt. door, painted gray surface, 57¾" H, 25" W $2,800.00

Blanket Chest, sm. PA, paint dec., ca. 1820 w/ lift lid & tilled int., dovetailed case, bold yel. & ochre sponge dec., 19¾" H, 30" W $300.00

Blanket Chest, PA, poplar, dated 1873, w/ lift lid over tilled int., dovetailed case, stenciled dec., retains overall orig. red paint & gold stencil dec., mkd. "W. S. 1873", 23" H, 41" W $2,000.00

Decoy, Am. carved & painted willet shorebird, ca. 1900, wooden stand, orig. paint & nail bill, 9½" H, 10" L .$850.00

Decoy, Am. carved & painted plover shorebird, ca. 1900, blk. stand, retains orig. paint & nail bill, 13" H, 8½" L $750.00

Man on Horse, wooden carved & polychrome paint dec. figure, ca. 1890, leather saddle, yoke, reins, bridle & bowler, horsehair tail & mane, wooden base, 13¾" H, 11¼" L .$1,800.00

Coffee Pot, PA, tin tole dec., ca. 1830, w/ hinged lid, red floral dec. on blk. ground, 10½" H $1,400.00

Watercolor, on paper by Hattie K. Bruner, farm scene w/ house & barn, Am., 1890-1982, 6" x 8" $1,000.00

Wall Plaque, PA folk art carved & painted, ca. 1920, owl on tree branch, half moon in sky, 22" H, 10¼" W . . .$1,500.00

Foot Stool, Sheraton hickory oval, ca. 1820, vibrant needlepoint seat & brass tack dec., 6½" H, 12½" L .$275.00

Sugar Bucket, Lehnware, late 19th C., w/ yel. & red grain painted surface, vine & berry dec., iron bands, 8½" H $1,100.00

Hooked Rug, pictorial, early 20th C., w/ 2 lions & colorful floral & leaf dec. w/ striped border, 20" x 61" $950.00

A-ME Jan. 1999   Cyr Auction Co. Inc.

Tall Case Clock, from Cordwell family of Norway, ME, 79" H $1,250.00

Wall Box, painted blue w/ drawer, 13½" T $275.00

Sign, Ingersol Watches, 2 sided, 34" $900.00

Weathervane, sheet metal fox, 9½" L $400.00

Weathervane, arrow, scroll dec., 32" L $350.00

Wall Box, gr., dovetail heart cut out, 12¾" x 8½" T x 5½" diam. $950.00

Weathervane, arrow, copper & iron, 34½" L $350.00

Gent Silhouette, w/ gold embellishments, 1850 pencil, 11" x 7" $300.00

Gent Profile, full length watercolor, 10" x 7" $400.00

Blanket Chest, mini., salmon painted, 7¾" x 9¾" x 15" $750.00

Box, round, wallpapered, 2¾" x 2½" D $100.00

Box, wallpapered, 5" H x 5¾" diam. $300.00

Pantry Box, painted red, 4½" x 8½" $125.00

Pantry Box, painted gr., 4½" x 8½" $200.00

Pantry Box, painted blue, 4½" x 8¾" $300.00

Spaniel, Rockingham glazed stoneware, 9¾" $200.00

Box, oval Bentwood, traces of tulip dec., 5¾" x 4¾" x 2" H $200.00

Gameboard, red & blk., 21" x 19" $150.00

Wing Chair, Chippendale, frame w/ molded legs, 45½" T $2,250.00

Bowl, round, mustard, 13½" $275.00

Bowl, wood, blue, 15" diam. $175.00

Bowl, burl, round painted, 16" diam. x 7" D $1,200.00

Bowl, wood, traces of gray paint, 18" diam. $200.00

Bowl, round, molded edge, 24½" diam. $225.00

Hooked Rug, 54" x 72" $750.00

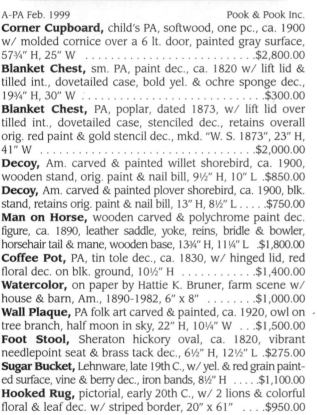

A-ME Jan. 1999   Cyr Auction Co. Inc.

Blanket Chest, 2 drawer, bracket base, gr., 17" x 38" x 35" $850.00

Crock, 2 gal. Hasdale, blue flower dec., 8½" x 10" . .$75.00

Chest, blue miniature, 7" x 11" x 12" $225.00

Church Models, 5" x 10" x 20" $150.00

Carriage Lamps, pr., 7" x 20" $300.00

Tap Table, red stretcher base, one board top mortised & pegged const., 20" x 32" x 28¼" $650.00

Sideboard, pine country, 21½" x 68" x 58" $3,500.00

Rocking Chair, red & blk. dec., 16" x 24" x 40" . .$150.00

A-PA June 1998   Pook & Pook Inc.

High-Top Drysink, PA, paint dec. walnut & poplar, ca. 1840 w/ 3 short upper drawers, retains fine grained & stipple dec. surface, 47" H, 50" W, 22¾" D $3,750.00
Portrait, Jacob Maentael, Am. 1763-1863, fully carved polychrome dec. frame, 19¾" x 16" $5,000.00
Painting, I.M. Lining, Am. late 19th C., oil on artist board, folk art scene, sgn. lower left, 7½" x 11" $1,000.00
Plate, Historical blue transfer dec. of "Gilpins Mills on Brandywine Creek", 9" diam. $325.00
Pitcher, Canary transfer dec. commemorative, together w/ 3 other examples, reprs. $2,100.00
Pitcher, lrg. copper luster, together w/ polychrome dec. teapot & a sm. pitcher & cup $100.00
Pitcher, Pearlware w/ polychrome relief mask of Bacchus, ca. 1800, grotesque face of wine god w/ pointed ears, minor age crack, 6⅛" H $550.00
Pitcher, Canary grotesque, early 19th C., w/ grinning mask w/ pointed nose, minor repr., 5" H $500.00
Pitcher, pink luster grotesque w/ grinning mask of Bacchus, 4¾" H $400.00
Staffordshire, group of silver resist, 19th C., incl. coffee pot, teapot, pitchers, waste bowl, 6 pcs., losses . . .$550.00

A-PA June 1998   Pook & Pook Inc.

Armchair, PA, Windsor, ca. 1760 w/ carved ear crest rail, retains a gr. painted surface . . . . .N/S
Blanket Chest, PA Bucks County, painted, from the "Deep Run Valley School", early 19th C., overall yel. & ochre feather grained dec., circle & star dec. lid w/ yel. molded edge, 26" H, 36" W, 19" D $16,000.00
Trinket Box, PA, painted w/ walnut paneled top, inlaid "M.E. 1886", overall red & yel. comb dec., inscribed "Ephrata", 7½" H, 10½" W, 6½" D $400.00
Table, N. Eng. pine, ca. 1810, top dec. w/ polychromed basket of fruit surrounded by grapes, retains orig. red wash, 28½" H, 17" W, 17" D $1,600.00
Fire Bucket, Am. leather, early 19th C., w/ blk. body lettered "Frenica Lentz", 13¼" H $750.00
Pitcher, PA, Remmey-type stoneware, 19th C., w/ extensive blue floral dec., impr. "1½", 12¼" H $750.00
Pitchers, two lrg. stoneware, 19th C., w/ blue floral dec., damaged, 13½" & 14" H $250.00
Sampler, PA, Berks Co., silk on linen, by "Charlotte Beck, Pine Grove School 1811" w/ pot of flowers, etc., 16¾" x 12" $1,900.00
Trade Sign, painted wood, bearing name "E.J. Trantow Storage Garage", 25½" H, 73½" L . . . . .N/S
Miniature Chest, PA, ca. 1830 w/ scrolled splashboard, 3 drawers flanked by scrolled columns & orig. gr. painted surface w/ gold pinstriping, 14½" H, 10¾" W, 9½" D . .$450.00

A-PA Feb. 1999   Pook & Pook Inc.

Portraits, Fr., 19th C., set of 4 watercolor on paper, ca. 1840 of mother father & two sons, sgn. lower left on one

"Manyett Fecit 1840", 13¾" x 10½" $1,600.00
Blanket Chest, PA, Lancaster Co., Amish, red stained & varnished softwood, ca. 1876, lift lid opening to dovetailed case, int. till, mkd. "S.L. 1876", 28" H, 48" W $750.00
Chair, N. Eng., fan back Windsor, ca. 1800 w/ crest w/ upturned ears, shield form seat & bamboo turned legs, retains a blk. painted surface w/ yel. highlights, 36" H $2,100.00
Hanging Wall Box, PA, walnut, ca. 1820, dovetailed const. w/ canted sides & heart cut-out back, 6¾" H, 13½" L, together w/ gr. paint & gold stencil dec. doll bed . .$550.00
Flowerpot, lrg. redware, attrib. to Peter Bell of Winchester VA, late 19th C., overall mottled glazing, 9½" H, 10½" diam. $250.00
Rocking Horse, carved & painted, mid 19th C., overall white coloring & leather bridle & saddle, missing rocker, 20" H, 33½" L $325.00

A-OH Sept. 1998　　　Garth's Auctions

Watercolor, theorem on paper, flower in many colors, br. ground is uneven, glued to mat, gold mat & bird's eye veneer frame, 22" H, 26¼" W $660.00

Table, Q.A., mah. w/ old faded finish, swing legs support leaves, oval top, repr., 10¾" x 35" w/ 14¾" leaves, 27½" H $605.00

Vegetable, Staffordshire covered, dk. blue transfer "A Ship of the Lines in the Downs", hairlines, 9½" x 9½" $715.00

Platter, Staffordshire, dk. blue transfer "Jedburgh Abbey, Roxburghshire", impr. "Adams", wear & deep knife scratches, 17" L $357.50

A-OH Sept. 1998　　　Garth's Auctions

Sewing Stand, Sheraton, mah. & curly maple veneer w/ old finish, two dovetailed drawers, top w/ fitted compartments, repl. pulls, missing castors, 15½" x 19¾", 27" H $2,420.00

Cup & Saucer, handleless, Gaudy floral dec. in blue, gr., yel. & yel. ochre, impr. "Wood & Sons", stains & wear $269.50

Pitcher, copper luster, canary band w/ white reserves & red transfer, blue, yel. & gr. enamel, minor wear, 5¾" H $841.00

Lamp, blue cut to white to clear font, opaque white base w/ fluted column, 13¼" H $935.00

Lamp, marble base w/ brass trim & fluted brass stem, clear pressed font w/ cut panels, engr. floral band, 12¼" H $110.00

A-OH Aug. 1998　　　Garth's Auctions

Rack, Euro. hanging plate drying, pine w/ old ora. stain, dovetailed scalloped ends, 25" W, 25½" H, 8" D $495.00

Blanket Chest, ref. pine & poplar, bracket feet, dovetailed case & lid, replms., till w/ lid has places for two drawers, 32½" W, 16¼" D, 18¾" H $440.00

Side Chair, Q.A., hardwood & softwoods w/ old mellow ref., repl. woven splint seat, repr., 40" H$385.00

Plates, pr. PA redware sgraffito, commemorative designs, early 20th C. reproductions of early plates, peafowl w/ "1792" & eagle w/ "1809", unmkd., edge chips, 8¾" diam. $412.50

Grease Lamp, wrt. iron hanging, sq. pan w/ one corner partitioned, ratchet trammel, adjusts from 28¼" H $302.50

A-OH Sept. 1998　　　Garth's Auctions

Chest, Fed., cherry w/ old finish, four dovetailed drawers w/ applied edge beading, walnut & poplar secondary wood, inlaid shield shaped escuts., reprs., 42⅝" W, 20" D, 39" H $1,540.00

Candlesticks, two similar Pittsburgh flint, hexagonal w/ round foot, pewter inserts, mismatched, one w/ sm. check, 9½" & 9¾" H $247.50

Shaving Mirror, Fed., mah. veneer on pine, four dovetailed drawers & beveled mirror, edge & veneer damage, one foot missing, 24¾" W, 9¼" D, 29¼" H $275.00

Lamp, cut overlay, white cut to cranberry stem insert & font, blk. ceramic base & brass fittings, mismatched base, 10" H $495.00

A-OH Sept. 1998　　　Garth's Auctions

Empire Chest, cherry w/ curly maple drawer fronts & old ref., three dovetailed drawers, poplar secondary wood, turned walnut pulls, 19¾" W, top 11⅜" x 20⅞", 19½" H . .$2,090.00

Press, wooden w/ drawer, cherry w/ old soft finish, punched detail, 6½" x 11¾" $605.00

Shaker Box, oval bentwood, finger const. & steel tacks, inscription on inside lid, old varnish finish, damage, 6¾" H $165.00

Cradle, doll size, walnut w/ old finish, 10¼" L $192.50

A-OH Aug. 1998   Garth's Auctions
Watercolor, on paper, "Schoener, Lidia...1807, Nicolas Cammillieri fecit", flying Am. flag, cut down slightly, gilt frame, 19⅞" H, 25⅞" W $1,980.00
Dressing Table, Q.A., walnut w/ old finish, mortised & pinned apron, two dovetailed overlapping drawers, two board top, edge damage, pine secondary wood, period brasses, one incomplete, repr., 21½" x 36", 30½" H $7,700.00
Candlesticks, pr. grass Q.A. w/ scalloped lip & foot, reprs., 8⅛" H $330.00
Butter Dish, blue & white Canton w/ domed lid & pierced insert, repr. & mismatched $440.00
Platter, blue & white Canton, 17½" L $550.00

A-OH Aug. 1998   Garth's Auctions
Stone Fruit, eleven pcs., mini. w/ polychrome, some old, some new .$605.00
Stone Fruit, five pcs. w/ polychrome, apple, pear, plum, yel. transparent apple, & stem w/ three cherries $275.00
Stone Fruit, five pcs. w/ polychrome, apple, pear, lemon, banana, chipped, & stem w/ three cherries . . .$220.00
Stone Fruit, five pcs. w/ polychrome, pear, lemon, fig, worn, apple & stem w/ two cherries $192.50
Stone Grapes, four bunches, two purple, 6½" L, two white, 8" L $247.50
Stone Fruit, six pcs. w/ polychrome, lemon, pear, fig, ora., tomato & apple $385.00

A-OH Aug. 1998   Garth's Auctions
Oil on Canvas, primitive scene of sailing ship flying Am. & Jap. flags, 20th C., framed, 25¾" H, 36" W $467.50
Table, Q.A., ref. maple base, cherry top, wear, pine & chestnut secondary wood, two board top w/ two board leaves, reprs., minor age cracks, 14¾" x 43½" w/ 14¼" leaves, 27¼" H $2,200.00
Candlesticks, pr., brass Q.A., sq. base w/ invected corners & well detailed stem & scalloped lip, 8" H . . .$1,045.00
Knife Box, dovetailed, walnut w/ old varnish finish, H sides & scalloped divider w/ heart cut out handle, 8¾" x 15¾" $880.00
Candlesticks, pr. of brass Q.A., sq. bas w/ invected corners, push ups missing, reprs., not seamed, 8⅜" H $605.00

A-OH Aug. 1998   Garth's Auctions

Paintings by William Rank
20th C., all have sponged dec. frames
Bowl of Fruit, w/ bird, sgn. "Bill Rank", 16" H, 18" W $55.00
Bowl of Fruit, w/ bird, sgn. "Wm. Rank", 21¼" H, 23¼" W $330.00
Crowing Rooster, sgn. "Bill Rank", 21" H, 19" W $577.50
Still Life, Chinese plate & fruit, sgn. "Bill Rank", 18¾" H, 22¾" W $110.00
Bowl of Fruit, w/ two birds, sgn. "Bill Rank", 16" H, 18" W $110.00
Horse & Buggy, landscape, unsgn., 21" H, 23" W $467.50

A-OH Aug. 1998   Garth's Auctions
Table, Chippendale to Hepplewhite, walnut w/ old finish, beaded edge apron & one board top, top has stains, 19" x 29¼", 28¼" H $8,250.00
Candlesticks, pr. pewter, similar, unmkd., 9¾" H $253.00
Tea Caddy, Chippendale, mah. w/ old finish, dovetailed case & molded edge lid, orig. brass bale handle, int. dividers missing, repr., 11¾" W, 6¾" D, 8" H $1,650.00
Mirror, Eng. Q.A., oak w/ old finish, old glass has some wear, silvering & backboards repl., 21¼" H, 13" W $330.00

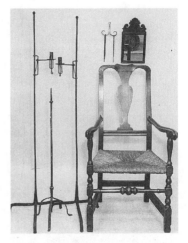

A-OH Aug. 1998   Garth's Auctions
Candlesticks, pr. of wrt. iron, tripod base, adjustable sockets w/ pushups, 54½" & 55¼" H $1,43.00
Pricket Candlestand, primitive wrt. iron w/ tripod base, pitted w/ rust, 36" H $412.50
Skewer Holder, wrt. steel & five skewers, simple detail, 14" L .$192.50
Mirror, Q.A., mah. w/ old finish, molded frame, minor split in bottom edge of frame, 16¼" H, 9" W .$550.00
Armchair, NH Q.A., maple & other hardwood w/ good old worn br. finish, old rush seat, 41½" H . .$2,475.00

A-OH Aug. 1998   Garth's Auctions
Highboy, Q.A., top refitted as chest of drawers, maple w/ some curl & old br. finish, added bracket feet, dovetailed case, six dovetailed overlapping drawers, orig. batwing brasses, pine secondary wood, insect damage, cornice 21¼" x 39½", 44¼" H . .$1,540.00
Tall Pot, pewter, "F. Porter, Westbrook No.1", touch, ME, finial wafer missing, 10¾" H $302.50
Candlesticks, pr., pewter, similar w/ slight variation, one has repr. to foot, one slightly battered, unmkd. Am., 9¾" H $192.50
Tall Pot, pewter, dents & repr., bottom is repl. & wooden finial very worn, 11⅜" H $93.50
Tall Pot, pewter, "T.S. Derby" touch, CT, corroded surface & reprs., 10¾" H $220.00

A-OH July 1998   Garth's Auctions
Mirror, w/ beveled mah. veneer frame, flaking in rev. painted sailboat, 22" H, 11⅝" W $275.00
Candlestand, Hepplewhite, ref. curly maple, carving on legs, reprs. to base, 14½" x 21", 27¾" H $990.00
Side Chair, PA ladderback, maple w/ old ref. & old rush seat, 43¾" H $605.00
Plate, blue spatterware, peafowl in blue, gr., red & blk., impr. "Adams", wear, 8⅞" diam. $302.50

A-OH Aug. 1998   Garth's Auctions
Highboy, Q.A., top refitted as chest of drawers, ref. maple facade w/ pine ends & secondary wood, traces of red paint, dovetailed case w/ added feet, dovetailed overlapping drawers, orig. brasses, cornice 20" x 37¼", 43" H $825.00
Candlestick, Dutch brass, domed base & baluster stem w/ mid-drip pan, 12⅜" H $3,520.00
Vase, Delft, blue & white floral dec. w/ oval scene of youth & windmills, chips, hairline & repr., 8¼" H $275.00
Bowl, Delft, polychrome floral dec. w/ butterfly, wear, rim hairline & sm. chips, 13" diam., 6" H $1,705.00
Candlestick, brass, mismatched parts, varying colors of brass, repr. to base, 9½" H $330.00

A-OH Sept. 1998   Garth's Auctions

A-OH Aug. 1998   Garth's Auctions
Wall Cupboard, two pc., ref. pine & poplar, base has three dovetailed drawers, mismatched top w/ H pie shelf, molded cornice is patched on ends, 64½" W, 18" D, 85" H .$2,530.00
Plates, two Staffordshire, red transfer "Waverly", stains & crazing, 10⅜" diam., & "Spanish Convent", impr. "Adams", 9½" diam. $165.00
Plates, two Staffordshire, red transfer "Milanese Villas", impr. "Dillon", crazing & sm. chips, 10½" diam., & "Florentine Fountain", stains, 9" diam. $137.50
Plates, two Staffordshire, red transfer "Columbus" wear & stain, 10⅝" diam., & "Palestine", sm. edge flakes, 8½" diam., both impr. "Adams . . .$148.50
Plates, two Staffordshire, red transfer, "Oriental", chip on back edge, 10¼" diam., & "The Sea", impr. "Adams", 8¾" diam. $165.00

Eagle, carved pine w/ old red, white, blue & gold paint, missing applied stars & damage, reprs., 30½" W $5,225.00
Hutch Table, cherry w/ old ref. on base, underside w/ old blk. paint, hinged seat lid, three board top, edge damage & reprs., age cracks, 43" x 45½", 28½" H $9,350.00
Bowl, ash burl w/ good old finish, detail at lip & base, minor age crack, 15½" diam., 6½" H $2,970.00
Jar, ovoid stoneware, applied shoulder handles, label "L. ...Toronto, Ont.", cobalt blue brushed flower & "2", hairlines & flakes at rim, 13" H . .$357.50
Jar, stoneware preserving, cobalt blue stenciled & freehand label "Hamilton & Co.... Pa.", 10" H $165.00

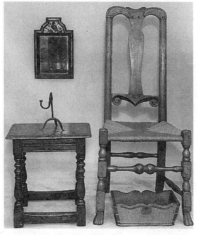

A-OH Aug. 1998 Garth's Auctions
Sampler, silk on linen, alphabet in blue, white br. & faded gr., "...by Farquar...1836", minor stains, modern frame, 25" H, 20¼" W $550.00
Thoerems, eight sm. on velvet all sgn. by "Bill Rank", 20th C., PA, two of ea. fruit, framed, 6½" H, 4½" W ...$247.50
Stand, ref. cherry w/ mah. veneer facade, two dovetailed drawers, top repl., 16½" x 23" w/ 9¼" leaves, 28¾" H $275.00
Armchair, Q.A. banister back, old blk. repaint w/ gold leaf on crest, repl. rush seat, mortised joints redoweled, wear & some damage, 45" H .$495.00
Pitcher, Pratt, molded pearlware w/ portraits of men, br., gr., gold & blue, reprs., 7½" H $110.00

A-OH Aug. 1998 Garth's Auctions
Mirror, wooden frame w/ rev. painted glass inserts, orig. mirror glass w/ worn silvering, penciled "restored 1914", retouch & restored, brass corner braces on back, 16½" H, 10⅞" W $935.00
Stool, early joint, oak w/ old finish, wear & age cracks, 11" x 16½", 17¾" H $990.00
Side Chair, Q.A., maple w/ old ref. w/ traces of red, repl. paper rush seat, 42" H $1,265.00
Rush Light Holder, wrt. iron, three feet & twisted detail, 7¼" H .$385.00
Box, dovetailed, curly maple w/ relief carved designs, poplar bottom, hole at compass star, 13¼" L $1,155.00

A-OH Aug. 1998 Garth's Auctions
Table, PA Q.A., walnut w/ old finish, mortised & pinned apron w/ beaded edge & two dovetailed overlapping drawers, removable one board top, completely orig. incl. brasses & pins, one missing pin, age crack in top, 16¾" x 30⅜", 29¾" H $27,500.00
Candlesticks, pr. brass mid-drip, not seamed, one has casting holes repr., 11¼" H $495.00
Mirror, sm. Q.A., figured walnut veneer on pine w/ rubbed down finish, molded frame, repl. glass, minor edge damage, repr. & age cracks, 15¾" H, 9" W $770.00
Tureen, blue & white Canton w/ boar's head handles, minor chips, 12¾" L $935.00
Trunk, oriental leather covered wood, worn painted scenes w/ figures, brass hardware, 15" L $275.00

A-OH Aug. 1998 Garth's Auctions
Work Table, Q.A., maple base w/ traces of old paint & a reddish br. finish, mortised & pinned apron, two board pine bread board top, good old patina, corner damage, 31¾" x 62½", 27¾" H $4,125.00
Lighting Stand, wrt. iron, round base w/ punched brass washer trim, adjustable betty lamp & candle socket on rod w/ ring top finial, wire link wick pick, 23" H $1,045.00
Rack, Euro. hanging plate drying, pine w/ traces of old finish, scalloped ends dovetailed, 30" W, 42" H $522.50
Candlestick, primitive wrt. iron w/ spring loaded splint holder on tripod base, 19⅝" H $467.50
Fireplace Fender, steel & wire w/ brass top rail, some battering & damage, 57" W, 19" D, 12" H ...$1,210.00

A-OH Aug. 1998 Garth's Auctions
Corner Cupboard, Eng. handing, mah. w/ old finish, base is missing drawer, 22¾" W, 39" H $770.00
Teapot, blue & white Canton, 6¼" H $495.00
Teapot, blue & white Canton w/ twined handle, mismatched lid, 6½" H $412.50
Sugar Bowl, blue & white Canton w/ ear handles, mismatched lid, 5⅞" H $275.00
Plate, blue & white Canton or Nanking, rim chips & short hairlines, 9½" diam. $49.50

A-OH Aug. 1998 Garth's Auctions
Painting, 20th C., cornucopia w/ fruit & bird, sgn. "Wm. Rank", plain pine frame, 28¾" H, 33¾" W $577.50

A-OH Aug. 1998   Garth's Auctions

Row 1, Left to Right

Portrait, on ivory, gentleman w/ white hair & dk. blue frock coat, ground is repainted, blk. lacquered frame w/ brass trim, 5¾" H, 5⅛" W $330.00
Butterprint, wooden, butternut w/ old scrubbed finish, "The Union" w/ heart & stars, added tin hanger, 3⅛" x 5" $357.50
Butterprint, wooden, pine w/ old patina, stylized tulip, added tin hanger, 3" x 4⅞" $247.50
Portrait, on ivory, woman w/ white lace bonnet & collar w/ blk. dress, minor edge damage, blk. lacquered frame w/ gilded band & brass trim, wear & edge damage, 5¼" H, 4½" W $357.50

Row 2, Left to Right

Tools, two wrt. iron, curling iron, 10" L, & tongs 6¾" L $137.50
Cookie Cutter, tin, woman w/ hat & long dress, 9" H $522.50
Roaster, wrt. iron, pierced pan has hinged lid, wooden handle, 12" L $357.50
Cookie Cutter, tin, man w/ pipe, hat & frock coat w/ tails, punched circle around hole, lt. rust, 8½" H . .$522.50
Cookie Board, pewter w/ fifteen segments w/ well detailed animals, flowers, buildings, etc., walnut back, 3⅞" x 7" $220.00

A-OH Aug. 1998   Garth's Auctions

Row 1, Left to Right

Tinder Lighter, flintlock, wooden pistol grip, engr. & cast detail, 7" L . .$495.00
Betty Lamps, three wrt. iron, two have wick picks, w/ hangers, 3¾" to 4¼" H $385.00

Row 2, Left to Right

Pease Jar, turned w/ lid, maple w/ old varnish finish, age crack in bowl, 4½" H $165.00
Box, burl veneer, int. has old gold paint w/ sponged colors, mirror in lid, some veneer damage, 5¼" L .$192.50
Carpet Balls, two, sponged star designs, one br. & one blk., 3¼" diam. $143.00
Carpet Balls, two, plaid, one blk. & one red, wear & chips, 3¼" diam. $220.00

Row 3, Left to Right

Two Pieces, treen sander, 3⅛" H, & pewter inkwell, repl. glass insert, 5" diam. $137.50
Desk Set, redware, molded edges, hollow int. & dog w/ urn, blk. brushed design w/ clear glaze, 5½" L, 6½" H $522.50
Candlestick, early bronze on sq. base w/ raised feet, & simple tooling, sm. casting hole, not seamed, 4¾" H $220.00

A-OH Aug. 1998   Garth's Auctions

Jelly Cupboard, ref. poplar, two dovetailed drawers, minor edge damage & age cracks, 39½" W, top 20½" x 42", 53" H overall . .$605.00
Box, dec. dome top, beech w/ worn polychrome floral dec. on blue ground, white edge stripe, wrt. iron lock w/ hasp, minor worm holes, 10⅝" L $770.00
Basket, woven splint buttocks, tightly woven w/ plaited medial band & bentwood handle w/ penciled inscription "Mrs. W.A. Brown.....", VA, 14" x 17", 8" H $1,430.00
Shorebird, root head & worn & weathered layers of br., blk. & white paint, 11" L $412.50
Quilt Squares, five applique, floral medallions in red, pink, yel. & gr., two have simple frames, three stapled to cardboard, 22½" x 23¼" $82.50

A-OH Aug. 1998   Garth's Auctions

Refrigerator, ref. pine, turned feet, paneled doors & lift top for ice, metal lined, 33¾" W, top 20¾" x 36¼", 48¼" H $440.00
Tea Kettle, sm. copper, dovetailed, lid repl., polished, 5" H plus swivel handle $192.50
Rush Light, wrt. iron w/ candle socket counter weight, twisted detail, turned wooden base has age cracks, 11½" H $385.00
Tea Kettle, copper, dovetailed, polished, dents & pinpoint holes in bottom, 6" H plus swivel handle .$192.50
Bedwarmer, brass w/ floral engr. lid, turned wooden handle has old finish, 40" L $412.50

A-OH July 1998   Garth's Auctions

Bicycle, balloon tires & med. blue paint w/ chrome trim, "Dayton, Huffman, Mfg. Co.", minor wear $330.00

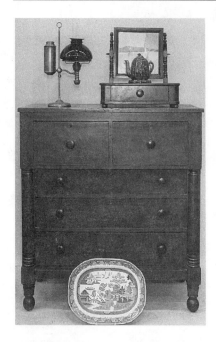

A-OH Sept. 1998　　　　Garth's Auctions

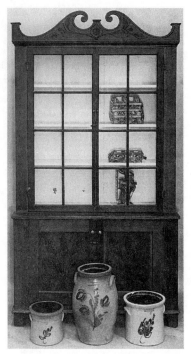

A-OH July 1998　　　　Garth's Auctions

Chest of Drawers, cherry & poplar w/ old cherry red finish, five dovetailed drawers, poplar & walnut secondary wood, 42¼" W, top 21" x 43⅛", 47¼" H $605.00

Student Lamp, brass, orig. oil burner w/ tubular wick, old gr. & white overlay shade has chips on base & one on top edge, 20½" H $330.00

Shaving Mirror, mah. & figured mah. veneer w/ old finish, one dovetailed drawer, 19¼" W, 10½" D, 19⅜" H $165.00

Teapot, Rockingham w/ stand, Rebecca at the Well, minor chips & mismatched lid, 7¼" H $60.50

Platter, blue willow, minor wear, 17¾" L $55.00

A-OH Sept. 1998　　　　Garth's Auctions

Row 1, Left to Right

High Top Boots, carved, good detail, old blk. & red paint, 5" H $577.50

Bank, carved folk art, mule kicks when button pushed, polychrome paint, edge damage & wear, mule's ears & tail missing, trap also missing, 8½" L $82.50

Boy's Head, papier mache, probably puppet head, blk., red & white paint, modern steel base $110.00

Row 2, Left to Right

Inkwells, three carved wooden, dog w/ log has glass eyes, bear & a bear w/ log pen holder both have bead eyes, glass inserts, 7" L $412.50

Cigar Lighter, cast white metal, traces of gilt, comic figure w/ top hat w/ oil burner in hat & stone bucket for matches, 5¼" H $412.50

Row 3, Left to Right

Buckets, two stave const. w/ metal bands, old worn patina, missing one band, 3½" H, other has partial paper label, 3⅝" H $71.50

Shaker Bucket, stave const., ca. 1875, laminated staves in three colors of wood, metal bands, worn & uneven varnish finish, 7½" diam., 5" H $1,375.00

Sugar Bucket & Shoe, bucket w/ dk. patina, 4½" H, carved wooden man's shoe, 5¾" L $71.50

Cupboard, one pc., cherry w/ old mellow finish, old glass, one cracked, dovetailed cornice, int. has old white paint, 16" x 46¼", 81¼" H . .$2,090.00

Chocolate Molds, three tin & steel, three rabbits, 9½" L, four chicks, 10" L, & rabbit w/ pack, 11¼" H, soldered reprs. $165.00

Crock, stoneware w/ applied handles, impr. label "E. & L.P. Norton, VT 1½", floral dec. in cobalt blue, 8" H $137.50

Churn, ovoid stoneware w/ applied shoulder handles, cobalt blue brushed tulips & "6", int. lime deposits & hairline, 18" H $220.00

Crock, stoneware w/ applied handles, impr. label "E. Norton & Co...VT 3", floral design in cobalt blue, minor chips & lime deposits, 10¼" H . .$137.50

A-OH July 1998　　　　Garth's Auctions

Shelves, pine w/ old red, one board ends, 43" W, 12½" D, 46" H . .$935.00

Row 1, Left to Right

Treenware, two pcs., Pease, footed jar, 6¾" H, & tapered jar, revarnished, 5" H $220.00

Two Pieces, cast iron spider pan w/ mismatched lid, 5¾" diam., Mallard hen decoy, old repaint & glass eyes, 16¾" L $165.00

Row 2, Left to Right

Footwarmer, poplar frame w/ turned corner posts in old red, tin has punched circle design, some damage, 7¾" x 8¾" $82.50

Doorstop, cast iron, full bodied alpine box w/ basket of flowers, old worn polychrome, 7¼" H $220.00

Bank, chalk bull, old worn br. & amber finish, edge wear & minor damage, 15¼" L $605.00

Row 3, Left to Right

Jug, stoneware, impr. label "F.B. Norton & Co....MA 2", cobalt blue floral design, 13¾" H $275.00

Jar, Pease treenware, old worn varnish finish, age cracks, 9½" H $962.50

Jug, ovoid stoneware w/ strap handle, impr. label "Cowden & Wilcox 2", cobalt blue brushed floral dec. 13⅜" H $220.00

Row 4

Sled, wooden w/ metal tipped runners, old worn red & white repaint w/ "Francis P. Drake", early auto, butterflies, etc., old repr., 37½" L . . .$55.00

A-OH Sept. 1998   Garth's Auctions
Gameboard, dec. folding box w/ worn old blk. & br. pain w/ yel., red & blue, 24" x 24" open $363.00
Blanket Chest, dovetailed, poplar w/ old red repaint, till w/ lid, minor nailed repr. to back edge, 42¾" W, 20" D, 24¼" H $330.00
Footwarmer, pine w/ old red paint, edge damage, sliding door repl., repr., 7" x 9", 7¼" H $165.00
Bowl, burl, dense ash burl, ref.,¼" hole in side, minor age cracks & wear, 11" diam., 5" H $550.00

A-OH July 1998   Garth's Auctions
Rag Rug, hooked, cat & kitten in faded colors of blk., white, gr., yel., red, blue & br., wear & repr., backed for hanging, 29½" H, 24" W . .$605.00
Chest of Drawers, ref. poplar & cherry w/ curly & bird's eye maple drawer fronts, three dovetailed drawers, cut down from a four drawer chest & top repl., 43" W, top 19½" x 44", 34" H $385.00
Bowls, four Rockingham, 9" & 9½" diam., & two sm. dishes mkd. "National", 4¼" & 5½" diam. . .$247.50
Hobby Horse, blk. stuffed cloth, head w/ br. fur name & button eyes, wear & repr., 47" L $110.00
Two Pieces, pine doll cradle w/ old red, good scrolled detail, 17" L & late hanging corner shelf w/ white repaint, 19½" H $165.00

A-OH Sept. 1998   Garth's Auctions
Bedwarmer, grass w/ turned wooden handle, engr. lid, age crack, 42" L $275.00
Checkerboard, pine w/ old patina & blk. stained squares, edge damage, 13" x 23¾" $192.50
Bedwarmer, brass & copper w/ turned wooden handle, engr. lid, old reprs., 43" L $220.00
Crock Stand, hardwood w/ old worn dk. red paint, 57" W, 41" H . .$522.50
Shorebirds, two, mkd. "Randall", weathered finish w/ blk. & white paint, driftwood bases, 12" H $165.00

A-OH Sept. 1998   Garth's Auctions

Row 1, Left to Right

Candle Box, pine w/ old red, 12" L $220.00
Treen, two pcs., nut br. finish, sander, 3½" H & nut cracker, 5" L $115.50
Baby Cradle, whale bone scrimshaw, good detail, minor crack, 5" L . .$522.50
Carpet Balls, three w/ stick spatter designs, red, br. & blk., minor wear, 3¾" diam. $313.50

Row 2, Left to Right

Biscuit Box, tin, shaped like books w/ strap, bright red, gold, blk. & tan, "Huntley & Palmer", 6¼" L $330.00
Carpet Balls, three w/ plaid stripe designs, red, br., & blk., minor wear, 3¼" diam. $214.50
Birds, two carved w/ polychrome paint, yel. throat warbler & nuthatch, one initialed. "G.P.J." $88.00
Two Pieces, chalk dog, hollow, worn surface w/ traces of blk. & red, chips, 8¾" H, & stoneware jar, cobalt blue brushed "2", four lines, 11¼" H . .$137.50

A-OH Sept. 1998   Garth's Auctions
Lithograph, handcolored by "Currier & Ives", "Harvesting the Last Load", dk. water stains in margins, modern curly maple frame, 14½" H, 18½" W $220.00
Lithograph, handcolored by "Currier & Ives", "The Western Farmer's Home", margins trimmed, minor stains, beveled frame, 12¼" H, 16" W $357.50
Stand, Hepplewhite, cherry w/ old finish, one dovetailed drawer, reworked top, poplar secondary wood, 17¼" x 20½", 29" H . . .$550.00
Side Chair, Windsor bowback, old dk. varnish stain over white paint, variation in spindles, 33¾" H .$192.50
Jug, ovoid stoneware, cobalt blue dec. w/ "3", 15½" H $192.50

A-OH Sept. 1998   Garth's Auctions
Chest, Hepplewhite, mah. veneer w/ cross banding & inlay, old ref., four dovetailed drawers, pine secondary wood, reprs. & replms., 39" W, top 17¾" x 40¼", 33¾" H $1,100.00
Knife Box, mah. veneer w/ inlay, inlaid oval on inside lid, veneer damage, 14½" H $220.00
Lamps, two similar astral, brass w/ stepped bases, one in blk. onyx & one in marble, chipped & collars repl., worn gilding, 14¼" & 12½" H $110.00
Lamp, marble base, ornate gilded brass stem & emerald gr. cut to clear font w/ brass collar, 20¾" H .$385.00
Knife Box, mah. veneer w/ inlay, short feet, banded corner inlay & inlaid star on lid & on inside of lid, edge & veneer damage, int. incomplete, replms., 14½" H $412.50

A-OH Sept. 1998   Garth's Auctions

Lithograph, handcolored by "Currier & Ives", "The Haunts of the Wild Swan", foxing & minor edge damage, new curly maple frame 15" H, 19" W $302.50

Lithograph, handcolored by "Currier & Ives", "A Home in the Wilderness", minor stains & sm. hole in center, molded frame, 13⅜" H, 17⅜" W $302.50

Table, Sheraton, curly maple w/ old mellow ref., two dovetailed drawers, one board top, top reattached, reprs., repl. brass pulls, 18⅜" x 18¾", 29" H $1,182.50

Side Chair, saber leg, curly maple w/ mellow nut br. ref., paper rush seat, 34¼" H $247.50

Crock, stoneware w/ applied shoulder handles, cobalt blue dec., glaze wear & pitting, 13¼" H $110.00

A-OH Sept. 1998   Garth's Auctions

Chest of Drawers, Hepplewhite bowfront, ref. cherry, facade of curly maple & mah. veneer & inlay, four dovetailed drawers, poplar secondary wood, damage & repr., 43" W, top 22" x 43¾", 39½" H $3,025.00

Lamp, marble base, brass fluted stem & purple cut to clear font w/ brass collar, 9⅛" H $357.50

Lamps, two, marble bases w/ brass trim, fluted brass stems & clear pressed font w/ wafer, one is thumbprint, 11½" H, one is heart w/ sawtooth & bull's eye, 11¼" H$302.50

Box, dovetailed, burl w/ old soft finish, int. has till w/ lid, old brass batwing escut., lock missing, minor edge damage, 14⅛" L $1,705.00

Lamp, opaque white base & white cut to cranberry font w/ brass connector & collar, minor chips, 10¼" H $346.50

A-OH Sept. 1998   Garth's Auctions

Chest of Drawers, Fed., ref. cherry w/ inlay, scrolled apron w/ inlaid heart, four dovetailed drawers, poplar secondary wood, replms. & reprs., 24" W, top 12¼" x 24¾", 26" H .$2,970.00

Book Flask, Bennington flint enamel, "Departed Spirits", minor edge wear, 5⅝" H $467.50

Book Flask, Bennington flint enamel, "Battle of Bennington", wear & one corner chipped, 6" H $385.00

Flasks, three, books, blue glaze "History of Burbon County", 7" H, "History of Holland", 5 ¾" H, "Coming thro the Rye", 5" H, all have chips $495.00

A-OH Sept. 1998   Garth's Auctions

Chest of Drawers, Empire mini., ref. cherry & curly maple, two top dovetailed drawers, other drawers secured w/ drawer bottoms & backs removed making hollow int., back board missing, 21½" W, 12½" D, 25½" H $2,310.00

Table, Hepplewhite, birch & maple w/ some curl in legs, base has worn old red, top scrubbed, replms. & additions, 18" x 39" w/ 10¼" leaves, 28½" H $550.00

Decanters, two pillar mold w/ applied collars & lips, some int. stain, 11½" & 13" H $165.00

Jug, ovoid stoneware w/ strap handle, impr. "N.A. White & Son, Utica, N.Y. 3", dk. cobalt blue dec., hairlines, repr. chips, 15½" H $330.00

Jug, stoneware w/ strap handle, impressed "F.B. Norton & Co. Worcester, Mass. 2", cobalt blue dec., chip $220.00

A-OH Sept. 1998   Garth's Auctions

Chippendale Chest, ref. curly maple, four dovetailed drawers, bottom backboard & feet repl., brasses repl., 41¼" W, top 19½" x 42", 37½" H .$2,420.00

Candlesticks, pr., pewter, unmkd., similar but not an exact match, 9¾" H $203.50

Teapot, pewter "Sellew & Co., Cincinnati", eagle touch, reprs., 7⅞" H $220.00

Lamps, two similar pewter w/ lemon fonts & whale oil burners, one mkd. "R. Dunham", dents, 8⅝" H . .$275.00

Plate, pewter, eagle touch w/ "Barnes, Phila.", wear, scratches & edge damage, 11¼" diam. . . . . . .N/S

A-OH Aug. 1998   Garth's Auctions

Candle Sconces, pr. tin w/ mirrored backs, some age, reprs., 12" H $412.50

Blanket Chest, PA, poplar w/ old brownish red finish, dovetailed bracket feet, three dovetailed drawers & case, hinged lid, till w/ lid, int. printed "Haus Segen", fraktur, bear trap lock, damage, 50½" W, 23" D, 30" H $2,090.00

Ewer, Euro. stoneware w/ pewter lid, incised floral design w/ birds & "G.H.", lid has damage & repr., 10¾" H $77.00

Band Box, wallpaper covered, cardboard w/ orig. wallpaper covering w/ scene of "Castle Garden" in red, br., white & gr. on blue ground, wear & bottom loose, sgn. "Joel Post", 23" L $3,300.00

Flagon, pewter w/ vintage finial, unmkd., reprs., 14" H $82.50

A-OH Sept. 1998   Garth's Auctions

Watercolor, theorem on paper, flowers & fruit, good color, tears & old reprs., old gilt frame, 25¼" H, 31¼" W $385.00

Table, Sheraton, ref. curly maple, dovetailed drawer & three board top, replms., 22½" x 35½" w/ 11½" leaves, 29¾" H $522.50

Doorstops, two cast iron, baskets of flowers w/ old worn polychrome paint, 9¾" & 10½" H $220.00

Mini. Blanket Chest, cherry w/ old finish, ca. 1847, VA, dovetailed case & dovetailed bracket feet, poplar secondary wood, 15¾" L $3,575.00

Doorstop, golfer, old polychrome has wear, 8" H $770.00

A-OH Sept. 1998   Garth's Auctions

Desk, Hepplewhite slant front, ref. curly maple, dovetailed case & drawers, fitted int. is cherry w/ ten dovetailed drawers, pine secondary wood, repl. brasses, repl. feet, reprs., 42" W, 19½" D, 41½" H $3,300.00

Lamp, astral, marble base, pierced stem w/ fluted brass collar around red insert, brass font & repl. collar, traces of gilding, 13¾" H . . . . .N/S

Lamp, astral, marble brass base w/ molded opal. stem & brass font, mkd. "Pat. by J.G. Webb, NY...1851", font altered & collar repl., 13" H . .$165.00

Lamps, two astral, one w/ marble base, frosted cut to clear globe, electric insert, brass stem & font, replms. & reprs., 20" H, one w/ marble base, fluted brass stem & brass font labeled "Cornelius & Co. Philad", replms., not pictured, 14" H $302.50

Lamp, astral, marble & brass base w/ molded cranberry stem, labeled "Pat. by...NY...1851", altered, has rings for prism & globe, chipped, 13½" H $192.50

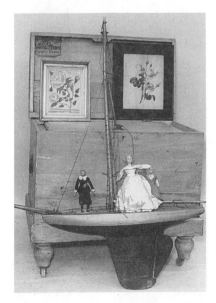

A-OH Aug. 1998   Garth's Auctions

Refrigerator, poplar w/ old worn ref., metal lined int. w/ double wooden lid, paper label "Eddy Refrigerator, Boston...", 34" W, 20½" D, 30¼" H $247.50

Watercolor, on paper, primitive roses in pink, yel. & three shades of gr., stains & some water damage, old gilt frame, 13" H, 11⅛" W $110.00

Watercolor, on paper, roses, reds & greens a bit faded, stains, old mah. veneer frame is worn, 17" H, 14⅜" W $137.50

Sailboat, model, wood & wire, some damage, old paint, 49" H $385.00

Dolls, lot incls. thirty five primitive wooden & cloth dolls, doll cloths, 5" to 11" H, six carved wooden animals, sm. tin kitchen, 6" W, 5" H & other child related items $1,760.00

A-OH Jan. 1999   Garth's Auctions

Table, Hepplewhite, cherry w/ old ref., inlay added & top repl., repr. 17¼" x 45¾" w/ 18" leaves, 28¾" H$605.00

Kugel, cranberry, brass hanger, 8" diam. $990.00

Kugel, blue, brass hanger, 10" diam. $1,045.00

Kugel, silver, brass hanger, wear to silvering, 8" diam. $137.50

A-OH Sept. 1998   Garth's Auctions

Shaker Items

Lithograph, "Shakers", but Kellogg & Comstock, faded coloring & stains, mah. veneer beveled frame, 13" H, 16⅞" W $495.00

Shaker Table, cherry w/ old dk. varnish stain finish, one dovetailed drawer, minor age cracks & nailed repr., pine secondary wood, 18½" x 18¾", 27" H $330.00

Armchair Rocker, Mt. Lebanon, ref. & repl. tape seat in brownish red & white, 41¼" H $412.50

Shaker Box, oval, MA, old varnish finish, finger const., steel tacks w/ some renailing, minor age cracks & edge damage, 10⅞" L $275.00

Shaker Bucket, w/ lid, stave const., old blue paint w/ blk. on metal bands & blk. stenciled "28", int. has worn lt. gr., wooden handle & wire bale w/ diamond attachments, 11" H $2,860.00

A-OH Sept. 1998   Garth's Auctions

Shaker Items

Lap Board, two tone pine & walnut slats w/ impr. rule, paper back rolls up for storage, side braces w/ brass clips make rigid, 19½" x 36" $192.50

Candlestand, Hepplewhite, OH, cherry w/ old varnish finish, one board top, revarnished, 15½" diam., 28" H $605.00

Sewing Rocker, Mt. Lebanon, NY, orig. dk. finish w/ revarnish, stenciled label, repr. split, repl. tape seat & back in red & blk., 34" H $412.50

Shaker Box, round Mt. Lebanon, NY, old br. finish, finger const. w/ steel tacks, minor edge damage & reprs., 9⅞" diam., 4⅛" H $357.50

Sewing Carrier, oval, four finger const., copper tacks, orig. varnish w/ blk. stenciled label, "Shaker Goods, Calfred, Me", repl. cloth lining, 6¼" x 9", 2⅞" H $247.50

A-OH Sept. 1998   Garth's Auctions

Shaker Items

Measure Stick, walnut w/ old patina, mkd. off in 4½" intervals, 39" L $165.00

Hanger, pine & poplar, 36½" L $192.50

Double Hanger, Mount Lebanon, NY, cherry, 15" L $302.50

Child's Rocker, Mount Lebanon, NY, old not orig. finish, repl. red tape seat & back, turned detail, 28½" H $550.00

A-OH Sept. 1998   Garth's Auctions

Shaker Items

Shaker Stand, cherry w/ old worn finish, one dovetailed drawer, false drawer front on rev., minor age cracks, 9¼" x 7½", 25" H $880.00

Shaker Side Chair, Canterbury, NH ladderback w/ tilters in back feet, ref. maple w/ woven tape seat in faded gr. & tan, 41¼" H $1,320.00

Shaker Box, old worn patina, finger const. w/ copper tacks, several worm holes, 12" L $385.00

Shaker Box, old worn patina, finger const. w/ copper tacks, partial printed paper label inside lid, hold in side, 10¼" L $357.50

Shaker Box, old worn varnish, finger const. w/ copper tacks, 6¼" L ...$247.50

A-OH Sept. 1998   Garth's Auctions

Shaker Items

Fork & Fly Swatter, both w/ turned wooden handles, 17" & 18½" L $121.00

Pie Lifter, wrt. steel w/ wooden handle, 13¼" L $93.50

Palette Box, w/ colored chalk, pine w/ old finish, 5½" x 7" $143.00

Three Pieces, two horse hair brushes & a wire pie lifter w/ wooden handle, 17" L $110.00

Whisk Brooms, two broom straw, 10" & 16" L $385.00

Brushes, two, horse hair w/ turned handle, 11" L & round bristle w/ turned handle, 5½" L $82.50

Two Pieces, bristle brush w/ scored wooden back, Mt. Lebanon, 5¼" L, & yel. paper seed envelope printed "Turnip, Enfield, N.H.", framed, 6½" W x 7½" H $60.50

A-OH Sept. 1998   Garth's Auctions

Shaker Items

Washstand, ref. cherry, one dovetailed drawer, breadboard top, top repl., 18" x 19", 28¾" H ..$440.00

Sewing Rocker, Mt. Lebanon, worn orig. dk. finish w/ stenciled gold label, old woven tape seat is blk. & sage gr., 34½" H $605.00

Box, oval, old worn lt. blue paint, finger const. w/ copper tacks, 11¾" L $2,970.00

Box, oval, Sabbathday Lake, MA, old worn dk. blue or lt. blue paint, finger const. w/ copper tacks, 10¾" L $1,540.00

Box, mah. veneer w/ maple & walnut on beveled edge lid, mirror in lid, ref. & minor veneer damage, age crack, int. lined w/ colored paper, tray missing, 11¼" L $93.50

A-OH July 1998   Garth's Auctions

Pie Safe, poplar w/ two layers of old blue over other colors, mortised frame, one nailed drawer, twelve panels all w/ circle & star design, three in end & three in ea. door, 39¾" W, 17½" D, 59" H $1,540.00

Jar, ovoid redware w/ shoulder handles, clear reddish br. color w/ blk., chips, 9½" H $220.00

Baskets, two woven splint buttocks, both damaged, 8" diam., 4½" H, & 13" diam. 9" H $192.50

Utensils, set of five, wrt. iron & polished brass, fork, dipper, skimmer, spatula, & smaller dipper w/ reprs. to bowl, 13½" to 19" L $247.50

A-OH July 1998   Garth's Auctions

Chest, Chippendale, walnut w/ old worn finish, dovetailed case, feet repl., brasses repl. & other restoration, poplar secondary wood, 35¾" W, top 20¾" x 37", 37½" H $3,025.00

Candlestick, early brass w/ domed base & baluster stem, 8¼" H .$357.50

Burl Bowl, ash burl w/ good figure & soft varnish finish, minor hairline crack, 13½" diam., 6" H $660.00

Butter Paddle, burl w/ bird's head handle, wear & repr., 8½" L . .$159.50

Candlestick, early brass w/ domed base & baluster stem, stem reattached to base, reprs., 8" H $137.50

A-OH July 1998   Garth's Auctions

Desk, walnut w/ old finish, one board ends, three dovetailed drawers, 37" W, 17" D, 44¾" H $605.00

Coffee Pot, pewter mkd. "Homan & Co., Cincinnati" OH, cast flower finial, minor dents, 8¾" H $77.00

Communion Flagon, pewter mkd. "Smith & Feltman, Albany", minor dents, 12" H $192.50

Coffee Pot, pewter, mkd. "Dunham", ME, cast flower finial, repr. to base, 8¼" H $165.00

Pots, three Eng. pewter, two mkd. "Lewellyn & Co.", wooden handles, one repr., 8" H, & one by "James Dixon & Sons", 10¾" H $192.50

A-OH July 1998   Garth's Auctions

Tea Table, Chippendale, ref. hardwood base & pine top, five board top is old replm., 29½" diam., 28½" H $467.50

Armchair, Windsor, old ref., reprs. & replms., feet have lost some height, 41½" H $522.50

Hurricane Shades, pr. of clear blown w/ folded rims, late, 13¾" H $247.50

Mirror, Hepplewhite bowfront, mah. veneer w/ inlay, ogee feet worn & incomplete, one dovetailed drawer, adjustable mirror, pine secondary wood, damage, glass repl., 14" W, 7" D, 15⅝" H $165.00

Shorebird, pine w/ worn old paint, repr., 9¼" plus stand $192.50

A-OH July 1998   Garth's Auctions

Hooked Rugs, two, one rag w/ "welcome" in reds, yel., gr., gray, purple, etc., wear & repr., 22" x 34½" & late yarn rung w/ six panels of pastel flowers on blk. ground, 24" x 36" $165.00

Sawbuck Table, pine w/ old blk. paint on base, top has natural finish, late 19th C., 23" x 48¾", 30" H$880.00

Bowl, turned poplar, old reddish br. stain on ext. & int. has wear & stains, edge damage, 27" diam., 8½" H $495.00

Jar, stoneware w/ applied handle, cobalt blue brushed floral design w/ "3", minor chip & crazing, 16" H $247.50

Jar, stoneware w/ applied handle, impr. label "J. Fisher & Co....NY", faint cobalt blue flower, 16" H $220.00

A-OH July 1998   Garth's Auctions

Barometer, Eng., mah. veneer w/ inlay, silvered dials w/ convex mirror, mkd. "Ballard Cranbrook", mercury tube broken, cornice restored, 37½" H $577.50

Barometer, Eng., mah. veneer, silvered dials, mkd. "Routledge, Carlisle", cornice restored, 37¾" H $682.50

Scroll Mirror, Chippendale, mah. veneer on pine, old dk. finish cleaned off in two places, minor reprs. & age cracks, orig. glass has worn silvering, 22¾" H $550.00

Tea Table, Eng. Chippendale, mah. w/ old dk. finish, two board top, 30½" diam., 27½" H $797.50

Side Chairs, pr. Hepplewhite, mahogany w/ old finish, reupholstered, 35¼" H $1,045.00

A-OH Sept. 1998   Garth's Auctions

Table, Hepplewhite, ref. pine w/ good color, two dovetailed drawers & one board top, 16½" x 20", 28⅝" H $330.00

Armchair Rocker, Mt. Lebanon, blk. paint worn to orig. finish, repl. tape seat is blue & gray, 40" H . . .$825.00

Swift, all wood in orig. yel. varnish, retied & four members are repl., 20" H $247.50

Shaker Box, oval, added red stain & orig. worn blk. stenciled label, "Sabbathday Lake Shakers", finger const. w/ copper & steel tacks, minor age cracks, 10½" L $495.00

Shaker Box, oval, worn patina, finger const. w/ copper & steel tacks, edge damage & age cracks, 8" L $192.50

A-OH Sept. 1998   Garth's Auctions

Reel, floor standing, hard & softwoods w/ old blk. paint, 54¾" H $220.00

Shaker Boudoir Side Chairs, pr., Mt. Lebanon, NY, old dk. reddish br. finish, new woven splint seats, 29¼" H $1,265.00

Scouring Box, poplar w/ dk. gr. repaint, worn w/ repr., edge damage, 9" x 12¾" $165.00

Worker's Leather Vise, all wooden, chestnut w/ old patina, OH, 28" H $115.50

Basket, round woven splint, good patina, 10¼" x 11½" $110.00

A-OH Sept. 1998   Garth's Auctions

Shaker Drying Rack, walnut w/ old worn finish, mortised const., shoe feet, one foot repl., 28" W, 39" H $165.00

Basket, sm. woven splint, good patina, 8½" diam., 6" H $330.00

Baskets, two woven splint buttocks, some age, 7" x 7½", 4" H & 4" x 4½", 2½" H $170.50

Armchair Rocker, Mt. Lebanon, old ref., br., repl. woven tape seat is gr., beige & blk., repr. split, 23" H $770.00

Armchair Rocker, Mt. Lebanon, w/ shawl bar, orig. dk. br. finish w/ touch up reprs. in base, orig. label "Shaker's... Mt. Lebanon,...", repl. tape seat in blk. & blue, 27½" H $330.00

A-OH Sept. 1998   Garth's Auctions

Work Table, cherry w/ old finish, one dovetailed drawer, three board top repl., age cracks, needs repr., pine secondary wood, 23" x 47", 30" H $495.00

Grain Measure, stave const., old sage gr. paint, two rings repl., 10¾" H $99.00

Table Top Cupboard, poplar w/ old red, nailed & screw const., 16" x 28", 21⅛" H $1,210.00

Bucket, stave const., pine w/ blk. over gr., steel bands & bale w/ wooden handle, no lid, 7" H $137.50

Basket, woven splint, bentwood handle, 15½" x 10" H $209.00

A-OH Sept. 1998   Garth's Auctions

Shelf, walnut w/ orig. varnish finish w/ ebonized detail & gilt, wear & repr., 16⅞" W, 19½" H $385.00

Sugar Chest, mini., cherry & walnut w/ old natural finish, repl. hinged lid, reprs., 17¾" W, 11¾" D, 22½" H $2,750.00

Windsor Side Chairs, set of four dec. bamboo, old br. grained repaint, 37" H $1,210.00

Skater's Lamp, brass & tin w/ emerald gr. globe, reprs. & gold paint retouch, 6¾" H $60.50

Skater's Lamp, two w/ clear globes, one all brass, 6¾" H, one brass & tin w/ mismatched top, 7" H . . .$132.00

A-OH Sept. 1998   Garth's Auctions

Shaker Cheese Ladder, hickory w/ old patina & worn white paint, 25" L $577.50

Shaker Stool, or arm rest, birch w/ old red, shaped ends w/ cutout feet, top is dovetailed into ends, 5½" x 16", 13½" H $1,265.00

Shaker Side Chair, Mt. Lebanon, NY, ladderback, ref. hardwood w/ soft finish, new woven tape seat in mauve, gray & beige, 40½" H $522.50

Pine Box, w/ blk. stenciled label "100 Shaker pipes & stems", wire nail const., edge damage, 9½" L . .$148.50

Bentwood Dipper, hard & soft woods, old br. finish, copper tacks, 7½" diam., 8" turned handle .$192.50

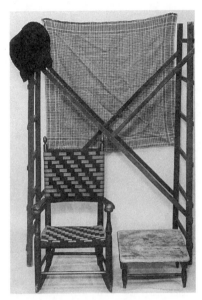

A-OH Sept. 1998　　　Garth's Auctions

Shaker Bertha Scarf, tan, blue & white w/ plaid center & woven border patt., initialed "A.P.", wear, edge damage & soiling, 29" x 30" $302.50

Shaker Drying Rack, Mt. Lebanon, ladder style w/ cross frame, poplar w/ old soft br. red paint, 30½" W, 16½" D, 43½" H $357.50

Amish Bonnet, blk. cotton & a white linen cap, both machine sewn, wear & some damage, 9" H $71.50

Armchair Rocker, orig. dk. finish w/ gold stenciled label "Shaker...Mt. Lebanon...", repl. woven tape seat is gr. & blk., 24" H $2,035.00

Cricket Stool, Mt. Lebanon, worn orig. dk. finish w/ bare traces of label, 11⅜" x 11⅝", 6½" H $247.50

A-OH Sept. 1998　　　Garth's Auctions

Pie Safe, ref. cherry, mortised frame & one dovetailed drawer, restoration & replm., 41¼" W, top 18" x 42", 60" H $1,045.00

Bentwood Box, round w/ lid, old patina, lapped seams w/ steel tacks, 10½" diam. $82.50

Basket, woven splint buttocks, old scrubbed patina, some damage, 10" x 11", 5½" H $60.50

Bentwood Box, round w/ lid, old patina, lapped seams w/ steel tacks, wooden handle w/ wire bale & oval attachments, 9½" diam. $110.00

Tub, stave const. w/ wooden bands, two shades of old gr. paint, impr. "C. Whitney", 17" diam., 6" H . . .$220.00

A-OH Sept. 1998　　　Garth's Auctions

Sugar Chest, ref. cherry, one dovetailed drawer, dovetailed case w/ divided int. & bread board lid, feet repl., reprs. & replm., 28" W, 16" D, 31¼" H $1,760.00

Salt Box, dovetailed, walnut w/ old refinish, dovetailed drawer in base w/ curly maple front, divided int. w/ slant top lid, reprs. & replm., 13" W, 7½" D, 12" H $247.50

Shaker Box, oval, yel. varnish repaint, finger const. w/ copper tacks, lid possibly mismatched, 11¼" L $302.50

Shaker Box, oval, old varnish finish, finger const. w/ copper tacks, 6" L $385.00

Basket, wooden splint buttocks, old gray scrubbed finish, 9½" x 10½", 5¾" H $159.50

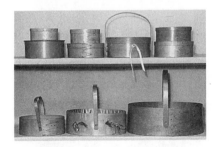

A-OH Sept. 1998　　　Garth's Auctions

Row 1, Left to Right

Bentwood Box, round, natural varnish finish, lapped seams w/ steel tacks, 6⅜" diam. $115.50

Shaker Box, oval, lt. natural finish, finger const. w/ copper tacks, 4¼" L $440.00

Shaker Box, oval, ME, natural varnish finish, finger const. w/ copper tacks, 5⅞" L $357.50

Shaker Box, oval, shiny varnish, finger const. w/ copper tacks, two fingers on base & one on lid, lined w/ pink satin, by George Robert, Mt. Lebanon, NY, 4⅝" L $225.50

Shaker Sewing Box, round w/ lid & swivel handle, natural varnish finish, lapped seams w/ copper tacks, relined w/ bright yel. satin w/ pincushions, etc. 6¾" diam. $181.50

Shaker Box, oval, natural varnish finish, finger const. w/ copper tacks, bottom impr. "8", 6" L $385.00

Shaker Box, oval, Canterbury, NH, old natural patina & worn varnish, finger const. w/copper tacks, 5½" L $440.00

Row 2, Left to Right

Shaker Sewing Box, oval, natural varnish finish, finger const. w/ copper tacks, swivel handle, mkd. "Sabbathday Lake Shakers, ME", 7" L $170.50

Shaker Sewing Box, oval, natural shiny lacquer finish, finger const. w/ copper tacks, lined w/ blue satin w/ pincushion, needle case, etc., mkd. "Sabbathday Lake Shakers, ME", 9⅜" L $605.00

Shaker Carrier, conversion from box to carrier, old varnish finish w/ med. color, finger const. w/ copper tacks, swivel handle, 12" L $231.00

A-OH Sept. 1998   Garth's Auctions

Oil on Canvas, mountain landscape w/ lake sgn. "Dixon", orig. gilt frame has damage, 21½" H, 31¾" W $220.00

Roulette Wheel, nickel plated cast steel & wood w/ mirrors & glass w/ red, white, blue & blk. paint, removable feet, reprs., 32½" diam., 50½" H $990.00

Roulette wheel, wood & plywood w/ blk. & gold paint w/ white, standard made in two pcs. & will disassemble, 47½" diam., 82" H $82.50

Steamship, stern wheel pull toy model, wood & wire w/ old br. patina, some damage & repr., 24" L .$440.00

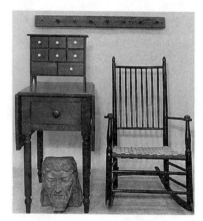

A-OH Sept. 1998   Garth's Auctions

Peg Board, poplar w/ seven maple pegs, old natural patina, 46" L$220.00

Work Table, cherry w/ old finish & good color, top & drawer repl., 17¼" x 26" w/ 13" leaves, 29½" H . . .$247.50

Armchair Rocker, old dk. finish & repl. woven tape in two-tone blue, slightly crooked, repr., 38" H . .$55.00

Chest of Drawers, mini., walnut & poplar w/ old finish, dovetailed drawers, rebuilt drawers, repl. porcelain knobs, one missing, 15¼" W, 7½" D, 13½" H $495.00

Wooden Head, carved bearded man, weathered natural finish w/ age cracks, 12½" H $165.00

A-OH Sept. 1998   Garth's Auctions

Row 1, Left to Right

Cow Nodder, compo. w/ worn br. & white cow hide, natural horns & glass eyes, wear & damage, tail missing, 12" L $192.50

Animals, four carved wooden, two dogs & sheep w/ old dk. patina & sheep w/ old white & blk. paint, glass eyes, damage & repr., 6⅜" H .$137.50

Elephant Nodder, papier mache w/ gray flocked coat, ora. felt blanket w/ gold trim & paper label "Ger.", wear & edge damage, 8½" L $192.50

Row 2, Left to Right

Whimsies, six carved, ball in cage, chains, etc., one has old red & blue paint, the rest have old patina, five have wooden bases, 3½" to 15" H $357.50

Whirligig, man chopping wood, old weathered brownish red paint, 20th C. folk art $220.00

Box, dovetailed, pine w/ old worn dk. grayish gr. paint, applied base & lid edge molding, repl. lock has key, edge wear & damage, 14½" L $247.50

Nutcracker, carved wooden head, worn old dk. patina, good detail w/ wear & edge damage, 7¾" L .$770.00

A-OH Sept. 1998   Garth's Auctions

Quilt, pieced youth size, star design in lavender, yel., coral & blue on pale gr. ground, wear & some color loss & stains, binding machine sewn, 48" x 64" $269.50

Duck, carved wood in landing position, orig. paint has wear, edge damage, 25½" wingspan $550.00

Tableaux, contemporary folk art w/ hunter in graveyard, unsgn., 14½" x 23½" $192.50

Cat Shaped Box, balsa wood w/ silver paint & blk. spots, 16½" L $181.50

A-OH Sept. 1998   Garth's Auctions

Lap Board, portable, two-tone pine & walnut slats w/ impr. rule, paper back allows board to roll up for storage & side braces w/ brass clips allow it to stay rigid, old shipping label attached to back "U.S. & Canada Express, ...MA", 19½" x 36" . .$220.00

Shaker Table, Hepplewhite, ref. walnut, mortised apron, one dovetailed drawer & one board top, orig. drop leaf table, top repl. & drawer added, 23¾" x 36½", 26½" H $770.00

Oval Box, natural patina, overlapping joints w/ wrt. iron tacks, 17½" L $137.50

Shaker Sewing Box, oval, orig. reddish tint varnish, Mt. Lebanon, NY, finger const. w/ copper tacks, int. lined w/ pale blue silk w/ woven straw needle case, etc., brass mono. medallion added to lid, 11½" L $880.00

Bee Skep, rye straw, wear, int. retains some bee's wax, 21" diam., 13" H $247.50

A-OH Sept. 1998   Garth's Auctions

Shaker Boxes, five oval bentwood, nesting set, Mt. Lebanon, NY, varnish finish, finger const. w/ copper tacks, four w/ poplar bottoms & lids, one pine, 7⅛" to 13⅝" L $1,430.00

Shaker Cheese Colander, tin w/ rim handles, split, 22" diam. . .$71.50

Mule Chest, pine w/ old red repaint, one board ends, two dovetailed drawers, two board top, reprs., rehinged, 43¼" W, 18¾" D, 41¼" H $880.00

Seed Box, pine w/ orig. finish & paper label, Mt. Lebanon, NY, 11½" x 23½", 3¼" H $770.00

Hardware Chest, poplar w/ old br. finish, 35 drawers, wire nail const. w/ plywood back, some worn tape labels, 16⅜" W, 5¼" D, 16⅜" H $330.00

Shaker Box, oval, Mt. Lebanon, NY, end of day box, finger const. w/ copper tacks, varnish finish w/ slightly red tint to lid & handle w/ yellowish tint to box, penciled verse inside lid "Charlotte Morrow, 1865", break & renailing, 13½" L $577.50

Sugar Chest, ref. cherry, one dovetailed drawer, dovetailed case divided into three compartments, bread board lid, poplar secondary wood, scraps of "Weekly Courier Journal, Louisville" from 1800's in bottom drawer, age crack in lid & nails disturbed, minor edge damage to feet, 27¾" W, 19¼" D, 40" H $4,675.00

Shaker Box, oval, old finish, finger const. w/ copper tacks, minor break in lid at nail, 14¼" L $1,100.00

Shaker Box, old red, finger const. w/ copper tacks, 13½" L $2,640.00

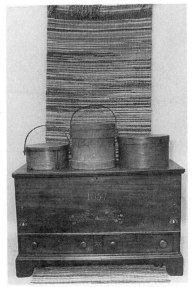

Rag Carpet, PA, multi-colored, mostly blue, br. & white, unused condition, 38½" x 506" $330.00

Blanket Chest, PA, poplar w/ orig. br. graining & gr. painted trim, stenciled dec. dovetailed bracket feet, two drawers & case w/ applied moldings, repr., 46¾" W, 20¾" D, 29½" H $3,025.00

Bentwood Box, round w/ lid & swivel handle, old varnish finish, copper tacks, 13½" diam., 6½" H $192.50

Shaker Sugar Bucket, Watervliet NY, stave const. w/ interlaced wooden bands, old yel. paint, lid & swivel handle, 12½" diam., 12½" H .$605.00

Shaker Box, round, red stain, steel tacks, age cracks, 15" diam., 8" H $220.00

Row 1, Left to Right

Bentwood Box, oval by Hersey, natural varnish finish, single finger const. w/ copper tacks, 5⅞" L $165.00

Bentwood Box, oval by Hersey, natural varnish finish, single finger const. w/ copper tacks, edge damage & rim loose, 5½" L $110.00

Basket, woven splint w/ rim handles, some breaks in weave, 10" diam. $165.00

Shaker Box, oval, red stain, finger const. w/ copper tacks, 6¼" L$715.00

Shaker Box, oval, good old dk. patina, finger const. w/ copper tacks, 5¼" L $770.00

Row 2, Left to Right

Shaker Box, oval, med. br. soft finish, finger const. w/ copper tacks, 10¼" L $577.50

Shaker Box, oval, old dk. patina w/ scratches on lid, left hand finger const. w/ copper tacks, 9" L .$522.50

Shaker Box, oval, old dk. patina w/ scratches & glue stain on lid, finger const. w/ copper tacks, 8" L .$550.00

Shaker Sieve, bentwood w/ woven horse hair, old patina, 9" H . .$357.50

Shaker Box, mah. veneer w/ bird's eye maple & walnut w/ line inlay, pine secondary wood, age crack, 11¼" L .$104.50

Game Board, inlaid, intricate marquetry in several colors w/ old alligatored varnish finish, back has inlaid horse & "F.C.B." & pencil inscription "2000 pcs. Jan. 17, 1911", 16⅝" H, 17¼" W $687.50

Blanket Chest, sm. dovetailed, ref. pine, restoration & feet repl., 31" L $495.00

Box, dovetailed, walnut w/ old worn finish, sliding lid has orig. brass bale handle, replacements & damage, 10½" x 11", 16½" H $110.00

Shaker Lap Desk, Hancock, MA, pine, poplar & walnut w/ old worn patina, hinged lid & pull out drawer for inkwell, 17½" x 12½", 4½" H $935.00

Basket, oblong woven splint, bentwood swivel handle w/ laced & end detail, old patina, 15" L $137.50

A-OH Jan. 1999   Garth's Auctions

Chest of Drawers, Fed., cherry w/ old dk. finish & inlay, five dovetailed drawers, cherry & walnut secondary wood, damage & replms., 40" W, top 22¾" x 41", 46½" H $1,402.50
Lamps, two pewter, time clock, 12¾" H, & bell shaped w/ ear handle, brass spout burner loose, 3" H plus burner $220.00
Charger, pewter, unmkd., pitted & somewhat battered, 14" diam.$192.50
Tumblers, two pewter, unmkd., 5¼" & 2¾" H $165.00
Pitcher, pewter, battered, unmkd., 7½" H $165.00

A-OH Jan. 1999   Garth's Auctions

Candle Sconces, two tin, similar w/ ribbed backs & crimped circular crests, one has double diamond punch work design, some damage, 13½" H $330.00
Table, Wm. & Mary gate leg, maple w/ dk. worn finish on base & top is curly w/ worn natural finish, mortised & pinned joints, butterfly hinged leaves, one dovetailed drawer, chestnut secondary wood, reprs., 15¾" x 45½" w/ 18½" leaves, 26½" H $19,250.00
Pie Plate, redware, coggled rim, three line designs in yel. slip, wear & old chips, 10" diam. $467.50
Pitcher, redware, ribbed strap handle, clear mottled gr. glaze w/ yel. slip dec. highlighted w/ br. & gr., br. glazed int., minor chips, old wooden lid, 10¾" H $9,900.00
Pie Plate, redware, coggled rim, three line designs in yel. slip, 10" diam. $55.00

A-OH Jan. 1999   Garth's Auctions

Watercolor, landscape "View from Mt Ida", OH, well detailed houses, people, trees, etc., stains & corner edge damage, old molded frame, 15" H, 23" W $1,100.00
Tavern Table, Q.A., birch w/ old worn red paint on base & oval pine top w/ traces of red, three board pine top, minor edge repr. & age cracks, 26"x 36¾", 25" H $2,860.00
Candlesticks, pr. brass, late 19th C. early 20th C., 10½" H $110.00
Bowl, ash burl w/ worn soft finish, deep bowl shape, 14" diam., 6" H $1,540.00
Crock, stoneware, applied handles, foliage & "5" in cobalt blue quill work, sm. edge chips, 13" H $110.00

A-OH Jan. 1999   Garth's Auctions

Bedwarmer, copper, tooled brass lid w/ center flower medallion & turned wooden handle, 36½" L $165.00
Hatchel, dec., two round medallions w/ nails, backing has compass scribed design in yel., red & worn dk. patina, 30½" L $660.00
Drying Rack, oak or ash w/ dk. worn finish, revolving top w/ six collapsing rods, 39" H $192.50
Herb Grinder, cast iron, boat shaped w/ wheel pestle, wooden handle repl., minor chip on one foot, 16" L $511.50
Corner Cupboard, ref. cherry & poplar, cut down from bottom & apron repl., 44¼" W, 79" H .$2,200.00

A-OH Nov. 1998   Garth's Auctions

Civil War Hat, Hardee, sgn. "U.S. Army...", has bugle "1" & "2" insignias along w/ brass eagle & shield plate, several reprs., 6" x 13½" . . .$1,540.00
Civil War Artillery Kepi, manuf. by "Bent & Bush-Boston", red wool w/ white piping & blk. band around base, has eagle "A" buttons, damage $605.00
Civil War Drum, w/ eagle, paint has flaked w/ wings & head remaining, hoops are red w/ early repr., "Edward Baack, NY" label, PA, sold w/ copies of war record $797.50

A-OH Jan. 1999   Garth's Auctions

Stand, Sheraton, ref. curly maple, one dovetailed drawer & two board top, top reattached, old brass pull, 18" x 19", 29¼" H $385.00
Side Chair, bamboo Windsor, ref., plank seat, 35" H $82.50
Student Lamp, brass, gr. shade cased in white, electrified, mkd. "The Belgium Lamp", 23" H plus chimney $467.50
Jar, ovoid stoneware, applied shoulder handles & impr. label "Hamilton, Greensboro, PA 4", cobalt blue dec., stains & hairlines, chip, 15" H $550.00

A-OH Nov. 1998   Garth's Auctions

Wall Cupboard, one pc. pine w/ old blue paint over lighter blue, two nailed drawers & molded cornice, MA, edge wear & damage, 23" x 55½", 78½" H . .$6,050.00

Cats, two, printed fabric labeled "Pat., '92", wear & fading, 13" & 6½" H . .$93.50

Cat, "Steiff", gray mohair w/ glass eyes & ear button, added red ribbon, wear, damage, 18½" L $330.00

Cats, three blk. velvet w/ glass eyes, one has ear button & cloth label "...Made in Japan...", one has tail pinned in upright position, 13¾" H $110.0

A-OH Jan. 1999   Garth's Auctions

Desk, school master's, ref. pine w/ old gr. on int. & inside of drawer, one dovetailed drawer, low gallery & simple pigeon hole int., damage & repr., repl. brasses, 32" W, 21" D, 41½" H . . .$440.00

Pie Plate, redware, coggled rim, splashed dots of yel. slip, wear, chips & hairlines, 9" diam. $148.50

Jug, redware ovoid, strap handle, greenish amber glaze w/ br. flecks, chips, 9¼" H $137.50

Pie Plate, redware, coggled rim, spots of yel. slip, wear & old chips in glaze, 11" diam. $220.00

Canada Goose, swimmer, realistic paint & good carved detail, sgn. "...by Clem Wilding", repr., 31" L $165.0

A-OH Nov. 1998   Garth's Auctions

Dry Sink, hutch top, poplar w/ old finish, three dovetailed drawers & well w/ shelf, top has four dovetailed drawers, repl. porcelain knobs & cast iron thumb latches, OH, 73¾" W, 23" D, 50½" H .$1,870.00

Basket, round woven splint, 33 ribs, good color, 12" diam., 7½" H $220.00

Basket, round woven splint, 33 ribs, good color, 13" diam., 7¾" H $137.50

Basket, round woven splint, 33 ribs, good color, 16½" diam., 9½" H $165.00

Basket, round woven splint, 33 ribs, good gray patina, 16" diam., 9¾" H $192.50

Crock, stoneware, blue & white spongeware, hairlines, 11" diam., 6" H . . .$71.50

"Butter" Crock, stoneware, blue & white spongeware, 9" diam., 6" H $302.50

A-OH Jan. 1999   Garth's Auctions

Checkerboard, pine w/ orig. mustard yel. paint, red & gr. striping & br. squares, wear, applied edge, 17" H, 16½" W $990.00

Tavern Table, Q.A., maple base cleaned down to traces of old red & pine top w/ old worn finish, mortised & pinned stretcher & apron, one pine dovetailed drawer & two board breadboard top, 28½" x 39", 27" $3,520.00

Footwarmer, punched tin, mortised hardwood frame w/ old patina, punched heart & circle design, 8" x 9", 5¾" H . . .$192.50

Brazier, wrt. iron, wear & edge damage, turned wooden handle, 9" x 10" .$220.00

Candle Mold, twelve tin tubes in poplar frame, old patina, repl. wire rods, 5½" x 17½", 15¾" H $770.00

A-OH Nov. 1998   Garth's Auctions

Cupboard, early two pc. open pewter, pine & poplar w/ old dk. finish, 57½" W, 17½" D, 73" H . . . . .N/S

Candlesticks, pr. pewter w/ push ups, one has repr. causing height variance, 10" H $302.50

Tall Pot, pewter, mkd. "Simpson & Benham, N.Y.", minor soldered repr., 11"H $385.00

Plate, pewter, crowned rose touch mark, "Jacob Whitmore", CT, wear & scratches, 8" diam. $220.00

Chamber Lamp, pewter, lemon font, "R. Gleason" touch, MA, orig. whale oil burner loose tube, 4¾" H .$198.00

Ewer, Euro. pewter w/ hinged lid, dents & repr., 8⅛" H $82.50

Bowl, pewter, eagle touch mark "B. Barns, PA", wear & scratches, 13¾" H $165.00

Loaf Pan, redware, worn yel. slip dec. w/ polka dot bird & foliage, coggled rim, wear & flaking, damage, 16" L $550.00

A-OH Sept. 1998   Garth's Auctions

Utensil Rack, wrt. iron, four birds, scrolled detail & six hooks, 24" W $357.50

Utensil Rack, wrt. iron, scrolled detail & five hooks, 20½" W $220.00

Bootscraper, cast iron in limestone block, 8½" x 18" $302.50

Bootscraper, wrt. iron in limestone block, 11¼" x 11¼", 15" H $385.00

Griddle, cast iron w/ wrt. bale handle, 14¾" diam. $110.00

A-OH Nov. 1998   Garth's Auctions
Work Table, Sheraton, walnut & cherry w/ mah. veneer facade & curly maple veneer on drawer fronts, three dovetailed drawers & one board top, poplar secondary wood, damage & repr., repl. brasses, 25" W, 17" D, 28¼" H $1,430.00
Chalk Deer, pr., old worn paint in red, blk. & yel., 5½" H $935.00
Chalk Cat, old worn paint in red, blk. & yel., 9⅞" H $1,430.00
Blanket Chest, pine w/ old worn yel. & br. graining, lid rehinged, 16¾" W, 7½" H $715.00
Chalk Cat, sleeping, old polychrome paint, wear & some edge damage, repr., 12" L $412.50

A-OH Nov. 1998   Garth's Auctions
Bellows, dec. turtle back, orig. white paint w/ smoked graining w/ yellowed varnish, stenciled & freehand flowers in red, gr., blk. & gold, brass nozzle, professionally releathered, 17½" L $357.50
Fraktur, OH, pen & ink & watercolor on heavy paper,, "Daniel Sehaey...", ca. 1854, old walnut beveled frame, 8¾" H, 10¾" W $577.50
Bellows, dec. orig. red paint w/ stenciled & freehand vintage in gold, bronze & blk., old worn releathering, brass nozzle, 18" L $192.50
Chest of Drawers, birch w/ old mellow ref., four dovetailed drawers, repl. brasses, pine secondary wood, 37" W, 17¾" D, 48¼" H overall $935.00
Andirons, pr., early brass, double lemon top, 17½" H $385.00

A-OH Nov. 1998   Garth's Auctions
Cupboard, one pc., pine w/ brownish red repaint, single board doors in base, edge damage, 44" W, 16¼" D, 74½" H $550.00

Row 1, Left to Right

Plates, three Eng. pewter, two "Townsend & Compton" & one "Samuell Ellis", wear & battering, 7½" to 8" diam. $192.50
Cups, two footed pewter, some wear & battering, 3¼" diam., 3⅛" H .$55.00

Row 2, Left to Right

Measures, five pc. assembled set, pewter, largest is "James Yates", two mkd. "Birmingham" & one "Glasgow", minor damage, 2" to 6¼" H ..$368.50
Plates, three pewter w/ angel touch & engr. initial's, pr. of pates 8¾" diam., & soup plate 8½" diam., all have wear & scratches $93.50

Row 3, Left to Right

Plates, three Eng. pewter, faint marks, 8⅝" diam., "John Townsend" touch, 9⅛" diam., & faint touch mark "SH", split in rim, 9¼" diam., all have wear & damage $165.00

Row 4, Left to Right

Two Pieces, pewter, pear shaped teapot w/ Neptune mark, damaged & repr., 7⅛" H, & octagonal jar w/ screw cap, battered, 9" H $82.50
Bowl, pewter covered, wear & repr., 9" diam., 10" H $170.50
Urn, pewter on scrolled legs, wooden handle & finial, repl. brass spigot mkd. "Buckeye Brass Works, Dayton, O", repr. $192.50

A-OH Sept. 1998   Garth's Auctions
Drying Rack, pine w/ old patina, two sections w/ canvas hinge, 31" x 40" $60.50
Drying Rack, pine w/ old patina, two sections w/ mortised const., steel

hinges are replm. for canvas hinges, 24" x 43" $88.00
Baskets, four sm. woven splint of various ages, 6" to 9" diam. $71.50
Stool, pine w/ br. repaint, 7½" x 26½", 7½" H $220.00
Shaker Sewing Rocker, Mt. Lebanon, worn orig. finish w/ gilt stencil label, repl. red & blue tape seat, 34" H $550.00
Peach Basket, woven splint, diamond design w/ old br. patina, 14½" diam., 11½" H $192.50
Shaker Measures, three bentwood, orig. finish w/ blk. stenciled labels, "...Sabbathday Lake, ME", 7½", 9½" & 11½" diam. $495.00
Box, round bentwood, old worn dk. gr. paint over lighter gr., minor edge damage, 10¼" diam. $192.50

A-OH Jan. 1999   Garth's Auctions

Baby Rattles

Rattle, silver w/ child's head & four bells, ivory handle has age cracks, & repr., 6" L $192.50

Rattle, silver plated brass, urn shaped, ivory handle loose, age cracks, 6" L $55.00

Rattle, w/ four nickel plated bells on leatherized cloth straps in white w/ red zig-zag, blk. painted turned handle, 6" L $148.50

Rattle, bone w/ four bells, ring glued & minor damage, whistle handle, 4" L $165.00

Rattles, two, one silver rooster w/ pearl handle, 3¼" L & one silver plated bell, bone ring handle glued, 3" L $132.00

Rattle, white molded rubber, bell embedded in end, 5⅛" L $82.50

Rattle, tin, colorful litho w/ girl & cat & boy w/ dog, soldered, 4½" L $165.00

Rattle, w/ turned whistle handle, two bells on repl. leather strap & soft rubber pacifier end, 6" L $27.50

Rattle, w/ twelve bells on leatherized cloth straps, turned handle, worn & flaked white paint, 6¾" L . . .$137.50

Rattle, twisted wire, turned wooden handle is blk. w/ four tin bells in worn japanning, 8¼" L $165.00

A-OH Nov. 1998   Garth's Auctions

Rugs, two similar hooked rag & yarn, loosely worked colorful scenes w/ flowers, one has two dogs, 21" H, 33½" W, & one has two horses & barn, 18½" H, 35" W, wear & damage $55.00

Apothecary, ref. pine & walnut, 44 drawers w/ white porcelain knobs, walnut top board added, wire nail const., 36¾" W, 14¼" D, 21¾" H $1,375.00

Bowl, burl, dk. finish has been rubbed down to a mottled shine, 9" diam., 3¾" H $33.00

Candle Box, hanging, poplar w/ worn bluish gr. paint, scalloped crest & slant top lid w/ staple & hinges, reprs., 10¼" W, 4½" D, 4½" H $198.00

Crock, stoneware w/ lid & applied handles, cobalt blue brushed design, base has stabilized cracks & lid has chips, 8" diam., 5¼" H $192.50

Watercolor, on paper theorem, flower & berries in shades of blue, gr., br., yel. & faded red, sgn. "W.P. Eaton...Boston...1843", stains & minor damage, orig. frame w/ transfer & gilded designs, 14½" H, 15¾" W $1,650.00

Stand, Sheraton, curly & bird's eye maple w/ mellow ref., front dovetailed, back nailed, repl. one board top, reprs., 17" x 19¼", 27¼" H $715.00

Side Chair, Windsor, worn reddish br. finish, repr. in front edge of seat, 36½" H $1,045.00

Bowl, hardwood w/ hand work, lt. worn natural patina, 10" x17½", 4" H $110.00

Churn, stoneware, applied shoulder handles, cobalt blue dec. & "5", crow's foot hairlines, 17¾" H $220.00

A-OH Sept. 1998   Garth's Auctions

Row 1, Left to Right

Spice Box, round bentwood, orig. varnish w/ blk. stenciled labels & tin trim, int. has eight canisters, labeled "S.C....Iowa", 9" diam. $467.50

Boxes, two round bentwood, old ref., one w/ traces of gr. paint, lapped

seams w/ steel tacks, 6⅜" & 5¾" diam. $110.00

Bucket, stave const., worn red graining w/ white int., steel bands are blk., bottom repl., 7½" diam., 6" H $220.00

Armand Marseille Doll, in Shaker costume, bisque head w/ glass eyes & open mouth, cloth body w/ maroon dress, woven poplar bonnet & red wool cape, moth damage, 11" H $412.50

Doll, Ger. in Shaker costume, celluloid over compo. head & body, gray dress w/ white lace trim & woven poplar bonnet w/ gray satin trim, some damage to skirt, 9¾" H $330.00

Row 2, Left to Right

Blanket Chest, cherry w/ old mellow finish, dovetailed case w/ turned

maple feet, bottom board poplar, lock w/ key, 13½" L $357.50

Baskets, two berry, bentwood w/ natural patina & stains, one has tin fastener at seam & other has wire, 6" diam., 4" H $180.00

Shaker Candy Boxes, four, "East Canterbury, NH", 4" to 9½" L . .$77.00

Boxes, two round, natural finish, lapped seams w/ steel tacks, stenciled label "S.B. Swan", tin edging impr. "Newark N.J.", 7½" diam. $192.50

Shaker Box, ref. mah. veneer w/ maple & walnut inlay on beveled lid, pine secondary wood, paper lined int. w/ mirror in lid, lift out tray missing, hinges loose, damage, 11" L . .$27.50

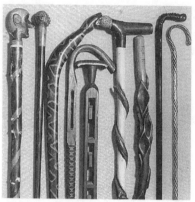

A-OH Sept. 1998   Garth's Auctions

Trade Sign, in old worn gold & blk., old repaint w/ same letters on both sides, 18" H, 24" W $165.00

Blanket Chest, dec., poplar w/ orig. red graining, dovetailed case, till w/ lid, wrt. iron strap hinges, pine secondary wood, repr., 45" W, 19½" D, 23" H $1,210.00

Decoy, swimming Brandt, old worn working paint, edge damage & crack, repr., 20½" L $253.00

Box, dovetailed, ref. pine, int. has deep till, brass side handles & escut. repl., 18¼" L $165.00

Weathervane, whale, wood w/ old worn & weathered repaint, traces of gilding, hinged tail, split, old hardware, 30" L $1,650.00

A-OH Sept. 1998   Garth's Auctions

Walking Stick, carved man's head, painted br., blk., red, yel. & ora., 20th C., 42" L $165.00

Walking Stick, carved head w/ good detail & glass eyes, blk. grained shaft, some wear, 35" L $330.00

Walking Stick, diamond back rattlesnake in br. w/ gold & blk. diamonds, glass eyes, 37" L ...$192.50

Canes, two, both have ball/or block cane design w/ carving, 34½" & 36" L $253.00

Cane & Walking Stick, cane w/ serpent & bird head handle wrapped w/ leather, 40" L, & stick w/ carved crooked shaft & carved initials, 36" L $357.50

Canes, two glass, one clear w/ spiraled blue & maroon, 34" L, & one dk. amber, sq. w/ twisted handle & tip, 38" L $99.00

A-OH Sept. 1998   Garth's Auctions

Work Table, ref. walnut & other wood, assembled from old parts, four nailed drawers, 39½" W, 28" D, 31" H $27.50

Coffee Pot, tin w/ pewter finial, 12¼" H $99.00

Shaker Reel, w/ table clamp, Hancock, MA, old yel. varnish, damage, 20" H $143.00

Shaker Dippers, two tin w/ tapered cylinder handles, one has ring hanger & other has added wooden plug w/ screw eye, lt. rust, 7¼" & 8½" diam. $93.50

Shaker Coffee Pot, tin oversize, rust damage & repr., swivel handle, 16" H $165.00

A-OH Sept. 1998   Garth's Auctions

Hanging Shelves, walnut w/ old worn dk. patina, four tiers, reprs. & back post repl., 24" W, 7" D, 19½" H $495.00

Baskets, two similar splint berry, half pint size, 4" diam., 2¼" H ...$165.00

Baskets, pr., splint berry w/ tin rims, traces of red, pint size, 4¼" diam., 3⅞" H $302.50

Shaker Sewing Box, Mt. Lebanon, NY, w/ lid & swing handle, old varnish finish, copper tacks, repl. blue lining & gold brocade w/ blue ribbons, pincushion, needle case, 5¾" diam. $137.50

Shaker Baskets, pr. of splint berry, quart size, 6⅜" diam., 3½" H .$242.00

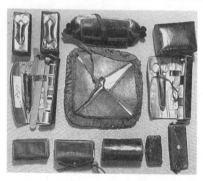

A-OH Sept. 1998   Garth's Auctions

All Shaker Sewing Items w/ Leather Cases

Sewing Box, dk. leather w/ bronze finish & pink silk lining, steel scissors & thimble w/ 3 spools of thread, wear & edge damage, 4¼" L $49.50

Sewing Box, dk. leather w/ bronze finish & blue silk lining, steel scissors & thimble w/ strawberry, needles & a bit of tatting, wear, 4¼" L $60.50

Sewing Case, blk. leather w/ purple knit binding, blk. pompons & ribbon tie, line in blue silk, wear & repr., 7½" L $60.50

Sewing Box, br. leather w/ br. silk binding & int., steel scissors, silver closure w/ three Shaker sisters in relief, 4¼" L $71.50

Sewing Case, rolls into cylinder, blk. leather w/ tan satin lining & maroon ribbon, contains five spools, steel scissors, pins & busk w/ "A.P. Little", wear, 7" L $49.50

Handkerchief Caddy, br. leather w/ br. silk trim & red silk lining, contains five hankies, worn w/ ribbon closure, 8" x 8½" $82.50

Sewing Case, blk. leather w/ gold silk lining, steel scissors, thimble, needles, etc. wear, 7" L $60.50

Sewing Cases, two leather w/ needles, thread, thimbles & steel scissors, worn black leather w/ blue & lavender silk lining, worn, 3¾" & 4" L $60.50

Sewing Cases, three leather, cylindrical w/ three spools of thread, 4" L, rectangular w/ nine sm. spools of thread, 3" L & rectangular pin case, 4¾" L $49.50

A-OH Sept. 1998   Garth's Auctions

Hunt Board, ref. walnut, three dove-tailed drawers, poplar secondary wood, reprs. to drawer & top repl., 22¼" x 49", 43¾" H $2,475.00

Knife Box, Bentwood, ash & chestnut w/ old varnish finish, turned handle, 8½" x 13" $137.50

Knife Box, pine w/ worn red repaint, 9½" x 17" $165.00

Child's Wagon, wooden bed & spoke wheels, old br. finish, reprs. & steel axle rods repl., 24½" L $822.50

Box, round, old gr., lapped seams w/ steel tacks, 10½" diam. $412.50

Box, round, old ref., lapped seams w/ steel tacks, int. has red repaint, 10½" diam. $49.50

Box, round, old blk. paint, lapped seams w/ steel tacks, wear & bottom has sm. holes, 9½" diam. $220.00

Box, round, old brownish red repaint, lapped seams w/ steel tacks, 8½" diam. $247.50

Box, round, old gray paint, lapped seams w/ steel tacks, 7½" diam. $247.50

Boxes, two round, old ref., lapped seams w/ steel tacks, 5½" pictured, & 6¼" diam. $203.50

A-OH Sept. 1998   Garth's Auctions

Shelves, poplar w/ worn old red, one board ends w/cut out feet, brass braces added to back, 26" W, 9½" D, 50" H $880.00

Basket, woven splint buttocks, old varnish, 11" x 11", 6¼" H $170.50

Shaker Sewing Box, oval, orig. varnish & blk. stenciled label, "...ME", finger const. w/ copper tacks, bentwood swivel handle, worn pink silk lining/ 10½" L $412.50

Basket, open work woven splint w/ lid, damage & hole, 11" diam. $137.50

Shaker Egg Carrier, Enfield, NH, bird's eye maple w/ old patina, wire fasteners w/ wooden spring clip, 13" x 13", 11" H $1,375.00

A-OH Sept. 1998   Garth's Auctions

Table, Hepplewhite, ref. pine & cherry, one dovetailed drawer, top repl. & drawer mismatched, 17" x 19", 24¾" H $275.00

Shaker Side Chair, Mt. Lebanon, old finish, repl. tape seat in mauve, yel. & sage gr., 40¾" H $770.00

Spice Cupboard, hanging, ref. bird's eye maple & mah., dovetailed case, porcelain knobs, wire nail const., 15¼" W, 5" D., 18⅝" H $467.50

Basket, woven splint buttocks, good patina w/ dk. br. color, 11" x 12½", 6" H $220.00

Bucket, stave const. w/ interlapping wooden bands, natural patina, old ink inscription on bottom "...1922", 11½" D, 8¼" H $165.00

A-OH Sept. 1998   Garth's Auctions

Shaker Letter, on Canterbury, NH stationery, two pages & envelope addressed to Rebecca A. Hathaway, Providence, RI, dated 12-7-'03, picture in corner of frame, 19" H, 21" W $137.50

Candlestand, cherry w/ old finish, two board removable top, 13¾" diam., 22½" H $275.00

Shaker Side Chair, New Lebanon ladderback, ref., repl. rush seat, 41" H $660.00

Shaker Box, oval, old finish, three finger const. w/ copper tacks, no lid, minor damage, 6¼" L $104.50

Basket, Woodland indian woven splint buttocks, faded colors, 11" x 12½", 6" H $93.50

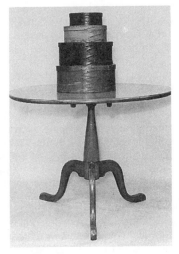

A-OH Sept. 1998   Garth's Auctions

Shaker Tea Table, tilt top, Watervliet, NY, maple w/ old refinish, wrt. iron catch, 36" diam., 26¾" H $2,310.00

Shaker Box, oval, old varnish finish, wear & stains, finger const. w/ copper tacks, wood burned inscription "Cloe Wattring, Berline, Ger. 1784 A.D.", crack, 13¾" L $495.00

Shaker Box, oval, old worn blk. over pale gr., finger const. w/ copper tacks, 12" L $770.00

Shaker Box, oval, old worn patina w/ traces of blk., tucked in finger const. w/ copper tacks, 9½" L$385.00

Shaker Box, oval, old worn bluish gr. over lt. blue, finger const. w/ copper tacks, 7¼" L $715.00

A-OH Sept. 1998   Garth's Auctions

Basket, woven splint open work, heavy gr. paint, flaking, 11" diam. $385.00

Shaker Dust Pan, tin w/ turned wooden handle, some soldered & glued reprs., 34½" L $330.00

Blanket Chest, mini., poplar w/ old red, dovetailed case, base & lid edge molding, 25¼" W, 14¼" D, 15½" H $385.00

Shaker Box, Enfield, NH, pine w/ orig. gr. paint, dovetailed, lid w/ applied edge molding & branded "S.T. Bradford", int. partially lined w/ Shaker blue paper, reprs. & damage, 19¾" W, 11¾" D, 10½" H $715.00

Gameboard, red & blk. w/ yel. foliage scrolls in corners, gallery has edge damage, 16" x 17" $577.50

A-OH Sept. 1998   Garth's Auctions

Drying Rack, shoe feet, pine w/ old med. gr. repaint, two mortised bars, 24¾" W, 34" H $110.00

Ladies Bonnet, woven poplar splint in natural & blk. w/ beige silk ribbons & trim, paper label "5", 9½" L $137.50

Baskets, two woven splint buttocks, one has fine weave w/ repr., 9" diam., 4½" H, one is coarser weave 8½" x 9½", 4" H $148.50

Armchairs, pr. of similar child sized, worn orig. dk. finish, orig. woven splint seats have damage, 24" H $550.00

Wooden Scoops, three, one w/ cut out handle & deep bowl is pictured, natural patina $110.00

A-OH Sept. 1998   Garth's Auctions

Box, oval bentwood by Hersey, old varnish w/ fruit & foliage in red, gr. & blk. added to top lid, finger const. w/ steel tacks, 5⅞" L $165.00

Shaker Box, Union Village, OH, cherry w/ old dk. finish, dovetailed, lid w/ orig. wire hinges & low crest that has old break held by added hinge, uneven feet have been leveled, 12½" W, 16" D, 7" H $770.00

Shaker Sewing Box, Enfield, CT, walnut w/ old varnish finish, dovetailed w/ lift out tray, 7½" x 9" x 14" $440.00

Box, poplar w/ worn orig. blk. paint w/ gold & silver stenciled floral dec., repl. two feet, wear & edge damage, 13½" W, 7" D, 6¼" H $110.00

Mini. Chest of Drawers, English, mah. w/ old finish, dovetailed drawers, extensive reprs., 10" W, 4" D, 10¼" H $165.00

A-OH Sept. 1998   Garth's Auctions

Drawers, hanging case, ref. oak, machine dovetailing, wire const., 20½" W, 9½" D, 22" H $605.00

Child's Rocker, Mt. Lebanon, orig. blk. paint, gold stenciled label "Shakers...NY", rockers repl., new woven tape seat in red & pale gr., paint retouch, 28½" H $605.00

Shaker Box, oval, old finish w/ reddish stain & darker graining on lid, faint paper label under varnish, finger const. w/ copper tacks, 15½" L $1,045.00

Shaker Box, Sabbathday Lake, ME, oval, old dk. blue paint w/ wear, finger const. w/ copper tacks, minor edge damage, 10½" L $1,237.50

Shaker Bonnet, & wooden doll bonnet mold, woven straw is damaged & ecru silk trim & ribbons worn, 4¼" L $412.50

A-OH Sept. 1998   Garth's Auctions

Shaker Table, Hepplewhite, Union Village, OH, cherry w/ old red & poplar top, one nailed drawer, one

board top worn, dk. varnish finish, 18½" x 28¾", 29" H $1,100.00

Shaker Side Chair, Mt. Lebanon ladderback, "3" impr. on top slat, old dk. alligatored varnish finish w/ traces of red & blk. paint, tilters & woven cane seat repl., 38½" H $440.00

Swift, w/ table clamp, old dk. br. patina, wrt. iron thumb screw, 20" H $192.50

Shaker Box, mah. veneer w/ inlaid patter on beveled edge top, fitted int. lined w/ printed paper & calico, mirror in lid & lift out tray, minor edge damage, 11⅛" L $55.00

Shaker Bucket, stave const., old gray paint, metal bands, 13¾" diam., 12" H $165.00

A-OH Sept. 1998   Garth's Auctions

Crock Stand, four tiers, pine w/ old worn gr. paint, porcelain castors, 24" x 48", 35¼" H $577.50

Hat Molds, three, one in blk., two w/ old varnish finish, w/ impr. sizes, two have repl. bases, 10¾" to 11½" H $165.00

Grain Measures, two round bentwood, blk. stenciled label "shaker Society, Sabbathday Lake, Me", 6" & 7½" diam. $247.50

Dipper, round bentwood w/ old varnish finish, copper tack const., 7¼" diam., 8" handle $55.00

Shaker Box Maker's Mold, w/ screw clamp, two sizes, one oval & one round, old patina, 14¾" H$412.50

Shaker Foot Warmer, oval tin, wooden base & top, punched pinwheel designs, old tag "Leavitt Collection", 11" L $797.50

Basket, round woven splint, gray scrubbed patina, wear & damage & rim wrap is incomplete, 11" diam., 7½" H $60.50

Basket, rectangular w/ radiating ribs, old patina, 9½" x 14", 7" H $148.50

Basket, round woven splint, old patina, 12" diam., 6" H $137.50

A-OH Sept. 1998   Garth's Auctions

Row 1, Left to Right

Food Molds, three copper w/ similar geometric designs, old patina, dents, 10" diam. $302.50

Salt Crock, yellowware w/ br. & grayish sponging, hinged wooden lid, faint worn gilt label "salt", 6" H $137.50

Food Molds, two sm. copper w/ geometric design, hammered finish & old patina, 4¼" & 5" diam. $192.50

Food Molds, three copper, all geometric, one has squirrel, 8½" diam., bunch of grapes, 7¼" diam., & fruit mkd. "Kreamer", 7¼" diam. . .$192.50

Row 2, Left to Right

Tobacco Can, cylindrical, blk. litho on ora., 6½" H $275.00

Box, dovetailed, pine w/ old varnish finish, velvet lining, 11½" L . . .$55.00

Child's Tea Set, three pc. in ironstone, br. transfer w/ stag, mkd. "Staffordshire Eng.", stains & lids have minor damage $55.00

Spice Box, round bentwood, worn orig. varnish w/ blk. stenciled labels & tin edges, int. has eight matching canisters, minor damage, 9½" diam. $220.00

A-OH Sept. 1998   Garth's Auctions

Shaker Drying Rack, folding w/ three sections, poplar w/ old worn grayish yel. repaint, ea. section 35" x 56" $192.50

Basket, oval woven splint, old grayish patina, wear & damage, 9½" x 13", 8¼" H $137.50

Shaker Work Table, maple & pine w/ reddish stain, mortised apron w/ one dovetailed drawer, two board top w/ drop leaf, pine & chestnut secondary wood, 25" x 49", 9¼" leaf, 28¾" H $1,925.00

Basket, round woven splint, bentwood rim handles, singed "Harvard 1916", old patina, rim wrap incomplete, some damage, 22" diam., 9" H $302.50

Basket, lrg. woven splint buttocks, grayish patina, some damage, 20" diam., 12" H $148.50

A-OH Sept. 1998   Garth's Auctions

Shaker Work Cupboard, Harvard, MA, ref. poplar w/ dk. br. stain, repl. hardware, 50½" W, 25¼" D, 44½" H .$1,595.00

Shaker Carry-All, dovetailed, walnut w/ old dk. finish, six compartments "& divider w/ handle, 7¼" x 14¾", 5¾" H $440.00

Shaker Dippers, three tin, similar const. w/ ring hangers, worn br. japanning, one has dents in handle, 3", 4½" & 6" diam. $143.00

Knife Box, walnut w/ worn old finish, shaped divider, 10" x 14½", 4½" H $60.50

Basket, round woven splint, good old br. patina, some damage & rim wrap incomplete, 11" diam., 6½" H .$220.00

Carrier, oval, poplar & chestnut w/ old worn finish, gallery edge & bentwood handle, minor edge damage, 15" x 20½" $302.50

Basket, round woven splint, old dk. patina, 10" diam., 6" H $258.50

Boxes, two round, varnish finish, lapped seams w/ copper tacks, larger w/ age crack in lid, 7¾" & 9¾" diam. .$82.50

Carrier, round bentwood, old worn patina, lapped seam w/ steel tacks, bentwood swivel handle, 10¾" diam., 6½" H $165.00

Boxes, two round w/ old finish, larger is varnished, lapped seams w/ steel tacks, minor damage & one lid loose, 9" & 11" diam. $132.50

A-OH Sept. 1998   Garth's Auctions
Shaker Blanket Chest, Union Village, OH, walnut w/ over varnish, dovetailed case w/ dovetailed bracket feet, has till w/ lid, minor reprs., damage, 38¼" W, 17¼" D, 22" H $1,100.00
Shaker Box, oval, ref., finger const. w/ copper tacks, age crack in lid, 13½" L $412.50
Shaker Box, dk. varnish stain on bottom, rest rubbed down to a soft finish, finger const. w/ copper tacks, puttied holes in lid, 12" L $357.50
Shaker Box, Union Village, OH, oval, three finger const. w/ copper tacks, no lid, old finish, 8½" L $192.50
Hanging Cupboard, ref. poplar, reprs. & hinges repl., 22½" W, 7" D, 25⅛" H $385.00

A-OH Sept. 1998   Garth's Auctions
Shaker Hearth Brush, old worn finish, blk. bristles are incomplete, 21½" L $71.50
Shaker Rag Rug, multi-colored center w/ border stripes of olive, red & blue, 30" x 58" $357.50
Shaker Hearth Tools, two, similar wrt. iron tongs & shovel, 21" & 22" L $99.00
Shaker Cradle, butternut & poplar w/ worn old red, 36" L $440.00
Footstool, pine w/ old red paint over earlier blue, wear & edge damage, 17" L $192.50

A-OH Sept. 1998   Garth's Auctions
Utensil Rack, wrt. iron, scrolled detail w/ four birds, six hooks, 24" W, 14¼" L $440.00
Fork & Trimmers, two pcs., roasting fork w/ adjustable tines & blk. turned handle, 20" L, & steel scissor wick trimmers, 7¼" L $27.50
Double Crusie Lamps, two wrt. iron, twisted hangers, 6" H . . .$55.00
Ember Tongs, wrt. iron, 10½" L $209.00
Baby Cradle, pine w/ old worn blk. paint, well made w/ mortised frame, 31" L $880.00

A-OH Sept. 1998   Garth's Auctions
Cookie Board, bear, cherry w/ old patina, branded "B.R.", & inscribed in ink "B. Raber", 5" x 7⅞" $192.50
Hand Mirrors, two, oval beveled glass has wear, worn finish, blk., 8¼" & natural, 12½" L $82.50
Treen, three pcs., lemon squeezer, 11" L, & two basket weaver's tools $71.50
Chopper & Fork, wrt. iron food chopper & cast iron fork, both w/ wooden handles, 16¼" L $93.50
Tobacco Cutter, dec., chip carved wooden base w/ turned handles & old worn finish, wrt. iron horse shaped blade has engr. flowers & "Fabriquado En Arcos", 14" L $220.00
Yarn Winder, & table clamp, all wood, old paper label "Pat. Applied For", 13" L $71.50

A-OH Sept. 1998   Garth's Auctions
Shaker Darner, good patina, 6" L $60.50
Marquetry Board, slab of figured mah. w/ colored wood inlay in floral & geometric patt. on both sides, wear, some repair & age cracks, 16" H $137.50
Child's Side Chair, Mt. Lebanon ladderback, ref. & new tape seat in red w/ olive stripes, 28" H $247.50
Candle Mold, 36 tin tubes in dovetailed cherry case, old surface varnished, 18¼" W, 7" D, 15" H . .$1,210.00
Boxes, three similar bentwood w/ lapped seams w/ copper tacks, ref., wear, 6½", 7¾", & 8½" diam. .$165.00

A-OH Sept. 1998   Garth's Auctions
Pie Safe, ref. poplar, one board ends, one nailed drawer, 40¾" W, 15" D, 49" H $1,375.00
Spice Rack, hanging, ash w/ natural finish & blk. stenciled labels on eight drawers, wire nail const., 10¾" W, 5¼" D, 15½" H $412.50
Spice Rack, hanging, ref. hardwood w/ traces of stenciled labels, 18" W, 4¾" D, 8¾" H $495.00
Tea Caddy, Eng., exotic wood veneer w/ satin wood edging at lid, ivory diamond inlaid escut., int. has two lids, 7¼" L $137.50
Flour Sifter, poplar w/ old finish, 10¼" x 14¾", 8" H $137.50

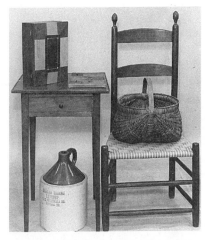

A-OH Sept. 1998   Garth's Auctions

Shaker Clock Shelf, hanging, Union Village, OH, walnut w/ old finish, one dovetailed drawer, secondary wood poplar, has label from Shaker medicine crate, 16" W, 42" H $962.50

Gameboard, painted, dk. br., ora. & red w/ gold & colored decals, 17½" x 17¾" $467.50

Grain Measures, three round bentwood, branded "Daniel Cragin... Wilton, N.H.", all impr. "T.J.D.", 5¾", 7¼", & 11½" diam. $132.50

Boxes, two round bentwood, worn dk. greenish paint, 6" diam., & natural finish, 8¾" diam., some edge damage $99.00

Rocker, Mt. Washington, old dk. finish & old faded ora. Shake made tape on seat & back, 28½" H $357.50

A-OH Sept. 1998   Garth's Auctions

Shaker Table, Mt. Lebanon Hepplewhite, cherry w/ old worn finish, one dovetailed drawer & two board top w/ applied gallery, renailed & reprs., 17" x 17¼", 26¼" H $550.00

Shaker Side Chair, ladderback, Watervliet, NY, old finish, old repl. tape seat has faded, 38¾" H .$715.00

Shaker Box, walnut veneer w/ walnut, maple & mah. inlaid beveled edge top, fitted int. lined w/ Shaker blue paper, red calico & gr. printed paper w/ mirror in lid & lift out tray, 8" x 11¼" $137.50

Basket, woven splint buttocks, newer, stained finish, 12½" x 13", 8¼" $93.50

Stoneware Jug, two-tone white & br., blue transfer label "Shaker Brand Ketchup...Portland, ME", minor chips, 14" H $880.00

A-OH Sept. 1998   Garth's Auctions

Shaker Peg Board, cherry w/ maple pegs & old worn finish, 54½" L $110.00

Settle Bench, ref. poplar, plank seat & half arrowback, reprs., 48" L $440.00

Basket, woven splint buttocks w/ boat shaped bowl & twisted twig handle, old finish, minor damage, 10½" x 17", 8" H $324.00

Basket, woven splint buttocks, scrubbed finish w/ bare traces of varnish, 12" x 15", 7¾" H $104.50

Basket, round woven splint, old varnish finish, 10" diam., 6¾" H ..$82.50

Shaker Footstool, pine w/ old patina, worn orig. fabric cover w/ padding, wire nail const., 10" x 14", 9" H $192.50

Baskets, two, woven splint, rectangular 9½" x 16", 5" H, & buttocks w/ faded multi-colored weaving, minor damage, 11" x 12", 6½" H ...$110.00

A-OH Sept. 1998   Garth's Auctions

Row 1, Left to Right

Shaker Sewing Box, oval w/ lid & swivel handle, varnish finish, finger const. w/ copper tacks, repl. pink satin lining, minor rim damage, 7" L $165.00

Shaker Sewing Box, tiered w/ one drawer, cherry & curly maple w/ mah. veneer on drawer, old finish, edge damage & finial missing, 6" H $247.50

Shaker Spool Holder, maple & chestnut w/ old finish, wooden spools (not Shaker) on pins & red velvet pincushion, 5¾" H $137.50

Row 2, Left to Right

Shaker Box, oval, old varnish, finger const. w/ copper tacks, chip out of top, 6¼" L $220.00

Shaker Box, oval, old worn putty colored paint, finger const w/ copper tacks, 5⅛" L $1,650.00

Bentwood Box, oval, old finish, finger const. w/ copper tacks, 4½" L $165.00

Round Box, old varnish finish, single finger const. w/ wrt. iron tacks, 7¾" diam. $82.50

Round Box, traces of old red, lapped seams w/ steel tacks, 6½" diam. $93.50

Round Box, old gr., lapped seams w/ copper tacks, 6¾" diam. $302.50

Round Box, old red, finger seam on lid & lapped seam on base w/ steel tacks, 5¾" diam. $357.50

A-IA July 1998   Jackson's

Row 1, Left to Right

1049-Jug, stoneware, 19th C., semi-
ovoid w/ lrg. brushed cobalt dec.,
13" H $247.50
1050-Field Basket, oak splint, ca.
1920, carved handle, VA region,
17" H $66.00

1051-Jug, stoneware, NY area, mid
19th C., 3 gal., oval shape w/ lrg. dec.
in cobalt, firing lines, chip on rim,
16" H $165.00
1052-Basket, ribbed hickory splint
buttocks, ca. 1950, eastern coast,
17" L $49.50
1053-Crock, stoneware, 4 gal. w/
molded rim & applied ear handles,

brushed cobalt dec., 12" H . . .$154.00

Row 2, Left to Right

1054-Crock, stoneware, ca. 1865,
1 gal., impr. "E & LP Norton...VT",
molded rim & applied ear handles,
brushed cobalt design, hairline crack,
7" H $71.50

1055-Basket, dec. wicker, ca. 1920, 13" H $60.50

1056-Butterchurn, stoneware, ca. 1850, 2 gal., impr. "Lyons", brushed cobalt blue floral design, 10" H $192.50

1057-Basket, oak splint, ca. 1900, Tennessee region, dk. patina, 13" H $82.50

1058-Syrup Jug, sponge dec. in blue & white for "Geo. Buente St. Louis, MO", emb. designs on top & shoulder, bail handle, some damage, 10" H $192.50

1059-Jar, stoneware, 2 qt., br. & white w/ Weirs pat. lid, chip on base, 9" H $13,75

1060-Batter Jug, blue-gray stoneware w/ emb. design of flowers over banded keg, 5½" H $60.50

Row 3, Left to Right

1061-Sugar Bucket, pine, all wood const. w/ bail handle & fitted lid, 11" H $82.50

1062-Jug, stoneware, 1 qt. white w/ br. lid, "The Weir Pat. Mar. 1st, 1892", chip on base, 8" H $19.25

1063-Basket, oak splint, ca. 1930's, Tennessee region, patina & coloring from use, 18" diam. $115.50

1064-Basket, oak splint, ca. 1930's, rib const., 19" L $60.50

Row 4, Left to Right

1065-Basket, ash splint, ca. 1950's, 28 rib const., 17" L $71.50

1066-Jug, Redwing Advertising, one-half gal., br. top w/ bail handle, "Williams Bros. ...Detroit, Mich.", 7½" L $137.50

1067-Tea Kettle, Rockingham, of "Rebecca at the Well", some minor chips, 8½" H $38.50

1068-Jug, stoneware, one-half gal., "Deodorizer-Pullman Co.", in cobalt blue, 9" H $33.00

1069-Holder, wrt. iron splint & rush, 19th C., w/ wood base, 19" H . .$49.50

1070-Bucket, child's, wooden 19th C., bail handle, brass hoops & 50% orig. blue paint, 5" diam. $93.50

1071-Shaker Boxes, pr., round w/ fitted lids, wood pegs & cooper tacks, 5½" diam. & 6½" diam. $55.00

1072-Box, Norwegian pine, lidded, ca. 1820, twist forged iron handle, remnants of orig. red & blue polychrome, early reprs., 14" x 6½" $247.50

Row 5, Left to Right

1073-Work Bowl, turned maple, 19th C., dk. honey colored patina, 17" diam. $49.50

1074-Sewing Basket, Chinese bamboo splint, dec. w/ glass rings & beads, coins & tassels on fitted lid, 10" diam. $33.00

1075-Egg Basket, ash splint, early 1900's, fine weave, New Eng. region, 12" L $93.50

1076-Egg Basket, ribbed reed, early 1900's, 10" L $71.50

1077-Basket, ash splint, ME, ca. 1920's, 8" L $44.00

1078-Egg Basket, ash splint, New Eng., ca. 1900's, br. & gr. stained dec., 10" L $93.50

1079-Indian Basket, splint ash, ME, ca. 1960's, 9" diam. $27.50

1080-Coiled Basket, straw & oak-splint, early 1900's, 11" diam. .$16.50

1081-Jug, stoneware, 2 qt., Albany glaze, 6½" H $13.75

A-PA Oct. 1998   Conestoga Auction Co., Inc.

Row 1, Left to Right

Trinket Chest, dome top w/ polychrome floral & foliage designs on ora. ground, 3" H, 4½" W, 3" D $330.00

Egg Cup, Lehnware, strawberry & vine dec. on blue ground, red, gr. & dk. blue pedestal base, yel. int. w. gr. rim, chips on base & paint loss, 2⅝" H . . .$962.50

Box, slide lid, polychrome floral dec., gr. ground, thumbpull & compartment int., 2½" H, 4" W, 7" L $3,025.00

Document Box, 18th C., red, yel. & white flowers w/ white outlines, "ICH"., wrapped & stapled tin hinges & clasp, 3" H, 9¾" W, 7¾" D $6,325.00

Row 2, Left to Right

Blanket Chest, w/ red, blk. & yel. designs on gr. ground, molded base & turned feet, dovetailed const., 6¼" H, 11" W, 6¼" diam. $1,980.00

Egg Cup, Lehnware, polychrome floral dec. w/ pink ground, gr., red & blue base, 2½" H $1,155.00

Saffron Box, Lehnware w/ Berry patt. on a mulberry ground, red, gr. & blue pedestal base, lid w/ blue finial & Strawberry patt., gr. trim & vine on red ground, sm. chip on base, 5" H $3,410.00

Cup & Saucer, Lehnware, mini. w/ strawberry design on pink/gray ground, cup 1½" H, saucer 3" diam. $907.50

A-OH Nov. 1998   Garth's Auctions

Row 1, Left to Right

Two Pieces, Euro. tôle chamber stick w/ old yel. repaint w/ gold, 6¼" H, & conical bank, yel. & gr. foliage & blk. inscription in Ger., 3¾" H, both w/ repr. $181.50

Tôle Box, dome top, worn dk. br. japanning w/ white band & dec. in red & yel., ring handle missing, 4¼" L $55.00

Tôle Creamer, w/ hinged lid, dk. br. japanning w/ floral dec. in yel., gr., red & white, some wear, 4¼" H $522.50

Row 2, Left to Right

Tôle Coffee Pot, dk. br. japanning w/ colorful floral dec. in red, gr., br., blue & yel., wear & old touch up repaint, reprs., 10½" H $495.00

Deed Box, tôle dome top, dk. br. japanning w/ colorful floral dec. in yel., red, gr. & blk., white band has painters mark, seams loose & repr., minor wear, 8¾" L $825.00

Tôle Coffee Pot, blk. ground w/ colorful floral dec. in red, gr., yel. & white, crusty surface has touch up repr., rust, battering, 9½" H . .$852.50

Row 1, Left to Right

1082-Wash Bowl & Pitcher, tealeaf ironstone by Alfred Meakin, sm. hairline in bowl, 13" H $126.50

1083-Pot & Lid, tealeaf ironstone by Alfred Meakin, some slight staining, 9" H $77.00

1084-Kitchen Clock, walnut, 19th C., rev. painted design of arch & florals, restored condition, 18½" H $93.50

1085-Shaving Mug, tealeaf ironstone by Anthony Shaw, Emb. Lily of Valley mold, minor stains, 3½" H $192.50

1086-Shoes, pr. ladies leather, ca. 1910, lace-up in mint cond., 8" H $44.00

1087-Spice Drawers, wood advertising "The Grange Store", 19th C., 8 drawers w/ stenciled titles, 18" L $313.50

1088-Recipe Box, oak advertising for Gold Medal flour, orig. card dividers w/ illus., 7" L $27.50

Row 2, Left to Right

1089-Gold Dust Box, w/ washing powder, unopened, 8½" H $49.50

1090-Gold Dust Box, scouring cleanser, missing bottom, 5" H $13.75

1091-Cookie Jar, yel. baker by Redwing, 12" H $77.00

1092-Spice Cabinet, oak, wall mount w/ 8 drawers, 18" H ..$115.50

1093-Baby Shoes, 3 pr. leather, white, 2 pr. w/ M.O.P. buttons, avg. 4" L $16.50

1094-Hat Form, 2 pc. basswood, ca. 1930, 14" diam. $55.00

1095-Store Canister, Japanned tin, hinged lid w/ porcelain knob, remains of gold dec. & woman's portrait, 10" H $27.50

1096-Bread Plate, tealeaf ironstone by Alfred Meakin, bamboo handle, 9" sq. $11.00

Row 3, Left to Right

1097-Inkstand, cast iron w/ swirled glass, wells w/ iron caps on ornate iron stand, 10" L $71.50

1098-Yarn Winder, wooden w/ expanding slates, 19" L $60.50

1099-Canister, Planter's Peanut w/ emb. peanut lid w/ enameled jar, chip on jar, 10" H $27.50

1100-Inkstand, pr. cut crystal wells w/ cork stoppers on oak base w/ nickel handle, 11" L $93.50

1101-Inkstand, pr. ribbed crystal wells w/ hinged lids on ornate iron stand w/ letter rack & pen rests, 8" L $55.00

1102-Shoes, pr. early leather high heels, Art Deco design, 11" L .$27.50

1103-Comb Case, walnut, wall mount w/ circular mirror, carved acanthus leaves, lamp brackets & cylinder cover, 21" H $126.50

1104-Door Knocker, cast iron of woodpecker, gr., blk. white & red polychrome, 4" H $16.50

1105-Ice Skates, pr. of wood & iron, ca. 1870, 14½" L $33.00

1106-Hat Stand, ca. 1920, 18" H, plus 2 identical stands & iron shoe display & folding wire shirt display not pictured, 5 pcs. total $192.50

Row 4, Left to Right

1107-Shoes, pr., natural calf skin uppers w/ pat. leather & 19 buttons, ea. very minor wear, 10" H . .$110.00

1108-Swiss Cow Bell, bronze, 19th C., w/ leather collar, emb. designs, mkd. "1875- Viglino", 7½" diam. $71.50

1109- Shoes, child's leather, 6 buttons ea. 6" L $38.50

1110-Shoes, pr. ladies leather in blk. w/ laced uppers, 13" H $71.50

1111-Boots, pr. child's leather in white w/ partial lacing, 6" H, & pr. of pigskin child's mucklics, 5" H .$49.50

1112-Decoy, carved wooden mallard, hollowed body, glass eyes, 16" L $38.50

1114-Shoes, pr. ladies high tops, ca. 1910, laced uppers, blk. leather, 10" H $60.50

1115-Ox Bells, India brass, 26 bells on brass hangers w/ figural bulls head, 32" L $77.00

1116-Gill Measures, set of 3, Eng. pewter, early 19th C., in full, half & quarter size, repr. to one $33.00

1117-Servants Bell, brass & iron, 19th C., wall mount w/ coiled return spring, 10" L $88.00

1118-Cow Bell, brass Swiss w/ leather collar, emb. designs & maker's name, 7" diam. $55.00

1119-Ornament, blown glass of sailboat dec. in red, white & blue, 5" H $22.00

Row 5, Left to Right

1120-Cow Bell, bronze Swiss emb. dec. w/ "1878 Chiantel Fondeur", 4½" diam. $27.50

1121-Cow Bell, early iron 19th C., hand forged & riveted seams w/ folded corners, 6" H $13.75

1122-Shoes, 2 pr. child's leather, ca. 1930, incl. art deco blk. & white pr., 4½" L $27.50

1123-Sleigh Bells, bronze, 14 bells w/ emb. design on leather belt, 40" L $115.50

1124-Cow Bells, pr. bronze Swiss w/ emb. designs & "1878", 3½" & 4" diam. $22.50

1125-Hames Bells, bronze w/ five bells in graduated size on leather hanger, 32" L $143.00

1126-Saddle Bag Bell, early brass, 19th C. dual tone w/ pendulum clapper on turned walnut handle, 9" L $121.00

1127-Transistor Radio, advertising "Sinclair Gasoline", gas pump form, 4½" H $16.50

1129-Sleigh Bells, brass 19th C., w/ 12 bells on leather strap, 2" H, 36" L $93.50

1130-Cow Bell, iron, 19th C., hand folded & riveted, oval shaped, 7" H $27.50

1131-Sleigh Bells, set of brass, 24 graduated w/ emb. design on leather strap, 70" L $143.00

1132-Ice Cream Molds, pr., pewter, hinged two pc., one strawberry & one cupid w/ bow, 4" L $77.00

A-IA July 1998   Jackson's

1024-Kettle, copper, wrt. iron bail handle, 17" diam. $143.00

1025-Water Barrel, primitive oak, 19th C., remnants of mustard yel. paint, repl. bands, 26" x 18" diam. $88.00

1026-Kettle, copper, 19th C., dovetailed const., wrt. iron bar handle, 17" diam. $110.00

1027-Butterchurn, wooden, 19th C., orig. lid & dasher, barrel 20" H $121.00

1028-Yarn Winder, early 19th C., pine & turned maple w/ geared counter mech., rich old dk. patina, 40" H $82.50

A-IA July 1998   Jackson's

1032-Penny Weighing Machine, ca. 1930's by "Peerless', white enameled cast iron w/ mirrored dial, up to 275 lbs., 70" . . . . .N/S

1033-Vending Machine, sports cards, 6 for 5¢ & post cards, 2 for 5¢, contains approx. 200 humorous valentine post cards, manuf. by "Calex Vending", 56" H $77.00

A-MA Aug. 1998   Rafael Osona Auctioneer & Appraiser

Left to Right

Library Steps, Am., Sheraton, mah., ca. 1815 w/ tooled leather steps, 2 have hinged compartments, 17½" W, 25" H $650.00

Library Steps, Eng., Sheraton, mah., ca. 1815 w/ tooled leather inset steps & 2 hinged compartments, 18⅜" W, 26½" H $1,100.00

A-PA Mar. 1999   Horst Auctioneers

Dry Sink, mid to late 19th C., softwood ref., wear, 32" H, 18½" D, 55" W . .$900.00

A-MA Sept. 1998   Craftsman Auctions

Magazine Stand, Stickley Bros., mkd. w/ paper label, 42" x 14" x 14" $900.00

A-PA Mar. 1999   Horst Auctioneers

Hanging Cupboard, PA, cherry ref. shelf repl., 36¼" W, 61½" H .$1,900.00

A-IA June 1998   Jackson's

Armchair, wicker, painted white, 40" H $86.25

A-IA June 1998   Jackson's

Bench, wicker w/ side tray, painted white, 43" H $69.00

A-IA June 1998   Jackson's

Ice Cream Parlor Set, 5 pcs. w/ oak top $201.25

A-NH Nov. 1998   Northeast Auctions

Etagere, NY Fed. mah., 60" H, 19" W $4,250.00

A-MA Sept. 1998   Craftsman Auctions

Cider Set, Clewell 5-pc., pitcher 9¾" H w/ hairline, all pcs. mkd. "Clewell Coppers" w/ heavy copper overlay $1,000.00